A HISTORY OF TEXTILES

Flemish linen damask from the seventeenth century. (Detroit Institute of Arts, gift of Miss Elizabeth Sundstrom)

A HISTORY OF TEXTILES

Kax Wilson

WESTVIEW PRESS / BOULDER, COLORADO

NOTE: Portions of Chapter 11 are from a thesis submitted to the graduate faculty of Colorado State University in partial fulfillment of the requirements for the degree of Master of Science.

Copyright © 1979 by Westview Press, Inc.

Published in 1979 in the United States of America by
  Westview Press, Inc.
  5500 Central Avenue
  Boulder, Colorado 80301
  Frederick A. Praeger, Publisher

Library of Congress Catalog Card Number: 79-3977
ISBN: 0-89158-491-9

Printed and bound in the United States of America

TO HOBE

CONTENTS

PART TWO
WORLD TEXTILES

FIGURES

PLATES

PREFACE

The purpose of this book is twofold: to serve as a text for college classes and to aid textile history researchers. It has grown out of more than ten years of research and teaching at Colorado State University. I hope readers will enjoy the book as well as learn from it.

Appreciation is due many helpful museum curators and librarians across the country and especially to the faculty and staff at Colorado State University's Morgan Library. Particular thanks go to Virginia Valaki for thoughtful editing, to Opal Moore for professional typing, and to Pat Dietemann for art work. I would also like to thank my family and my friends for their support and encouragement. Extra credit for encouragement belongs to Dr. Frances Duffield of Auburn University.

Kax Wilson

A HISTORY OF TEXTILES

1. SOME RELATIONSHIPS

Textile history has many facets. It can involve archaeology, inasmuch as fabrics provide a record of ancient man, or anthropology, inasmuch as fabrics form part of the material culture of a primitive people. It can involve a study of religion and symbolism in order to decipher motifs, or it can mean using chemistry to identify fibers, analyze dyes, or properly clean an old textile. Politics and economics are also intricately woven into textile history. Artistic analysis is very important, as identification and dating often become the work of an art historian. Some textiles are considered fine art and exhibited with great paintings; others are classed as folk art and housed with crafts. There is also "tourist art," representing a degeneration in traditional weaving, with its interesting sociological and psychological implications. Hence, textile historians are involved with many disciplines, and textiles are studied from various viewpoints.

Handwoven fabrics have now become an art form and are well removed from everyday life. This was not always so, and as we study something old—commonplace in its time—we wonder who was personally involved in its making and use. How was it made? How can it be described? What are the terms to use? Appreciation of old fabrics is enhanced if one can "read" them well in terms of material, structure, and design as those elements relate to sociological, economic, and artistic concepts. For example, one sees a Navajo rug in an airport shop; it typifies 200 years of weaving certain designs in wool tapestry on a primitive loom; it also tells a story of economics, first Indian commerce, then Anglo trader control of a reservation industry; and yet, there is an intangible element—the psychological value of tribal prestige earned by the weaver.

A textile is considered to have five components: 1) the fiber—the basic unit—suitable material from many sources, mainly vegetable and animal; 2) the yarn—the structure made by spinning or twisting the fibers together; 3) the fabric construction—woven if the yarns are interlaced at right angles, done by some other

1

method if the yarns are twisted, looped, or knotted; 4) the finish, including processes such as bleaching and pressing; and 5) color—fibers, yarns, or cloth can be dyed or the cloth may be printed. Textiles from all over the world, past or present, are often similar yet different. There are some variables that make each group distinct, however.

1. *The raw materials.* Certainly, not all fibers could be raised in all parts of the world nor were they always available in trade. Fiber content determined fabric characteristics (such as handle and texture) and also put limitations on what could be done in spinning, weaving, dyeing, and finishing. Interesting things sometimes happened when an unfamiliar material was imported and used in the way of a traditional fiber.

2. *The technology.* Different materials required different tools and techniques for spinning and fabric construction. Limitations imposed by lack of technical knowledge often put restrictions on what could be made. Hawaiians had no loom, so they made cloth by beating bark fibers into a mat. The ancient Chinese were ahead of the rest of the world in making patterned fabrics of silk because they had an advanced loom technology. In the seventeenth century dyers and printers in India knew methods for coloring cotton cloth not known anywhere else. Europeans invented and used the machines that made mass production possible.

3. *The reason for production.* The amount of effort and skill put into weaving has varied according to the intended use of the product and the value placed on that use by a society. If clothing and protection from the elements were primary concerns, people sought economical and fast methods. Cloth made for trade might be woven very carefully for a sophisticated buyer—or less so for a casual tourist. Often designs were modified from the traditional to meet the needs of the buyer. On the other hand, many hours might be spent making patterns for aesthetic reasons. Textiles made for religious purposes were important for their symbolism; a belief in life after death resulted in fabrics of intricate design and fine quality.

4. *Influences from other cultures.* It is very difficult to identify what might be considered a "pure" textile, that is, one developed solely within a group and never changed by the ideas of new weavers coming into the area, or by people of different religion taking over and changing motifs, or by new plant materials being introduced to change colors. Cultural diffusion is very evident and often several influences can be identified in a single historic fabric.

*   *   *

In Part One material and technology will be covered with a view towards tying them to people, places, and different periods. Emphasis will be placed on fiber, yarn, construction, finish, and color and their historical relationships. Part Two will discuss textiles of selected places and times. Examples can be seen in museums,[1] and at least some published information about them is available. Bibliographical essays included with each chapter will provide important references in English for each topic, following the order of presentation used in the chapter.

NOTES

1. For information about museums with textile collections see Cecil Lubell, ed., *Textile Collections of the World,* 3 vols. (New York: Van Nostrand Reinhold, 1976-). Lubell's first volume deals with the United States and Canada, the second with the United Kingdom and Ireland, and the third with France. Others to come.

PART ONE

HISTORY OF MATERIALS AND METHODS

2. SPINNING AND RAW MATERIALS

Loose fibers have little value as textile material unless they can be made into yarn. At least ten thousand years ago women were able to identify the materials that were strong and long enough to spin. Although many materials were spun, the ancients mainly used four that served the world's major textile needs until the twentieth century. Each of the great civilizations can be associated with at least one fiber—Egypt with flax, India and Peru with cotton, China with silk, and Mesopotamia with wool.

Tools for spinning developed slowly. Fiber preparation and yarn making were never-ending tasks until the nineteenth century.

SPINDLES AND WHEELS

Spinning can be accomplished without any instrument by simply rolling the fibers between the palms or along the thigh. Using a spindle makes the process much easier. Although there are many kinds of primitive spindles, the basic device is a thin stick between seven and eighteen inches long, tapered at both ends (Figure 2.1). At the top there is usually a notch to hold the yarn while it is being spun. Somewhere between the middle and the lower end will be the *whorl*, made of clay, wood, bone, pottery, or even precious metal. The whorl keeps the spindle in motion once it has been set to turning. The *distaff* (a word sometimes used erroneously to mean "spindle") is also a stick, but it is used to hold the fibers that have been prepared for spinning (Figure 2.2.). It can be tucked under the spinner's arm or attached to a spinning wheel.

The steps in spinning are about the same for all fibers except filament silk. First,

FIGURE 2.1 (*above*) / Spindle.
FIGURE 2.2 (*left*) / Spinning with Distaff.

they must be cleaned of seeds, vegetable matter, and dirt. Then they are laid parallel, or in some order, and formed into a strand. This is called *roving*. Next, the strand is attenuated by stretching (from the hanging weight of the spindle), drafting (pulling out with the fingers), or a combination of the two. The next step, *twisting*, is the vital part of the process, because it is the twist that holds the fibers together and gives the yarn strength. The twist is imparted by the rotation of the spindle. After twisting the yarn must be wound onto the spindle or into a ball.

If the spindle is turned in one direction, an "S" twist results; if it is turned in the opposite direction, a "Z" twist is produced. To see the difference, visualize these letters superimposed on yarns or twist some cords together (Figure 2.3). Some fibers are consistently spun either "S" or "Z," and certain groups of spinners spin all fibers in one direction. "S" and "Z" identification is used in textile analysis for a number of determinations like possible fiber content, place and date of manufacture, or washability. If the fibers are spun only once, a *single* or *one-ply yarn* is the result. If two or more singles are twisted together, the result is a *two-ply, three-ply,* etc., yarn. If several strands are then twisted together, the result is a *cord* (Figure 2.4).

Sometime around 750 A.D. in India[1] the spindle was mounted on a frame and rotated by turning a wheel that held a cord attached to the spindle. Called a *charkha* (Figure 2.5) in India, and a *Jersey wheel* (or great wheel) (Figure 2.6) elsewhere, it was only a little bit faster than the hand spindle, but the product was more uniform. The Chinese added a treadle that accelerated the process, but many wheels of this type continued to be turned by hand. Spinning on the charkha or Jersey wheel was intermittent; the spinner had to stop periodically to wind the yarn on the spindle.

9

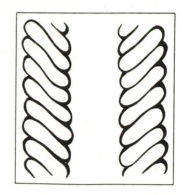

FIGURE 2.3 (*right*) / "S" and "Z" Twists.
FIGURE 2.4 (*below*) / Single Ply, and Cord.

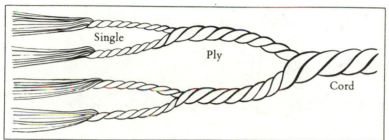

Single

Ply

Cord

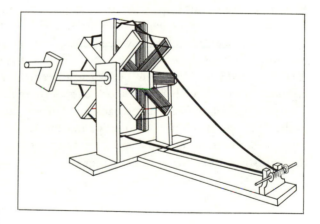

FIGURE 2.5 (*above*) / Charkha (Indian spinning wheel). FIGURE 2.6 (*left*) / Jersey Wheel.

FIGURE 2.7 / Saxony Wheel.

A major advancement occurred in the sixteenth century when Saxony or *Brunswick wheels* came into use in Europe. This important innovation was the flyer, a "U"-shaped device fixed on the end of the hollow shaft holding the spindle. Two pulleys, activated by the wheel, turned the flyer and spindle at different rates, enabling the yarn to be wound on the spindle as the twist was being made (Figure 2.7). Leonardo da Vinci has been given credit for the invention of the flyer, although it may have been the work of a German from Brunswick named Jurgen. The principle, however, dates back to fourteenth century Italian silk throwing mills. Spinning machines, the jenny, and the water frame, greatly speeded yarn production by using multiple spindles. They were not, of course, developed until the Industrial Revolution (see chapter 8).

THE MAJOR FIBERS

There is not a great deal of information, other than archaeological, about textiles before the Christian Era. The Bible, a few ancient writings, and some cave murals are the best references. Archaeological samples are sometimes biased because conditions in an area have preserved only the vegetable, or only the animal, fibers.[2] A predominance of material has been preserved in desert regions, but that does not necessarily mean that more fabrics were made there. And even in very recent times, historians have often been confused about or unconcerned with fiber content: cotton has been called linen, flax and hemp have been used interchangeably, and wool and cotton have been mistakenly identified.

The textile historian is aided in educated guesswork by a knowledge of the physical and chemical properties of the fibers. Physical properties determine the

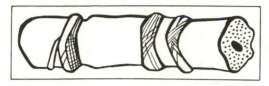

FIGURE 2.8 / Flax Fiber (microscopic view).

methods that must be used for spinning and weaving in order to achieve a successful product: for example, certain constructions are not suitable to wool. Chemical properties of fibers determine finishing and dyeing techniques as well as survival rates.

Flax

Flax (the word is derived from the Teutonic *flacks*) may well have been the first plant used for fiber. The wild variety, *Linum angustifolium,* grew as a perennial in many parts of the prehistoric Old World; it was used by Swiss lake dwellers as early as 8000 B.C. *Linum usitatissimum,* the annual variety, was cultivated extensively in the Mediterranean region at least as early as neolithic times and is the variety historically grown throughout the world.

Flax is a *bast* fiber; that is, it is part of the inner bark (phloem) of the stem of a dicotyledonous plant. The bast fibers, which grow as bundles held together by pectins, waxes, and gums, support the plant and transport nutrients. Composed of cellulose (as are all plant fibers), flax is grown for its seed, which supplies oil, as well as for its fiber (Figure 2.8).

High strength is one of the outstanding properties of flax fiber, and it gains strength when wet—helpful when linen fabric received primitive laundering. As the fiber dries, it rotates in an "S" direction. This is thought to be the reason why flax was consistently spun in that direction.[3] Most spinners will moisten flax to aid spinning (Figure 2.9). Another property, *wicking,* or moving moisture along the surface, means that flax is comfortable to wear in hot climates but difficult to dye. Therefore, linen is usually bleached and left white, or it is printed.

Preparation for Spinning

About a hundred days after planting, flax is pulled up by the roots so as not to waste fiber. Then it is gathered into bundles and stood upright in the field to dry. Next, the seeds are removed by *rippling*—drawing the heads of the plants through a comb—or by threshing—beating the flax with a heavy tool (as the ancients must have done). At this stage the flax can be tied into bundles and stored in a dry place for a fairly long time.

Retting is the most important part of the process; its purpose is to decompose the pectins and gums that hold the fibers together and free them from the straw. Retting has been done in various ways; by spreading the flax on dewy fields and leaving it for several weeks, by immersing bundles in special ponds or slow-running rivers for several days, or, more recently, by using tanks and careful controls. (In

FIGURE 2.9 / Spinning Flax.

ancient Egypt long lines of slaves were used to pass buckets of water from the river so that the flax could be kept damp.)

Breaking (Plate 1) is the first pounding operation used to free the fiber from the woody stems. The flax is laid across the brake, and the upper blade is brought down sharply. Any *shive* (stem particles) that remains is removed in a process called *scutching* or *swingling*. The flax is laid over the edge of an upright board and tapped with a wooden knife. *Hackling (hatchelling* or *heckling)* is a combing process; the flax is pulled through a series of boards with different-sized protruding pins (Figure 2.10). The *line*, or long fibers, are separated from the short *tow* fibers. Then the fiber is ready to be bound on a distaff and spun with a drop spindle that falls to the ground as it rotates (Figure 2.9), or with a Saxony wheel (Figure 2.7).

Flax in Egypt

Flax was cultivated in Mesopotamia, Assyria, and Babylonia, but Egypt was known as the "land of linen." Linen was woven there at least six thousand years ago; fragments of Egyptian cloth have been dated to 4500 B.C.[4] Tomb models (Plate 2), paintings, and texts, as well as the writings of Herodotus and Pliny, have supplied many details about the ancient industry. There were centers for linen production operated by the state using slave labor. Airless work pens and "holes" have been described.

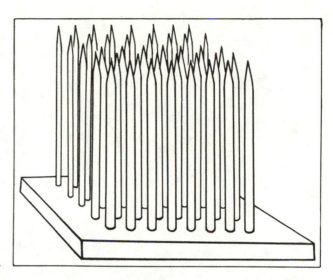

FIGURE 2.10 / Hackle.

Different grades of cloth were made. The higher one's place on the social scale, the finer the weave in one's mummy wrappings—sometimes over five hundred threads to an inch. As much as three hundred yards of cloth was used to wrap one mummy. Linen was the universal clothing fabric, and some extremely sheer versions have been recorded in paintings. Flax was considered to be a symbol of divine light and purity and it was the only fiber worn by priests. Egypt exported many yards of linen for sails. The flax retted in the Nile was reputed to be much softer than other kinds, and sails did not wear out from abrasion as quickly if made from Egyptian linen.

In early Egypt yarn was made a little differently than in other areas.[5] Bundles of fibers were overlapped slightly and rolled on the thigh to make a splice, as one joins knitting yarn. This roving was then wound into a ball and placed in a pot of water. Then two or three rovings were drawn out and *twined,* that is, twisted in an "S" direction with a spindle. (Figure 2.11)

The Holy Land

Although the Hebrews usually wore woolen robes, they did weave linen for inner garments. It is thought that they learned linen manufacture while held captive in Egypt; some of the people led out by Moses may have been former textile slaves. The Hebrews, however, spun the flax and did not twine it. As in Egypt, linen was regarded as pure and was worn by priests. Part of the idea that flax was pure may actually be related to the belief that people who wore linen next to the body were less likely to contract leprosy than those who wore wool.

Weaving was the work of the Hebrew woman in her home. The virtuous woman in Proverbs (31:13, 19, 24) "seeketh wool and flax and worketh willingly with her hands. She layeth her hands to the spindle, and her hands hold the distaff. She maketh fine linen and selleth it, and delivereth girdles unto the merchants."

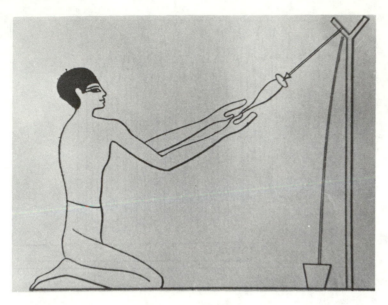

FIGURE. 2.11 / Twining Yarn in Egypt.

Thus, the Bible serves as the oldest textile source book, although interpretation is difficult because the Hebrews were prone to record the unusual, rather than everyday events like weaving.[6] The sackcloth that Jacob wore when he mourned his son (Genesis 37:34) may have been made of tow. The curtains of the tabernacle were made of fine twined linen (Exodus 26:1), and the body of Jesus was wrapped in fine linen (Mark 15:46).

The Hebrews had laws about when and where flax could be planted, probably because it impoverished the soil. In the earliest Old Testament texts the Hebrew word for linen was *peshet*; later books use *pishta* or *pishtan*. In the *Mishnah* (coded laws of the second century A.D.) linen was called *kittan*, which developed into the Greek word *chiton*, the name of a woman's garment.

Phoenicia, Greece, and Rome

The Phoenicians were the real shipping magnates of the Mediterranean world. In the first millennium B.C. they warehoused Egyptian linens to be traded all over the known world and may even have introduced flax into Britain and Flanders.

The Greeks concentrated on wool growing, although they did raise flax in the Peloponnesus—an especially white kind came from Elis in the northwest. Linen is mentioned twice in the *Iliad,* and this illustration from a fifth century B.C. vase gives an idea as to how it was spun (Figure 2.9). Linen was considered effeminate in Greece, but it was necessary for some things. Aristophanes told of Greek ladies who adopted linen napkins as handkerchiefs even though some diehards stayed with their foxtails. There was a fairly extensive household industry in the fifth and fourth centuries B.C., but more linen was manufactured in the Greek colonies than in Greece proper.

The situation was similar in ancient Rome. A little flax was raised, most of the industry was in the home (although there were a few factories or workshops), and the colonies furnished the largest quantities of linen. The Romans were credited with founding *colleges,* the first agriculture experiment stations, where the best methods of flax and wool production were developed and disseminated throughout the Empire.

In the first century A.D. Pliny wrote of three kinds of linen: common flax, *byssus* (from Old Testament *bus* and *shesh,* meaning fine linen), and *asbestinon,* an incombustible type. Pointing out the value of linen for sails, Pliny wrote a glorious passage in his *Natural History*:

> How audacious is life that out of so small a seed springs a means of carrying the whole world to and fro, a plant with so slender a stem and rising to such a small height from the ground when broken and crushed and reduced by force to the softness of wool, afterwards by this ill-treatment attains to the highest pitch of daring.[7]

Flax in Northern Europe

The Romans had linen factories in Britain and Gaul to supply their armies, but production dwindled for a time after the barbarian invasions. What manufacture there was between the sixth and ninth centuries was either in the household or an occupation of small groups within each community. Surplus was insignificant and not of a quality worth trading. In the eighth century Charlemagne ordered each family in his realm to learn to process, spin, and weave flax, because he recognized the sanitary value of linen garments and also saw a potential market for Christian liturgical vestments.

Flanders (see Figure 6.1) became the first important center for the medieval linen industry. The climate was ideal for growing flax, and the labor was skilled. The luxury diaper (a type of figured linen) and damask industries developed in the early sixteenth century in Ghent, Bruges, Ypres, and Courtrai. The Dutch also wove linens, but they imported their yarn from Germany. Holland was more famous for its bleaching works at Haarlem, and in the seventeenth and eighteenth centuries linens were sent there from all over Europe so that they might receive the best whitening available. Some districts of Germany—Dowlas, Silesia, Osnaburg, Tecklenburg—were important producers from the fourteenth century on. Russia, too, had some linen industry by the seventeenth century, but that country was more a flax exporter.

The English linen industry had little significance until the late sixteenth century when thousands of skilled workers fled to England from the Low Countries to avoid Spanish persecutions. Coarse linens and lace were manufactured in some quantity, although the industry was not allowed to really prosper in England because favor was shown toward the wool industry.

In Ireland, however, linen manufacture was a major industry—one that continued into the twentieth century. The beginning might be traced to the Phoenicians, who went to Ireland in 1000 B.C., but more likely it dates back to the Normans who settled there in the seventh century A.D. There is little information

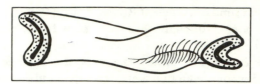

FIGURE 2.12 / Cotton Fiber (microscopic view).

until the twelfth century when the Norman king, Henry II, promoted the industry. By the thirteenth century Irish linens were being exported to England. In the seventeenth century English laws repressed the industry there, to the advantage of Ireland, but the Irish woolen industry was ruined by English tariffs that practically prohibited any foreign wool imports. Thus, the wool industry in Ireland's Catholic south suffered, while the linen industry in the Protestant north prospered. Belfast was one of the leading linen centers of the world, and in the early part of the nineteenth century the old cottage industry was displaced by a factory system.

Cotton

Cotton, the other major cellulose fiber, may be as old as flax, but archaeological evidence gives it a "textile birth" sometime around 3500 B.C. in India and 3000 B.C. in Peru. To anyone who has ever played with a cotton boll, or the seed pod from milkweed, it seems quite possible that prehistoric people would have realized cotton's potential more readily than that of the bast fibers.

The cotton fiber, a seed hair, is a single cell that grows from the outer skin of the seed. As many as twenty thousand fibers grow from one seed, and a boll (the fruit) may contain over a hundred and fifty thousand fibers that serve to accumulate moisture for germination of the seed and also to protect it as nature distributes it for planting.

When the plant matures the boll opens, the fibers dry, and as their cell walls collapse, they flatten and twist (Figure 2.12). These characteristic twists, or *convolutions,* one to three hundred per inch, are responsible for cotton's spinning qualities—the fibers will hold together even though some varieties are only three-eighths of an inch long. The longest cotton is about two-and-a-half inches in length. The shortness of the fibers made spinning difficult, so the ancients used a supported spindle (Figure 2.13), because the yarns would pull apart if a drop spindle was used. This was also one of the reasons why cotton was not used extensively in Europe prior to the Industrial Revolution; it was hard to spin on the Saxony wheel. Traditionally cotton has been spun "Z," because that is the direction it twists as it drys. "Z" yarns stay intact when washed, "S" yarns are more apt to untwist.

The genus *Gossypium,* because of its commercial value, has been the object of study since it was first mentioned by Pliny in his *Natural History.*

The upper part of Egypt lying in the direction of Arabia grows a bush which some people call cotton (gossypion) but more often by a Greek word meaning

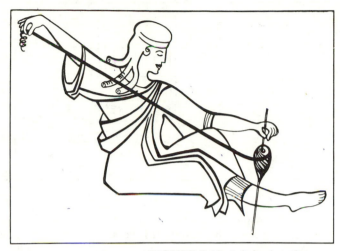

FIGURE 2.13 / Spinning Cotton.

wood (xylon) hence the name xylina given to linens made from it. It is a small shrub and from it hangs a fruit resembling a bearded nut with an inner silky fibre from the down of which thread is spun. No kinds of thread are more brilliantly white or make smoother fabric than this. Garments made of it are very popular with the priests of Egypt.[8]

Gossypium includes many plants, varying in height from ten inches to six feet (the tree cottons of India and Brazil). There are both perennial and annual varieties, but all need high temperatures and large amounts of water during the main growth period. Cotton thrives in tropical and semi-tropical regions.

Preparation for Spinning

After cotton is harvested the first step is to remove dirt, leaves, and other trash, and to separate the fibers (called *lint*) from the seeds. For over five thousand years millions of patient hands have performed this step, often to the happy sounds of singing and gossiping (Plate 110a). A roller gin (Figure 2.14) was invented in India, probably in the Middle Ages. Rotation of two closely set rollers drew lint between them but stopped the seed from passing through. It was not suitable for all types of cotton but was the only gin in use until Eli Whitney invented the saw gin (see chapter 10).

Carding, getting the fibers in order, was also a hand process: fibers were pulled into little bunches and lapped. In India, and some primitive societies, bows were used to fluff the fiber and remove some of the dirt and knots. A workman struck the taut string with a mallet and its vibrations fluffed the cotton. In some places split sticks, or switches, were used for the same purpose. Combing, an additional process of fiber alignment, was not practiced widely until the nineteenth century.

Cotton in India

There is little doubt that India was the ancient world's "cradle of cotton." Spun

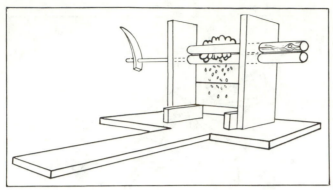

FIGURE 2.14 / Roller Gin.

cotton yarns, dated at 3000 B.C., were found in the ruins of Mohenjo-Daro, the great city in the Indus valley. It is possible that the earliest variety was tree cotton, but shrub varieties were also cultivated in India. The cotton industry was well developed by 1500 B.C., and there was no significant change in methods noted from Roman times until very recent attempts to industrialize.[9] It was primarily an individual domestic activity.

Cotton in the West

Cotton spread westward from India, first as an object of trade, then as a plant and an industry. It was reported in Assyria by 700 B.C. and soon after in Babylonia. Cotton was well known in the Near East by Hellenistic times, although it was cultivated only on a small scale throughout the Roman period. Called *carbasina* after Sanskrit *karpasa,* it was first used in Rome about 71 B.C. for tents. There is no record of cotton cloth being manufactured in Rome, but in the last centuries B.C. and first centuries A.D. some cotton was woven in Roman colonies in the Near East and in the Sudan.

Cotton was grown in Elis in Greece in the second century A.D., and the women made hair nets from it. At the end of the same century the scholar Pollux described a fabric made with a linen warp and a cotton filling, the first reference to what was later called fustian.

Trade declined with the fall of Rome, to pick up again under Arab domination in the ninth and tenth centuries (the word cotton was derived from the Arabic *qutn*). The Muslims encouraged the cotton industry in the Near East and established it in Spain. Cotton flourished in Spain, and by the fourteenth century fabrics of superior softness were being woven in Granada. Catalonia became a fustian weaving center at an early date.

By the thirteenth century the cotton industry was well established in Italy. Milan, Padua, and Genoa were important weaving towns and trading centers. In the fourteenth century Venice and Milan were manufacturing fustians and dimities. Some of these fabrics found their way to the early medieval fairs in France, and the industry, mainly fustian weaving, moved northward. As early as 1300 cotton was imported into Flanders, but it was not used for warp. Much was used for quilt or garment waddings and for candlewicks. Cotton played a minor role in the medieval European textile industry because of spinning and supply problems. These problems were alleviated when supplies of longer staple cotton were brought from the New World. There is no record of cotton yarn being woven into cloth in Europe, except on a warp of another fiber, until the close of the eighteenth century.[10]

On the other hand, all-cotton fabrics from India were known in England as early as the eighth century. Sources (mostly church inventories) indicate that dyed and painted Indian cottons were not rare in Europe prior to the opening of sea trade in the 1500s.[11] It was the sea trade, initiated by the Portuguese, that brought large quantities of cotton goods to Europe in the form of exotic prints and utilitarian types of goods. By the seventeenth century Indian cotton became a substitute for linen, and India continued to supply both Europe and America with fabrics until the Industrial Revolution brought the cotton industry to England.

Silk

Once upon a time (about 2700 B.C.), the Chinese princess Si-Ling-Chi was walking in her garden. She idly picked a fuzzy white cocoon from her favorite mulberry tree, which had been covered with caterpillars a few days before. She toyed with the cocoon awhile, accidently dropped it into her tea, and found that she could pull out a long strand. Thus began a textile industry. Si-Ling-Chi became the patroness of Chinese silk, and a day in her honor was celebrated annually until 1911. Her Province of Shantung was the "cradle of silk weaving."

Silk is an animal fiber composed of protein called *fibroin*. The silkworm, really a caterpillar, eats voraciously of mulberry leaves for almost five weeks, expanding tremendously and shedding its skin four times. When "ripe," the creature begins to secrete a double-stranded filament that is held together with a gummy protein called *sericin*. The silkworm moves its head in a figure-eight pattern and winds the silk around itself. Making the cocoon takes two to three days. Inside the cocoon the caterpillar, now much smaller, changes into a chrysalis and in ten to twelve days to a moth that will emerge and break the filament if not killed first by steam or hot air. The moth mates, lays its eggs, dies within four days, and the cycle begins again. Silkworms are touchy and require proper temperatures and absence of both bad odors and loud noises—although they like to listen to good music. (See Plate 3).

It is usually *Bombyx mori,* the species grown first in China, that has been cultivated commercially. It feeds on mulberry and makes the finest and whitest silk. There are a number of wild varieties, some reputed to make colored silk because of what they eat. Usually the filaments of wild silk cocoons are broken when the moth emerges, but *Antheraea pernyi* (Tussah) leaves an opening in the cocoon that it seals with sericin, and the filament remains intact.

Silk is a strong and fairly elastic fiber, one that is absorbent and comfortable to wear. Its luster gives silk a special appeal that has never been matched by other natural fibers.

Making Yarn

The Chinese discovered that sericin could be softened by boiling water and the filaments loosened and pulled from the cocoons. A worker would whip the water

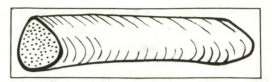

FIGURE 2.15 / Silk Fiber (microscopic view).

with a branched stick to which the filaments would adhere, or the ends of several cocoons would be run through the eyes in small porcelain discs and combined to make yarn. This process, called *reeling,* has always required skill and is still best done by hand, because each filament is narrower toward the beginning and the end, and as each cocoon is exhausted a new one needs to be joined carefully. Individual filaments can be a thousand yards long. Reeled silk is also called *grege* or *raw silk.* It has no twist and can be used for weaving only if left in the gum and the sericin is not boiled off.

The next step, *throwing,* is a twisting operation. Yarns to be used for different purposes are thrown as singles, "S" or "Z," with different amounts of twist, giving organzine, crepe, tram, or grenadine yarn. Thrown silk is made from filaments, while *schappe,* or *spun silk,* is made by carding, combing, and spinning waste silk. Schappe makes heavier and duller textiles than those made of reeled or thrown silk.

Silk in China

Ancient Westerners thought Chinese silk (serica) was a type of cotton scraped from tree bark in the gloomy forests of the Seres (Chinese). Aristotle wrote of the wild kinds that grew around the Mediterranean and on the island of Cos where the fiber was probably woven, but he knew nothing of Chinese silk culture. Pliny also described the industry on Cos, but by then the women may well have been raveling silk fabrics from China to get yarns for their famous transparent fabrics.

Some very old Chinese chronicles described the silk industry, but very little is known about the period prior to the Han dynasty (202 B.C. to 220 A.D.), except that silk was used widely and worn by all classes, served as a medium of exchange, was hoarded, and was used to pay tribute. During the Han dynasty the Chinese started to move westward and in 110 B.C. sent an embassy to the Parthians in Persia. Soon long camel caravans crossed the vast desolate regions of Central Asia with goods for the West. A network of routes known as the Great Silk Road (Figure 2.16) linked China with Syria, Asia Minor and India (where silk had been traded since the fourth century B.C.). Zones of settlement grew along these routes, and as goods passed from one territory to the next they were heavily taxed, often in kind. The Chinese exported silk yarn and fabrics but not the knowledge of how they were made.

Silk in Other Lands

Silk was seen by the Romans for the first time in 53 B.C. at the battle of Carrhae

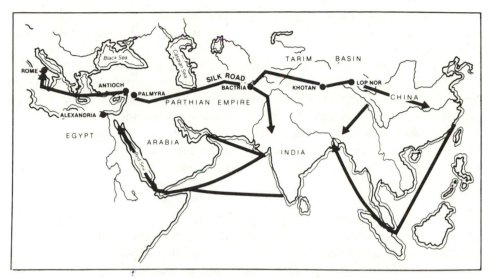

FIGURE 2.16 / Silk Trade in Early Centuries A.D.

in Persia.[12] Marcus Lincinius Crassus led seven legions out from Syria across the Euphrates in pursuit of an enemy that persistently eluded him. At Carrhae the Parthians turned and attacked with a dreadful frenzy. They killed twenty thousand and captured ten thousand more (men who vanished into history somewhere in Central Asia). The Romans fought hard and tried to hold, but their ranks finally broke at the very moment the Parthians unfurled their silken banners. The sudden dazzle, amid the din of the battle, proved too much.

About 45 B.C. silk was brought to Rome by Caesar for his canopies, and from then on it became an expensive and desirable luxury, one that the Senate banned in the first century A.D. It was not considered decent attire for Romans—but demand did indeed grow.

Alexandria, Antioch, and Jerusalem were silk weaving centers by the fourth century. Silk was very expensive by the time it got there: duties were especially high as it passed through Persia. Sea routes down the Red Sea and over to India were developed, but they were used more after the third century when upheavals in Central Asia made the Great Silk Road unsafe. The Sassanid Persian silk weaving industry was probably developed by weavers brought from Syria after the fourth century. A state-monopolized weaving industry was also on the rise in Byzantium before sericulture was known.

The secret of the silkworm could not be kept forever. The Japanese learned it sometime around 200 A.D., when, according to one story, they offered a large reward and some Koreans kidnapped four Chinese concubines who were forced to tell. According to another, the secret was on its way west in 400 A.D. with a Chinese princess who was to marry a Khotan prince. She hid silkworms in her hair as part of her dowry, but she neglected to tell the part about stifling the moth before it emerged—so the Khotans never had continuous filament. One hundred and fifty years later Emperor Justinian in Constantinople rewarded two Nestorian monks who had smuggled eggs and mulberry seeds from either China or Khotan by hiding them inside their canes.

Learning sericulture was a great stimulus to silk weaving in the Near East. Industries for throwing yarn grew up in Tyre, Sidon, and Beirut. After the seventh century all the Near Eastern silk industry outside of Byzantium was controlled by the Muslims, who also introduced silk to Spain in the eighth century.

There were some interesting medieval legends about silk: it was really made by fairies who lived on a mysterious island; it never sat right upon a faithless woman; a young woman caught in a storm had no fear of lightning if she wore a silk chemise. Perhaps a bit more scientific was the belief that wearing silk garments protected against disease—vermin would not lodge in them.

Through late medieval and early modern times the silk industry gradually spread throughout Europe, moving from south to north—the great centers were in Spain and Italy, then France, and finally England (see chapters 6 and 8). France gave up sericulture in the mid-nineteenth century when a disastrous epidemic of pebrine disease swept the industry. Japan, free of the disease, then became the world's supplier of silk. Today, China is again a major producer of silk, a product with a dwindling demand except from the luxury market.

The silkworm, however, is not yet extinct, although one wrote her will a long time ago:

The Silk-Worm's Will
by
Miss H. F. Gould

On a plain rush bundle a silk-worm lay,
When a proud young princess came that way:
The haughty child of a human king,
Threw a sidelong glance at the humble thing,
That took, with a silent gratitude,
From the mulberry leaf, her simple food;
And shrunk, half scorn and half disgust,
Away from her sister child of dust—
Declaring she never yet could see
Why a reptile form like this should be,
And that she was not made with nerves so firm,
As calmly to stand by a "crawling worm!"

With mute forbearance the silk-worm took
The taunting words, and the spurning look:
Alike a stranger to self and pride,
She's no disquiet from aught beside—
And lived of a meekness and peace possessed,
Which these debar from the human breast.
She only wished, for the harsh abuse,

To find some way to become of use
To the haughty daughter of lordly man;
And thus did she lay a noble plan,
To teach her wisdom, and make it plain,
That the humble worm was not made in vain;
A plan so generous, deep and high,
That, to carry it out, she must even die!

"No more," said she, "will I drink or eat!
I'll spin and weave me a winding-sheet,
To wrap me up from the sun's clear light,
And hide my form from her wounded sight.
In secret then, till my end draws nigh,
I'll toil for her; and when I die,
I'll leave behind, as a farewell boon,
To the proud young princess, my whole cocoon,
To be reeled and wove to a shining lace
And hung in a veil o'er her scornful face!
And when she can calmly draw her breath
Through the very threads that have caused my death;
When she finds, at length, she has nerves so firm
As to wear the shroud of a crawling worm,
May she bear in mind, that she walks with pride
In the winding-sheet where the silk-worm died!"[13]

Wool

Wool was probably the last of the major fibers to be spun. Nomads, the early herdsmen, would have learned spinning from sedentary people who spun the vegetable fibers for textiles because they lacked pelts. Shears were unknown until the Iron Age, about 1000 B.C. Before that time the fiber was plucked with a comb-like device or hacked off with a stone knife.

Wool, a modified hair fiber composed of the protein *keratin,* developed from the inner coat of wild sheep that originated in Central Asia. Like many animals, these sheep had outer coats of coarse fibers (hair) and inner coats of soft finer fibers (wool). Over time, the wild sheep of Asia were domesticated and bred to have a predominance of inner coat. Wool fibers are much crimpier than hair and so are generally easier to spin.

Fibers from different breeds of sheep vary greatly in size, length, and color, but common to all wool and hair fibers is their external structure. Under the microscope a wool fiber shows a surface covered with scales (Figure 2.17). Scales vary in size and prominence according to wool type. If a mass of wool or hair is rubbed while it is damp the fiber scales will interlock, making felt. Probably wool was felted earlier than it was spun, and felting would have occurred unintentionally if pelts were worn fur side in.

*FIGURE 2.17 / * Wool Fiber (microscopic view).

Preparation for Spinning

Wool from different breeds contains varying amounts of grease (a mixture of fats), suint (dried perspiration), and extraneous matter such as burrs, plant leaves, and excrement. In some places sheep are washed in a nearby river before shearing, or the wool is spun "in the grease." In other places the fleeces are scoured with various cleaning agents. Usually water is used, but in desert regions wool may be cleaned with sand.

After scouring the wool is *picked,* a mechanical process now, but as early as Roman times fiber was spread on a mesh surface and beaten with sticks. Any remaining trash fell through the mesh, and the matted wool was fluffed and made ready for *carding.* The purpose of carding is to align the fibers. It can be done with the fingers, with a bow (as cotton is ginned), with *teasels* (carding comes from the Latin *carduus*, meaning thistle), with hand cards set with bent metal wire (first made in thirteenth century France), or by machine (Plate 4). After carding the wool is ready to spin for *woolens*—fabrics with large, fluffy yarns.

Another aligning process is *combing,* but only long wools are combed. Early Roman combs had iron teeth set into wooden frames. Until the mid-nineteenth century combing remained a skilled hand operation. Combs were heated and worked in pairs, and as the wool was pulled through, the short fibers, or *noils*, were removed and the long strands of *top* made ready to spin for *worsteds*—fabrics with small, smooth, slightly lustrous yarns.[14]

Wool does not twist in a certain direction as the vegetable fibers do, so in some regions it was spun "S" after the fashion of flax, in other regions "Z" after the fashion of cotton. In ancient times it was spun on a drop spindle. The added weight of the spindle helped to attenuate the fibers (Figure 2.18). In medieval and early modern times, wool was spun on the Jersey wheel.

Wool in Ancient Lands

Mesopotamia was the "land of wool" and the first place where sheep were domesticated. The tablets of Ur (2000 B.C.) tell of huge flocks of white and black sheep, of hundreds being shorn in a single day, of wool being sold and the prices received. They tell of 127 slave girls and thirty children working the wool, and of 165 women and girls weaving.

More is known about wool in the ancient Holy Land. It was mentioned frequently in the Old Testament and in Jewish law, and wandering Hebrews measured their wealth in sheep and goats. The Hebrews made jackets for some of

FIGURE 2.18 / Spinning Wool.

their sheep to protect fleeces from the yellowing effects of sunlight and became famous for pure white wool. There was extensive spinning and weaving of wool in the Holy Land and Asia Minor by about 1000 B.C., and in the seventh century B.C. the Phoenicians bought homespun from the Israelites and traded it for British tin. Jerusalem was a major wool market, and weaving remained an important industry in Palestine until cheap European textiles flooded the markets in the late nineteenth century.

Early Egyptians spun and wove wool. Skeletal remains and murals of hairy steppe sheep and balls of spun yarn date from 2000 B.C. The wool industry seems to have died out in favor of flax, but it was reinstated during the late centuries B.C. by the Syrians.

Some of the oldest surviving wool fabrics, dated 300 to 500 B.C., have come from the frozen graves of the Scythians, nomads who roamed the steppes of Eurasia. Ancient Greeks pictured the Scythians as griffins, with heads of eagles and bodies of lions, guarding their gold. The Scythians made outstanding felt appliqués for hangings and horse trappings and pile rugs with some 230 knots per inch.

Wool was the major fiber worn in Greece; as early as the sixth century B.C. the Greeks made woolens that were fulled and napped and worsteds called *trita*. Most of the spinning and weaving was done by women in their homes, but in many towns there were specialists for finishing the cloth. During the Greek period some sections of Asia Minor were noted for clips of fine wool, textiles, and embroideries.

Syria exported considerable quantities of woolens.

Wool was also the fiber used most commonly by the Romans. They were expert sheep breeders and were thought to have produced the ancestors of the fine-wooled Spanish Merino. In Rome there were mills that employed three hundred or more *textores*, and many tasks were specialized. Pompeii had extensive fulleries, and other factory-like operations were located throughout the empire. Both fine goods from Asia Minor and very coarse ones from Gaul were imported by Rome, but old-fashioned leaders, like Augustus, made a point of wearing homespun. Columella, a soldier and farmer of the first century A.D., considered home weaving essential:

> Nowadays when wives so generally give way to luxury and idleness that they do not deign to carry the burden of manufacturing wool, but disdain clothing made at home, and with perverse desire are pleased with clothing that costs great sums and is bought at a whole year's income we have to appoint stewardesses on the farm to perform the offices of the matron.
>
> On rainy and cold days when the slave-woman can not do farmwork in the open, let the wool be ready-combed and prepared beforehand so that they may be busy themselves at spinning and weaving, and the steward's wife may exact the usual amount of work. It will do no harm if clothing is spun at home for the stewards, overseers and the better class of slaves so that the owner's accounts may bear the less burden.[15]

After Rome fell in the fifth century the wool industry continued as a very simple cottage industry.

Medieval and Modern Centers

When the Muslims occupied Spain in the eighth century they were already familiar with working wool. Their knowledge, combined with supplies of fine wool developed by the Romans, served to build one of the greatest wool industries of the early Middle Ages. Operating under a guild system, the Catalan industry grew to a peak in the fifteenth century, but when the Muslims were expelled from Spain at the end of that century, the industry declined.

After the thirteenth century two basic types of sheep were raised in Spain: *Transhumantes,* or migrating sheep, and *Estantes,* stationary flocks. The Merino was developed from the *Transhumantes* in the fourteenth century, and lighter and softer fabrics could be woven as a consequence. From the *Estantes* came the *Churro* (the common meat variety) brought to the New World by the conquistadores (see chapter 11).

Fourteenth century Italians gained fame as the best dyers and finishers of woolens that were purchased in Flanders, the leading woolen exporter from the ninth to the fourteenth century. Flemmish-grown wool was coarse, and when open land became scarce in the thirteenth century, the Flemmings gave up growing wool and imported finer kinds from Britain, Spain, and Germany. They did continue to weave and finish some very high quality fabrics.

Just as Mesopotamia had been the capital of wool in antiquity, England held the title in the late medieval and modern periods. The long history of wool in Britain is represented by an extant piece of Yorkshire cloth at least four thousand years old. The Romans had woolen factories there to supply their armies. Manufacture declined with the barbarian invasions but apparently did not die altogether, because there are reports of woolen exports in the eighth century. William the Conqueror took weavers to Britain with him in 1066, and in 1080 the first guild of weavers was established near Bristol. By 1200 England was the main wool growing country in Europe. The monasteries and large landowners kept huge flocks, and wool merchants, who became very wealthy, traveled from place to place making contracts for clips a year or two in advance. At first the English concentrated on growing wool for export; in fact, they had poor reputations as weavers until some Flemmings were induced to immigrate and teach their skills. But by the seventeenth century England was shipping wool cloth all over the world, and during the eighteenth and nineteenth centuries could not supply enough raw wool for her own mills.

Australia, started as a penal colony in 1788, sent great quantities of wool back to England in the magnificent clipper ships of the mid-nineteenth century. South America and South Africa also became large producers of wool for English mills.

A story about Christopher Columbus, born to a Genoa weaving family, can be used to sum up the major natural fibers. He discovered America, because he was looking for the East and a source of marvelous Chinese silks. He was financed by Spanish wool interests. He found cotton growing in the West Indies. And surely, he was wearing a linen shirt at the time.

MINOR TEXTILE MATERIALS

A large variety of natural fibers have been used locally by different cultures throughout history. Most have come from plant stems or leaves and the undercoats of fur bearing animals. Historic information is scanty; specific identification of charred or decayed fibers from archaeological sites is usually impossible, and ancient writers seldom distinguished the minor materials.

Bast Fibers

Bast fibers, from plant stems, have been widely used in bagging and cordage as well as apparel. Of the little information about them most concerns their production after the nineteenth century. Now most have been replaced by man-made fibers.

Hemp comes from *Cannabis sativa,* an annual with a very long history as a narcotic. The Latin word has given us canvas, camp, canopy. The word hemp came from the Teutonic *hänaf,* or *haenif,* first in use sometime between 500 and 250 B.C. Hemp probably originated in western Asia and India and was cultivated by the first millennium B.C. Coarse, strong, and durable, it was used extensively for ropes and sails in ancient times and also for clothing, especially by the poor.

Hemp is a dioecious plant: ironically, the male plants are called *fimble* hemp (from the Latin *femmella* or female) because they are shorter and thinner than the females, which are called *carl* hemp (from the Old Norse meaning man). The males are picked for fiber two or three weeks ahead of the females, which supply both fiber and seed.

Historically, hemp was retted like flax, but fibers were usually stripped by hand. After the fourteenth century a flax brake was used in some areas. Hemp fibers were pounded with a mallet to soften them and were then *swingled*—thrown over a board and beaten with a wooden sword to remove the straw.

Fibers from a number of other plants have been called hemp: *sunn,* a bast fiber that grew in India in prehistoric times; *kenaf* from Africa and India, and *apocynum* from the American Southwest. *Esparto grass,* a rush known in ancient Mesopotamia, and fiber from the *papyrus* plant, used for blankets, mats, ropes, and sails in early Egypt, were also known as hemp.

Jute is another very old bast fiber, common in India and called Calcutta hemp. Jute (the word comes from Indian *jhot,* meaning entangled) is prepared for spinning in the same manner as hemp. Coarse, strong, but brittle, jute is most suitable for bagging cloth and carpet backing, but it has been worn by the poor in India. Jute was first seen in Europe in the mid-eighteenth century when the British East India Company persuaded the government of the Netherlands to substitute jute yarn for flax in coffee bags. Dundee Scotland was an important jute spinning center in the early ninetenth century, when the Napoleonic Wars cut off the supply of Russian hemp and flax. The industry was enlarged when the Crimean War again cut off Russian fibers and when the American Civil War made cheap cotton unavailable.

Bast from *nettle* plants supplied fiber to northern Europeans as early as the Bronze Age. It was used for sails in Scandinavia. Several varieties of nettle grew in the temperate climates of both the Old and the New Worlds. Instead of retting, the bark was boiled to release the fiber, which was then combed.

Egyptian mummies dated to 5000 B.C. were found wrapped in *ramie,* or China grass, a plant that belongs to the nettle family. Ramie was spun and woven in early Mediterranean civilizations and during the Middle Ages in Europe. It is now produced commercially in many parts of the world, especially the Orient where it is used in clothing.

Bamboo fibers, extracted from young plants by soaking the stems, then peeling off the skins and chewing the mass, were used in Borneo and Java. The short fibers were knotted together and woven into sarongs, jackets, and trousers.

Other Plant Fibers

Abaca, a fiber indigenous to the Philippines, has been known as Manila hemp even though it comes from the leaves of a banana plant. It was important in the Western world as a cordage fiber after the mid-nineteenth century, because it was strong and water resistant.

Sisal is a leaf fiber from the agave family indigenous to Central America; the name came from the Yucatan port of Sisal. It was used by the Aztecs for clothing; now it is a carpet fiber. A closely related plant is *henequen.*

The Ceylonese coconut is an interesting source of fiber. That derived from it is called *coir.* It probably never reached the ancient Near East, but in the thirteenth century Marco Polo wrote of ropes made of coconut fiber. The Arabs taught the natives of Ceylon how to spin the fiber, recovered from the husks by retting and beating.

Animal Fibers

Man has always used fibers from the animals domesticated for his food supply and his transportation. The *camel* has proved useful for thousands of years. Fiber comes from the undercoat of the two-humped Bactrian variety, a common beast of burden in Asia. Trailers go along behind the caravans and pick up the hair that is shed in the spring. (Sometimes, if the camel is agreeable, the fiber can be plucked.) The trailer loads the clumps into baskets carried by the last camel and sells it in the towns along the route. Camel's hair cloth became popular in England about 1840, even though it cost $100 a yard. It was introduced by an army captain who had served in India.

New World members of the camel family, the *llama, alpaca, vicuna,* and *guanaco* furnished fiber in pre-Columbian South America (there were no sheep until the Spanish brought them). Today, the most commonly used of the four is the alpaca. Its fiber, which varies in color from black to white with many shades of tan and grey, has been made into dress fabrics, tropical suitings, and knits. The fleece of the llama does not grow as long as that of the alpaca, and the fibers are more brittle and coarse, but the color range is about the same. Llama is used for carpets and heavy fabrics. Both the guanaco and the vicuna are wild animals that must be killed to get the fiber, and the Peruvians are working to conserve and domesticate them. Vicuna is the softest, rarest, and most expensive fiber; it is used for shawls and coating fabrics.

The goat is another animal that has furnished fiber for thousands of years. *Cashmere* is the most elegant and expensive; its soft fiber is combed from domesticated goats of China, northern India, and central Asia. The finest fiber, *pashmina,* was used in the famous Kashmir shawls (see chapter 7).

Mohair, from Angora goats, is much coarser than cashmere but easier to spin because of its length. It makes durable fabrics. Until the early nineteenth century mohair was raised only in Turkey, but now several countries, including the United States, produce it. Hair from many other animals has at times been used for textiles: deer, reindeer, moose, rabbits, dogs, and even people.

One fiber, *byssus,* has been a real challenge to textile historians. Pliny called byssus a type of very fine linen, and other authors seem to have used the word to mean cotton cloth. At times "byssus" meant a particular shade of purple. Most interesting is the byssus filament secreted by several bivalve mollusks, one of genus *Pinna:* bundles of fibers extrude from a gland in the foot of the creature and serve to hold it to rock surfaces. Much speculation can be raised about ancient spinning and weaving methods for byssus.

Mineral Fibers

Another fiber, once considered magic, could be cleaned by fire. Pliny reported its use in shrouds for royalty so their ashes would be kept separate from those of the funeral pyre. The Arabs used it for protective suits to wear into towns put to the torch, and Charlemagne is supposed to have awed the barbarians into retreat by tossing his tablecloth into the fire, then pulling it out undamaged. This fiber is thought to have originated in China at a very early date, and it "grew" in that part of India so hot and dry that only snakes could live there. The Chinese called it stone wool; Pliny called it *asbestinon*. The fibers are mineral crystals.

As early as 1600 B.C. the Egyptians drew *glass* filaments to ornament vases. Both Robert Hooke in the seventeenth century and the Frenchman Reaumur in the eighteenth century speculated on the possibility of making cloth from glass, but it was not until 1842 that any was actually woven. The first glass to be used for clothing was woven on a silk warp for a stage star in America in 1893.

Metallic Yarns

It is impossible to know just how much gold and silver was woven into the sumptuous ancient and medieval textiles. Tons of cloth were melted for their gold content by conquering armies or impoverished monarchs. Silver is thought to have been used as early as 2000 B.C., and reference is made in the book of Exodus (39:3) to a robe interwoven with wire made from beaten gold. Darius I of Persia (fifth century B.C.) wore a mantle with gold hawks, and Henry VIII met Francis I on the Field of the Cloth of Gold in 1520.

Aurum battutum, pure gold, pounded out into very thin sheets and cut into strips, was probably the oldest type of metallic yarn. Fragments have been found from the third century B.C. in the Crimea, and it was used in medieval Europe. The Egyptians used narrow strips of pure gold wound around a linen core. *Aurum Tracitium,* drawn gold wire, has been found in Viking graves, and it was the type used in the fifteenth century brocaded velvets from Italy. *Aurum filatum,* known as skin gold in eleventh century Cyprus, was made by winding a narrow strip of gilded animal gut around a linen core. The Chinese gilded paper and wrapped it around cotton or silk. These core yarns were lighter and more flexible than the drawn wire thread. Now gold yarn is made from aluminum and polyester.

NOTES

1. W. Born, "The Spinning Wheel," *CIBA Review* 28 (December 1939):989.

2. R. J. Forbes, *Studies in Ancient Technology,* Volume 4, *Textiles,* 2nd rev. ed. (Leiden, Netherlands: E.J. Brill, 1964), p. 1; and J. P. Wild, *Textile Manufacture in the Northern Roman Provinces* (Cambridge, England: Cambridge University Press, 1970), pp. 41-44.

3. Forbes, *Studies,* 4:152; and Louisa Bellinger, *Textile Analysis: Early Techniques in Egypt and the Near East,* The Textile Museum Paper No. 2 (Washington, D.C.: The Textile Museum, June 1950).

4. Grace Crowfoot, "Textiles, Basketry, and Mats," in *A History of Technology,* 5 vols., ed. Charles Singer et al. (Oxford: Clarendon Press, 1954-1958), 1:413.

5. Louisa Bellinger, "The History of Threads: Natural Fibers and Elements," in *Threads of History* (New York: The American Federation of Arts, 1965), p. 28.

6. Louisa Bellinger, *The Bible as a Source Book for the Study of Textiles, Workshop Notes,* The Textile Museum Paper No. 18 (Washington D. C.: The Textile Museum, November 1958).

7. Forbes, *Studies,* p. 35.

8. Ibid., p. 47

9. John Irwin, "Indian Textile Trade in the Seventeenth Century," *Journal of Indian Textile History* 1 (1955):5. This journal is a publication of the Calico Museum of Textiles, Ahmedabad, India.

10. Thomas Ellison, *The Cotton Trade of Great Britain* (1886; reprint ed., New York: A. M. Kelley, 1968), p. 3.

11. Agnes Geijer, "Some Evidence of Indo-European Cotton Trade in Pre-Mughal Times," *Journal of Indian Textile History* 1 (1955):39.

12. See "Introduction" of Luce Boulnois, *The Silk Road* (New York: Dutton, 1966).

13. Clinton G. Gilroy, *The History of Silk, Cotton, Linen, Wool, and Other Fibrous Substances; including Observations on Spinning, Dyeing and Weaving* (New York: Harper and Brothers, 1845), pp. 117-118.

14. For a detailed account of combing in the eighteenth century see James Bischoff, *Comprehensive History of the Woollen and Worsted Manufactures and the Natural and Commercial History of Sheep* (1842; reprint ed., New York: A. M. Kelley, 1968). The differences in spinning methods for woolen and worsted yarns are discussed in K. G. Ponting's introduction in *Baine's Account of the Woollen Manufacture of England,* 2nd ed. (New York: A. M. Kelley, 1970), pp. 37-42.

15. Forbes, *Studies,* pp. 22-23, as quoted from *Columella 12.*

BIBLIOGRAPHY

Review in any general textiles text such as Norma Hollen and Jane Saddler, *Textiles,* 4th ed. (New York: Macmillan, 1973) or Marjory L. Joseph, *Essentials of Textiles* (New York: Holt, Rinehart, and Winston, 1976) would be helpful for the reader unfamiliar with fibers and their properties.

The oldest general history of textiles is James Yates, *Textrinum Antiquorum: An Account of Weaving Among the Ancients* (London: Taylor and Walton, 1843). In 1845 Clinton G. Gilroy considered it the only competent work available when he wrote *The History of Silk, Cotton, Linen, Wool, and Other Fibrous Substances: including Observations on Spinning, Dyeing and Weaving* (New York: Harper and Brothers, 1845). Although somewhat tedious for the twentieth century reader, Gilroy does present some interesting information.

The most scholarly and complete publication covering ancient fibers and spinning is R. J. Forbes, *Studies in Ancient Technology,* Volume 4, *Textiles,* 2nd rev. ed. (Leiden, Netherlands: E. J. Brill, 1964). J.P. Wild, *Textile Manufacture in the Northern Roman Provinces* (Cambridge, England: Cambridge University Press, 1970) is also well documented and is easier to read, although less complete. For a thorough explanation of fiber differences in regard to spinning and weaving methods see Rene Batigne and Louisa Bellinger, "The Significance and Technical Analysis of Ancient Textiles as Historical Documents," *American Philosophical Society Proceedings* 97, no. 6 (1953):670-680. Some of their theory is covered elsewhere: see Louisa Bellinger, *Textile Analysis: Early Techniques in Egypt and the Near East,* The Textile Museum Paper No. 2 (Washington D. C.: The Textile Museum, June 1950), and "The History of Threads: Natural Fibers and Filaments," in *Threads of History* (New York: The American Federation of Arts, 1965).

Primitive hand spinning methods are presented in helpful outline form in Mary Lois Kissell's old text *Yarn and Cloth Making, An Economic Study* (New York: Macmillan, 1918). A fairly good short history is "The Spinning Wheel," *CIBA Review* 28 (December 1939). See also "The Reel," *CIBA Review* 59 (August 1947). Hand spinning is explained simply in W. English, *The Textile Industry: An Account of the Early Invention of Spinning, Weaving, and Knitting Machines* (London: Longmans, Green, 1969). More current and scholarly work on spinning technology can be found in various articles in *Textile History,* a journal published by The Pasold Research Fund, Ltd., Becketts House, Edington, NR Westbury, Wilts., U.K.

There are two major histories of flax: Alex J. Warden's *The Linen Trade* (1864; reprint ed., London: Frank Cass, 1967); and William F. Leggett's *Story of Linen* (Brooklyn: Chemical Publishing Co., 1945). Neither cites sources or is very concise. Warden is especially verbose. Virginia D. Parslow, "Spinning Fibers in Early New York," *New York History* 29, no. 4 (October 1948): 428-435 is complete on the process used on nineteenth century farms. Also see her (under the name of Virginia Parslow Partridge) "Flax From Seed to Yarn," *Handweaver and Craftsman* 3, no. 2 (Spring 1952). The European industry is discussed in John Horner, *The Linen Trade of Europe During The Spinning-Wheel Period* (Belfast, Ireland: The Linenhall Press, 1920); Conrad Gill, *The Rise of the Irish Linen Industry* (1925; reprint ed., Oxford: Clarendon Press, 1964); and N. B. Harte and K. G. Ponting, eds., *Textile History and Economic History, Essays in Honor of Miss Julia de Lacy Mann* (Manchester, England: Manchester University Press, 1973).

Helpful pieces in *CIBA Review* include: "Cloth Making in Flanders," 14 (October 1938); "The History of the Textile Crafts in Holland," 48 (May 1944); "Flax and Hemp," 49 (April 1945); and "Textiles in Biblical Times," no. 2 (1968). *CIBA Review* (later *CIBA-GEIGY Review*), an important serial in the area of textiles and their production, was published from 1937 until 1975 by CIBA Limited (later CIBA-GEIGY Limited) in Basel, Switzerland. An index covering most of the articles of interest to textile historians was published in issue no. 4 (1970).

A classic source on cotton is M. D. C. Crawford, *The Heritage of Cotton* (New York: Grosset & Dunlap, 1924). His style is outdated, but the information is generally good. (Perhaps Crawford's best statement is "You can no more explain spinning than you can describe how Fritz Kreisler plays a violin.") The other classic is Edward Baines, *History of the Cotton Manufacture in Great Britain* (London: H. Fisher, R. Fisher, and P. Jackson, 1835). This also includes some ancient history. The second edition of Baines (New York: Augustus M. Kelley, 1966) is more valuable than the first, because it contains a bibliographical introduction by W. H. Chaloner giving sources for the cotton industry in the British Isles. An important scholarly article is Andrew M. Watson, "The Rise and Spread of Old World Cotton," in *Studies in Textile History,* ed. Veronika Gervers (Toronto: Royal Ontario Museum, 1977), pp. 355-368.

Indian cotton is covered by Rustam J. Mehta, *Masterpieces of Indian Textiles* (Bombay: D. B. Taraporevala Sons & Co. Private Ltd., 1970); and John Irwin and P. R. Schwartz, *Studies in Indo-European Textile History* (Ahmedabad, India: Calico Museum of Textiles, 1966). The latter study discusses the seventeenth century trade.

Also see R. Marsden, *Cotton Spinning* (London: George Bell and Sons, 1909); and Carl Johan Lamm, *Cotton in Mediaeval Textiles of the Near East* (Paris: P. Geuthner, 1937). *CIBA Review* articles include "Cotton and Cotton Trade in the Middle Ages," 64 (February 1948); "Cotton," 95 (December 1952); and "Manchester—The Origins of Cottonopolis," no. 2 (1962).

There are many books on the British cotton industry. Three that are useful for the period prior to the Industrial Revolution are Thomas Ellison, *The Cotton Trade of Great Britain*; C. H. Lee, *A Cotton Enterprise, 1795-1840; a history of M'Connel and Kennedy fine cotton spinners* (Manchester, England: Manchester University Press, 1972); and a classic by Alfred P. Wadsworth and Julia de Lacy Mann, *The Cotton Trade and Industrial Lancashire, 1600-1780* (1931; reprint ed., Manchester, England: Manchester University Press, 1965). See also bibliography for Chapter 8.

Overviews of silk include William Leggett, *The Story of Silk* (New York: Lifetime Editions, 1949); and Joseph Schober, *Silk and the Silk Industry* (London: Constable, 1930). Scholarly and very interesting, especially for its account of ancient trade, is Luce Boulnois, *The Silk Road* (New York: Dutton, 1966).

CIBA Review is quite extensive on European silk history. See "Silks of Lyons," 6 (February 1938); "The Early History of Silk," 11 (July 1938); "Venetian Silks," 29 (January 1940); "Lucchese Silks," 80 (June 1950); and "Silk Moths," 53 (November 1946). Peter Thornton, *Baroque and Rococo Silks* (New York: Taplinger Publishing Co., 1965) is complete on European silk weaving centers. An interesting section on silk throwing can be found in George S. White, *Memoir of Samuel Slater* (1836; reprint ed., New York: A. M. Kelley, 1967). An excellent economic study is Min-hsiung Shih, *The Silk Industry in Ch'ing China,* Michigan Abstracts No. 5 (Ann Arbor, Michigan: The University of Michigan Center for Chinese Studies, 1976).

Ancient wool is covered most thoroughly in Forbes, Wild, and "Textiles in Biblical Times," *CIBA Review* no. 2 (1968). Shelagh Weir, *Spinning and Weaving in Palestine* (London: The British Museum, 1970), relates to old methods in describing twentieth century weaving. Sergei I. Rudenko, *Frozen Tombs of Siberia, The Pazyryk Burials of Iron Age Horsemen* (Berkeley and Los Angeles: University of California Press, 1970) is excellent for both historical background and costume and textile information. See also M. I. Artamonov, "Frozen Tombs of the Scythians," *Scientific American*, May 1965 pp. 100-109.

General surveys are provided by William Leggett, *The Story of Wool* (Brooklyn: Chemical Publishing Co., 1947) and chapter 1 of H. S. Bell, *An Introduction to Wool Production and Marketing* (Bath, England: Pitman Publishing, 1970). Bell is very clearly written. Another general history, but one that is very detailed and involved, can be found in James Bischoff, *Comprehensive History of the Woollen and Worsted Manufactures and the Natural and Commercial History of Sheep* (1842; reprint ed., New York: A. M. Kelley, 1968). Bischoff contains an abridgement of John Smith, *Chronicon Rusticum—Commerciale: or Memoirs of Wool & Being a*

Collection of History and Argument Concerning the Woolen Manufacture and the Woolen Trade in General (London, 1747). Smith's book was reprinted by A. M. Kelley in 1969.

The medieval wool industry is covered very well by E. Carus-Wilson, *Medieval Merchant Venturers,* 2nd ed. (London: Methuen, 1967). She is fairly complete on England. Also important is K. G. Ponting's introduction in *Baine's Account of the Woollen Manufacture of England,* 2nd ed. (New York: A. M. Kelley, 1970). Ponting's bibliography in this helpful second edition lists the major sources, of which there are many, on the English woolen and worsted industries. Baines, also author of *History of Cotton Manufacture,* was a noted nineteenth century English economist and journalist. One of the classics is Herbert Heaton, *The Yorkshire Woollen and Worsted Industries from the Earliest Times up to the Industrial Revolution* (Oxford: Clarendon Press, 1920). A second edition with a new preface appeared in 1965.

Some of the sources that cover later periods in England are Frank Atkinson, *Some Aspects of the 18th Century Woollen & Worsted Trade in Halifax* (England: Halifax Museums, 1956); John James, *History of the Worsted Manufacture in England* (1857; reprint ed., New York: A. M. Kelley, 1968), which is very detailed; E. Lipson, *The History of the Woollen and Worsted Industries* (London: Frank Cass, 1965); and Harte and Ponting, eds., *Textile History and Economic History.* Scotland's industry is discussed in Clifford Gulvin, *The Tweedmakers: A History of the Scottish Fancy Woolen Industry 1600-1914* (New York: Barnes & Noble, 1973).

CIBA Reviews on wool are "Australia, the Land of Wool," 74 (June 1949); "The English Wool Industry," 130 (January 1959); and "The Catelan Textile Industry," no. 3 (1963).

Several of the ancient minor fibers are discussed briefly in Forbes, in Warden, and in Adele Weibel, *Two Thousand Years of Textiles* (New York: Pantheon Books, 1952). J. Gordon Cook gives brief histories for many in the first volume of *Handbook of Textile Fibers,* 2 vols., 4th ed. (Watsford, Hertsfordshire, England: Morrow Publishing Co., 1968).

CIBA Review seems to be the best source for the minor materials: "Flax and Hemp," 49 (April 1945); "Hard Fibers," 99 (August 1953); "Jute and its Substitutes," 108 (February 1955); "Coir," 116 (August-September 1956); "Ramie," 123 (November 1957); "Gold and Textiles," no. 3 (1961); "Hemp," no. 5 (1962); ; "Glass Fibers," no. 5; "Bamboo," no. 3 (1969); and no. 5 (1963); "Asbestos," *CIBA-GEIGY Review* no. 2 (1972).

In addition, see H. Godwin, "The Ancient Cultivation of Hemp," *Antiquity* 41, no. 161 (March 1967):42-48; and 41, no. 162 (June 1967):137-138. Some economic and political aspects are considered in Alfred W. Crosby, *America, Russia, Hemp, and Napoleon: American Trade with Russia and the Baltic, 1783-1812* (Columbus: Ohio State University Press, 1965).

Three little pamphlets, written by Sylvan I. Stroock, were published in New York by S. Stroock and Company: *The Story of Camel Hair,* 1936; *Llamas and Llamaland,* 1937; and *Vicuna, the World's Finest Fabric,* 1937. Although old and quaint, they contain some useful information.

3. FABRIC CONSTRUCTION

Textiles are identified and named by their construction. Construction is dependent upon material and equipment and often determines design and finish. Anthropologists study old construction methods in order to establish ancient trade and migration routes, while artists study them to find new ways to make fiber structures. Some techniques are practiced only in certain cultures, while others are known more widely.

Weaving is the most universal construction method. It probably developed after basket, mat, and net making sometime before 6000 B.C. when early neolithic people settled into permanent dwellings and started to farm and to domesticate animals. Weaving, interlacing two or more sets of strands at right angles to each other, was a simple concept for rigid materials like reeds, but it afforded complex problems when flexible yarns were used. The first record of a weaving device is a picture of a horizontal loom on an Egyptian dish dated 4400 B.C. The loom, one of mankind's simplest and most useful tools, has not changed in basic structure since its prehistoric invention.

LOOMS

The purpose of a loom is to hold one set of elements (warp, ends, lengthwise yarns) evenly, without tangling, and under varying amounts of tension depending on the fiber used, while the other set of elements (weft, filling, woof, picks, shot, crosswise yarns) are interlaced. Most looms have only a few basic parts, and a small one can be made very easily by attaching one end of a group of warp to a fixed point and holding the other end with the fingers. But usually one end of the warp is tied to or rolled around a *warp beam* (back beam or warp bar), and the other end is fastened to the *cloth beam* (front beam) on which the finished fabric can be rolled.

35

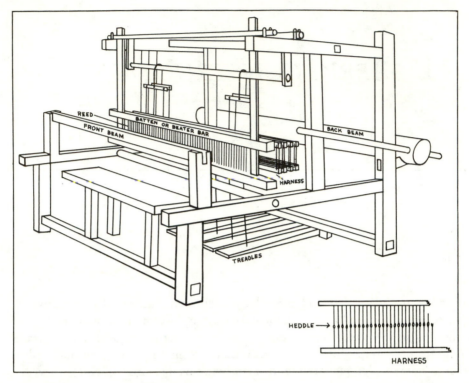

FIGURE 3.1 / Parts of the Loom.

Looms are generally distinguished from other frames used to make openwork and twined fabrics by the addition of *heddles* (healds, headles). One heddle, a loop of string or wire, is attached to one warp yarn. A group of heddles is looped on a heddle rod or held in a frame called a *harness* or *shaft* (Figure 3.1).

Horizontal looms often have *reeds* made of strips of wood, metal, or reed set into a frame as long as the width of the cloth. The warp pass through *dents*, or slots, in the reed and can thus be spaced as desired. On a treadle loom the reed is held in the *beater bar*.

Weaving is a three-step process. During the first, called *shedding*, some of the warp are lifted by raising the harnesses or heddle rods to form a *shed*, that is, a triangular space between the warp that are up and the warp that are down (Figure 3.2). In the case of plain weave, simple "over one/under one" interlacing, half the warp are up and half are down; alternate warp are raised each time the shed is changed. The second step is called *picking*, or *making the shot*. During it the weft, generally wound on some sort of *shuttle*, is passed through the shed. In the third step, *battening* or *beating*, the weft is packed back with a comb, sword-like rod, or the reed.

A precise evolution of the loom cannot yet be given because there is not enough archaeological information available. Very often loom construction has to be deduced from study of the weaves of archaeological finds. Probably different types of looms were in use simultaneously to serve varying purposes. Certain types, however, do tend to belong to specific periods, regions, or fibers.

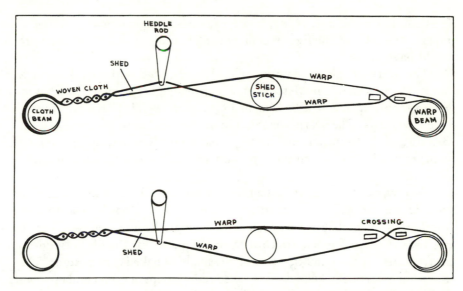

FIGURE 3.2 / Shedding.

The Backstrap Loom

The backstrap (hip strap, waist, band, or belt) loom is a two beam loom with warp held at a slant anywhere between the near horizontal and the near vertical (see Plate 129 and Figures 11.4 and 12.2). The warp beam is attached to a fixed point and the cloth beam is connected to the weaver by a belt around the waist or hips. As the weaver adjusts body position, the proper tension is applied to the warp. Generally the fabrics woven on a backstrap loom are quite small; there is no way to make yardage by rolling long warp on the warp beam. Pieces with four selvages may be woven on this loom, however.

One heddle rod plus a shed rod behind it speeds plain weaving (Figure 3.2). Extra heddle rods can be tied on to make pattern weaves, or a rigid hole and slot heddle can be used (see Figure 9.2). The backstrap loom is very versatile and textiles made on it are limited in complexity only by the weaver's skill. The loom's ready portability is a great asset. It was known all over the ancient world and was important in northern Europe, China, Japan, and Southeast Asia. It is still a major tool in South and Central America where intricate patterns are woven (see chapter 12).

The Warp-Weighted Loom

The most faithful woman of all time was Penelope, wife of the Greek hero Odysseus. While awaiting his return from the Trojan War, she was besieged by several suitors. Penelope put off choosing one for a husband by insisting that she be allowed to finish the shroud she was weaving for her father-in-law, Laertes. Each night Penelope unraveled what she had woven during the day, and the suitors did not find out until she was betrayed by her maids. Scholars agree that she worked on a warp-weighted loom (Figure 3.3), but they do not all agree on the fiber or the construction technique. Many, however, think Penelope was weaving a woolen tapestry because of the figures depicted and because it was the slowest project she could have chosen.

The warp-weighted loom was closely associated with Greek wool weaving, but it was also known in Mesopotamia. Loom weights arranged at what must have been a loom site date to 2500 B.C. in Troy. Loom weights have been found in Swiss lake dwellings. The warp-weighted loom was the most commonly used type in Britain and the Rhineland, definitely predating the Roman conquest. It is still found in Scandinavia and Iceland and is presumably the same as the ancient type.[1] (Figure 3.4).

Two wooden uprights at a slant against a wall held the cloth beam that revolved to hold the finished cloth. In ancient times a starting border was first woven on another loom, probably a belt loom with a rigid heddle, and was then sewn to a perforated strip of wood attached to the cloth beam. Bundles of odd-numbered warp were loosened and tied to weights made of baked clay or stone. Those same warp hung vertically behind a fixed shed rod. Groups of even numbered warp were then weighted and hung in front of the rod. The warps were spaced across the top of the loom with a cord, as it was not possible to use a reed. Next, a heddle rod was attached to the odd warps (the rear system). This heddle rod was brought forward for alternate sheds (Figure 3.5).

Many times two weavers (who had to stand) were needed to handle the heddle rod and put in the weft. The major difficulty came with beating the weft up against gravity. Three different devices were employed as beaters. Used mainly in Britain were pin-beaters, made from sheep or goat bones cut diagonally to a point on one end. One was thrust into the warp from the front, or drawn across the surface. Bone or antler weaving combs were also used from the front. Swords, long flat blades pushed into the sheds before they were changed, are illustrated on Greek vases, but they would have been the hardest kind to use on a warp-weighted loom.

The warp-weighted loom was generally replaced by the two-beam vertical loom and the horizontal loom in the early centuries of the Christian era, although it was retained into the eleventh century for weaving special linen tunics for boys and brides. It had a distinct advantage over other looms in that fabrics could be made quite wide and had three finished edges.

The Horizontal Ground Loom

The horizontal ground loom, associated with linen weaving in early Egypt, consisted of warp stretched between two beams staked out by four pegs pounded into the ground. Its size was probably the same as the length of the cloth to be woven. Because some very long pieces of fabric have been found, however, it is thought that the Egyptians may have used roller beams. A major source of information about this loom, in use until around 1200 B.C., is the tomb painting of Chnem-hotep (Figure 3.6).[2] The loom appears to be vertical, because the Egyptians did not employ perspective. Tomb models give a better concept (Plate 2). The early Egyptians did not have a reed.

FIGURE 3.3 / Penelope's Loom (originally on a fifth century B.C. Greek vase).

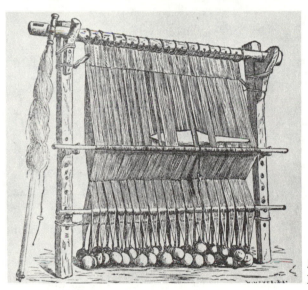

FIGURE 3.4 / Warp-Weighted Loom (from Kissel, 1918).

The Egyptians first measured the warp on spaced pegs, then put it on the loom. Because linen yarns were strong and smooth, they were set closely together. A construction called *rep*, with two to three times as many warp as weft, resulted. Ratios of 80 to 100 warp to 40 weft per inch were common in mummy wrappings. No doubt rep construction was chosen because it was hard to make each

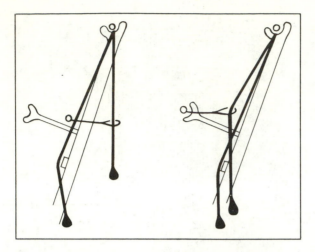

FIGURE 3.5 / Shedding on
a Warp-Weighted Loom.

FIGURE 3.6 / Egyptian Loom.

pick: If more warp were used, sufficient cover (density) could be attained with fewer picks. Early Egyptian fabrics had fringe along the side and selvages did not appear until about 1600 B.C.[3] Tomb paintings show a fringe on the left. Bellinger suggests that its purpose was to keep the web straight during the difficult beating-in process, something that required two weavers.[4]

Scholars have determined that the ground loom was used in ancient Palestine from the story of Samson (Judges 16:13-14). Delilah wove Samson's hair into a web, and since he was asleep at the time, the loom must have been a horizontal one.

Bedouins use the same loom today.[5] It can be staked out to the size needed for a

PLATE 1 (*above*) / A flax brake from nineteenth century Nova Scotia. (Courtesy of the Royal Ontario Museum, Toronto)
PLATE 2 (*below*) / A tomb model of a weaving shop from Upper Egypt in the period of the Middle Kingdom. (Courtesy of The Metropolitan Museum of Art. Anonymous Gift, 1930)

PLATE 4 / A water-powered carding machine. (Courtesy of Old Sturbridge Village. Photo by Donald F. Eaton)

PLATE 3 (*facing page*) / Sericulture in Japan (each frame runs right to left). From a set of prints by Utamaro published in Shojiro Nomura's *Historical Sketch of Nishiki and Kinran Brocades* (circa 1914).

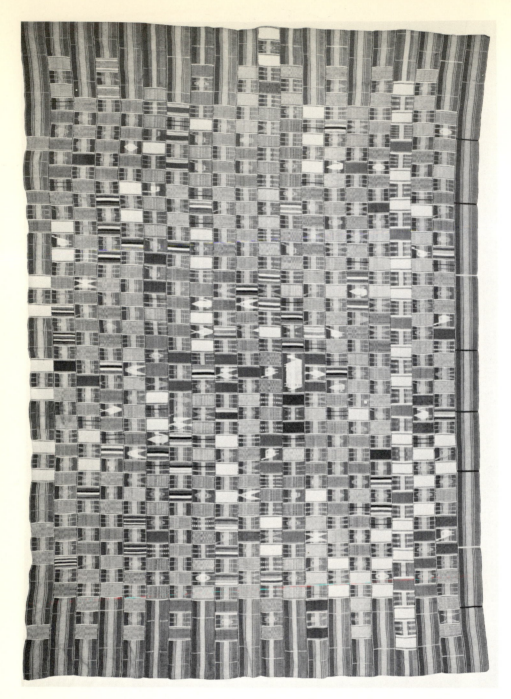

PLATE 5 / A man's cloth from the Ewe tribe, early twentieth century Ghana. Plain weave in cotton with supplementary weft patterning. 8'8" x 6'4". (Courtesy of The Textile Museum, Washington, D.C. 1975.17.12 Gift of Fred M. Fernald)

PLATE 6a (*left*) / A streamer of a mitre from twelfth century Germany. An elaborate variant of tablet weaving. 15¾″ x 3″. (Courtesy of The Detroit Institute of Arts. Founders Society-Octavia Bates Fund) PLATE 6b (*above*) / A detail of the reverse side of the mitre. (Courtesy of The Detroit Institute of Arts. Founders Society-Octavia Bates Fund)

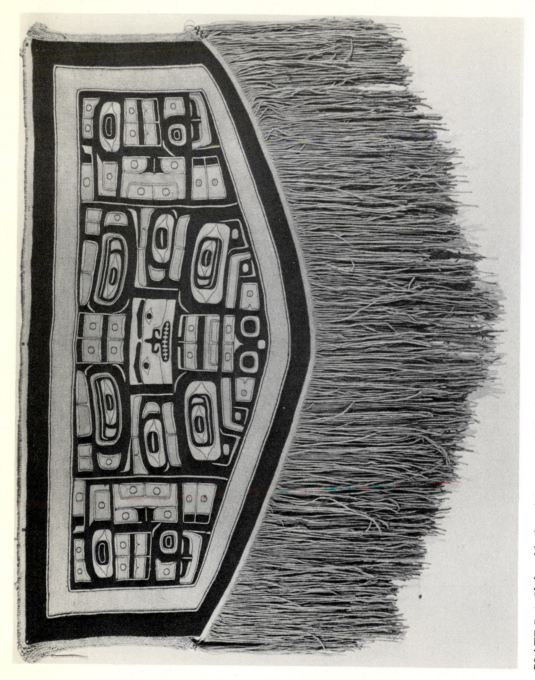

PLATE 7 / Chilcat blanket. (Courtesy of The Denver Art Museum)

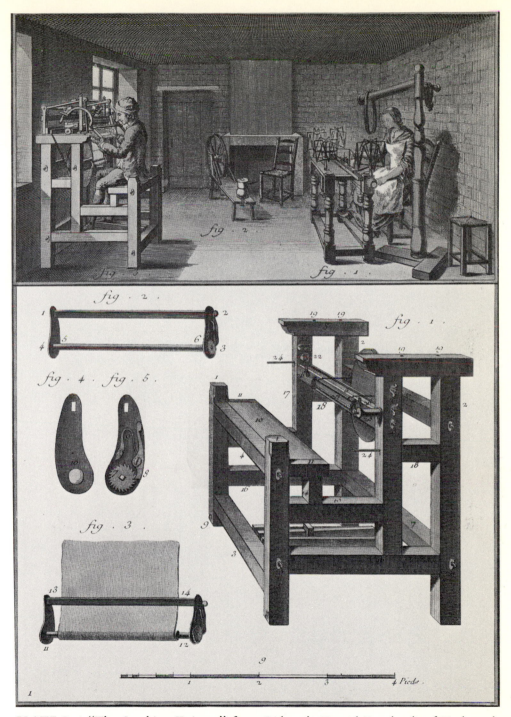

PLATE 8 / "The Stocking Knitter," from Diderot's *Pictorial Encyclopedia of Trades and Industry*. Top of plate: Fig. 1—Filling the bobbins with silk yarn; Fig. 2—Common spinning wheel for preparing the silk yarn; Fig. 3—Knitting the silk yarn into stockings. Bottom of plate: Fig. 1—Detail of the hosiery knitting machine (also called a stocking frame); Figs. 2–5—Details of the fabric take-up device. (Courtesy of Groz Beckert, U.S.A., Inc.)

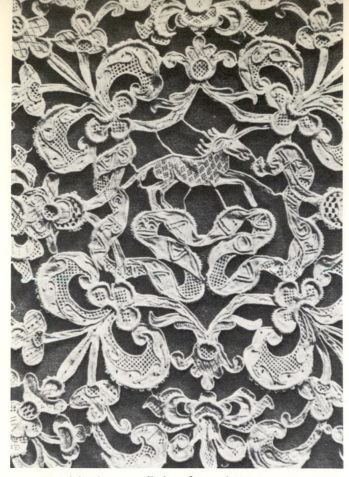

PLATE 9 (*above*) / Needle lace from *The Mentor*, 1 May 1917.
PLATE 10 (*below*) / Bobbin lace from *The Mentor*, 1 May 1917.

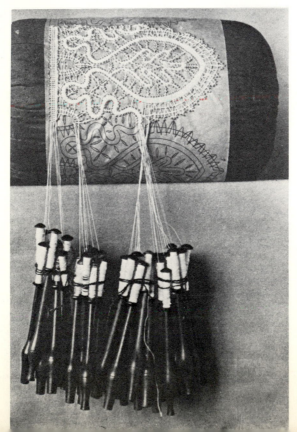

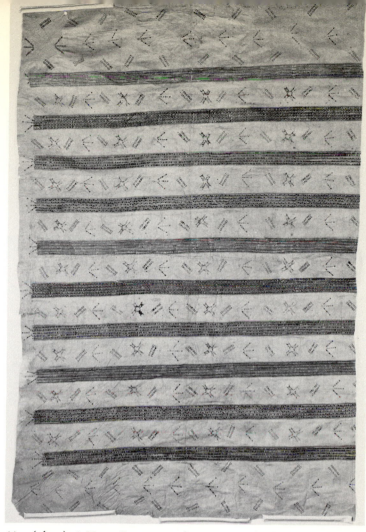

PLATE 11a (*above*) / Hawaiian tapa. (Courtesy of The Denver Art Museum)
PLATE 11b (*below*) / A detail of the Hawaiian tapa. (Courtesy of The Denver Art Museum)

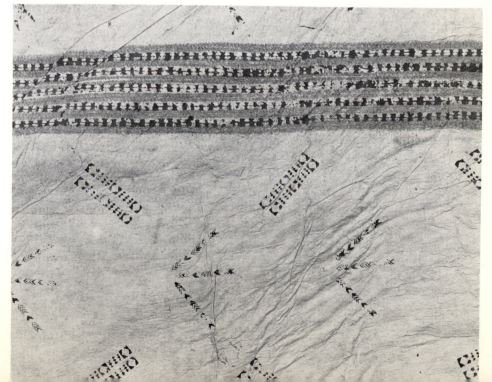

PLATE 12 / Cloth press from about 1860, Antioch, West Virginia. (Courtesy of Merrimack Valley Textile Museum, North Andover, Massachusetts)

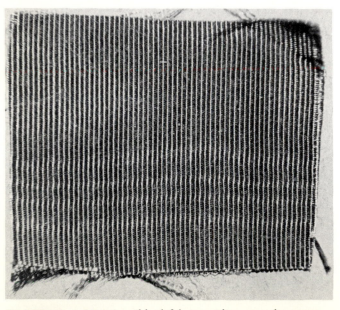

PLATE 13 / Moiré—ribbed fabric with watered pattern.

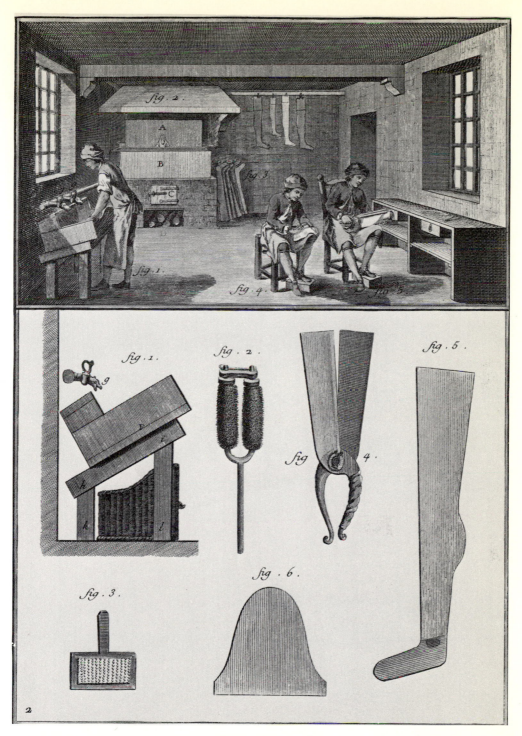

PLATE 14 / "A Fulling Mill," from Diderot's *Pictorial Encylopedia of Trades and Industry*. Top of plate: Fig. 1—A worker soaks the woolen pieces in hot water (see Fig. 1 below); Fig. 2— The furnace and boiler that supply the essential hot water; Fig. 3—Forms for shaping the stockings as they dry; Fig. 4—A worker uses a fuller's "thistle" to nap and shape a knitted cap over a form; Fig. 5—A worker shears a piece after it has been napped and shaped. Bottom of plate: Fig. 1—Tub for soaking the knitted pieces; Fig. 2—The fuller's "thistle" used to nap and shape the fabric; Fig. 3—A brush to clean the "thistle"; Fig. 4—Shears; Fig. Fig. 5—Stocking form; Fig. 6—Cap form. (Courtesy of Groz Beckert, U.S.A., Inc.)

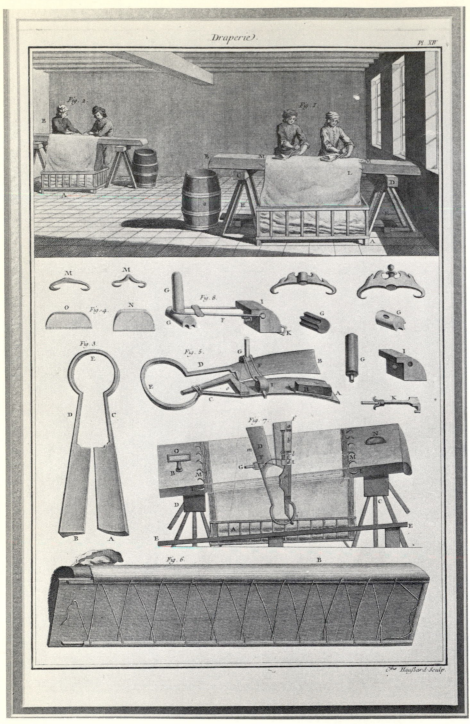

PLATE 15 / "Shearing," from Duhamel du Monceau's "Art de la draperie," in
Descriptions des Arts et Metiers (Paris, 1765). (Courtesy of the Merrimack Valley Textile
Museum, North Andover, Massachusetts)

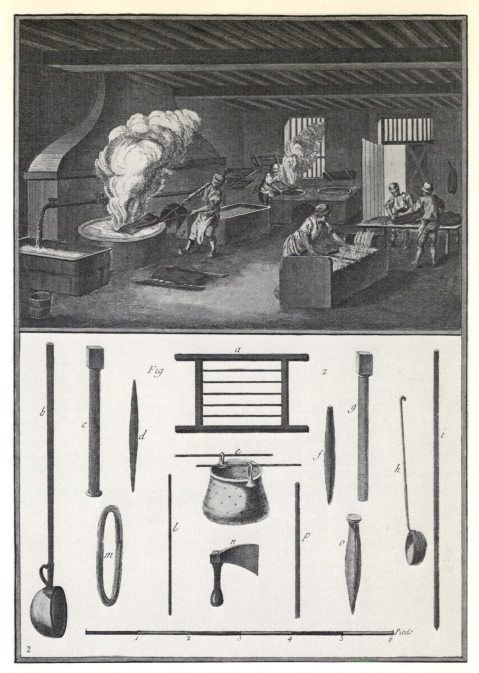

PLATE 16 / "The Dye House," from Diderot's *Pictorial Encyclopedia of Trades and Industry.*
Top of plate: Fig. a—To bring out the special lustre of silk, the skeins, packed in cloth sacks
to prevent tangling, were boiled in soapy water. After three hours or more the film of
grease and other impurities, which gave some buoyancy, would dissolve and the bags would
sink to the bottom, indicating the silk was clean and ready to "take" a dye; Fig. b—Here a
worker places the skeins, several of which are arranged on a wooden rod, into the heated
dye vat. Dipping the silk in and out he watches carefully until the right coloring is achieved;
Fig. c—After the skeins have been boiled this worker arranges them on the wooden rods, by
which they will be suspended in the dye vats; Fig. d—The skeins are packed into cloth sacks
by these workers and are removed again after boiling. Bottom of plate: Figs. a-p—The
simple utensils of the dye house include an axe (n) for cutting pieces of the raw dye material,
a bowl (e), and ladles (b and h) for mixing, and various wooden rods for handling the skeins
while being processed, and for twisting them after boiling and after dyeing, so as to wring
out the excess liquids. (Courtesy of Groz Beckert, U.S.A., Inc.)

PLATE 17a (*left*) / Indonesian batik. (Courtesy of The Denver Art Museum)   PLATE 17b (*below*) / A detail of the Indonesian batik. (Courtesy of The Denver Art Museum)

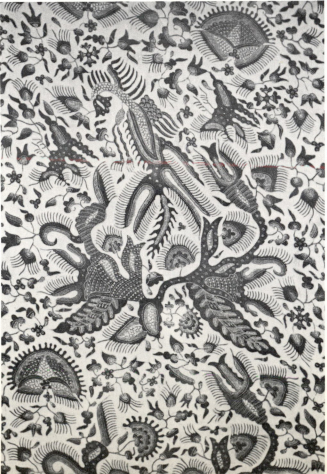

PLATE 18 (*above*) / Shibori. (Courtesy of Pat Dietemann)   PLATE 19 (*below*) / Double ikat.

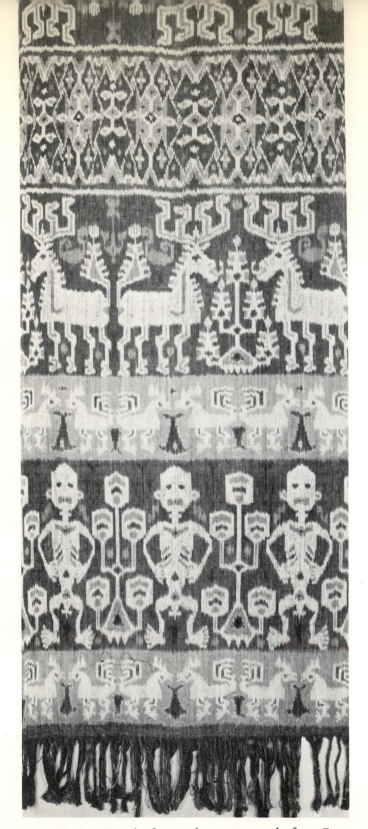

PLATE 20 / Detail of a man's cotton mantle from East
Sumba showing warp ikat technique. Moving up from the
fringe, the figures are roosters, human figures alternating
with abstract plants, and deer. (Courtesy of The Textile
Museum, Washington, D.C., T. M. 6.267)

carrying bag, cradle, or rug and warped directly with wool, camel hair, or cotton yarn. If the group moves before the weaving is finished, the loom can easily be rolled up and taken along. Knotted carpets are made on the horizontal ground loom in parts of Iran. The horizontal loom was the type that was to become most highly developed over time.

The Two-Beam Vertical Loom

Around 1500 B.C. side supports were added, and the Egyptians turned their horizontal ground loom to the vertical and propped it against a wall or fastened it to posts. The idea may have originated in Syria or Palestine, and this type was known in Scandinavia before the Christian era. The weavers could sit comfortably on benches in front of the loom, and it was easy to beat the weft down. It is possible that in Egypt the warp beam, set into the framework, was adjustable and could be lowered as the finished cloth was rolled up on the lower beam. The weaver always worked in the same place and the work was adjusted.

The upright loom is best suited to plain weave and constructions that do not require very many harnesses. It is still used in Africa, Greece, the Near East, and the American Southwest (see Figure 11.3) to make rugs and tapestries. At the beginning of the Christian era it traveled slowly westward from the Near East to replace the warp-weighted loom.

The Two-Harness Loom and the Pit Loom

The horizontal loom that was developed for weaving cotton had two harnesses. Cotton made a relatively weak warp and so, instead of making a cross and using a heddle rod, two harnesses were used, one controlling the even-numbered warp, the other, the odd warp. A wide shed could be made without breaking the warp, but the weaver was limited to plain weave. Cotton was, and still is, generally woven in plain weave.

The harnesses were operated by cords attached to the weaver's toes, and later, by treadles. It was common practice in India and the Near East to dig pits for the treadles, and the weaver sat on the edge. The pits may even have held water to increase the humidity and make it easier to handle the cotton (Figure 3.7).

The two-harness loom traveled to the Roman world via the silk routes and was adopted by the linen weavers. By the third century A.D. Syrian wool weavers had added a third harness to make twills.[6] There is some evidence that treadles were in use in Egypt in the sixth century,[7] although they were not found in Europe before the late twelfth century.

The Raised Horizontal Loom

The treadle loom, also known as the horizontal frame loom, handloom, barn loom, etc., is the form associated with medieval Europe and early America (Figure 3.8). It had harnesses, treadles, and roller beams. To historians, it seemed to have

FIGURE 3.7 / Pit Loom
(from Marsden, 1895).

FIGURE 3.8 / Treadle Loom
(sixteenth century woodcut).

just appeared, fully developed, in thirteenth century Europe. There are, of course, some missing links. The harness system involved cords and pulleys attached to the loom frame or to the ceiling and treadles operated by the weaver's feet. In the fifteenth century a very heavy closed frame was introduced and a batten could be swung from the top of the frame. Numerous variations of the raised horizontal loom evolved to handle different kinds of cloth. It is, of course, still used by handweavers.

Some Variations

Among the very primitive variations of the horizontal loom is the one used in West Africa to weave narrow strips (Figure 3.9). The loom is easily movable because only a scanty frame supports the harnesses and beater. Wooden disks held between the weaver's toes are tied to cords that control the harnesses, which are made of simple string heddles. The warp is not tied to the back beam but, rather, extends many feet behind it and is weighted with a rock or rolled up and held in place with a rock on a sledge that is pulled toward the weaver as he needs more warp. Very narrow patterned fabrics, usually between four and ten inches wide, are woven on these looms. For marketing the newly woven fabric is wound into large wheels.[8] The strips are cut and then sewn into garment widths (Plate 5).

Another variation is the loom called an *inkle*—one popular with weavers today (Figure 3.10). *Inkle* was the word used for narrow linen bands and tapes, and the loom was used in England from the seventeenth century on. Fabrics can be woven very quickly and additional pattern heddles can be added.

Tablet weaving was known throughout the ancient world, although probably not in the pre-Columbian New World. It is thought that the method was invented in Egypt before 4000 B.C. and was highly developed by around 3000 B.C. Tablets were used in prehistoric Scandinavia; a pack of fifty-two wooden ones was found in the Oseberg ship burial of 850 A.D. Small square or rectangular tablets of bone, horn, or leather were used as heddles on very narrow looms. Tablets were punched in each corner, the warp run through the holes in sequence, and the tablets turned in consistent order as the weft was inserted (see Figure 3.11 and Plate 6).

Pattern Looms

After Syrian wool weavers adopted the horizontal loom and added a harness to make weft-faced twills, they learned to use that third harness in a different way— to control warp that would act as binders for pattern weft laid in between the regular picks that formed the background of the cloth. This is known as inlay and brocaded design, and the equipment for doing it was in use by the first half of the third century.[9] Excavation of Dura-Europos, an ancient city on the Euphrates River and a Roman fortress when it fell in 256 A.D., yielded many textile fragments that support the theory that a three harness loom was well known by then. The textiles are the only evidence; no looms survive.

The next logical step was to increase the number of harnesses in order to make

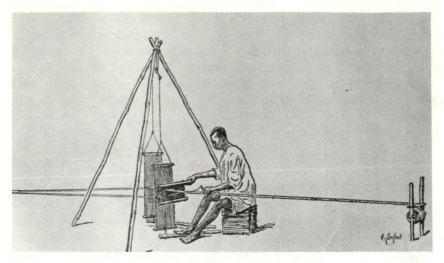

FIGURE 3.9 / West African Loom (from Kissel, 1918).

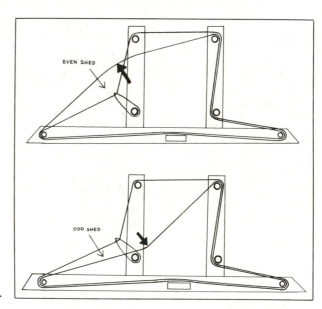

EVEN SHED

ODD SHED

FIGURE 3.10 / Inkle Loom.

more complicated structures. Too many harnesses were unwieldy, however, and the drawloom became the answer to the problem.

The Drawloom

Fragments of twill damasks dated to the second century B.C. in China suggest that some sort of pattern loom was known by that time. The often published picture of the Han prototype for the drawloom (shown in Figure 3.12 and Plate 62) supports

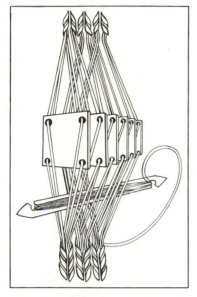

FIGURE 3.11 (left) / Tablet Weaving.   *FIGURE 3.12 (right)* / Chinese Pattern Loom.

this suggestion. The picture originally came from a twelfth century Chinese encyclopedia.

On the other hand, there is a strong possibility that the drawloom was the invention of Syrian tapestry weavers, perhaps as early as the third century A.D. and that it was more completely developed during the sixth and seventh centuries when Syrian wool weavers were moved to eastern Persia to weave silk. There is a marked difference between early Chinese and early Near Eastern patterned silks; Chinese were warp-faced and Near Eastern were weft-faced. In addition to patterned silks, some woolen textiles of apparent drawloom patterning have been found in fourth and fifth century Egyptian burying grounds.

The drawloom was used to weave the most elaborate textiles ever known. It was in use for some fifteen hundred years until replaced by the jacquard loom in the early nineteenth century. Regular harnesses were worked by the weaver sitting at the front of the loom, and the pattern sheds were controlled by the "drawboy" sitting on top of the loom. Strings were tied to the warps, and the ones for the warps to be raised for each different pick (shed) were grouped and tied to a cord that went through one of many holes in a comber board. As many different sheds were possible as there were combinations of draw cords. Cords were numbered and each shed had a code. The cords were pulled in sequence.

In the seventeenth century the invention of the *simple,* by a Frenchman named Simplot, allowed the drawboy to stand on the floor and pull down a series of cords rather than perch atop the loom (Figure 3.13). Nevertheless, the work was still very tedious and unhealthy for the children who tended to be employed at it.

FIGURE 3.13 / Drawloom
(from Glazier, 1923).

The complexity of the drawloom required skilled workers and workshops, or at least permanent positioning of the loom. A "mass production" of patterned fabrics was now possible, even necessary, because of the time consumed in setting up the drawloom. Fabrics remained expensive because they were made of silk, and it was the clergy and royalty who used them. Textile designers became important because of the necessity to plan repeats that would best utilize the drawloom.

The Jacquard Loom

The jacquard loom, or rather the jacquard attachment to the handloom, was a direct descendant of the drawloom. The goal was to replace the drawboy, who could, and did, make mistakes. Sympathy for his plight may also have been a reason for a series of inventions leading to the jacquard loom.

One report, not substantiated, stated that an Englishman, J. Mason, was in 1687 able to weave drawloom type fabrics without the help of a drawboy. In 1725 Basile Bouchon used a system of perforated paper and needles to select the cords to be drawn, and in 1728 another Frenchman, Falcon, used perforated rectangular cards instead of paper and laced them together as an endless chain. In 1745 Jacques de Vaucanson mounted the cards above the loom, and for the first time the device could be operated without an assistant. Joseph Marie Jacquard perfected that invention.

There are many different stories about Jacquard. He was born in Lyons in 1752 and at the age of ten ran away from his job as his father's drawboy to become an apprentice to a bookbinder. His father's death brought him home to become a weaver and inventor. In 1793 Jacquard joined the unsuccessful defenders of Lyons against the Army of the Convention and then escaped with his teen-aged son to join the Army of the Rhine. The boy was mortally wounded during a battle and died in Jacquard's arms. Jacquard then returned to Lyons to find that his house had been burned and that his wife was missing. He found her plaiting straw hats in a garret, and for a while did that work himself.

Jacquard turned to inventing and demonstrated a final version of the drawloom at the Paris Industrial Exhibition in 1801. For that he received a bronze medal. He next invented a fishnet machine and received several thousand francs. In 1805 he introduced his major invention, the punched card device that could be attached to a regular handloom and be operated simply by two treadles (Figure 3.14). The machine was given to the public in 1806, and Jacquard received a small pension. His invention was greeted with hostility by Lyon weavers who thought it would destroy their employment; many models were burned and Jacquard was attacked several times. By 1812, however, there were over eighteen thousand looms equipped with jacquard heads. The great French silk industry was revitalized enough to challenge Spitalfields in England (see chapter 8). In 1819 Jacquard received the Legion of Honor, and the next year saw his invention introduced into England. Jacquard died in 1834, and a statue honoring him was erected in Lyons.

The jacquard weaver did have to be skilled in setting up the loom. First, the design was copied onto squared drafting paper. Then a card was punched for each pick to show the warp to be raised; the number of cards equaled the number of picks in one design repeat. The cards were laced together and placed on a cylinder. As the cylinder turned, each card was pressed against a set of horizontal needles, each connected to a separate vertical hook that raised or lowered the warp it controlled. The cards could be taken off the loom, stored, and used again whenever that particular pattern was wanted.

The Dobby Loom

Little is known about the history of the dobby, a revolving device with a series of wooden pegs that contact and activate levers that control multiple harnesses. The mechanism is more closely associated with power weaving, although some crude handloom versions probably preceded the jacquard. Dobbies (the word meant household sprite) were called witch looms and were in use at Spitalfields in 1830.[10] Allover patterns with small repeats were made.

The horizontal loom has proved to be the most practical type not only for pattern weaving but also for plain weaving, mainly because it will support the greatest number of harnesses. Rotating beams make it possible to do large quantity weaving, and it is the only type that has been adapted to power (see Figure 10.1).

WOVEN CONSTRUCTIONS

Terms in this section are ones commonly used by textile historians. Nomenclature, however, is not set by law, and there is often disagreement about

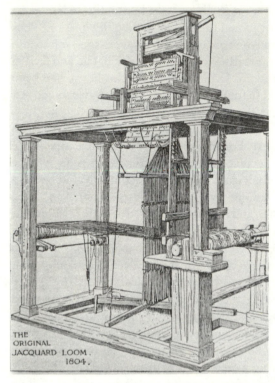

THE
ORIGINAL
JACQUARD LOOM.
1804.

FIGURE 3.14 / Jacquard Loom
(from Glazier, 1923).

exact meanings of words. Scholars have recently taken a greater interest in this
particuar aspect of textile study and considerable work has been done to bring
order to fabric classification and nomenclature.[11]

Simple Weaves

Simple weaves employ only two sets of elements—one set of warp and one set of
weft. (A single set of elements equals a group of components—yarns—all used in
the same way.) At any one point of interlacing (where warp and weft cross) the
warp will be on top on the right side and the weft will be on top on the reverse side;
or, if the weft is on top of the right side, the warp will be on top on the reverse.

Plain Weaves

The most widely used woven construction is *plain weave*. The sequence of
weaving (what the weft does as it interlaces with the warp) is over one, under one
(Figure 3.15). A number of other terms have been used for plain weave: *linen weave*
and *cotton weave* (because these fibers were most frequently woven in plain weave),
canvas weave, cloth weave, and *checker weave.* Today weavers use the term *tabby,*
derived from the Arabic *attabi,* a rich watered silk (moiré taffeta) made in Attabiya
(a weaving quarter just outside the Damascus gate).[12] A tabby cat is streaked, just

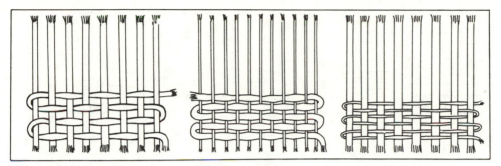

FIGURE 3.15 (left) / Plain Weave.   *FIGURE 3.16 (center)* / Rep Weave.
FIGURE 3.17 (right) / Tapestry Weave.

like the silks of Attabiya. Plain weaves can be varied in a number of different ways: by changing size, texture, color, direction, and amount of twist in the yarns, and by changing the *balance,* the ratio of the number of warp to the number of weft per inch—the over one, under one interlacing remains.

When the balance is changed so that the fabric has more warp than weft a construction called *rep*, repp, rib, or cord, results (Figure 3.16). Rep is warp-faced, the weft is generally hidden, and a crosswise rib results. This was the construction used for the early Egyptian linens made on horizontal ground looms, and taffeta is a modern example. Aside from the fabrics made on ground looms, ribbed textiles were not woven in quantity until the fifteenth century in the Near East and a little later in Europe. At that time silk was used and durability was poor because of slippage (sidewise movement of warp) and warp breakage.

The construction just the opposite of rep is *tapestry weave* (Figure 3.17). The weft are much more numerous than the warp, which do not show. Ribs form in the lengthwise direction. This construction developed on the vertical wool looms, because the wool yarns, with many protruding fibers ready to entangle, had to be set rather far apart and held under constant tension. The weft was woven in by small sections, rather than having the whole shed open at once. This leads to another definition, the more important one, for tapestry. In addition to usually meaning weft-faced plain weave, tapestry implies *discontinuous wefts*, that is, different colored wefts can be used in limited areas to produce pattern. The term tapestry has also been used to identify any pictorial weaving, not necessarily woven in plain weave.

Discontinuous wefts can meet or join in several ways. If they meet but do not join, *slit tapestry* is the result (Figure 3.18). Examples of this are seen in the kilim rugs of Persia, Turkey, and North Africa, and in Chinese k'o-ssu (see chapter 7). Discontinuous wefts can be joined by *interlocking*, linking between warp (Figures 3.19a and 3.19b), or they can share a common warp and be *dovetailed* (Figure 3.20). These constructions are found in Navajo and Peruvian textiles (see chapters 11 and 12).

Another variation of plain weave is called *basket* or *matt weave.* Two or more

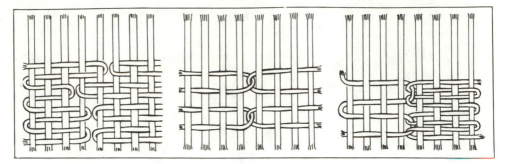

FIGURE 3.18 (left) / Slit Tapestry.   FIGURE 3.19a (center) / Interlocking Tapestry, Single.   FIGURE 3.19b (right) / Interlocking Tapestry, Double.

warp and/or weft are used as one (Figure 3.21). A modern example is *monk's cloth*. In semi- or half-basket weave only one of the two sets of elements is multiple. Oxford cloth is an example of this. Linen basket weaves were woven in the eastern provinces of the Roman Empire.

Float Weaves

Float weaves employ only two sets of elements also, but the sequence of interlacing is different from that of plain weave. The weft goes over, or under, more than one warp for an interlacing. Weft floats result when the weft goes over more than one warp; warp floats result when the weft goes under the same warp in successive picks.

Twill is a float weave associated historically with woolens. The weave makes a thick construction suitable for napping, and twill is the best construction for fulling. The sequence of weaving in a twill is over one, under two, or over two, under one, or over two, under two, etc. *Progression* of successive picks to the right or left causes a diagonal *wale* that is characteristic of all twills.

There are three kinds of twill based on weaving sequence and thread count. If the weft goes over more warp than it goes under, a weft-faced, or *reclining twill* is produced. The wale lies at less than a forty-five degree angle, and there are more weft than warp (Figure 3.22). Weft-face twills were made on the three harness looms of the third century Near East.

The opposite to the weft-faced twill is the *steep* or warp-faced variety (Figure 3.23). The angle of the wale is more than forty-five degrees, and there are more warp than weft. Denim and gabardine are modern examples; they show weaving sequences of under tw, over one. If the warp and weft counts are about equal, and the weft goes under two, over two warp, an *even-sided* (and reversible) *twill* is produced. These were woven on the warp-weighted looms of Bronze Age Europe. The even-sided twill allowed for an equal division of the warp between the front and the back of the fixed shed rod (Figure 3.4).

Most twills are *continuous*—the wale goes from one corner to the one diagonally

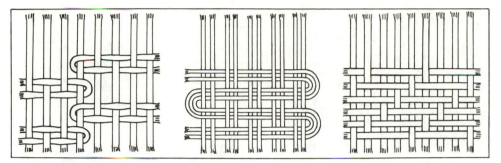

FIGURE 3.20 (*left*) / Dovetailed Tapestry.   FIGURE 3.21 (*center*) / Basket Weave.
FIGURE 3.22 (*right*) / Reclining Twill.

opposite. Pattern, however, can be achieved by periodically changing the direction of the wales. These weaves are called *broken twills*; herringbone is one example, *diamond twill* (from Roman Britain) another. (See Plates 96 and 97).

Satin weave is like twill in that it is a simple float weave, but it is different in that the progressions are intermittent (Figure 3.24). Sometimes satin is referred to as *skipping* or *rearranged twill*. For warp satin weave (usually called just *satin*) the sequence of weaving for the weft is over one, under four (or more) warp. This, of course, causes the warp to float on top of the weft on the right side. The construction is warp-faced, and there are many more warp than weft. The opposite, weft satin, is known as *sateen*. Here, the sequence of weaving is over four, under one. The fabric is weft-faced, and there are many more weft than warp.

Historically, satin has been associated with silk. Its origin is unknown, but it did require at least a five harness loom. The word may have come from the Latin *seta* (meaning silk), from the medieval European pronunciation of the Chinese *ssu tuan* for satin, or from the name of the Chinese port, Zaytun. Satin also came to mean any woven fabric with a lustrous and silky appearance, not necessarily one of satin construction.

Simple Pattern Weaves

Patterns can be formed by using different combinations of floats: the fabrics are called *fancies* and are made now with dobby looms. *Huck*, or huckaback, named because it was sold by English hucksters, is a modern example. Others, with names like fisheye or "Ms and Os," were made on early American multiharness looms. *Diaper* is a term used for allover, small scale patterning.

Damask, named after Damascus in Syria where it was once woven of silk, is an example of the combination of warp-faced and weft-faced twill or satin sections. Damask has been called a *turned weave*; other turned weaves were simple checks. Damask is characterized by flat design, because the floats are all the same length, and by design that is reversible, because a design area with warp floats on one side has equal weft floats on the other. The Crusaders were probably responsible for

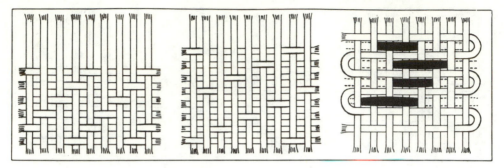

FIGURE 3.23 (*left*) / Steep Twill.   FIGURE 3.24 (*center*) / Satin Weave.
FIGURE 3.25 (*right*) / Brocading.

introducing damask into Europe, and some elegant linen damasks were woven in the Low Countries and Ireland. Damask was especially important in the sixteenth and seventeenth centuries (see Frontispiece).

Compound Weaves

Compound weaves have three or more sets of yarns, with at least two sets in either the warp or the weft. These extra sets are *supplementary* and can be removed leaving the base fabric intact, or the extra sets are *complementary* and cannot be removed without causing destruction of the fabric. Compound weaves also include *combined weave* structures, the double cloths. When there is more than one set of warp or weft the sets will usually be different in size or color.

Supplementary Sets of Yarn

Extra weft can be woven in to form patterns that stand out from the surface of the cloth (Figure 3.25). Commonly the technique is referred to as *brocading*, and it is sometimes confused with embroidery. Brocading can be *continuous*; that is, the extra weft are carried the full width of the fabric in the pattern shed, come to the surface only where needed, and float between design areas on the back. In *discontinuous* brocading, known as *space weaving*, a group of small shuttles is used for each pattern area, and the pattern has to be put in by hand. Yarns float on the back only within pattern areas. This method allows the conservation of expensive materials. Although brocading is a technique used with all fibers and in many different older and contemporary textiles, it is preferable to limit the fabric name *brocade* to the luxurious gold or silver patterned silks made on drawlooms or jacquards. The most narrow and exact definition of brocade includes discontinuous weaving.

The term *inlay*, or *laid-in*, refers to patterning with extra wefts that are placed in the ground weave sheds and float only in design areas (they do not float freely between design areas as do brocaded wefts). *Overshot*, seen in American coverlets, is a weave using supplementary weft that float first on one side, then on the other, so that design is formed on both faces (Plate 86). It is also possible to have supplementary warp patterns, but they must be continuous. Both supplementary warp and weft can serve as backing or reinforcement for a textile.

Some three-dimensional textiles, with looped or cut *pile*, are *supplementary weft compound weaves.* As early as 2000 B.C. the Egyptians made linen fabrics with extra linen weft pulled out into loops for both pattern effects and warmth (Plate 24). Corduroy (Corde du Roi—woven for kings' servants in the Middle Ages) has extra wefts that form lengthwise rows of floats that are cut to form the pile. This cloth was called *thickset* in the seventeenth and eighteenth centuries, and it is related to *fustian,* a sturdy wool or linen/cotton fabric dating back to the early centuries A.D.

Early velvets were good examples of *supplementary warp pile* textiles. Fragments of twill velvet have been dated to ninth century France, but it is not known where velvet was first woven (although it was probably Persia or Italy). The extra warp beam necessary to make velvet was not in use much before the fourteenth century; it held the extra pile warp that were looped over rods as the fabric was woven. In *pile-on-pile*, one of the oldest techniques, pattern was achieved by using two or more pile heights. Pile was cut or left looped. *Voided* velvet had areas without pile, and *Cisele* had both cut and uncut pile. During the Renaissance, the heyday of velvet, many sumptuous ones were brocaded in gold.

A similar construction is terry cloth. Although the pile warp are looped by slack tension weaving, no rods are used. Terry was first made by machine in England in 1848, and in the late eighteenth century, it was probably a simple uncut cotton velvet.

Complementary Sets of Yarns

Compound textiles can have *complementary* sets of warp and/or weft that are coequal with the base yarns and cannot be removed without destruction of the textile. These are the weaves most often, called compound by older authors. Usually one set of the warp or weft appears on the face of the fabric while the other (or others) appear on the back. Sometimes the extra warp are called *inner warp* or pattern warp; they are hidden from view and serve to make heavier fabric and bind pattern wefts (Figure 3.26). The compound weave technique is associated with the drawloom. It was important in Persian and Syrian textiles after the fourth century, and it was especially important in European silks from about the thirteenth to the eighteenth century. There were compound satins, twills, and damasks. *Lampas* and *brocatelle* were eighteenth century names for compound weave textiles.

Combined Weave Structures

Combined weave structures have at least four sets of yarns, that is, two sets of warp and two sets of weft. Two textiles will actually be formed, one above the other, with each set of warp being interlaced with its own set of weft. Each pair of warp and weft will change sides at design edges (Figure 3.27). This is seen in matelassé, some Peruvian textiles, and in jacquard coverlets (Plate 88). These

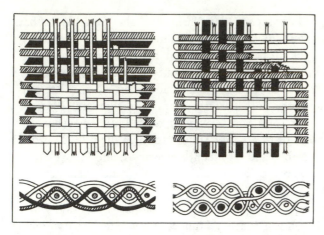

FIGURE 3.26 (*left*) / A Compound Weave.
FIGURE 3.27 (*right*) / Double Cloth.

structures are generally termed *double cloth*. A variant of double cloth uses an extra warp or weft (five sets in all). Sometimes this is called true double cloth, as the fabric can be cut apart yielding two separate pieces. Modern velvet, invented in France in 1838, is an example.

Weaving presents numerous possibilities for variation in color and texture as well as structural design. The nonweaving techniques are more limited in construction, but they also present some interesting structures and textures.

NONWEAVING TECHNIQUES

Fabrics made by methods other than weaving have served some specific functions throughout history. Several techniques predate weaving and include twining two sets of yarns and interlacing, looping, knotting, or linking a single set of yarns or a single yarn. It is also possible to make fabrics directly from fibers, and no yarn is used.

Twining

Twining is the technique most closely related to weaving because it uses two sets of yarns. Indeed, it is often called weaving. Twining is a finger manipulation that cannot be easily duplicated mechanically. It seems to have evolved simultaneously with weaving, until the invention of heddles made the latter more efficient. Both twined and woven fabrics came from the same early sites in Anatolia and Peru (Plate 112).

In *weft-twining* the warp is hung from a frame or stretched between two bars, and the weft is worked crosswise in pairs. As one ("A") of the pair goes over a warp, the other ("B") goes under. Then they traverse one another so that "A" goes under the next warp and "B" goes over it (Figure 3.28). There are many variations possible; working yarns closely or making openwork, working with multiple

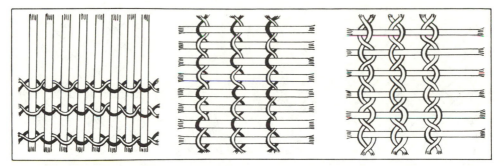

FIGURE 3.28 (*left*) / Weft-twining.   FIGURE 3.29 (*center*) / Warp-twining.
FIGURE 3.30 (*right*) / Leno Weave.

strands of weft, enclosing more than one warp at a time, working wefts back and forth within design areas (like tapestry weaving), or even braiding and knotting the warp.

The Chilkat ceremonial robe (Plate 7) was the triumph of the weft-twining art developed by the indians of the Pacific Northwest coast. Although there has been something of a revival of twining among the indians,[13] the ceremonial robe is no longer being made. An extant one is a rare treasure indeed, because most were allowed to disintegrate at grave sites of the chiefs or the well-to-do. Others were cut up and made into bags or articles of clothing. Worked so closely as to resemble tapestry, highly symbolic abstract animal designs were executed with mountain goat wool dyed black, yellow, and a pleasing and unusual shade of green-blue made by oxidizing copper in urine.[14] A characteristic three-strand twining was used to outline designs.

Warp-twining, as old as weft-twining, was commonly used to make narrow bands. Pairs of warp were twisted around each other as the wefts were inserted (Figure 3.29). Warp-twining should be differentiated from *leno*, or gauze, *weave*.[15] Leno weave, important in Chinese Han dynasty silks, has warps that cross and recross between picks (the same warp is always on top of the weft). (Figure 3.30 and Plate 53). Leno can be made with a simple heddle rod.

Braiding

Unlike weaving and twining, braiding is a technique that uses only one set of elements. The strands are interlaced diagonally from either the outside in or the center outward. Braids can be round, square, or flat (Figure 3.31). They are usually narrow, although some fairly wide fabrics were made in Peru and Egypt. In the prehistoric American Southwest shirts were braided. It was a technique used widely in prehistoric and in later times for slings, trump lines, ties, fringes, and cords. The indians of the Great Lakes region made very complicated patterned braids, and one type was adapted as an elaborate sash by the French Canadians in the nineteenth century.

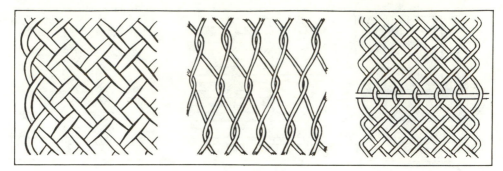

FIGURE 3.31 (*left*) / Braiding.   FIGURE 3.32 (*center*) / Plaiting.
FIGURE 3.33 (*right*) / Sprang.

Plaiting is a term often used interchangeably with braiding, although *plaiting* is best reserved for a method of interlinking whereby elements simply turn around each other as in a chain. (Figure 3.32 and Plate 90). Braiding is more like weaving in that yarns are interlaced.

Sprang

Sprang, also known as frame or loom plaiting and meshwork, is a method for making openwork by intertwining, interlinking, or interlacing yarns that are stretched on a frame. Because the warp are fixed at both ends of the frame, mirror image patterns will form simultaneously top and bottom as the yarns are manipulated with the fingers. During the process, the linkages may be temporarily held in place by rods, but no extra yarns are used to stabilize the structure (Figure 3.33).

The oldest specimen of sprang dates to the early Bronze Age (1400 B.C.), in Denmark, and others have been found in Peruvian graves from 1100 B.C. Several specimens from Coptic Egypt have survived. Sprang was practiced widely in northern Europe, especially during Roman times. The word itself came from the Swedish *sprangning*, meaning an openwork textile.

Netting, Knotting, and Looping

Netting is a general term that includes both the knotting and looping of yarns. These techniques predate weaving and twining and were especially well developed in ancient Peru (Plate 110b) and the American Southwest. Netted openwork fabrics were used for fishnets, snares, bags, and hairnets.

The present term for *knotted* work is *macrame*, originally from the Arabic word *migramah* (meaning embroidered veil) and coming more directly from a Turkish word *makrama* (napkin, kerchief, or towel). These items were probably fringed, because the use of knotting as an ornamental fringe developed in Arabia during the thirteenth century and spread to Europe with the Muslims. Gradually, macrame moved northward and was introduced into England in the seventeenth century. It became a court pastime for Queen Mary of England who had learned it in Holland. Knotting enjoyed a revival near the end of the Victorian period.

In the simplest *looping* a thread is spiraled around a support, thread, or rod. After the first row is completed the yarn is turned back and spiraled through the loops already formed. This back and forth looping is continued until the fabric is complete. *Crocheting* is looping with a hook, and the fabric is built both horizontally and vertically. Little is known about its history, although archaeological finds indicate that finger crochet is a very old technique. Crocheting was a popular activity for nuns in the Middle Ages, and in the nineteenth century the Irish started to make crocheted lace.

Knitting

Now the knitter interloops one strand of yarn with a pair of needles in order to build vertically a sweater, hat, or sock. The two faces of the fabric vary according to the way the loops are taken off the needles. In *stockinet*, stocking stitch knit, the loops are all on one side and so the faces are not alike (Figure 3.34). With two needles this is "knit a row, purl a row." In garter stitch knits alternate rows have loops on the right side and on the reverse, so both faces are alike (Figure 3.35). This is continuous knitting with two needles.

The oldest form of knitting, however, is *crossed knitting*. In it, stitches are rotated a half turn. Crossed knitting was done with a relatively short length of yarn threaded into a needle of bone or cactus thorn, and the work was more like sewing. Loops were successively made and tightened against the previous stitch. The work did not run (ladder) as other knits.[16] This method has also been called *single needle knitting* and *pseudo knitting*[17] and advanced development of it can be seen in figured Peruvian fringes (Plate 111). Other cross-knitted fabrics were found in the ruins of Dura-Europos (third century). They consisted of two small fragments of ribbed knitting and a larger patterned one.[18] Some socks and other items recovered from fourth or fifth century Egyptian burying grounds display the crossed knitting technique.

Samples of *uncrossed knitting* made with a continuous yarn have been attributed to the tenth century, and some stockings with Arabic inscriptions exist dating to the early twelfth century. Knitting was introduced into Europe sometime around the fifth century. Knitted woolen caps were very common in England after the fifteenth century, and several silk knitted garments survive from the sixteenth century.

In 1589 the Reverend William Lee made a knitting frame so perfect that few improvements were needed for 250 years (Plate 8). Because Queen Elizabeth would not give him a patent, Lee emigrated to France where he died in poverty. Lee's brother James took some knitting frames back to England and founded a prosperous hosiery industry.

Knits were probably more plentiful in the seventeenth century than is generally thought, for they have not received the same attention from scholars as that given

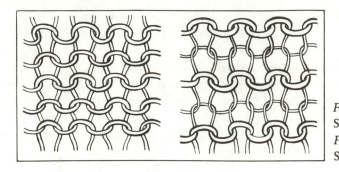

FIGURE 3.34 (*left*) /
Stocking Stitch Knit.
FIGURE 3.35 (*right*) / Garter
Stitch Knit.

to other fabrics. This is perhaps because knits were used for rather mundane purposes and were seldom treasured and preserved. In the seventeenth century patterning in knits was developed, and in the eighteenth century shaping of hosiery and garment sections was refined. By the nineteenth century knitted underclothes were common.

Lace

Lace is a very general term for a number of different ornamental openwork fabrics that can be made by interlacing, looping, twisting, and knotting threads, and also by embroidering net. Some kinds are made by machine but *real lace* is always handmade. Lace-like fabrics date to prehistoric Egypt, Peru, and the American Southwest, but lace was more completely developed during the Renaissance in southern Europe. Lace took two general forms, *needle lace* and *bobbin lace.*

Needle lace (needlepoint or point lace), is a looping technique worked with a needle and thread. It is essentially a sewing technique (the buttonhole stitch), and it is thought to have grown out of decoratively darning worn clothing. Needle lace developed before bobbin lace. (Plate 9).

Bobbin lace is made from a large number of fine yarns each wound on a small reel, or bobbin, to prevent their entangling. The lace is worked on a pillow or fabric-covered frame on which a paper pattern is laid. The pattern has many holes into which pins are stuck as the lace is being worked. The yarns are twisted around the pins and are interlaced and intertwined to make the pattern. (Plate 10).

Fabrics Made Directly from Fibers

When the word *felted* is used in the broadest sense—that is, fibers matted and adhered together—it can mean that wool, hair, or vegetable fibers from the bark of certain trees and shrubs have been used. The technology is much simpler than that for other textile techniques, and felting probably predated most of them in some regions.

Felt

More specifically *felt* means the dense fabric formed from wool and other hair fibers by application of heat, moisture, and agitation. Fiber scales become interlocked and the process is irreversible. Few tools are needed.

Feltmaking was known in Asia and Europe in ancient times, but the method was probably not used in America or Africa. One of the oldest specimens comes from a 1400 B.C. German grave. Felt was most important among the nomads of Central Asia where coarse wooled sheep were first domesticated. Scythian burials from the fourth century B.C. have yielded applique work done in multicolored felts, and felt was recorded in China, Tibet, and Turkey in the early centuries after Christ. By following word derivation, it has been assumed that feltmaking reached Western Europe from Turkey and Central Asia via the Slavs.[19]

At one time the steppes of Asia were known as the Land of Felt, and the fabric was essential to the life of the nomads there. Flocks were large and vast quantities of wool were consumed in making the typical round tent (yurt), mats, rugs, blankets, hats, footwear, and waterproof cloaks and coats. In earliest times feltmaking was women's work; it was necessary only to card the wool by hand, spread it out on an old piece of felt, sprinkle with water, roll it into a bundle, and roll the bundle back and forth while applying pressure. Feltmaking became a craft, and organized work for men, when the cotton bow was adapted for carding the wool. A special spreading fork was also developed to dispense the carded wool onto a reed mat.

The traditional shop method is still followed to some extent in Turkey and Iran. Wool is first cleaned of extraneous matter by children or old people. Then it is carded with the bow: the worker beats on the taut cord with a mallet, and the vibrations fluff the wool and remove any impurities that have missed the hands of the pickers. The carded wool is spread on a reed mat on which colored pattern pieces are first positioned if a rug is to be made. The mass is sprinkled with water, rolled up, and tied. Then the bundle is stepped—walked back and forth across the workroom floor by several men who put pressure on it by pressing on their knees.[20] This *hardening* process takes about half an hour, and it may be repeated. Hardening is followed by *fulling,* a very important part of feltmaking. Generally the felt is shrunk in hot water to which soap is added, then it is worked back and forth by rolling and unrolling, something like kneading bread, or it is treaded with bare feet.

Carding machines and felt presses replaced the old methods just as new synthetic fabrics are taking the place of felt for many uses. Felt is still the preferred material for heavy rain cloaks in the Near East.

Beaten Bark Cloth

While Europeans were weaving sumptuous silk damasks on drawlooms, women in Polynesia were beating strips of bark with wooden clubs to make their cloth. It was cloth suitable for garments and bedding, some as soft and drapable as muslin. This bark cloth was called *tapa* in most of Polynesia and *kapa* in Hawaii where the greatest variety was made (Plate 11).

The inner bark of several trees and shrubs in the *Moraceae* family, including the paper mulberry and breadfruit trees, was stripped from branches with a piece of shell and soaked in sea water for a week. The soft, pulpy strips were laid over a stone anvil and beaten with rounded clubs to form pliable sheets of bark cloth.

For the next stages of beating, there were special houses and long wooden anvils with grooves carved into the bottom so the sounds of the beating would be amplified. This was also the island communication system, and there was a well-known code. Grooved beaters were used first, then smooth ones, and finally beaters with incised patterns that "watermarked" the tapa.

Tapa was dyed in a wide range of colors made from tropical plants, or colored sections were overlaid and joined to a new cloth by beating. Designs were also painted on with tapa swabs or block printed with bamboo stamps. Taut cords impregnated with dye were snapped over the tapa to make straight lines. Delicate scents could be imbued by powdering sandalwood and sprinkling it between sheets of tapa or by using fragrant ferns and flowers.

There are reports of bark from paper mulberry being beaten into cloth in China during the third century. Bark cloth was made in Africa and South America, and the art was highly developed in the Indonesian archipelago. Polynesian tapa is best known, because very good records were made by Captain Cook and other white seamen who visited the Pacific islands in the late eighteenth century. In the nineteenth century whalers established bases in Polynesia and collected some fine pieces of tapa that are now in New England museums. Missionaries recorded the last of real tapa making while they dispensed calico Mother Hubbards.

NOTES

1. J. P. Wild, *Textile Manufacture in the Northern Roman Provinces* (Cambridge, England: Cambridge University Press, 1970), pp. 61–68.

2. H. Ling Roth, *Ancient Egyptian and Greek Looms* (Halifax, England: Bankfield Museum, 1951). Roth gives a history of the interpretation and misinterpretation of the painting.

3. Ibid., p. 10.

4. Louisa Bellinger, "The History of Threads: Natural Fibers and Filaments," in *Threads of History* (New York: The American Federation of Arts, 1965), p. 28.

5. Shelagh Weir, *Spinning and Weaving in Palestine* (London: The British Museum, 1970), p. 16.

6. Louisa Bellinger, *Textile Analysis: Early Techniques in Egypt and the Near East, Part 2,* The Textile Museum Paper No. 3 (Washington, D.C., April 1951).

7. R. J. Forbes, *Studies in Ancient Technology, Volume 4, Textiles,* 2nd rev. ed. (Leiden, Netherlands: E. J. Brill, 1964), p. 219.

8. See Kate P. Kent, *Introducing West African Cloth* (Denver: Museum of Natural History, 1971); Venice and Alastair Lamb, *The Lamb Collection of West African Narrow Strip Weaving,* ed. Patricia Fiske (Washington, D.C.: The Textile Museum, 1975); Venice Lamb, *West African Weaving* (London: Duckworth, 1975); Roy Sieber, *African Textiles and Decorative Arts* (New York: Museum of Modern Art, 1972); and Cheryl Plumer, *African Textiles: an Outline of Handcrafted Sub-Saharan Fabrics* (East Lansing, Mich: Michigan State University African Studies Center, 1971).

9. Louisa Bellinger, *Textile Analysis: Developing Techniques in Egypt and the Near East,*

Part 6, The Textile Museum Paper No. 14 (Washington, D.C., November 1957).

10. W. English, *The Textile Industry: An Account of the Early Inventions of Spinning, Weaving, and Knitting Machines* (London: Longmans, Green and Co., 1969), p. 105.

11. Irene Emery, *The Primary Structures of Fabrics: An Illustrated Classification* (Washington, D.C.: The Textile Museum, 1966). Emery is the current authority for all constructions and has been followed in this chapter.

12. See the article on tabby in George S. Cole, *Cole's Encyclopedia of Dry Goods* (Chicago: Cole, 1900), pp. 529-530.

13. Oliver N. Wells, *Salish Weaving: Primitive and Modern* (Sardis, British Colombia: O. N. Wells, 1969).

14. George T. Emmons, "The Chilkat Blanket," *American Museum of Natural History Memoir* 3, no. 4 (1907):320-350.

15. Emery, *Primary Structures,* p. 190.

16. Dorothy Burnham, "Coptic Knitting: An Ancient Technique," *Textile History* 3 (December 1972):116-124.

17. Verla Birrell, *The Textile Arts* (New York: Harper & Row, 1959) p. 303.

18. R. Pfister and Louisa Bellinger, "The Textiles," in *The Excavations at Dura-Europos, Part II* (New Haven: Yale University Press, 1945), p. 4.

19. Forbes, *Studies,* p. 93.

20. Michael and Veronika Gervers, "Felt-making Craftsmen of the Anatolian and Iranian Plateux," *Textile Museum Journal* 4, no. 1 (December 1974):19.

BIBLIOGRAPHY

There is no single history of looms and weaving. Charles Singer, et al., eds., *A History of Technology,* 5 vols. (Oxford: Clarendon Press, 1954-58) is helpful inasmuch as it discusses weaving in conjunction with other technological developments. Note especially volume three. Mary Kissell, *Yarn and Cloth Making, An Economic Study* (New York: Macmillan, 1918) outlines various types of looms and points out advantages of each. H. Ling Roth, *Primitive Looms* (1918; reprint ed., New York: Burt Franklin Reprints, 1974) is useful for descriptions of weaving processes and equipment. Considered an authority by some authors is Luther Hooper, *Hand-Loom Weaving: Plain and Ornamental* (London: Sir Isaac Pitman and Sons, 1910). Easier to obtain is Luther Hooper, "The Loom and Spindle: Past, Present, and Future," *Annual Report of the Board of Regents of the Smithsonian Institution for 1914,* pp. 629-678. This is valuable for diagrams and explanations, although some of Hooper's statements are not accurate.

An interesting early book is Clinton G. Gilroy, *The Art of Weaving By Hand and By Power with an Introductory Account of its Rise and Progress in Ancient and Modern Times for the Use of Manufacturers and Others* (New York: George D. Baldwin, 1844). Another wordy nineteenth century book is R. Marsden, *Cotton Weaving: Its Development, Principles, and Practices* (London: George Bell, 1895).

"The Loom," in *CIBA Review* 16 (December 1938) is a brief general history. Lili Blumenau, *The Art and Craft of Handweaving* (New York: Crown Publishers, 1955) gives an overview of the evolution of spinning and weaving and also includes information on contemporary handweaving. Verla Birrell, *The Textile Arts* (New York: Harper & Row, 1959) has some history of many textile techniques as well as modern adaptations. Well illustrated, Birrell's book includes directions for several projects. Shirley Held, *Weaving, a*

Handbook for Fiber Craftsmen (New York: Holt, Rinehart and Winston, 1973) is similar, with both historical background and weaving instructions. Some of the many readily available books on handweaving may be helpful to the historian, especially if it teaches weave drafting, which in turn helps in understanding construction.

Although history is not given, various primitive looms are described in R. A. Innes, *Non-European Looms in the Collections at Bankfield Museum* (Halifax, England: Halifax Museums, 1959).

A brief history of the waistloom is given in Barbara Taber and Marilyn Anderson, *Backstrap Weaving* (New York: Watson-Guptill Publications, 1975), although most of the book is devoted to instructions for setting up a loom and weaving.

The warp-weighted loom is discussed thoroughly in J. P. Wild, *Textile Manufacture in the Northern Roman Provinces*. Wild cites the important work of Marta Hoffman who wrote *The Warp-Weighted Loom: Studies in the History and Technology of an Ancient Implement* (Norway, 1964). More readily available is Marta Hoffman's "Manndalen Revisited: Traditional Weaving in an old Lappish Community in Transition," in *Studies in Textile History*, ed. Veronika Gervers (Toronto: Royal Ontario Museum, 1977), pp. 149-159. The best explanation of warp-weight weaving is given by A. E. Haynes, "Twill Weaving on the Warp Weighted Loom: Some Technical Considerations," *Textile History* 6 (1975):156-164. For a very detailed study of Penelope's loom see Agnes Geijer, "The Loom Representation on the Chiusi Vase," *Studies in Textile History*, pp. 52-55.

The most detail about ground looms can be found in H. Ling Roth, *Ancient Egyptian and Greek Looms* (Halifax, England: Bankfield Museum, 1951); *Threads of History* (American Federation of Arts, 1965); Shelagh Weir, *Spinning and Weaving in Palestine*; and R. J. Forbes, *Studies in Ancient Technology, Volume 4, Textiles*, 2nd rev. ed. (Leiden, Netherlands: E. J. Brill, 1964).

Tablet weaving is covered in Birrell, *The Textile Arts*, and in *CIBA Review* 117 (November 1956). Quite technical is Otfried Staudigel, "Tablet-Weaving and the Technique of the Rameses-Girdle," *Bulletin de Liaison du Centre International D'Etude Des Textiles Anciens* (1975), pp. 71-98. (The *Bulletin* is issued approximately once a year and contains articles in both French and English. It is published by the Centre International D'Etude Des Textiles Anciens, 34 rue de la Charite, 69002 Lyons, France. The latter is a worldwide organization of textile historians.) See also Marjorie and William Snow, *Tablet Weaving, Step by Step* (Racine, Wisconsin: Western Publishers, 1973). Weaving with a rigid hole and slot heddle is considered by Otis Mason in "A Primitive Frame for Weaving Narrow Fabrics," *Annual Report of the U.S. National Museum for 1899* (Washington, 1901), pp. 485-510.

W. English, *The Textile Industry* provides one of the best descriptions of the pattern loom. For specific information about the drawloom see Adèle Weibel, *Two Thousand Years of Textiles* (New York: Pantheon Books, 1952); J. F. Flanagan, "The Origin of the Drawloom in the Making of Early Byzantine Silks," *Burlington Magazine* 35 (October 1919):167; and Hans E. Wulff, *The Traditional Crafts of Persia: Their Development, Technology, and Influence on Eastern and Western Civilizations* (Cambridge: The M.I.T. Press, 1966). For instructions on how to build a drawloom see Alice Hindson, *Designer's Drawloom: An Introduction to Drawloom Weaving and Repeat Pattern Planning* (Boston: Charles T. Branford, 1958). Leslie J. Clarke, *The Craftsman in Textiles* (New York: Frederick A. Praeger, 1968) is rather general, but helpful, especially for the development of the jacquard loom. An excellent study with historic illustrations is Natalie Rothstein, "The Introduction of the Jacquard Loom to Great Britain," *Studies in Textile History*, pp. 281-304.

Irene Emery, *The Primary Structures of Fabrics: An Illustrated Classification* (Washington, D.C.: The Textile Museum, 1966) is very detailed and best used as a reference volume. Its bibliography is extensive. There are, however, many early works on textile history, and the researcher needs to be familiar with other terminology. In 1964 CIETA (Centre International D'Etude Des Textiles Anciens) in Lyon published the very helpful *Fabrics: A Vocabulary of Technical Terms* in English, French, Italian, and Spanish. Some of the work was taken from Nancy Reath, *The Weaves of Hand-Loom Fabrics: A Classification with Historical Notes* (Philadelphia: Pennsylvania Museum, 1927). Nancy Reath and Eleanor Sachs applied Reath's system in *Persian Textiles and Their Technique from the Sixth to the Eighteenth Centuries Including a System for General Textile Classification* (New Haven: Yale University Press, 1937). Weibel has a clear, but brief, section on weaves in *Two Thousand Years of Textiles*, and Ethel Lewis has a helpful glossary in *The Romance of Textiles* (New York: Macmillan, 1937).

Harold Burnham, *Chinese Velvets: A Technical Study,* Art and Archaeology Division Royal Ontario Museum Occasional Paper 2 (Toronto: University of Toronto Press, 1959) and "Velvet," in *CIBA Review 96* (February 1953) give technical background on that fabric. "Damask," *CIBA Review* 110 (June 1955) is also helpful. An interesting aspect of jacquard weaving is discussed in Wilma Baker, *The Silk Pictures of Thomas Stevens: A Biography of the Coventry Weaver and His Contribution to the Art of Weaving* (New York: Exposition Press, 1957) and in Geoffrey Godden, *Stevengraphs and Other Victorian Silk Pictures* (London: Barrie & Jenkins, 1971).

In addition to Emery, Birrell's *Textile Arts* is especially helpful for the nonweaving techniques. Birrell gives more information on history and how a technique is done than Emery, who concentrates on structure. An important book, Raoul d'Harcourt, *Textiles of Ancient Peru and Their Techniques* (Seattle: University of Washington Press, 1962) has some excellent diagrams in addition to information about many different techniques. For an early classification system see "Basic Textile Techniques," *CIBA Review* 63 (January 1948). The chart from that article has been reproduced in Marjory Joseph, *Essentials of Textiles* (New York: Holt, Rinehart & Winston, 1976), pp. 158-159.

Richard Conn published a series of articles on finger weaving (braiding) in *American Indian Crafts and Culture* 6, no. 10, 7, nos. 1 and 2 (1972-3) that make it seem quite simple. Some of the illustrations are of historical interest. Peter Collingwood, *The Techniques of Sprang: Plaiting on Stretched Threads* (New York: Watson-Guptill, 1974) is mainly a "how-to-do-it" book, but it has some history and chronology of pictorial and written records of sprang fabrics and equipment. See also Odd Nordland's *Primitive Scandinavian Textiles in Knotless Netting* (Norway: Oslo University Press, 1961). One of the best for knotting is Virginia Harvey, *Macrame: The Art of Creative Knotting* (New York: Van Nostrand Reinhold, 1967).

A concise history of knitting is given in S. M. Levey, "Illustrations of the History of Knitting Selected from the Collection of the Victoria and Albert Museum," *Textile History* 1, no. 2 (December 1969):183-205. Milton Grass' *History of Hosiery* (New York: Fairchild, 1955) is an easy to read overview. An old (1867) classic reprinted is William Felkin, *A History of the Machine-Wrought Hosiery and Lace Manufacturers* (New York: Burt Franklin Reprints, 1967). Felkin has two chapters on Reverend Lee. A scholarly study is E. W. Pasold, "In Search of William Lee," *Textile History* 6 (1975):7-17. In the same journal issue (pp. 18-51) there is a discussion of uses for early knits by Jane Rapley entitled "Handframe Knitting: The Development of Patterning and Shaping." Another article reflecting the increased interest by researchers' in knitting is I. Turau and K. G. Ponting, "Knitted Masterpieces," *Textile History* 7 (1976):7-59. It has illustrations of some knitted tapestries.

Lacemaking is a specialized study and references are plentiful. A few include *CIBA Review* 73 (April 1949); Ernest Lefebure, *Embroidery and Lace* (Philadelphia: J. B. Lippincott, Co., 1889); Mrs. (Emily) F. Nevill Jackson, *A History of Hand-Made Lace* (New York: Charles Scribner's Sons, 1900); Mrs. Fanny Palliser, *History of Lace* (London: Sampson Low, Marston and Co., 1910), previous editions in 1869 and 1875; Clara Blum, *Old World Lace or a Guide for the Lace Lover* (New York: E. P. Dutton, 1920); Marian Powys, *Lace and Lace-making* (Boston: Charles T. Branford, Co., 1953); David W. Schwab, *The Story of Lace and Embroidery* (New York: Fairchild Publications, 1951); and Patricia Wardle, *Victorian Lace* (New York: Frederick A. Praeger, 1969).

For felt, see B. Laufer, "The Early History of Felt," *American Anthropologist,* n.s. 31 (1930):1-18; and *CIBA Review* 129 (November 1958). The classic work on bark cloth is W. T. Brigham, "Ka Hana Kapa: The Story of the Manufacture of Kapa (Tapa), or Bark-Cloth, in Polynesia and Elsewhere, but Especially in the Hawaiian Islands," *Memoirs of the Bernice P. Bishop Museum, Volume 3* (Honolulu: Bishop Museum Press, 1911), pp. 1-273. A more recent leading and detailed study is Simon Kooijman, *Tapa in Polynesia*, Bernice P. Bishop Museum Bulletin 234 (Honolulu: Bishop Museum Press, 1972). A shorter, more concise work is leading Polynesian anthropologist Te Rang Hiroa's (Peter H. Buck) "Arts and Crafts of Hawaii, Section V Clothing," *Bernice P. Bishop Museum Special Publication 45* (1964), pp. 165-252. Especially good for illustrations is "Bark Fabrics of the South Seas," *CIBA Review* 33 (May 1940). For samples of tapa see Adrienne L. Kaeppler, *The Fabrics of Hawaii (Bark Cloth)* (Leigh-on-Sea, England: F. Lewis, Publishers, 1975).

4. FINISH AND COLOR FOR TEXTILES

Finishing and color processes give textiles certain characteristics that frequently determine the names given to them. Color processes, especially, are sometimes closely associated with particular historic textiles.

FINISHING

Less is known about finishing methods than about other phases of textile production. Early methods were time consuming, sometimes employed some rather exotic ingredients, and were often held secret. Progress was generally slow until the late nineteenth century when scientists learned enough about the chemical and physical properties of the fibers to be able to apply scientific methods.

The history of finishing up to the nineteenth century is comprised mainly of odd bits of information. Pliny and other Romans left some, but it was not until the late Middle Ages that much was recorded—and that generally concerned wool finishing. That something needed to be done with woven cloth before it could be sold was recognized in *Piers Plowman* (fourteenth century):

> Cloth that cometh fro the wevying is noght comly to were
> Tyl it is fulled under fote, or in fullying stokkes
>   (fuller's stocks)
> Wasshen wel with water and with tasles (teazles)
>   cracched (scratched),
> Y-touked (finished) and y-teynted (stretched), and under
>   tailloures hande.[1]

Common Finishes

Sizing was used both to strengthen warp yarns for weaving and to enhance the finished fabric. The Indian Institutes of Manu (circa 200 B.C.) stated that rice water could be employed only to strengthen warp, not to hide defects of weaving. Pliny mentioned the use of cereal starch, and clay was frequently used. The English wove a very low count cotton fabric, *coolie cloth,* and sized it heavily with clay for the China trade.

Cleaning was always necessary, even if the cloth was to be dyed. Egyptian papyruses tell of the poor laundrymen who worked by the crocodiles. They rubbed the cloth with a detergent (potash or natron) and beat it with wooden clubs—the method still used in primitive societies. In the Near East the leaves and roots of several alkaline plants—soapwort was one—were crushed to make lathers. The Phoenicians prepared soap from goat fat and wood ashes in 600 B.C., and, although soap was made in England in the twelfth century, it did not come into general use until the nineteenth century. Another cleaning agent, used throughout the world and commercially even well into the nineteenth century, was stale urine from animals and humans. Decomposition of the urine produced ammonia which did the cleaning. Combined with wool fat, the ammonia made soap by partial saponification. As an industry, dry cleaning belongs to the nineteenth century, although spirits of turpentine were used as early as the late seventeenth century to remove spots. The major dry cleaning agent, benzene, was not in use until 1857.[2] Cloth was dried by spreading it out on the grass or hanging it on frames outdoors. During the Industrial Revolution superheated rooms were used.

Until the eighteenth century when calenders, or cylinders, were developed, fabrics were pressed by pulling wooden or metal rods or smooth stones across the surface. Cloth presses (Plate 12) were in operation as early as Roman times. The cloth was folded accordion fashion and laid between the plates and a giant screw turned to tighten the plates against the cloth. In fifteenth century Europe heat pressing with sheets of hot cast iron inserted between the cloth folds was considered a method for hiding defects, and hence illegal, but the method was also used for glazing. Glazing, or polishing, is most often associated with eighteenth century chintz, made by applying beeswax and polishing with flintstones.

Finishes for Linen

Linen and hempen cloths were never considered attractive unless bleached, and many different methods have been used throughout history, most of which consumed long periods of time. The traditional method, used in eighteenth century England, involved soaking the linen in sour milk and cow's dung, then steeping (*bucking*) it in waste lye for about a week. After washing, the cloth was held in vats of buttermilk for another week, then washed and spread on the grass (*grassing, crofting*) where it was exposed to sun and rain until white.

The Dutch were the best bleachers in eighteenth century Europe. Sometimes they used ryemeal or bran instead of milk, and the sequence of souring, washing, bucking, and watering was repeated several times for a period of six to eight months. The Irish speeded the process somewhat by boiling the cloth in lye, and they also milled (fulled) the bleached cloth. In the mid-eighteenth century the use of diluted sulfuric acid instead of milk cut the time to three months.

Ancients pounded the linen with wooden mallets and polished it with stones or linen rubbers (flattened glass balls). The *beetling* machine was invented in 1850. It had a pair of wooden rollers with hammers that pounded the cloth for hours in order to get a smooth, soft finish. The high strength of the flax fiber was an important asset. The Egyptians *goffered*, or fluted, linen with a special wooden instrument. It gave a pleated effect to garments.

Finishes for Cotton

Because cotton is a vegetable fiber, it was bleached by the same methods used for linen, although the time required was less. Probably the most dramatic breakthrough in cotton finishing was the discovery of the bleaching effect of chlorine by the Swede Carl Wilhelm Scheele in 1774.[3] In 1785 the Frenchman Berthollet suggested its use in the form of chlorine water (*eau de Javel*) for bleaching textiles. A process that had taken six to eight months could now be completed in hours. Bleaching powder, calcium hypochlorite, was first used in America around 1810.

Mercerization is important to the success of cotton fabrics, that is, the chemical finish that improves strength, luster, and dye affinity. The process was named after John Mercer who investigated the effects of strong caustic soda (sodium hydroxide) on cotton in 1840 and in 1850 patented a process for mercerizing without tension being held on the fabric. This method was a failure, because the cloth shrank 20 to 25 percent. It was, however, used in Lyons in 1884 to produce crimp effects on combination fabrics of silk and cotton by shrinking only the cotton. The method was used in a similar manner in calico printing in the 1890s to achieve crepon effects. In 1895 a practical process for mercerization with tension was developed in Krefeld, Germany. The process, applied first to yarn, then to piece goods, produced an almost new material. The *schreiner calender* finish was also invented in 1895. It used rollers engraved with fine lines, heat, and pressure to give luster to cotton fabrics and make them more like silk.

Finishes for Silk

Bleaching methods used for vegetable fibers are not suitable for animal fibers. Silk was bleached in the Middle Ages by spreading it over a cage in which lamp sulfur was burned. Later, sulfurous acid was used.

Watering (moiréing), another medieval finish (and a modern one also), gave a wave-like or veined pattern to ribbed silks (and later to worsteds). Sometimes the term *watered* was restricted to patterns in parallel lines, while *moiré* meant a nondefined pattern (Plate 13). Both patterns were achieved by pressing the ribs down in certain areas to cause a difference in light reflection. In medieval Europe and the Orient, moiré was made by placing two layers of cloth on a wooden block and beating them with mallets. In the nineteenth century calenders were used either to press together two layers of fabric laid off grain or to impress a single layer with a pattern from an engraved roller.

According to *Chambers Dictionary* (1784-1788) silk taffeta was brought to perfection by water and fire. The silk had to be of the finest kind and worked a long time before use, the water given only lightly, and the fire, passed under the taffeta to dry the water, handled skillfully. Possibly the Chinese, or else sixteenth century Europeans, discovered that silk had a very strong affinity (up to seven times its weight) for certain metallic salts—tin, lead, or iron—that gave the fabric a stiff hand. In the second half of the nineteenth century weighting was practiced extensively in Germany and France. England was slower in adopting the practice but considered it necessary for colored silks toward the end of the century. For a long time it was considered legitimate in the United States to replace 25 percent weight loss incurred when the sericin was boiled off. But after World War I, weighting, called "loading" and "dynamiting," became a definite abuse. A decrease in durability related directly to increasing amounts of metallic salts.

Finishes for Wool

Wool's chemistry causes it to yellow rather than to whiten in sunlight, so the ancients bleached it with sulfur fumes as they did silk. The bleaching was not always uniform, and sometimes white fuller's earth or gypsum was rubbed into the fabric to even out the whitening effect. In the eighteenth and nineteenth centuries sulfuring was called *stoving,* because the process was carried out in small, tightly sealed rooms or small buildings where the cloth was hung on wooden racks.

Fulling was essential to woolen manufacture and was used on some worsteds. It was a cleaning, shrinking, and felting operation that gave wool fabrics a softer surface for raising and shearing and made them thicker and more weather resistant (Plate 14). Probably more information has been recorded about fulling than about any other finish.

In 1826 a *fullonica,* milling factory, was discovered at Pompeii, an important Roman clothing trade center before its very sudden demise with the eruption of Vesuvius in 79 A.D. Murals and remaining structures give us an idea of the fulling that was done by treading the cloth held in vats.[4] Guilds of fullers throughout the Roman Empire formed one of the world's first service industries; their work included fulling homespun and cleaning dirty clothing.

The medieval process is representative of the ancient one. The cloth was first scoured with a lathering agent and hot water, then, after wringing out, it was treated with fuller's earth (a hydrated aluminum silicate clay) that removed the

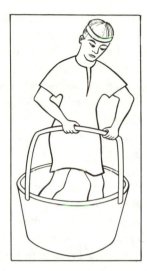

FIGURE 4.1 / Medieval Fulling.

natural grease and any oil added for spinning. Sometimes the cloth was soaked for several days in the fuller's earth and water before it was rinsed. The next step was *waulking,* or tramping the wet cloth in vats (Fig.4.1), beating it with clubs, or waulking it by hand. This could be done to the tune of special songs by a dozen or so women who sat divided between two sides of a bench and worked the wet cloth back and forth.[5]

Fulling mills, operated first by human power then by water power, were in operation in England sometime late in the eleventh century but were not widely used until the thirteenth.[6] Early mills had small wooden beams that were raised by cams. The beams fell to knead the cloth in a vat lined with pebbles to soften the blows. It was a harsh method and one used only for rougher goods. Hammer type mills were developed in the sixteenth century, and the cloth was kneaded more gently as it rotated slowly through the mill. The seventeenth and eighteenth century process called *currying* was related to fulling. Worsted cloth was rolled tightly on rods that stood in a kettle of boiling water for an hour. After draining and cooling, the cloth was rolled in the opposite direction and the process repeated. The worsted improved in appearance and was set in dimensions. After fulling woolens were *burled.* Any knot that had been tied in the yarns during weaving was pulled to the surface and clipped off. Burling also removed any vegetable matter remaining in the cloth.

After fulling the woolens were napped while still wet, or they were dried on tenter frames—arrangements of posts and rails that could be adjusted. The cloth was attached to "L"-shaped hooks on the upper and lower rails; over-stretching was a common abuse to be diligently restricted by guild inspectors. (Nerves are stretched tightly if one is "on tenterhooks.")

Raising, napping, or *gigging* served to raise the nap for shearing and to give the cloth a soft finish. In ancient times it was done by drawing teasels held in wooden frames over the cloth. Leonardo da Vinci invented a napping machine (gig mill) in 1490, but it proved impractical. Other versions—such as one with two teasel-covered cylinders rotated by a wheel that was turned by a workman as the cloth was pulled through slowly—were not generally in use until the 1830s due to the resistance of handworkers who feared loss of their jobs. Velour, melton, or doeskin finishes resulted from slightly different gigging methods.

Cropping (shearing) was a highly specialized craft requiring great physical stamina (Plate 15). The cloth was stretched over a padded bench and held taut by hooks. The shearman placed his shears across the bench and guided them with his left hand while operating a lever that opened and closed the blades with his right hand. Leonardo da Vinci designed some crank systems to open and close the shears, but shearing machines did not actually appear until 1784 and 1787, when Delaroche of Amiens and J. Harmer of Sheffield, respectively, produced inventions with several pairs of shears united by a crank and moved by power.

Frizing, a fashion finish of the seventeenth and eighteenth centuries, gave the woolen a granular (curly) appearance. It was originally a hand method. The cloth was moistened with honey or egg white, and the nap was rubbed in a circular fashion with a sandstone slab or a plank coated with coarse sand. Later, water or horse powered mills had two long planks that were circulated; one held the cloth and the other was covered with burrs.

COLOR

Throughout history color has often been associated with the supernatural and with superstition. Certain colors were sacred and could be worn by only a few people. Dyeing practices were intricately meshed with the mores and taboos of primitive societies. For example, pregnant women could not go near the dye pots lest they spoil the brew, and dyeing in some colors was reserved to specific persons. Similar restrictions were enforced by medieval guilds. Colors held special significance for ancient and primitive people, and even in modern Europe there are superstitions concerning color. Physicians who prescribed red medicine at one time wore red cloaks. Yellow purportedly cured jaundice, and blue was good for rheumatism.

Dyeing

Information about dyeing practices prior to the sixteenth century is limited, although recipes were recorded starting with the papyruses of the Coptic period (see chapter 5) and perhaps earlier. Often recipes contained useless ingredients and nonsensical instructions. In the tenth century a Byzantine monk who had fled to Cologne wrote *Schedula Diversarium Artium,* a description of various Byzantine crafts including dyeing. Other medieval works were *Divers secrets curieux, Secretum Philosophorum,* and an Englishman's *De Proprietatibus Rerum* (On the Properties of

Things). Perhaps five hundred books on dyeing were published between 1500 and 1856, when William Perkin discovered synthetic mauve. Thirteen are considered to be of major importance.[7] (See Plate 16.)

Dye and *dyestuff* are synonymous terms for colored materials applied to textiles from solutions or dispersions. *Pigments* are coloring compounds that are not soluble in water, that do not combine chemically with the fiber, and that are generally used with adhesives for painting or printing. Any color can be printed on any fiber, while all fibers cannot be dyed with all colors.

Most dyes are organic compounds with color-bearing groups called *chromophores*. But not all colored compounds will dye textiles; there must be *auxochromes* (salt-forming groups) present. Many dyestuffs will not directly color a fiber so *mordants* (from the French *mordre*, "to bite") must be used. Mordants are salts of aluminum, iron, tin, or chrome that combine with the dye and the fiber to make the color insoluble. Some common mordants are potash made from leaching wood ashes, the alum that is very common in many parts of the world, and caustic soda. Changing the mordant can give different colors or shades from one dyebath. Mordants are applied to the fibers before dyeing, added to dyebaths, or printed on the fabric before dipping.

Vat dyes (woad and indigo being the oldest) are insoluble in water. They are applied by a method of reduction, known as vatting, in which the dye is changed in dilute alkali to a colorless, or *leuco,* form that has affinity for the fiber. After dipping, the cloth is removed and the color develops by oxidation in the air. Vat colors are especially fast to light.

Although a very large number of mineral, vegetable, and animal materials have been used for dyeing, a few major ones have emerged as the most important and have been used and traded almost universally. Expensive dyestuffs traveled the Great Silk Road and the trade routes of medieval Europe. Vasco da Gama sought a sea route to Asia in the quest for dyes, and the New World proved to be a rich source for dye materials. All dyes were natural products until the late nineteenth century.

Mineral Dyes

Mineral pigments were probably the first materials used for dyeing. They were generally not fast to water. Natural ochre, a yellow (sometimes red) clay containing iron oxides, was one of the most common. Reds and browns could be obtained by dipping cloth in springs containing iron salts. American colonists used scraps of iron in vinegar and water. The indians of the American Southwest dyed yarn pink in the rainwater puddles on the red sandstone mesas. Limestone or lime was used for white, and some black dye was made from manganese dioxide, although charcoal and soot were more common as sources.

Other minerals have, at times, been used for dyestuffs: cinnabar, a bright red-orange mercury sulfide; several copper minerals, including blue azurite and green malachite; yellow orpiment, a sulfide of arsenic; litharge (lead oxide), a product of silver extraction; and even lapis lazuli. In the Middle Ages some of these pigments were mixed with oily or resinous adhesive mediums such as linseed oil or boiled amber and used for printing.

Vegetal Dyes

Woad, the high fashion blue of the European Middle Ages, was perhaps the world's most important dyestuff. It was known to the Egyptians and Mesopotamians long before the Hellenistic period when it was cultivated extensively. Widely distributed over Europe, Asia, and North Africa, woad was most closely associated with the Britons who, according to the Romans, dyed their bodies with it. The word is of Saxon origin.

> Molly, of the woad, and I fell out,
> O, What do you think it was all about?
> For she had money and I had none
> And that is how the strife begun.[8]

Woad comes from a yellow-flowered plant of the mustard family, *Isatis tinctoria.* Although it belongs to a different plant family than indigo, the coloring matter, indican, is the same but weaker. No doubt, what has been identified as indigo in some archaeological specimens is actually woad. Woad dye comes from the leaves, and the stage at which they are harvested determines the intensity of the color, from rather light blue to the deepest, most intense, called *perse.*

In thirteenth to sixteenth century Europe leaves were ground into paste by huge wooden rollers turned round and round by horses. The pulpy mass was drained and kneaded into loaf-like balls, called *pastel* (a name also used for the dye), and allowed to dry for a couple of weeks. The woad was then ground into a fine powder, moistened, and allowed to ferment for a month or two. The resulting dyestuff, with only a ninth the bulk of the original leaves, went into the dyer's vat, most often with urine as the reducing agent. As with other vat dyes, the color developed when the cloth was exposed to air.

In medieval England woad was so valuable it was used as a medium of exchange, and its composition and methods of use were carefully regulated. Only *indigo* proved to be a better source of blue. Woad was superseded by indigo, the "devil dye," in the seventeenth century after some bitter opposition from European woad interests. By then indigo could be imported cheaply by sea from India, and in the eighteenth and nineteenth centuries much came from West Indian plantations.

Indigofera tinctoria, a bush of the pea family, is the most important of the 350 different plants that produce indigo. The dye was used prehistorically in India where it probably originated. The word is derived from *Indicum,* the Latin word for imports from India. The Sanskrit for blue or indigo was *anil,* giving the word *aniline.* Indigo was a universal dyestuff. During the eighteenth and nineteenth centuries, the industry was of great importance in India, Java, and Guatemala and of lesser significance in Africa, China, Japan, and South Carolina. Indigo was not synthesized until 1880.

FIGURE 4.2 / Indigo Production in India (seventeenth century drawing).

In the production process, the indican was extracted from the leaves, reduced by fermentation to the white and water insoluble *indigotin* that was subsequently oxidized into a blue flaked precipitate. The process was carried out in tiered tanks (Figure 4.2) with the fermented mass being run off into the lower tank where it was beaten with paddles to incorporate the air needed for oxidation. (The stench has often been noted by historians.) The precipitate was then dried into cakes that were broken into chunks for sale. Various grades, from fine blue to inferior purples, were available. The indigo was frequently adulterated with ashes, sand, or starch, or allowed to absorb moisture to increase its weight.

Dyeing with indigo, like dyeing with woad, was a matter of reduction in an alkaline vat. The fabric emerged yellow, and the color gradually oxidized from green to blue, the latter a rich navy fast to light and water. The very practical urine vat was commonly used throughout the world and was especially useful for home dyeing. As late as 1890 peasants in Switzerland allowed urine collected during the summer to ferment, set it with indigo, and kept it warm on the oven in the living room for any clothes that required touching up.

The blossoms, leaves, and stems of many plants can be used for yellow. They color the fiber directly, although mordants are frequently used for good coloring. Four yellows were, and still are especially important.

Pliny wrote about *saffron, Crocus sativus* of the iris family, in use in Egypt since 2000 B.C. Saffron was the principal dye used by the Greeks and Romans, and it was an important trade item in the Near East. The golden yellow from the three stigmas handpicked from each purple flower was dried, then dissolved in water. Saffron was the official color for Buddist robes. After the Crusaders introduced it to northern Europe, saffron was used for a wool and silk dye, food coloring and flavoring, and perfume. The dye was always expensive and was for that reason often adulterated with safflower.

Safflower, Carthamus tinctorius of the thistle family, is native to many parts of Asia and Africa. Its flowers contain two coloring materials: safflower yellow (weak and water soluble) and carthamic acid (red and insoluble). It is a commonly used yellow in southern Asia, but the red dyeing is more complex, requiring treatment with alkalis.

Weld, Reseda luteola, one of the oldest dye plants of the Mediterranean region, was very common in medieval and early modern Europe. Because the coloring material came from the long spiked flowers, the stalks, and the leaves, the whole plant was pulled and dried for future use. Large amounts of the plant were required to get a rich, bright yellow. Weld, also called *dyer's weed,* was replaced by fustic from the New World.

Fustic could be used to dye cotton as well as wool and silk. The best, *old fustic* (yellow wood or dyer's mulberry), came from *Chlorophora tinctoria,* a tree native to tropical America. Chips of the logs were tied in bags, placed in the dyebath, and soaked for a few days before the alum mordant was added. Other mordants varied the color from golden to light yellowish tan. *Young fustic,* from a sumac plant, produced a more fugitive yellow.

In the late eighteenth century British soldiers and fox hunters wore coats of *madder* dyed wool in an effort to promote the industry. By that time tin mordants were used to get bright red on wool, something not possible previously.

Just when madder dyeing began is unknown. Certainly it was very early, because madder dyed fabrics were found at Mohenjo-Daro and in early Egyptian tombs. It could have been almost anywhere, as about thirty-five species of the family *Rubiaceae* were indigenous to many parts of Asia and Europe. *Rubia tinctorum,* the species of the Near East, was the most common variety. The roots were dug in the autumn, washed, dried, and ground into powder. The dye, ruberythric acid, was contained between the outer skin and the woody heart of the root, and the intensity of the color depended on the type of soil the madder was grown in. Madder was a cheap and fast dye for all the natural fibers, but the color was often a rather dull terra cotta, not the bright scarlet of the expensive insect dyes.

Turkey red dyeing, madder on cotton, was bright. The exact process was a secret of the Near East until the French figured it out and published the method in 1765. By then Europeans were no longer willing to pay the exorbitant prices charged for brilliant red cotton yarns from Greece and Asia Minor. The process was involved and used many different treatments and mordantings. After desizing and bleaching, the cotton cloth was oiled with olive oil, lard, fish, or rapeseed oil and treated with dung to animalize the fiber (i.e., make it like wool). The next step was "sumaching,"—really the addition of tannins. Nut galls were also used. After drying, the cloth was alumed and finally dyed. An important step, clearing, came after dyeing and involved boiling the yarn or cloth in potash soap baths and drying in sunlight. Often the various steps were repeated and each dyer had a preferred method.

The *redwoods* have been used for dyes since ancient times. Diverse trees belonging to the leguminous family *Caesalpiniaceae* are suitable; *echinata,* called *Brazilwood,* is the most common. The wood is cut into pieces, rasped into powder, and fermented for five to six weeks. When used on wool mordanted with alum the color is bright red.

Prior to the sixteenth century, Europe got its redwoods from India, Sumatra, and Ceylon courtesy of Venetian traders. After Vasco da Gama's discoveries, the dyes traveled in Portuguese ships. The Portuguese applied their word *braza,* meaning fire, to the wood. When they found the same trees growing in northern South America, they named the new land "Terra de Brazil."

Logwood was a material of such good quality that it was used as a black dye long after synthetic ones were available: it has even been used on nylon. Logwood came from a Mexican tree discovered by the Spanish early in the sixteenth century. The port of San Francisco de Campeche, from which logwood was shipped in 400 pound blocks to Europe, gave the dye another name, *campechy wood.* The wood had to be chipped, fermented, placed in a bag, and boiled for a short time, then removed from the dyebath before the cloth was immersed. To avoid adulteration the customer usually bought the dye in log form. In one Philadelphia jail inmates were for a time kept busy chipping it.[9] Upon cutting, logwood turned red on contact with air, but it was a fast black dye when a complicated method involving iron, aluminum, and copper salts was employed. Logwood could also be used to make a fugitive blue-black and a plum-blue.

A gum resin called *cutch* or *catechu,* a rich brown dye important in Indian calico printing, came from the heartwood of acacia trees of southeast Asia. Cutch was also extracted from betel nuts. Other browns and blacks came from walnut hulls, used first in Persia and Asia Minor and later in Europe and America. Butternut hulls made a good colonial American and Confederate tan.

Soft colors could be obtained from *lichens,* thallophytic plants composed of algae and fungi growing in symbiosis on rocks and trees. Wool could be dyed directly, although sometimes lichens required fermentation. *Archil,* orchil, or orseille (as it was known to Pliny) grew on Mediterranean marine rocks and was used as a substitute for indigo in making a red-purple. Lichens were used frequently in Norway and Iceland for delicate tints ranging from yellow through red. *Cudbear,* a combination of lichens from the British Isles, produced a fugitive purple.

Animal Dyes

Since very ancient times insects and mollusks have provided brilliant red and purple dyes for the protein fibers. In the past these dyestuffs were expensive, as their sources and processing show, but they made deep, rich colors that have survived to this day.

In the time of Moses ladies got up before daybreak to pick by lamplight the dead lice off the branches of oak trees. They grew their fingernails long for the job. The female of the shield louse laid her eggs, spread herself over them in protection, and died. The Hebrews called the dye *tola,* the Armenians, *kermes*—both meaning worm—although the ancients believed it to be a fruit of the oak. The insect bodies were pulverized for dyeing or were dried and sold as what appeared to be tiny seeds. Hence, kermes was known as *grain*. An old definition of ingrain dyeing implied the use of kermes. Known throughout Asia and the Near East, and in medieval Europe, kermes was the best red dye for wool and silk until it was superseded by cochineal.

When the Spanish conquered Mexico they found that the Indians paid Montezuma tribute in a dyestuff like kermes. They quickly observed that *cochineal* (from the Spanish *cochinilla* for little female hog, the name for the shield louse) was more prolific than kermes and that three crops, instead of one, could be harvested each year. The Europeans also recognized the superior dyeing qualities of cochineal and the possibilities for a profitable industry. They took over the business in Oaxaca and were able to keep the source of the new dye a secret. So, until the early eighteenth century, most Europeans believed cochineal to be the seed of some tropical plant. In the years between 1796 and 1820 the exports of cochineal through the port of Vera Cruz averaged over a million dollars a year, even though some was being grown in Europe.

Cochineal is still used for coloring foods and lipstick. *Dactylopius coccus cacti,* similar to several other dyeing insects of South and Central America, lay their eggs on the branches of cactus, mainly on the prickly pear. Before most do lay their eggs, they are scooped from the cactus and killed by drying in the sun or an oven. When scalded the tiny dried bodies yield carminic acid, the same coloring material as that in kermes. *Lac,* another red dye, came from southeast Asia. This was a resinous extrusion of several shelled insects that burrowed into trees to reproduce.

The best ancient purple was reddish with violet overtones. Sometimes it was actually blue. It is best to think of old purple as ranging from the blue-reds through the red-purples. The coloring material, dibromoindigo (found in several shellfish), has a chemical formula very similar to that of indigo.

The story of the origin of purple resides in legend. One day (about 1500 B.C.) Melgarth, a god of the Phoenicians, walked his dog along the shores of the Mediterranean. The dog suddenly crunched up a shellfish, and his mouth oozed with a red stain so brilliant that the god decided to dye a tunic for his beloved Tyros (a nymph).[10] This was the famous Tyrian purple (bleeding mouth purple, or Turk's blood), so special that it was reserved for royalty and the clavi on Roman senators' tunics. Thus began the famous Phoenician dye industry. To this day mounds of spent shells are visible on the eastern Mediterranean coast where ancient dye installations have been excavated. The complicated knowledge of purple dyeing passed from the Phoenicians to the Greeks, then to the Romans, and finally to the Byzantines—the last of the great purple dyers. After Constantinople was lost to the West in 1453, the secret was lost and the so-called cardinals' purple, the stamp of the church, was made from kermes.

The process of obtaining the dibromoindigo was not simple. The secret lay with the secretion of a small gland adjacent to the respiratory organ of the whelk. On exposure to air this yellow fluid changed through several stages to a purplish red or scarlet, depending on the length of exposure and variety of shellfish. The liquid had to be used immediately (and in the fall and winter), so textile centers grew near the sites where the shellfish were plentiful. Sometimes the fluid could be extracted from individual mollusks if they were large enough, but more often masses of small ones were crushed, soaked in salt for three days, washed, and boiled. This concentrated the dye and got rid of the meat and extraneous matter. Cloth was dipped, and if the proper color did not develop on exposure to the air, the dyebath was boiled a little longer.

According to Pliny, *real Tyrian purple* was double dipped, a process that made it especially expensive. First, it went into a solution that was barely ready, then it was dyed in the liquid of different shellfish. The result was a shimmering bright red. Silk dyed with Tyrian purple was worth its weight in gold.

Mixing Dyes

Dyestuffs were often mixed, either to extend expensive ones or to make colors not possible with one dye. The animal dyes were the ones most often imitated. Indigo and madder made a fairly good purple. One recipe for green comes from the sixteenth century *Plictho of Gioanventura Rosetti:*

To Dye Silk in Green Color

First one must alumate as one does for black and for grain. Then take two pounds of weld, that is a grass that grows in Bologna that is similar to corniola, for each pound of silk. Make it boil one hour and a half, and when it has boiled, you take that liquor in a tub and you take your silk out of the aluming and squeeze it by hand, strongly. Then treat it in said water until it takes the color to your liking. When you have given the yellow, treat the silk in the cauldron and take it out and know ye that silk is more yellow or light green. When it is needy, treat the said silk in the cauldron with flower of indigo. When it is strongly yellow, the color becomes darker green. When it lacks yellow, the color becomes more open and less loaded. Take it out and spread it in the sun.[11]

Design by Dyeing

Printing, the application of color to the surface of a textile, was, for the most part, a development of modern times. Pattern could, however, be achieved by dyeing and some methods are very old. Most were *resist* (reserve) procedures and perhaps began with the redyeing of dirty clothing. Material such as mud, clay, starch, or wax, was applied to the cloth as a pattern. The cloth was dyed, and the resist agent removed, yielding an undyed pattern on a colored background.

Other kinds of resist dyeing included the use of stencils to apply the resist pastes, shields pasted or sewn to the cloth, and the folding and tying of parts against the dye. In a process called *ikat,* yarns were wrapped with bast or cords to protect certain areas against dye penetration. Pattern could also be achieved by two methods that were not resist procedures. *Mordant printing,* known in ancient Egypt, was the application of mordants in certain areas before the cloth was dyed: the color took only where there was mordant. *Discharge,* the method for removing color from patterned areas of dyed fabrics with bleaching pastes, was an early nineteenth century development.

Resist Dyeing

Batik

The term *batik* is sometimes used to mean any kind of resist process. More specifically, it means paste or wax resist. Most specifically, it means the wax resist of Indonesia. Batik is derived from the Javanese word *ambitik,* meaning to mark with small dots, used first in the seventeenth century.

Batik reached its highest development in Indonesia (Plate 17), but it was also known in India, China, Japan, Egypt, West Africa, and Peru. Similar methods were probably developed independently in different parts of the world. If more data were available, it might be possible to relate batik development to ancient migrations. Although batik reached Java sometime between the tenth and the thirteenth century, it did not become a great national activity until the seventeenth century, when a sultan became so enthralled with the art that he had the ladies of the court designing and executing symbolic and heraldic designs. The craft soon spread to the lower classes who eventually turned batiking into a thriving business for the Dutch trade.

The process went slowly. Cotton cloth was cut to the proper size for a sarong, kerchief, shawl, or ceremonial wrap. After washing and sun drying, the cloth was soaked in coconut oil for several days and boiled to remove the oil. After drying again it was pounded with wooden beaters to "mellow" it and was sized with rice water. The design was drawn with pencil or charcoal, then spread on a frame for the hot beeswax application. By the seventeenth century the *tjanting,* a small copper cup with a thin spout and a handle of reed or bamboo, had replaced the old bamboo sticks and quills. The tjanting made it possible to draw very thin lines and details. Around 1850 the *tjap,* a stamp made of metal strips, speeded the wax application by about twenty times and also shifted it from a woman's activity to a man's business. Heavy cloths were waxed on both sides, while lighter ones were waxed on one side only and left in the sun a short time for the wax to melt through to the other side. Occasionally, the whole cloth was waxed and holes were made with a bamboo tool to give dotted designs on the finished cloth. The characteristic crackle that is associated with modern batik occurs when the wax cracks and the dye seeps through. This was not considered good form in traditional batik.

The Javanese worked with a limited color range in dyeing. All parts not to be blue, black, or green were waxed, and the cloth was held in a cold indigo vat for almost three weeks. After boiling to remove the wax and washing, the cloth was rewaxed for dyeing with sogan, the characteristic Javanese brown made from tree bark. Black came with several dyeings in indigo. A certain amount of Turkey red, yellow extracted from the rhizome of the creeping *curcuma* plant, and green made by overdyeing yellow on indigo, were used in polychrome batiks, usually of silk. Most Indonesian cotton batiks were indigo or brown with cream backgrounds because only cold, or at best lukewarm, dye baths could be used so as not to melt the wax.

The success of Indonesian batik design depended on balancing light and dark areas. There were a number of traditional motifs; some have been degraded, or combined with new patterns not indigenous, to serve the tourist market. The oldest designs included trees of life, ships of the dead, bird, animal, and plant forms. Flowers were drawn as seen from above. Some motifs were the province of royalty, and commoners could not use them.

The Yoruba of Nigeria are masters of a related type of resist dyeing. They paint cotton cloth with starch made from cassava flour and alum and dye it in indigo. Designs are simply done with straight lines, spirals, and leaves arranged in squares.[12]

Tie-Dyeing

Tie-dyeing is called *plangi* in Malaysia, *kokechi* or *shibori* in Japan, and *bandhana* in India. Portions of lightweight fabric are picked up with the fingernails or small hooks and wrapped with dye resistant bast or waxed cord. In India, China, and Turkestan heavy fabrics are arranged in a series of folds and tied. In some parts of the world seeds, pebbles, or other objects are tied in to make interesting shapes, but most patterns are simple arrangements of white circles or squares with dyed centers. Some rather complicated patterns, called "fish egg" or "eye" or "deer spot," are executed by the Japanese, who use nailed or pegged boards and purchased patterns to tie with. (See Plate 63.)

Dyeing is done quickly so that the wrappings are not penetrated, and most involve only one dye bath. Indigo is very closely associated with tie-dyeing, but lac, madder, and safflower are also typical. Several layers of thin cloth can be tied and dyed together. If these are silk, the characteristic crimped or bumpy surface that represents true plangi results. This crepe effect should not be ironed out (Plate 18).

By a related technique, called *tritik* in Java, threads are sewn as patterns in the cloth, then pulled up to force the cloth into closely packed folds. In Africa tritik is sometimes combined with plangi.

Ikat

From the Malayan *mengikat,* meaning to bind, tie, or wind around, comes *ikat,* the name given to the process for resist dyeing of yarns before weaving. The parts of the yarns that are to remain undyed are bound with a material impervious to the dye. Ikats are characterized by a hazy effect that results when the colors of the ikat dyed yarns merge irregularly into each other (Plate 19). Warp ikats with only the warp yarns resist dyed are fairly common. They are generally rep construction (see chapter 3), because the ikat effect is enhanced by the warp-faced weave. Weft ikat and double ikat with warp and weft dyed are more rare.

Ikats have been made in many parts of the world; no single place of origin can be identified. India, Indonesia, and Japan are perhaps the most important, but warp ikat was well developed in Peru, Guatemala, Mexico, and Africa. It was also made along the silk routes in Afghanistan, Persia, and Turkey. Ikating was a vigorous industry in Europe. Rouen made cotton weft ikats, Lyon wove silk warp ikats, and Spain was noted for misty ikat velvets. Patterns were usually simple warp stripes, but some ikats could be extremely complicated and could take years to complete. These were the ikats made on a few islands in Indonesia (Flores, Sumba, Rote) by noble women for ceremonial purposes or for a store of wealth. Patterns of stylized plant and animal forms—crocodiles, birds, fish, deer, humans, and skull trees for heads captured in war—were traditional (see Plate 20).

The method used in Indonesia to make warp ikat is complicated. Yarns are first stretched on a bamboo frame, grouped, and tied so that they will remain together during dyeing. Then, strips of palm bast are wound twice around each set of yarns in areas determined by the pattern to be made. Skilled workers have memorized the patterns, passed on from one generation to the next. If more than one color is to be dyed, the tying is more intricate and certain units have to be marked with special knots so they can be untied in proper sequence. Sometimes areas already dyed will be bound for protection in future dipping. Weaving also goes slowly because the yarns have to be carefully adjusted on the loom.

Conventional societies tend to encourage the development of one particular skill to a high degree. This was certainly true in Southeast Asia where a plentiful food supply and a comfortable concept of time allowed for the creation of marvelous batiks and ikats that were real documents of traditional cultures. After the purposes for which they were made changed from social and religious to economic, and the textiles were produced mainly for foreign trade, quality and pattern deteriorated. The same thing was true in India.

Painted and Printed Cottons of India

It is not known when the Indians started to make the elaborately figured court and temple hangings that came to be called chintz. Animal, bird, and plant designs were drawn from an abundant natural scene, and the tree of life became a common motif (Plate 21). The colors in extant examples show a subtle balance of soft reds and indigo blue, with touches of olive and blue-green.

In the early seventeenth century these textiles were trade items in the East Indies; the Portuguese and Dutch picked them up in India and exchanged them for spices in the islands to the east. A few were taken back to Europe, mainly as curiosities, but the reception by the color-starved ladies was sensational, and demand for them was soon considerable. Color that would not fade but actually improve with washing was something new to Europe. The impetus given to the French and English textile industries was far-reaching (see chapter 8). Chintz was used for bed hangings as well as for garments.

Chintz was derived from *chit, chitte,* and *chittes,* European trade terms of the seventeenth century derived in turn from the Indian *chitta,* meaning spotted cloth. Chintz was called *sarasa* by the Japanese, *pintados* by the Portuguese, and *indiennes* by the French. *Palampore* (Plate 21) was the European version of *palangpush,* Persian and Hindu for bed cover. Sometimes the word *kalamkar,* derived from the Persian, was used for an all painted palampore.

The methods for painting cottons, first recorded in the eighteenth century, have been published several times. M. de Beaulieu, a naval officer whose manuscript was found in the 1950s in a Paris museum, observed the process while in India around 1734. By cutting a sample at each stage, he was able to obtain a complete fabric record of chintz painting. Father Coeurdoux, a Jesuit missionary, also studied the process in India and is often quoted as saying it was like "the crawling of snails." In 1795 William Roxburgh, an English botanist, published a somewhat different account.[13]

Chintz painting was basically a combination of mordant printing and indigo resist dyeing (batik). For preparation the cotton cloth was first bleached, then treated with fat (buffalo milk) and myrobolan (a dried tree fruit containing tannin). A series of washings, dryings, and beatings with wooden blocks to soften the surface went on for several weeks.

A perforated paper pattern was laid on the cloth and pounced with powdered charcoal. The outlines to be red were traced over with a reed pen dipped in an alum mordant solution. The cloth was then dyed in *chay,* a dye made from a root of the madder family.

All of the cloth not to be blue was waxed with a special tool made of a bamboo stick wound with a thick ball of bast that held the wax. The stick had an iron point. After the indigo vat dyeing the wax was removed in boiling water. Next came another waxing to protect white areas within the red outlines and drawing with different mordants to give varying shades of red. The cloth again went into the chay dyebath. Then it was repeatedly soaked in a dung bath and bleached in the sun for several days. Finishing touches of yellow were added where desired and over some of the indigo to make green.

By the late seventeenth century chintz design had become quite different from traditional Indian design. It was a curious mixture of Indian, Chinese, and European designs, classified in Europe as "Oriental Style."[14]

At least as early as 1678, blocks—one for outline, one for ground, and one for details—were used to apply wax and mordants. Blocks speeded the process, and export fabrics could be made more cheaply. However, they lost much of their originality.

Block Printing

Wooden printing blocks, cut with designs standing up in relief from the nonprinting background, were known in India and China by 400 B.C. They were predated by clay cylinder stamps used in Mesopotamia by 3000 B.C. and in Egypt by 1500 B.C. to apply dyes or mordants in very simple patterns. Block making in itself was a specialized craft requiring the carving of fine grained hardwood. Eventually metal bands were inserted to make outlines, and in the late eighteenth century in Europe blocks were set with fine brass pins to make spotted patterns.

Cloth was spread out on a cloth-covered table, and for each application of a pattern the block was coated with color, laid on the cloth, and struck with a mallet to force the color into the cloth. Each color required a different block. Small pins in the corners of the blocks facilitated alignment of the patterns.

Block printing was important in Europe from the fourteenth century until the nineteenth. At first oil based pigments were applied to linens in imitation of costly Oriental and southern European silks, but these prints were stiff and not washable. Later, gold or silver dust was scattered over a print before it dried, and powdered wool flocking was used to simulate velvet. In the sixteenth century the Swiss learned to print with dyes and fixing agents (tannins), although the colors were seldom fast. Toward the end of the seventeenth century Europeans started to imitate Indian chintz by using blocks to print thickened mordants for the Turkey-red madder process and hot wax for the indigo resist. Fine lines were brushed in by hand. In England block printing reached a peak in the period 1790 to 1810, when increasing knowledge of dye chemistry brought development of a full range of colors, and there was not yet competition from other methods of printing. (Plate 75).

Blocks continued to be used well into the nineteenth century. In 1834, a Frenchman invented the Perrotine, a block printing machine. The machine could print three colors four times as fast as a hand printer and register was more accurate, but the repeats were very small. The machine was cumbersome and not a success.

Copperplate Printing

Copperplate printing was introduced in 1752 by Frances Nixon and Theophilus Thompson at a printworks near Dublin, and by 1760 the method was well known in London. The golden age of copperplate printing extended from 1760 to 1790, although the method was still used in the 1850s.

Copperplate printing was a type of intaglio work. Fine lines were engraved into copper plates. A dye or mordant paste mixture was applied to the plate and the excess wiped off, so that only the engraved lines held color. The cloth was pressed against the plates that were held in crude presses. Copperplates were used to print large floral repeats (Plate 76) and complex scenes of battles, political events, fables, or everyday life (Plate 73). Generally copperplate prints were monochrome—red, purple, sepia, blue, and occasionally green. Additional colored details were added with blocks or by brush.

Roller Printing

Although there were several prototypes, it was the machine patented in 1783 by Thomas Bell, a Scot, that was credited with being the first successful cylinder printing machine. It was different from earlier models in that it employed doctor blades to scrape off the excess printing ink and copper instead of wooden rollers.

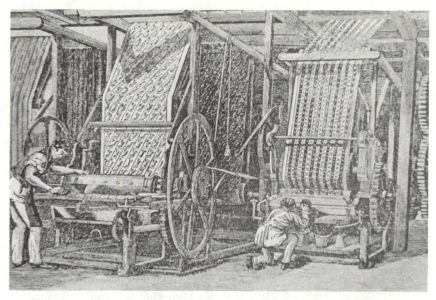

FIGURE 4.3 / Calico Printing in 1835 (from Baines).

The early machines were powered by water, and highly skilled people were needed to keep them in operation (Figure 4.3). The main problem was one of design misregistry caused by the rollers not being properly aligned. Hence, some of the first prints had small allover vines and geometric figures that disguised the problem. Many nineteenth century writers bemoaned the quality of roller prints, but there was variety. The first ones were small scale monochrome designs, and from 1820 to 1850 floral stripes were common (Plate 22). Throughout the first half of the twentieth century roller printing remained the principal commercial method.

NOTES

1. Charles Singer et al., eds., *A History of Technology,* 5 vols. (Oxford: Clarendon Press, 1954-1958), 2:220. Quoted from W. Langland, *The Vision Concerning Piers Ploughman* (1924).

2. See Sidney M. Edelstein, "The Origins of Drycleaning," *American Dyestuff Reporter* 46, no. 1 (14 January, 1957):1-8; and "Drycleaning," *CIBA Review* no. 1 (1964).

3. J. Schroeter, "Discovery of Chlorine and Beginnings of the Chlorine Industry," *CIBA Review* 139 (August 1960).

4. R. J. Forbes, *Studies in Ancient Technology, Volume 4, Textiles,* 2nd rev. ed. (Leiden, Netherlands: E. J. Brill, 1964), pp. 86-90.

5. Another relationship, that of music to textile history, can be appreciated by reading J. Campbell, *Hebridean Folksongs: A Collection of Waulking Songs, by Donald MacCormick, in Kilphedir in South Uist in the year 1893* (Oxford: Clarendon Press, 1969).

6. E. M. Carus-Wilson, *Medieval Merchant Venturers,* 2nd ed. (London: Methuen and Co., 1967), p. 210.

7. Sidney Edelstein, "The Thirteen Keys—Hints on Studying the History of Dyeing and Bleaching," *American Dyestuff Reporter* 48, no. 9 (4 May 1959):35-39. One of these books, *The Plictho of Gioanventura Rosetti,* 1548 edition, was translated by Sidney Edelstein and Hector Borghetty (Cambridge, Mass.: M.I.T. Press, 1969).

8. An English plucking chant. Jamieson B. Hurry, *The Woad Plant and Its Dye* (1930; reprint ed., New York: A. M. Kelley, 1973), p. 69. Quoted from *Aunt Judy's Journal* (1883).

9. Rita J. Adrosko, *Natural Dyes in the United States* (Washington, D.C.: Smithsonian Institution Press, 1968), p. 46.

10. Franco Brunello, *The Art of Dyeing in the History of Mankind,* tr. Bernard Hickey (Cleveland: Phoenix Dye Works, 1968), p. 58. Brunello says this was technically incorrect, but the legend has often been repeated in various versions.

11. *The Plictho of Rosetti,* p. 58.

12. For references on African textiles see note 8, chapter 3.

13. John Irwin and Katharine B. Brett, *Origins of Chintz* (London: Her Majesty's Stationery Office, 1970) has all three accounts. They can also be found in *Journal of Indian Textile History* 2 (1956); 3 (1957); and 4 (1959).

14. John Irwin, "Origins of 'Oriental' Chintz Design," *Antiques,* January 1959, pp. 84-87.

BIBLIOGRAPHY

Some of the few available sources on ancient and medieval finishing are the encyclopedias of technology. The best for textiles is *A History of Technology,* eds. Charles Singer et al., 5 vols. (Oxford: Clarendon Press, 1954-1958). More general are Maurice Daumas, *A History of Technology and Invention: Progress Through the Ages,* 2 vols. (New York: Crown Publishers, 1969) and Albert Neuburger, *The Technical Arts and Sciences of the Ancients* (New York: Barnes and Noble, 1969).

R. J. Forbes, *Studies in Ancient Technology, Volume 4, Textiles,* 2nd rev. ed. (Leiden, Netherlands: E. J. Brill, 1964) has a section on ancient finishing methods, mostly concerned with fulling. The fullonica of Pompeii is described in detail in "Dyeing and Tanning in Classical Antiquity," *CIBA Review* 9 (May 1938). E. M. Carus-Wilson has extensive information about fulling in *Medieval Merchant Venturers,* 2nd ed. (London: Methuen and Co., 1967). Harry Weiss, *The Early Fulling Mills of New Jersey* (Trenton, New Jersey: New Jersey Agricultural Society, 1957) has good diagrams.

There are a number of nineteenth and early twentieth century industry manuals that are helpful: Thomas Love, *The Art of Dyeing, Cleaning, Scouring, and Finishing, in the Most Approved English and French Methods* (Philadelphia: Henry Carey Baird, 1869); Frederick H. Green, *Practice in Finishing; The Art of Finishing Woolens and Worsteds in all its Details, A Complete Handbook for the Finishing Room* (Philadelphia: The Textile Record, 1886); Roberts Beaumont, *The Finishing of Textile Fabrics: Woolen, Worsted, Union and Other Cloths* (London: Scott, Greenwood & Son, 1909); and Friedrich Polleyn, *Dressings and Finish—for Textile Fabrics and their Application: Description of all the Materials Used in Dressing Textiles* (London: Scott, Greenwood & Son, 1911). The last was translated from the third German edition. These books often relate the fabric name to a specific finish.

Two scholarly articles on bleaching can be found in *Textile History* 1, no. 2 (Newton

Abbot, Devon, England: David & Charles, 1969). They are Enid Gauldie, "Mechanical Aids to Linen Bleaching in Scotland," pp. 129-157; and Jennifer Tann, "The Bleaching of Woollen and Worsted Goods 1740-1860," pp. 158-169. See also Sidney M. Edelstein, "A Frenchman Named O'Reilly—Modern Bleaching—150 Years Ago," *American Dyestuff Reporter 47,* no. 8 (21 April 1958):253-257; and "Two Scottish Physicians and the Bleaching Industry: The Contributions of Home and Black," *American Dyestuff Reporter* 44, no. 20 (26 September 1955):681-684. These last two have been reprinted in Sidney M. Edelstein, *Historical Notes on the Wet-Processing Industry* (Bronx, N.Y.: Dexter Chemical Corporation, 1972).

Interesting insights into color theory and its relationship to historic textiles can be gained from William and Doris Justema, *Weaving and Needlecraft Color Course* (New York: Van Nostrand Reinhold Co., 1971). Background on symbolism will be found in Faber Birren, *Color Psychology and Color Therapy,* (rev. ed. New Hyde Park, N.Y.: University Books, 1961). Birren's bibliography is extensive. In 1949 L. G. Lawrie published *A Bibliography of Dyeing and Textile Printing—Comprising a List of Books from the Sixteenth Century to the Present Time* (London: Chapman & Hall). It is very helpful to researchers although there are some errors in entries.

Probably the best and most complete current source on the history of dyeing is Franco Brunello, *The Art of Dyeing in the History of Mankind,* tr. Bernard Hickey (Cleveland: Phoenix Dye Works, 1968). Brunello takes a chronological approach and research on individual dyes is a little difficult, but there is a helpful dictionary. Older, easier to read, but containing some inaccuracies, is William F. Leggett, *Ancient and Medieval Dyes* (Brooklyn, N.Y.: Chemical Publishing Co., 1944). Another general survey is Stuart Robinson, *A History of Dyed Textiles* (Cambridge, Mass.: The M.I.T. Press, 1969). Robinson also covers resist methods in detail.

There are several good sources that give brief histories as well as recipes for dyeing. See Ethel Mairet, *Vegetable Dyes: Being a Book of Recipes and Other Information Useful to the Dyer* (London: Faber and Faber, 1948) and *Dye Plants and Dyeing—a Handbook* published by the Brooklyn Botanic Gardens, 1964. Rita J. Adrosko, *Natural Dyes in the United States* (Washington, D.C.: Smithsonian Institution Press, 1968) is an authoritative source and includes a revision of Margaret Furry, *Home Dyeing with Natural Dyes* published by the U.S. Department of Agriculture in 1935. See also the weaving periodicals such as *Shuttle, Spindle and Dyepot* and *Handweaver and Craftsman.*

An excellent and thorough study of one dyestuff is given by Jamieson B. Hurry in *The Woad Plant and Its Dye* (1930; reprint ed., New York: A. M. Kelley, 1973). An important scholarly study is Dena S. Katzenberg, *Blue Traditions: Indigo Dyed Textiles and Related Cobalt Ceramics from the 17th through the 19th Century* (Baltimore: The Baltimore Museum of Art, 1974). This is good for resist methods and indigo printing. Forbes has a complete section on Tyrian purple in *Studies in Ancient Technology.*

Numerous *CIBA Reviews* feature dyeing. See "Medieval Dyeing," 1 (1973); "India, Its Dyers, and Its Colour Symbolism," 2 (October 1937); "Purple," 4 (December 1937); "Scarlet," 7 (March 1938); "Madder and Turkey Red," 39 (May 1941); "Dyeing Among Primitive Peoples," 68 (June 1948); "Indigo," 85 (April 1951); "Sir William Henry Perkin," 115 (June 1956); "Textiles in Biblical Times," no. 2 (1968) (*CIBA Review*); and "Black," no. 2 (1973) (*CIBA-GEIGY Review*).

American Dyestuff Reporter has published many articles on dye history. Of special interest are Elise Pinckney, "Indigo," 65, no. 3 (March 1976):36-39, an account of the founding of the South Carolina indigo industry by the author's ancestress, Eliza Lucas Pinckney; and N.

Pelham Wright, "A Thousand Years of Cochineal: A Lost But Traditional Mexican Industry on Its Way Back," 52, no. 17 (19 August 1963):635-639. Sidney M. Edelstein has written several of note: "The Dual Life of Edward Bancroft," 43, no. 22 (25 October 1954):712-735; "Spanish Red—Thiery de Menoville's Voyage A Guaxaca," 44, no. 1 (13 January 1958):1-8 about cochineal; "Sir William Henry Perkin," 45, no. 18 (27 August 1956):598-608; and "Dyestuff and Dyeing in the Sixteenth Century," 52, no. 1 (7 January 1963):15-18. Edelstein's articles have been reprinted in *Historical Notes on the Wet-Processing Industry.*

An interesting review of the literature concerning quality of dyeing can be found in Stanley D. Forrester, "The History of the Development of the Light Fastness Testing of Dyed Fabrics up to 1902," *Textile History* 6 (1975):52-88. Also for color performance see J. J. Hummel, *The Dyeing of Textile Fabrics* (London: Cassell and Co., 1898). William Crookes, *A Practical Handbook of Dyeing and Calico Printing* (London: Longmans, Green, & Co., 1874) is a valuable source for research on dyeing and printing methods, natural and early aniline dyes, bleaching, and various fibers.

Two books are especially good for modern adaptations of old methods of applied fabric design: Meda Parker Johnston and Glen Kaufman, *Design on Fabrics* (New York: Reinhold Publishing Corp., 1967); and Verla Birrell, *The Textile Arts* (New York: Harper & Row, 1959). They both give some history.

For resist dyeing see Alfred Buhler, *Ikat, Batik, Plangi,* 3 vols. (Basel, Switzerland: 1972). Another important author is Alfred Steinmann. See his *Batik: A Survey of Batik Design* (New York: F. Lewis, 1958); and "The Art of Batik," *CIBA Review* 58 (July 1947). Monni Adams has a scholarly article "Symbolic Scenes in Javanese Batik," *Textile Museum Journal* 3, no. 1 (1970):25-40. Another important source is Laurens Langewis and Frits A. Wagner, *Decorative Art in Indonesian Textiles* (Amsterdam: Van Der Peet, 1964). This is a well-organized study of several decorative techniques, including batik and ikat. *Decorative Art* is also good for historical background. Two "how-to-do-it" books on batik include some history: Ila Keller, *Batik: The Art and Craft* (Tokyo: Charles B. Tuttle, 1921); and Nik Krevitsky, *Batik Art and Craft* (New York: Reinhold Publishing Corp., 1964).

For overviews on ikat see "Ikat," *American Fabrics,* Fall 1975; and A. Buhler, "Ikats," *CIBA Review* 44 (August 1942), which shows how the resists are tied. The current authority on Indonesian ikat is Marie Jeannie (Monnie) Adams whose *System and Meaning in East Sumba Textile Design: A Study in Traditional Indonesian Art* (New Haven: Yale University Southeast Asia Studies, 1969) is important as a complete cultural study. Adams also wrote "Designs in Sumba Textiles, Local Meanings and Foreign Influences," *Textile Museum Journal* 3, no. 2 (1971):28-37, which is good for design analysis. Indian double ikat is discussed in two articles in the *Journal of Indian Textile History* (Ahmedabad, India: Calico Museum of Textiles): Pupul Jayakar, "A Neglected Group of Indian Ikat Fabrics," no. 1 (1955):55-59; and Alfred Buhler, "Patola Influences in Southeast Asia," no. 4 (1959):4-46. For modern patola weaving see Mary Golden De Bone, "Patolu and Its Techniques," *Textile Museum Journal* 4, no. 3 (1967):49-62. Japanese ikat is illustrated in the Royal Ontario Museum's *Japanese Country Textiles* (Toronto, 1965) and "Japanese Resist-Dyeing Techniques," *CIBA Review* no. 4 (1967). See also "Plangi—Tie-and-Dye Work," *CIBA Review* 104 (June 1954).

A very large portfolio, well worth tracing, is George P. Baker, *Calico Painting and Printing in the East Indies in the XVII and XVIII Centuries* (London: Edward Arnold, 1921). The colored plates are superb, and Father Coeurdoux's letters are included. The three best available sources on Indian painted and printed fabrics are John Irwin and Katharine B. Brett, *Origins of Chintz* (London: Her Majesty's Stationary Office, 1970), a catalog for the Royal Ontario and Victoria and Albert Museum's collections; John Irwin and Margaret Hall, *Indian Painted and Printed Fabrics, Vol. 1 Historic Textiles of India at the Calico Museum* (Ahmedabad, 1971), especially good for textiles made before the seventeenth century; and Alice Baldwin Beer, *Trade Goods: A Study of Indian Chintz in the Collection of the Cooper-Hewitt Museum of Decorative Arts and Design, Smithsonian Institution* (Washington, D.C.: Smithsonian Institution Press, 1970), an account of the Southeast Asian trade and a summary of painting techniques. See also the bibliography for chapter 7.

The transition between Indian and English chintz is noted in MacIver Percival, *The Chintz Book* (London: W. Heinemann, 1923), which also has Father Coeurdoux's account. Percival gives a good overview of English prints aimed at people who want to select the right textiles for period furniture. See also the bibliography for chapter 8.

Good general surveys of various printing methods include Joyce Storey, *Van Nostrand Reinhold Manual of Textile Printing* (New York: Van Nostrand Reinhold, 1974); Stuart Robinson, *A History of Printed Textiles* (Cambridge, Mass.: M.I.T. Press, 1969); and Florence H. Pettit, *America's Printed and Painted Fabrics, 1600-1900* (New York: Hastings House, 1970). The most complete world bibliography on printing is C.O. Clark, "List of Books and Important Articles on the Technology of Textile Printing," *Textile History* 6 (1975):89-118. Again, see also the bibliography for chapter 8.

PART TWO
WORLD TEXTILES

5. PATTERNED TEXTILES OF THE NEAR EAST

Near Eastern cloths are found in the fine art museums of the world. Their opulence, their vibrant colors, their intricate designs executed in complex weaves earn them a place with great painting and sculpture. Near Eastern weavers have been masters of design and material since ancient times and have utilized both to enhance patterns taken from mythology, religious symbolism, and other art forms. Many of the ancient fabrics were greatly valued—and are often regarded as priceless today, for they reflect the ancient weaver's intelligence and devotion to his art. Near Eastern textiles reflect the awe, the delight, the visual enjoyment experienced by people not satiated with color and glitter.

THE NEAR EAST

The Land and the People

In the broadest sense, the Near East includes all the countries of southeastern Europe (i.e., Greece, Yugoslavia, Bulgaria, and Romania), southwestern Asia, the Middle East, and North Africa (Figure 5.1). Textile historians are most interested in Egypt, Syria, Iran, and Anatolia (during both the Byzantine and Turkish periods). For thousands of years Near Eastern peoples were integrated by nothing more than trade routes, along which cities and towns developed. Three different populations have characterized the region: multiethnic and multilinguistic groups living in the large urban centers, peasants following centuries-old patterns of rural life, and nomads, who became much less nomadic as political boundaries became more fixed.

Most Egyptians have lived for thousands of years as peasants and simple craftsmen in the narrow green belt of cultivatable land made by the Nile in its flow to the sea. Because Egypt was cut off geographically, it enjoyed more years of

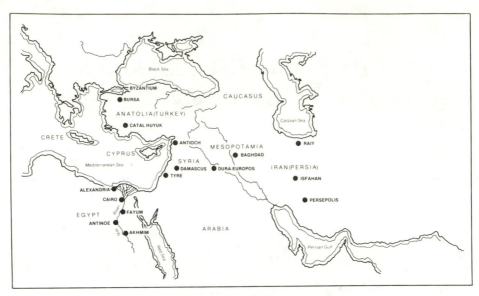

FIGURE 5.1 / The Near East.

peace than the rest of the Near East, but it also suffered somewhat from cultural stagnation. Egyptians, however, traded by land and sea beginning in the days of the Old Kingdom (2500 B.C.). Ancient Egyptians worshipped many gods, and certain animals were held to be sacred. Of all their religious convictions, the one most fortunate for the archaeologist and the art historian was the belief in an afterlife.

Ancient Syria, which included Palestine, lay in the large strip of land between the eastern Mediterranean, Anatolia, Mesopotamia, and the desert of northern Arabia. Syrians and Palestinians evolved from Mesopotamian and Arabian Semitic groups and were primarily agriculturalists. By the second millenium B.C. Syria possessed some fairly large urban centers where numerous products from Mesopotamia, Egypt, Anatolia, and Syria were traded. Ancient Syria knew little peace: conquering armies also traveled the trade routes. In addition, desert nomads frequently menaced unprotected settlements.

Iran has been called the driest place on earth, and one of the hottest, but it is a land bathed by an ethereal haze of light that has given inspiration to its artists. The Iranian plateau, an important land bridge linking Mesopotamia with the Indus-Ganges region and Central Asia with the West, was settled during the mass migrations of Aryans from the Caucasus around 1000 B.C. Some groups stayed on the vast plateau, others went on to the Indus. A little later Scythians from Central Asia moved into northwest Iran. This accounts for the strong Persian-Scythian textile linkage. (The western part of what we call Iran today was Persia to the Greeks and Fars to the Arabs.) The native Iranian religion was Zoroastrianism. Some Persian textile designs represent the eternal struggle between good and evil characteristic of that faith or depict the fire altar, a Zoroastrian symbol of truth.

The Anatolian peninsula was a homeland to many peoples prior to the coming of the ancestors of today's Turks. Discoveries made in the 1960s at Catal Huyuk in south-central Anatolia showed that people were living in the area in mud-brick houses as early as 7000 B.C. Among the many artifacts recovered were fragments of textiles and spinning and weaving tools. Anatolia, with its agricultural and pastoral economy, was a great melting pot for ancient Indo-Europeans, among them the Hittites, Phrygians, and Parthians. Greek, Roman, and Mongol blood also flows in the modern Turk, whose more immediate ancestors came from the east in the eleventh century.

The most important Anatolian city, curiously enough, is located outside it. Present-day Istanbul, the capital of several Anatolian empires, lies on the European side of the straits dividing Europe and Asia. For three thousand years the city has served as both a bridge and a barrier for religions, cultures, and armies. Orginally settled by Greeks, it was called Byzantium until 330 A.D., when the emperor Constantine made it the eastern capital of the Roman Empire and changed its name to Constantinople. After the decline of Rome in the West, the Eastern (and Greek) portion of the empire became an independent Greek political entity known as the Byzantine Empire. It is customary to refer to the textiles and other art coming from the city and the surrounding area before the middle of the fifteenth century as "Byzantine." The city gained the name Istanbul when the Turks captured it in 1453.

Historical Overview

Between 334 and 323 B.C. Alexander the Great conquered all of the lands between Greece and the Indus River, as well as Egypt. The Macedonian Empire broke up soon after his death, but Alexander's conquests had nonetheless ushered in a new cultural age in the Near East. The Hellenistic Age, so-named because of its predominantly Greek character, persisted throughout Near Eastern antiquity and was never quite supplanted by the influence of pre-Christian Rome. During this period, which lasted into the fourth century A.D., classical Greek culture made its way into the lives of most Near Eastern peoples, fostering practical and intellectual advances and creating a unity previously unknown in that part of the world.

Although very much a period of advance in secular perspectives and material culture, the Hellenistic Age saw the development and spread of new religions, among them Mithraism and the pagan cults of Iris, Baal, and Bacchus. Some clung to and further developed pre-Hellenistic religious notions of man in complex and dependent relationships with numerous gods, while others, more in the spirit of the age, moved toward monotheism and the separation of the realms of god and man. Some of the symbolism of these early religions is recorded in textiles.

Ptolemaic Egypt, the last of the Hellenistic monarchies, came under Roman rule in 30 B.C. The Ptolemies developed the district of Fayum (al-Fayyum), an oasis in the huge arid depression southwest of present-day Cairo. Fayum was a textile manufacturing center, and its burying ground has been important for the fabric remnants found there. Akhmim, a very ancient city in Upper Egypt, was also important during the Ptolemaic period as a textile center.

By the middle of the second century B.C. the Roman republic already had an extensive overseas empire, and many generals gained wealth and prestige fighting on its frontiers. When they returned to Rome (especially from the East), the generals frequently staged dazzling displays of captured slaves and treasure (including textiles). Although such displays often signalled the beginnings of Roman acquaintance with and trade in such things, they primarily served as a means of distracting the discontented masses in Rome. Twenty-seven B.C. marked the birth of the Roman Empire and the beginning of the great Pax Romana, two hundred years without war throughout the Western world. The Emperor Octavian (Augustus) introduced a new system of highly centralized government with paid civil servants and other innovations. Although less innovative in intellectual ways, the Romans nonetheless cultivated Greek culture and exhibited much enthusiasm for religious ideas coming out of the Hellenized Near East. Manichaeanism was popular and several forms of Christianity spread rapidly through the empire after the second century.

Diocletian, who ruled in Rome from 284 to 305, vigorously persecuted Christians, ended any pretext of obedience to the Roman Senate, and attempted to create an image of himself as divine by borrowing the pomp and trappings of the Persian courts. (As can be imagined, the market for sumptuous textiles boomed.) During Diocletian's rule, the empire was split along a line that passed through the Adriatic Sea. To the west Latin was spoken, to the east, Greek. Each part of the empire developed differently in politics and culture. Constantine the Great granted tolerance to all Christians in 313 A.D., after which the Roman and Christian worlds quickly approached congruity. At the same time, the Monophysitic Coptic church grew rapidly in Egypt.

Meanwhile the Parthians, once mortal enemies of the Romans (and an important link in the silk trade), were weakening under the stress of internal economic and political difficulties on the Iranian plateau. A force in the ancient world since the third century B.C., the Parthians were overthrown in 224 A.D. by the Sassanians, a powerful native family. The Sassanian period, which lasted until the mid-seventh century, was a time of constant war, first against the Romans to the west and later against the nomadic tribes of the East. During the turmoil of the Sassanian period, however, a renaissance in the arts occurred, manifested in the great limestone cliff sculptures found in many parts of Persia, huge barrel-vaulted buildings of baked clay, magnificent metal work, and intricately woven textiles. Kingly power and aspiration toward divinity were reflected in and reinforced by elaborate display in court dress and furnishings. Textiles were produced in royal workshops, the antecedents of the famous Muslim *Hotels de Tiraz*.

The great expansion of the Byzantine Empire under the Emperor Justinian (527-564) paralleled the Sassanian growth. Justinian effected conquests in Persia, Africa, Spain, and Italy, and the Byzantine Empire became a major power in the Mediterranean. As in many other instances, the Byzantines gained strategic advantage through economic policy when they learned the secret of silk cultivation and were able to monopolize silk textile production in the West. Justinian's court, under Persian influences, was a lavish one. There, one could discover among other innovations the growing use of the arts—and, with that, textile making—in the teaching of Christianity.

As Christian solidarity was building, a new religious movement emanated from Arabia. The Hijrah, Muhammad's flight from Mecca to Medina in 622, marked the start of Islamic chronology and the beginning of the Middle Ages in the Arab Near East. Within ten years of his death in 632 Muhammad's followers had conquered Persia, Palestine, Syria, and Egypt, and in the next hundred years the Muslims were to gain control of most of the Near East, Central Asia, Sicily, and Spain.

According to the tenets of Islam, there was only one God and man must submit to His will. On earth, social equality should reign. The righteous, wearing silken garments, could gain an eternal life of peace and joy in the garden of Allah, while the wicked would be cast into a fiery ditch and tormented forever.

Islam produced a regime of political and spiritual stability that enabled scholars, artists, and craftsmen to work with concentration. The zenith of early Islamic civilization was reached during the reign of Harun al-Rashid (786-809), who, incidentally, sent Charlemagne some very fine textiles. Harun's lavish court at Baghdad is described in *A Thousand and One Nights.*

Around the year 1000 Egypt came under the rule of the Fatimids, a Shiite (Muslim fundamentalist) sect that claimed descent from Muhammad's daughter, Fatima. By that time Anatolia, Crete, and Cyprus had become parts of the Byzantine Empire and Baghdad and Persia were controlled by the Buyids (or Buwayhids), a native Iranian family (945-1055). The Buyids were in turn replaced by the Seljuks (1055-1231), a Turkish tribe that invaded western Asia in the eleventh century and by the twelfth had gained control of Anatolia, Syria and Palestine, Mesopotamia, and most of the Iranian plateau.

Christian pilgrimages to the Holy Land and the Crusades that followed them in the eleventh century are of great interest to the textile historian, because they mark the beginnings of a great commercial and cultural exchange betweeen the Near East and Northern Europe. Christians began to visit Jerusalem in numbers during the third century. During Harun al-Rashid's rule in the late eighth and early ninth centuries, Muslims were especially hospitable to pilgrims, not least because they found a lively market among them for the bones of martyrs (wrapped, of course, in fine textiles).

A quiet existence was impossible on the Iranian plateau during the thirteenth, fourteenth, and fifteenth centuries. Mongol (and other) invasions from the East began with Ghengis Khan in 1219 and included the sack of Baghdad in 1258 and the push of Timur the Lame (Tamerlane) through the Near East to the Mediterranean in the fourteenth century.

Meanwhile, the Turkic peoples, pressured by the Mongols in Central Asia, were forced ever more westward into Anatolia. Although most groups remained nomadic, one tribe, the Osmanli, founded a state in northwestern Asia Minor. The

Ottomans, as they have come to be called, forced the Byzantines to withdraw until their empire shrunk to Constantinople and its environs. In 1453, of course, the city became the new capital of an empire that would include in time Anatolia, southeast Europe, the Middle East, and parts of North Africa. The golden age of the Ottoman sultans came with the reign of Suleiman the Magnificent (1520-1566). A sharp decline in wealth and power was not long in coming thereafter, but the empire endured until World War I, after which the modern (and much smaller) Turkish state was created.

At the beginning of the sixteenth century, while the Ottomans concentrated on extending their rule into the Balkans, Egypt, and Syria, the Safavids rose to power in Iran. This local dynasty, which lasted from 1501 to 1736, put an end to foreign domination and initiated a renaissance in all phases of intellectual and artistic life. The peak of the Safavid period was reached during the reign of Shah Abbas (1587-1629). His court, with its sumptuous costumes and hangings from the weaving centers at Yazd, Kashan, and Isfahan, surpassed even that of Harun al-Rashid. Then learning gradually diminished, creativity declined, and Persia, along with much of the Muslim world, weakened.

EGYPTIAN TEXTILES

Weaving had a very long history in Egypt, and patterned fabric (namely, linen tapestry from the tomb of Thutmose IV) dates to the fifteenth century B.C. During the Ptolemaic period the state controlled a large and important industry that utilized home, public, and temple workshops.[1] Town officials collected yarn from peasants and delivered it to the weavers who had to work for a fixed sum and produce the amounts ordered. Temple workshops were especially noted for finely woven *byssus* (probably linen) and *polymita,* a textile believed to be embroidered.

In the Roman period Egypt was the world center for the mass production of linen garments, particularly the nearly universal tunic. Government control was even more rigid than before, in part to meet requisitions by the Roman army.[2] Workshops in some towns specialized in wool tapestry weaving, and others, mainly in Alexandria, produced figured silks. Alexandria was also a world trade center: textiles from as far away as India were brought there. Weavers moved around the world of antiquity, too.

Coptic Textiles

The world Copt came from the Arabic *Kipt,* which was a corruption of the Greek *Aigptios*, the name given to the inhabitants of the Nile Valley. Although most of these native Egyptians were Christian by the time of the Muslim invasions in the seventh century, their textiles were strongly pagan in design.

Coptic textiles are widely available; thousands can be found in museum and private collections. In the late third century, the ancient embalming procedures

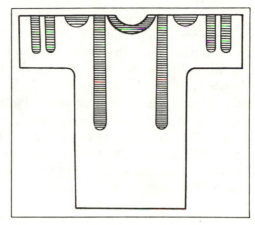

FIGURE 5.2 / Egyptian Tunic.

were abandoned, and the body, wearing everyday clothing, was tied to a board and wrapped in mantles, hangings, and curtains. Often rags and small cloths were rolled and stuffed in the hollows around the body. The dry sands of the necropolises of Antinoe, Fayum, Akhmim, and other places preserved the bodies and textiles. It is unfortunate that the burying grounds were "dug" in the last century without benefit of modern archaeological method. Much relevant data have been irretrievably lost. Local "miners" were also guilty of splitting large pieces, and fragments became scattered among different collections. Thus many Coptic textiles can be given only tentative dates and sources.

Fibers and Yarns

Flax was the principal fiber used for warp, and wool was used for weft. It was not until the Hellenistic period that wool became a common fiber in Egypt, although sheep had been raised there for many centuries. The idea for using it for weft, along with dyeing methods, probably originated in Syria. Cotton was sometimes used for pile weaves, and silk was woven in increasing amounts from the Roman period, although rarely in tapestry. Some simple handspinning tools have been found in Coptic graves.

Constructions

Tapestry was the major Coptic weave (Plate 23). It is assumed that warp-weighted, vertical two-bar looms, or small frames were utilized, although none have been found. Large hangings and curtains were woven, but it is mostly the narrow clavi and patches used to decorate tunics that have survived (Figure 5.2). Decorations were executed in three different ways. The small sections of tapestry could be woven separately, then sewn to a tabby weave tunic. Or, certain areas of a linen tunic were left unwoven, and the wool pattern wefts were then inserted. By a similar method linen wefts, cut and pulled out of a fabric, were replaced by wool. It was common practice to cut decorations from worn garments and sew them on new ones.

The tapestry was sometimes embellished by using a "flying shuttle" (or bobbin) moving in great leaps lengthwise, to work in an extra pattern yarn for facial features or dot patterns. Embroidery was also employed for special effects. *Hachure,* shading with different colors, was more characteristic of early, rather than late Coptic work.

Other Coptic construction techniques included knitting and plaiting as well as pile weaving. The latter was done by pulling extra linen, cotton, or wool wefts out into loops (Plate 24). The pile yarns were inserted in alternate sheds or drawn in from behind loose warp. Pile fabrics were also made by knotting. After the fourth century twills of wool and patterned twills of both wool and silk, like the ones of other Near Eastern countries, were woven in Alexandria.

Color

Some Coptic fabrics were vivid orange, blue-green, and gold polychromes, while others were somber monochromes with purple or brown designs or backgrounds. Two major sources on dyes used during this time are Pliny's *Natural History* and the *Uppsala Papyrus,* written in Greek in the third century A.D. and found in the necropolis at Thebes.[3] The papyrus includes twenty-six recipes for purple, as well as the method for dyeing saffron yellow over indigo or woad to get green, and several ways to combine kermes or madder with woad. Other dyes came from amaranth, pomegranate, and lichens. Pliny gives recipes using the juices of *Purpura* shellfish, but the purple color popular with the masses was most likely made by dyeing madder over indigo. Pliny reports what was probably mordant dyeing, that is, the application of alum, iron salts, or copper salts to cloth, then dyeing with madder to give varigated patterns. Printing blocks were used and resist patterns made with wax or the clay mud of the Nile.

Design

Although dating of specific Coptic textiles is not wholly accurate, there is a progression in styles that proceeds from the Greek, through the Roman (Byzantine) and Persian, to the Islamic. During the Roman period (to 400 A.D.), designs were Hellenistic and pagan, with reproduction of classical motifs in realistic fashion— Greek gods (Plate 24) and goddesses, Nilotic scenes, vines, scrolls, animals, and human figures, often very realistic portraits. Superior weaving molded figures into the third dimension.

The more typical Coptic style (in evidence from the fourth to the seventh century) shows the symbolism of Christianity (often derived from Hellenistic design): the ankh (cross), the vase, the tree of life, the fish (symbolizing Christ), the hare, the lion (meaning power and Satan). Faces with great goggling eyes (Plate 25) were woven. Textiles from this period, termed folk art,[4] show rather coarse texture and disportionate figures. Some authors say there was a degeneration in weaving technique, while others call it a new method of adapting technique to design by distorting the angle of the weft, using embroidery and outlining, and employing vivid colors to emphasize abstraction. This crude style was retained after the Muslim conquest by the Christian weavers, many of whom worked in monasteries. It continued well into the Fatimid period.

Islamic Textiles in Egypt

Meanwhile, figured silks were becoming more important and reflected Byzantine and Sassanian influences. Silk weaving merged more readily with Islamic style, while tapestry remained a peasant art.

Until the tenth century, when there was rapid expansion in the Muslim Egyptian textile industry, the *tiraz* (palace factory) was a symbol of prestige. Any prince rich enough had his own corps of weavers. The origin of the tiraz system is uncertain. It may have started with the Sassanians, because the word is borrowed from the Persian and originally meant embroidery. Then it came to mean the workshop where embroidery was done, and finally a weaving workshop. Textiles characterized by banded design often carried inscriptions identifying the tiraz where they were made (Plate 26). The tiraz was not exclusive to Egypt but was found throughout the Muslim world.

SYRIAN TEXTILES

The history of early Syrian textiles has not been well documented nor have there been the large finds like those in Egypt. Two major excavations, one at Palmyra, a trading city since the time of the Seleucids (312-64 B.C.) and one at Dura-Europos, a Roman fortress on the Euphrates, have yielded some fabrics from the second and third centuries A.D. Dura-Europos is the more important, because its textiles can be dated rather precisely to the last part of the third century. Fragments in a variety of plain, twill, and pile weaves recognized as being dyed with indigo, madder, and kermes have been found. All four major natural fibers were represented, although wool predominated.

Preserved wall paintings at Dura-Europos have given considerable information about the costume worn there. The main garment was a tapestry woven white wool tunic, made to shape and size on a loom as wide as the length of the back plus the length of the front.[5] When worn, the warp ran crosswise, and any colored band, inserted as weft, ran vertically. It was this vertical band that preceded the Coptic clavus.

Antioch, a leading cultural and silk manufacturing city, was a major early Christian center where some outstanding heavy silk twills depicting various biblical scenes were woven (Plate 27). Syrian textiles were so famous in the fourth century that Bishop Asterius of Pontus in Anatolia exclaimed at the skill of weavers in making animals that appeared as though they had been painted. But the bishop was scandalized by the biblical scenes and indignant at the haughty and frivolous persons who wore the gospel on their backs rather than carrying it in their hearts.

Damascus was another great weaving center where richly colored silk twills with biblical scenes, garments for Roman consuls, and (later) magnificant banners and flags for Muslim warriors were produced in large quantities. In the late Middle Ages, Damascus was an important source for silk damasks and compound weaves sold in the markets opened by the Crusaders. Syria was "in the middle" geographically. Its centers furnished textiles and weavers for Egypt, Byzantium, and Persia.

PERSIAN TEXTILES

Persia was another commercial crossroad. Trade routes from China, Central Asia, India, and the West intersected the Iranian plateau, and so Persia looked both eastward and westward for design inspiration, technical assistance, and markets. Relatively few Persian textiles are available for study because of the frequent rampages of destruction in Iran, and because burial customs served to destroy them. In Iran bodies were most often burned or exposed to birds of prey, although royalty was sometimes entombed. Hence, there were no large caches of burial fabrics like the ones found in Egypt and Peru. However, early commerce served the cause of preservation, and most surviving early Persian fabrics can be found in European church reliquaries or in collections that originally belonged to European royalty.

Persian weavers concentrated on a few constructions and developed them to perfection, surpassing the medieval Europeans. It was not until the decline of the Safavids that European textiles became more elaborate, although they were never as rich in color nor as resplendent with metallic threads as were the Persian.

Sassanian Textiles

The Sassanians (226-651 A.D.) were indebted to the Parthians before them for initiating the silk trade with China during the Han Dynasty. The few extant textiles that can be attributed to the Sassanians are dated after the fifth century. By that time sericulture was known on the Iranian plateau, and Syrian weavers had been settled there.

Weaves

Silks identified as Sassanian are compound weft-faced twill (*samit*), the major Near Eastern patterned silk weave used until the tenth century. Although compound tabby and warp-faced twill, also known in that period, could have been made on a pattern loom with multiple heddle rods, a drawloom was required to make samit. Although it is still debated, the consensus is that the drawloom and compound weft twill developed in one center in Egypt or Syria and spread from there.[6] The characteristic stair-step design contours in Sassanian textiles indicate that the drawloom was not yet fully developed or that weavers were unskilled in its use.

Compound weaves have more than two sets of yarns, and the early weft-faced compound twills (samit) varied in arrangement of the inner (pattern) warp; some were used singly, others in pairs, some in groups of three or four. The main (binding) warp bound the weft in the same twill in both the pattern and the background, so that design was essentially the result of color changes in the weft, not texture difference. There were at least two sets of weft. Some Sassanian fabrics had as many as six or seven different colored wefts, used with such skill as to give subtle vibration in greens, blue-greens, yellows, reds, and purples. Silk's excellent affinity for dye made rich colors easy to achieve.

Design

The dominant theme of Sassanian design was the animal, real or mythical, which had served to avert evil when used in various Iranian art forms over the centuries. Enchanting creatures were positioned in large framing circles (*roundels*) arranged in vertical rows and joined horizontally by small circles. Frequently the roundels were constructed of pearls (Plate 28) or heart-shaped leaves (Plate 29). Elephants, rams, winged horses, lions, and birds (some with ribbons around their necks to signify royal power) were lined up, facing in one direction or alternating. Two figures were occasionally used in doublet form facing either a fire altar or a *hom,* the ancient Assyrian tree of life symbolizing eternal renaissance and reincarnation. Rosettes represented eagerly awaited early spring flowers, and medallions signified the North Star and four cardinal points of the universe.

The Sassanian *senmurv* (or *simurgh*), also known as the *hippocampus,* is delightfully ferocious (Plate 28). Sometimes he is called the dragon-peacock because of his tail and dragon-like (or dog-like) head. This truculent beast is thought to have protected the young hero Zāl and is a bird of good omen. The senmurv is documented as a fabric pattern by the Sassanian royal garments depicted in the rock sculptures at Taq-i-Bostan located near Kermashah in western Iran, which were commissioned by King Khrosros II in the seventh century. Only a few Sassanian senmurv patterns survive, but a whole caftan was very recently discovered in the northern Caucasus.[7] Most extant senmurv pattterns date from later periods. The *cock,* symbol of Mithra, the sun god and definitely a bird of good omen, is also to be found at Taq-i-Bostan (Plate 29). If you heard him crow in the morning, it meant you had survived another dark night.

Sassanian textiles are important for their technical advancements and designs, but they are more important as the source of a style of shape and contour arrangement that outlived the symbolism (note Plate 35). Some typically Sassanian fabrics can be attributed to Antioch and Antinoe. They were copied faithfully in Byzantium, found their way to Central Asia, and were copied in Japan during the eighth century. Elements of Sassanian design appeared in many a medieval European textile.

Textiles of Early Islamic Persia

Long after the Muslim conquest in the seventh century, textiles continued to be made with traditional constructions and designs, because the Arabs had no particular style that could compete with the Iranian. It was not until the eleventh century that the influence of Islamic design was felt to any large degree in Iran. By contrast, the arabesque was well established in Spain by that time. Islam had a proscription against the depiction of living things, mostly to avoid their serving as idols. So in time the Sassanian animals became more ornamental and graceful. The old symbolism was lost, and stylized plant forms came into use.

Muslim burial rites were responsible for the preservation of sumptuous shrouds and coffin covers woven to exact shape on the loom and carrying inscriptions in Kufic asking for the mercy and compassion of God (Plate 30). In 1925 an important find was made at Raiy, a leading Buyid city.[8] One of the textiles shows the senmurv in total bird form (Plate 31). The Buyid double-headed eagle (Plate 32) was another imagined (not realistic) motif and was in conformity to Islamic proscriptions. The Buyid style merged into the Seljuk.

Persian Textiles of the Seljuk and Mongol Periods

More textiles survive from the Seljuk (1055-1231) than from earlier periods, and they illustrate some new weaving techniques. Design was enhanced because a difference in texture between the background and the pattern had developed, something not true with the weft-faced compound twills. This was achieved by using a plain weave compound construction probably derived from Egypt. The pattern was brought into relief by a vertical ribbed ground and a looser binding in the design. Another innovation was single cloth warp twill, brocaded with a supplementary weft. Seljuk textiles seem to have been the first Persian examples of discontinuous brocading (space weaving), and it is interesting to find this technique coming later than the more complex compound weaves.

Some of the rare extant examples of double cloth, representative of a technique thought to have flourished in Persia during the twelfth and thirteenth centuries, come from the Seljuk period. Satin, too, originated during this period or a little earlier, but it was a compound weave with brocaded patterns, rough and loose in construction—not satin as it is today.

Seljuk textiles, clearly Islamic in design, are characterized by Kufic lettering, often in bands of birds and animals. Foliation is common and the arabesque stalks and leaves combine into continuous elements that flow in all directions to produce allover patterns. Repeating motifs and endless pattern appealed to Muslims who believed life originated in the unknown and returned to it. Ogives replaced the roundels as framing devices for figures *adossé* (back to back) or *affronté* (facing). Double-headed eagles are reminiscent of the Byzantine and Buyid, while pomegranates anticipate sixteenth century Italian design.

Little can be said about Persian textiles from the Mongol period because few survive, but the assumption is that the old forms of construction continued because they were still in use in the Safavid period. The few examples that do exist show strong Chinese influence in design.

Persian Textiles of the Safavid Period

Now came the golden age. No contemporary European textiles equaled those of the Safavid period (1501-1736) in the lavish use of metallic yarn, excellence and delicacy of design, and subtle blending of color. Court costume, horse trappings, and tent hangings were magnificent, and Persian fabrics were coveted by the world's rich. Living in a society where they were accorded high status, weavers were able to perfect the compound weaves of earlier periods along with new techniques.

Safavid textiles are distinguished by metallic yarns, not found in extant Sassanian or Seljuk work. The yarns generally consisted of strips of silver or gilded membrane wound on a silk core. Occasionally flat strips of metal were used, most often in the backgrounds of velvets. In certain constructions the background appeared as a solid sheet of silver. Nancy Reath mentions one point useful for purposes of identification: in Near Eastern fabrics the metal tended to wear away from the yarn, leaving the silk core intact, while in European fabrics the metal strip and silk core broke at the same time. A larger amount of copper in the European alloy accounts for the difference.[9]

Safavid compound satins belong with the world's great textile art. This structure, sometimes mistaken for twill because of the way extra wefts are bound, gives weight and body to the exquisite and delightful figures inspired by the miniature paintings of the period. Designs with human figures (Plate 33) not only depict poems; they are poetic in execution with motifs placed in such a way as to flow, one to another, with perfect harmony in color. Salmon reds, turquoise blues, beiges, and yellows color a paradise garden of roses, lilies, carnations, and irises, while hares, lions, leopards, or griffons frolic here and there by a cyprus tree with its wind-bent tip—all presided over by human figures outlined in black. Small details might be enhanced by brocading.

One particular Safavid weaver, Ghiyath of Yazd, specialized in the tragic love story of Laila and Majnun. Laila's parents would not hear of a match so the distraught Majnun wandered off into the desert to write poetry and commune with the wild creatures. One of Ghiyath's textiles showed the princess, who has journeyed on camel to see Majnun, now quite emaciated. Another showed Laila walking toward the meagerly clothed poet, who is nursing a gazelle with doleful eyes that remind him of Laila.

Human figures were depicted in velvet too—velvet very fine in texture and unequaled in color variation (Plate 34). None date earlier than the sixteenth century, but those are so well refined technically that it is certain that velvet weaving must have been known for a long time in Persia. Indeed, it may have originated there. Safavid velvets show special technique—as many as five different colored warp used in addition to the foundation warp make small areas of supplementary hues possible. Safavid velvets are characterized by small scale human and floral and animal designs in several colors, while European velvets show larger floral motifs, fewer colors, but a greater variation in surface treatment (see chapter 6). Persian velvets are either the cut solid or cut voided type, and some have twisted loops or gilt or silver thread standing up from the surface.

Silk double cloth reached perfection in Safavid Persia and even evolved into triple cloth with a layering of different weaves that introduced subtle contrast in texture and shading of colors. Six different kinds of double cloth have been identified, some with complex human figures.[10]

The fabric made in greatest quantity for costume material was taffeta. Several weights were made, all of simple (not compound) ribbed plain weave. Most were brocaded with delicate floral sprays, and after weaving, the backgrounds might be stamped with geometric patterns. Some Persian taffetas even found their way to colonial America.

Tapestry weave was used in Safavid Persia to make silk carpets; different colored wefts were dovetailed, and the figures were outlined in black. The interlocking twill tapestry weave, found in Kashmir shawls, has been attributed to seventeenth century Persia.[11]

BYZANTINE SILKS

As Alexandria and Antioch declined as textile centers under the Muslims, Constantinople began to draw the world's merchants to her great workshops. For over a thousand years the city was a major trade center and an important link between East and West. Luxury goods from all over—silk from China, cotton and spices from India, tapestry from Egypt, art work from Syria and Persia, furs from Europe, and plenty of gold—were brought to exchange for the costly silks, jewelry, and metal and ivory liturgical art of Byzantium. Foreign merchants, usually sequestered under tight controls, had their visits limited, but the profits to be earned at home were well worth the harassment. Silk was a powerful political tool; a foreign government in disfavor might be denied trading privileges, another might be rewarded (or bribed) in precious silks.

The tenth century *Book of the Prefect,* a compilation of trade ordinances for commerce and industry, is the major source on the Byzantine textile industry.[12] The prefect was the highest ranking city official in Constantinople and represented the state in relations with the guilds. His crew of subordinates inspected everything and everybody. The work of the five silk guilds (the merchants, dealers in Syrian silk, dealers in raw silk, spinners, and weavers) was carefully regulated and the penalties severe. A hand was to be cut off for dyeing raw silk with murex. Flogging was the penalty for selling silk to Hebrews, confiscation of goods for selling materials to strangers without the knowledge of the prefect.

From the fourth to the eleventh centuries Byzantine emperors were able to retain a monopoly on the silk industry by controlling imports of silk and exports of fabrics. Figured textiles were woven in royal workshops (*gynaecea*)

PLATE 21 / Palampore (painted and dyed cotton) made for the European market during the first half of the eighteenth century. (Courtesy of the Royal Ontario Museum, Toronto)

PLATE 22 / A roller print, circa 1824. Red with yellow, blue, and overprinted green on tan ground. (Courtesy of The Henry Francis du Pont Winterthur Museum)

PLATE 23 (*left*) / Coptic tapestry. (Courtesy of The Denver Art Museum. Neusteter Institute Purchase) PLATE 24 (*below*) / A depiction of Hermes on a fourth or fifth century Egyptian looped woolen pile roundel. Diameter 15″ and 17″. (Crown Copyright. Victoria and Albert Museum)

PLATE 25 (*left*) / Third or fourth century Coptic portrait of a man. Panel 10½″ x 7¾″. (Courtesy of The Detroit Institute of Arts. Founders Society-Octavia Bates Fund)   PLATE 26 (*below*) / A wool and linen tapestry panel from an Egyptian tiraz of the Abbasid period (first half of the ninth century). (Courtesy of The Cleveland Museum of Art. Purchase from the J. H. Wade Fund)

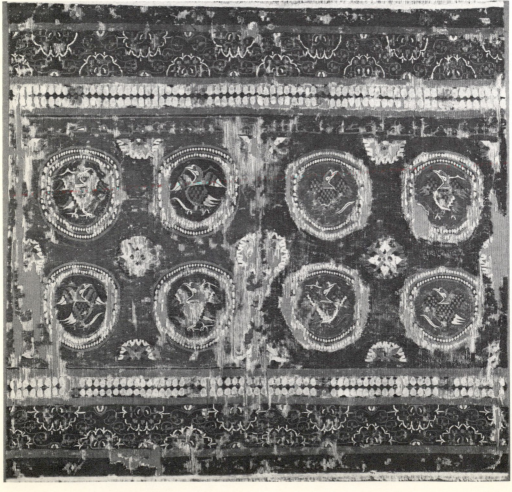

PLATE 27 / Hero and lion; an eighth or ninth century silk from Alexandria, Antioch, or Damascus. (Crown Copyright. Victoria and Albert Museum)

PLATE 28 / Sassanian *senmurv* (winged monster); a Near Eastern silk from the eighth or ninth century. 14" x 20¼". (Crown Copyright. Victoria and Albert Museum)

PLATE 29 (*above*) / A sixth or seventh century Sassanian silk twill. (Courtesy of the Biblioteca Apostolica Vaticana)

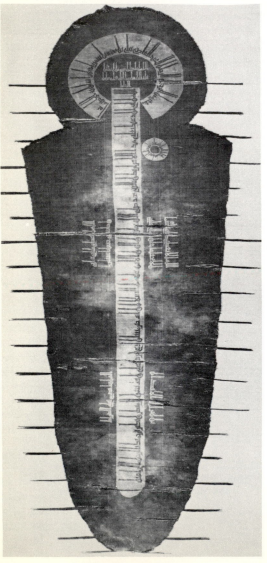

PLATE 30 (*left*) / Silk tomb cover (compound twill) from Iran's Buyid period (tenth century). A complete loom piece woven to shape. (Courtesy of The Cleveland Museum of Art. Purchase from the J. H. Wade Fund)

PLATE 31 / A fragment of a Buyid silk textile in a lampas weave, with a *senmurv* motif. (Courtesy of The Cleveland Museum of Art. Purchase from the J. H. Wade Fund)

PLATE 32 / Buyid double-headed eagle silk. (Courtesy of The Denver Art Museum. Neusteter Institute Purchase)

PLATE 33 / "Men Leading Prisoner in a Garden," from Persia, probably created in the seventeenth century. (Courtesy of The Museum of Fine Arts, Boston. Ross Collection)

PLATE 34 / An Iranian cut velvet on a cloth gold ground, from the Shah
Abbas period (early seventeenth century). (Courtesy of The Cleveland
Museum of Art. Purchase from J. H. Wade Fund)

PLATE 35 (*above*) / Byzantine silk medallion with quadriga design, found in Aachen Cathedral. (Copyright Ann Münchow)   PLATE 36 (*left*) / Turkish kaftan from Tahsin Oz's *Turkish Textiles and Velvets.*

PLATE 37 / Tunic fragment of the Infante Felipe, from the second half of the thirteenth century. (Courtesy of The Hispanic Society of America, New York)

PLATE 38 (*left*) / Brocaded cut voided velvet in pomegranate patterns from the late fifteenth century. (Courtesy of The Hispanic Society of America, New York) PLATE 39 (*below*) / Brocade from thirteenth or fourteenth century Granada. (Courtesy of the Museum of Fine Arts, Boston. Harriet Otis Cruft Fund)

PLATE 40 / "Tree of Life and Lions," a fancy compound satin from the fifteenth century. (Courtesy of The Hispanic Society of America, New York)

PLATE 41 *(left)* / Silk lampas with gold from Italy or Sicily in the first half of the fourteenth century. (Courtesy of The Cleveland Museum of Art. Purchase from J. H. Wade Fund.)

PLATE 42 *(right)* / Fourteenth century Lucchese silk brocade. (Courtesy of the Museum of Fine Arts, Boston)

PLATE 43 / Fourteenth century Italian silk and metallic woven fabric. (Courtesy of the Cooper-Hewitt Museum, New York. Gift of J. P. Morgan, 1902-1-329)

PLATE 44 / Fifteenth century Italian velvet. Pattern in green pile on crimson satin ground with floral devices in gold thread. (Crown Copyright. Victoria and Albert Museum)

PLATE 45 / Late fifteenth century Italian velvet. Scrolls and artichoke patterns on gold boucle and red velvet on a gold background. (Crown Copyright. Victoria and Albert Museum)

supervised by minor nobles, the procurators. During Justinian's reign illegal workshops made silks for a lucrative black market, and Justinian tried to counteract the traffic by selling fabrics from the *gynaecea* to Byzantine women (at that time sumptuary laws prohibited silk to men). After the sixth century silk became very plentiful and was worn by common people, although certain colors and the patterned fabrics were reserved to royalty.

The eighth and ninth centuries saw some very fine weaving, but the golden period came in the tenth, eleventh, and twelfth centuries under the Comnenus dynasty. By the era of the Palaeologus dynasty (1261-1453) a degeneration in weaving had occurred, but the art of embroidery flourished. Byzantine church vestments, embroidered in gold, were glorious.

Byzantine silk textiles, preserved mainly in European church treasuries, are quite similar to Alexandrian, Syrian, and Persian silks. Typically, they are compound weaves with animal designs—griffons, lions, elephants, and eagles are most representative—but they show greater sophistication. Colors are less vivid than those in Alexandrian silks and are sometimes rather dark and somber, with blues, violets, and red purples predominating, yet there are some light peaches and greens. In the eleventh century two-color patterns were made especially for export to Germany, and in the twelfth, monochrome green, grey, gold, or blue-black fabrics, with textured designs called "engraved" or "incised," were popular.

Pictures of a few well-known Byzantine works have been published many times. One of the earliest is the Quadriga Cloth in the Aachen Cathedral (Plate 35). It dates to the eighth century and was taken from Charlemagne's tomb. The charioteer, a very common motif, is reminiscent of the Iranian sun god, Mithra.[13] Another twill, with toy-like elephants, was placed in Charlemagne's tomb in the year 1000 by Emperor Otto II. It has a brick red ground and gold, blue, green, and pink patterns in large medallions. Most magnificent are the imperial eagle textiles. Sassanian motifs were still so popular they predominated even in the twelfth century, although certain renditions of circular bands with palmettes and devices between roundels were of Byzantine invention.

Gold was important in Byzantine silks made after the eleventh century. Most of it came from Cyprus, whose textile industry was considered almost a branch of the Byzantine. Cyprus was, however, noted more for its embroidery than for its weaving.

Expert handweavers were fully appreciated by almost all rulers in medieval and early modern times. So, when Constantinople was captured in 1453, the Christian weavers who had not fled westward were absorbed into Turkish workshops. The Ottomans were strict in enforcing Islamic proscriptions. The textiles from Istanbul showed few vestiges of Christian influences.

TURKISH TEXTILES

Most of the Turkish textiles that survive date from the sixteenth and seventeenth centuries; the best sources of information about earlier ones are European paintings from the fourteenth century on. Prior to the early twentieth century, there was very little interest in the preservation of old textiles in Turkey, and consequently, many coffin covers, mosque and palace hangings, and especially cushion covers, were exported to Europe. Fortunately, a valuable collection of both fabrics and documents remained in Istanbul at the Topkapi Saray (the seraglio of the sultans), made into a national museum after the republic was established in 1923. Kaftans (outer garments) and other clothing have been wrapped and labeled as to owner and occasion of wear. Because the wrappers were changed from time to time there are some problems of identifcation, but the textiles have been kept clean and well preserved. The archives include inventories, rules and regulations for weavers, and reports on market conditions and the problems concerning maintenance of quality.

In Turkey construction methods were standardized by law, especially in the fourteenth and fifteenth centuries. In the sixteenth the problem of quality was very real; the state was forced to fix standards and prices in order to meet the competition in foreign markets from Italian fabrics. However, a growing free market took almost anything and paid well for it; hence, the quantity and quality of the silk was reduced, yarns were not spun as carefully, thread counts were reduced, and dyes cheapened. The gorgeous shade of red, made by using lac and filtered indigo, became a red-violet when the amount of lac was reduced and the indigo no longer filtered. Some, but not all, of the extant sixteenth century work shows this lowering of standards.

Bursa, a major sixteenth century weaving center, made almost a hundred different kinds of cloth, many from cotton, but it was most noted for its brocaded silks and cut pile velvets. *Kemha* was a Bursa velvet brocaded with many colors, and *catma* a velvet with gold thread.

Turkish textile designs are similar to those on stone, metal, and ceramic work, because artists, subsidized by the state, created the patterns that were then turned over to different craftsmen for adaptation. Floral and stem patterns, featuring carnations, tulips, artichokes, and pomegranates, were common. After the sixteenth century the ogive was used widely, and designs were very much like those of Venice. One characteristic Turkish pattern is the *Chintamani,* two wavy lines with three balls (Plate 36). Probably Chinese in origin, it was a favorite with the Ottomans. Crescent and star patterns are also associated with the Turks.

NEAR EASTERN CARPETS

Since carpets require separate study, only a brief review will be given here. Almost every group of Near Eastern people specialized in one or another type of carpet weaving. Extremely versatile, these heavy products of simple vertical or horizontal looms have long served as floor and wall coverings, bags, cushion tops, and for a multitude of other domestic uses. Carpets, of course, were important export items as well.

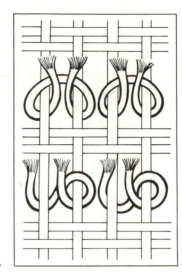

FIGURE 5.3 / Ghiordes (*top*) and Sehna Knots.

Carpet making is an ancient craft, dating at least to the seventh century B.C. according to Greek literary sources. A knotted pile rug with 230 knots per inch was discovered in a fifth century Scythian grave. Carpet fragments, probably Sassanian, were found at Dura-Europos, and the early Copts and Syrians produced heavy tapestries that were used as floor coverings. A number of Seljuk rug pieces surviving from the thirteenth century indicate an advanced knotted pile rug industry, one that perfected arabesque design. Ottoman Anatolia was, and is, a very important area for carpet weaving. Turkish carpets were especially valued in colonial America.

Oriental carpets, a category that includes Chinese, Central Asian, and Indian rugs as well as the Near Eastern, have been made with wool, silk, or cotton warp. Pile has usually been of wool or silk. Some camel and goat hair has been used, in spite of the fact that both are inclined to emit a distinct odor when wet. The silk carpets woven in Safavid Persia are perhaps the most exquisite of the oriental rugs with their garden scenes brocaded in gold and silver with birds, animals, and flowers—designs similar to those of lighter weight textiles.

The two basic types of oriental carpet construction are the flat woven tapestry (*kilim*) with or without slits and appearing the same on both sides; and pile weave, made with either the *ghiordes* (Turkish) knot or the *sehna*, or *senna* (Persian) knot inserted between rows of tabby weave (Figure 5.3). Pile construction makes very complicated structural design possible, and oriental carpet designs can be quite intricate. In kilims, however, tapestry technique restricts pattern more to geometric designs. Near Eastern rugs are also embroidered in imitation of the more expensive pile constructions. Unfortunately, textile experts have not, as yet, analyzed the construction of the famous flying carpets.

Connoisseurs value the rich, subtle colors employed in Oriental rugs. These resulted from the use of vegetable dyes such as indigo, madder, pomegranate, saffron, and others, in combination. The introduction of aniline dyes toward the end of the nineteenth century resulted in some garish color combinations. (The Navajos exhibited the same lack of restraint when they encountered a large selection of bright new hues. See chapter 11.) Aniline dyes were not fast to water, so there was often bleeding of colors.

Carpet weaving, although dying out, has endured into the twentieth century, although the weaving of sumptuous silks and velvets has not. The Near East was a direct source of materials, methods, and design for the medieval European textile industry. Renaissance design also owed much to Persia and Byzantium.

NOTES

1. Muhammad A. Marzouk, *History of Textile Industry in Alexandria 331 B.C.-1517 A.D.* (Alexandria, UAR: Alexandria University Press, 1955), p. 18.
2. Klaus Wessel, *Coptic Art* (New York: McGraw-Hill, 1965), p. 182.
3. Franco Brunello, *The Art of Dyeing in the History of Mankind,* tr. Bernard Hickey (Cleveland: Phoenix Dye Works, 1973), p. 97.
4. Wessel, *Coptic Art,* p. 231.
5. R. Pfister and Louisa Bellinger, "The Textiles" in *The Excavations at Dura-Europos, Part II* (New Haven: Yale University Press, 1945), p. 14.
6. Nancy Reath and Eleanor Sachs, *Persian Textiles and Their Technique from the Sixth to the Eighteenth Centuries including a System for General Textile Classification* (New Haven: Yale University Press, 1937), p. 13. For the most up-to-date discussion on Sassanian samit see Krishna Riboud, "A Newly Excavated Caftan from the Northern Caucasus," *Textile Museum Journal* 4, no. 3 (1976):21–42.
7. Riboud, *Caftan,* p. 21.
8. Dorothy Shepherd, "A Pall from the Tomb of 'Ali ibn Muhammad," *Bulletin of the Cleveland Museum of Art* 49, no. 4 (April 1963):75.
9. Reath and Sachs, *Persian Textiles,* p. 9.
10. Ibid., p. 30.
11. Ibid., p. 43.
12. Arthur E. R. Boak, "Notes and Documents: The Book of the Prefect," *Journal of Economic and Business History* 1 (1928-29):597-619.
13. Otto von Falke, *Decorative Silks,* 3rd ed. (New York: William Helburn, 1936), p. 9.

BIBLIOGRAPHY

A major and important source on early Near Eastern textiles is Otto von Falke, *Decorative Silks,* 3rd ed. (New York: William Helburn, 1936). Von Falke is still considered an authority, although some of his facts have been refuted. More recent, shorter, and more readily available is W. Fritz Volbach, *Early Decorative Textiles* (New York and London: Paul Hamlyn, 1969). The colored plates in Volbach are excellent. Adele Weibel covers the same ground in *Two Thousands Years of Textiles* (New York: Pantheon, 1952) and is often quoted by other authors. Ethel Lewis offers a general survey in *The Romance of Textiles* (New York: Macmillan Co., 1937). George Hunter's *Decorative Textiles* (Philadelphia: J. P. Lippincott, 1918) shows some interesting relationships between different Near Eastern textiles and their designs. Another survey is "Early Oriental Textiles," *CIBA Review* 43 (May 1942).

Chapter 1 of Phyllis Ackerman, *Tapestry: The Mirror of Civilization* (1933; reprint ed., New York: AMS Press, 1970) sets the stage for a study of Egyptian textiles with a summary of the period from 2900 B.C. through the Coptic—with some sensual descriptions of hedonistic Alexandria and its fabrics. Muhammad Abdelaziz Marzouk wrote about that city in his thoroughly researched *History of Textile Industry in Alexandria 331 B.C.-1517 A.D.* (Alexandria, UAR: Alexandria University Press, 1955). Textiles from 2000 B.C. are discussed in Winifred Needler, "Three Pieces of Unpatterned Linen from Ancient Egypt in the Royal Ontario Museum," in *Studies in Textile History,* ed. Veronika Gervers (Toronto: Royal Ontario Museum, 1977), pp. 238-251. Another important study is Elizabeth Riefstahl, *Patterned Textiles in Pharaonic Egypt* (New York: The Brooklyn Museum, 1944).

Several books on Coptic textiles are available, but there is no general agreement on dating sequences. Ludmila Kybalova, *Coptic Textiles* (London: Paul Hamlyn, 1967) is one of the best surveys for both religious history and design chronology. Klaus Wessel, in his *Coptic Art* (New York: McGraw-Hill, 1965), discusses several well-known textiles and various styles, but he is obviously an art historian and not a textile technician. Pierre du Bourguet, *The Art of the Copts* (New York: Crown Publishers, 1971) does a better job with technical aspects. A noted art historian, John Beckwith, wrote a fine overview: "Coptic Textiles," *CIBA Review* 133 (August 1959). Beckwith refutes some of the work done by R. Pfister, an archaeologist who published a number of works on Near Easten textiles in French in the 1930s. Pfister's book on Coptic textiles in the Louvre will be found only in rare book collections. Another rare book, or rather a large portfolio, but one worth tracing, is Kunisuke Akashi, *Coptic Textiles from Burying Grounds in Egypt* (Kyoto: Kyoto-Shain Co., 1950). The text is in Japanese, but the colored plates are exciting. A scholar earlier than Pfister was A. F. Kendrick, whose *Catalogue of Textiles from Burying-Grounds in Egypt,* 3 pts. (London: Victoria and Albert Museum, 1920-1922) has been an important reference.

Catalogs of collections in the United States include Suzanne Lewis, *Early Coptic Textiles* (Stanford, Calif.: Stanford University Art Gallery, 1969) with its four-page introduction, and Deborah Thompson's more informative *Coptic Textiles in the Brooklyn Museum* (Brooklyn, N.Y. The Brooklyn Museum, 1971). A frequently cited reference is Lillian May Wilson, *Ancient Textiles from Egypt in the University of Michigan Collection* (Ann Arbor, Mich.: University of Michigan Press, 1933). Wolfgang Volbach, *Late Antique Coptic and Islamic Textiles of Egypt* (New York: E. Weyhe, 1926) has an introduction by Volbach and Ernst Kuehnel and a hundred plates.

A few authors have written about specific fabrics. Paul Friedlander, *Documents of Dying Paganism, Textiles of Late Antiquity in Washington, New York, and Leningrad* (Berkeley and Los Angeles: University of California Press, 1945) discusses the *Hestia Polyolbos* (Honored Lady of Many Blessings) tapestry, which has been preserved for study in the Byzantine collection at Dunbarton Oaks in Washington, D.C. Rudolf Berliner wrote several articles for *Textile Museum Journal:* "A Coptic Tapestry of Byzantine Style," 1, no. 1 (1962); "Horsemen in Tapestry Roundels Found in Egypt," 1, no. 2 (1963); "Tapestries from Egypt Influenced by Theatrical Performances," 1, no. 3 (1964); "Remarks on Some Tapestries from Egypt," 1, no. 4 (1965); and "More About the Developing Islamic Style in Tapestries," 2, 1 (1966). An understanding of the close relationship between Egypt and Constantinople can be gleaned from Dorothy Shepherd, "An Icon of the Virgin, A Sixth-Century Tapestry Panel from Egypt," *The Bulletin of The Cleveland Museum of Art* 56, no 3 (March 1969). Lisa Golombek and Veronika Gervers, "Tiraz Fabrics in the Royal Ontario Museum," in *Studies in Textile History* considers technical characteristics, sociological implications, and epigraphical style of Muslim fabrics.

Background on Persia can be gained from reading the authoritative books *Persia from the Origins to Alexander the Great* (1964) and *Iran, Parthians and Sassanians* (1962) written by the archaeologist Roman Ghirshman and published in London by Thames and Hudson. The illustrations and maps are excellent. For the Islamic period see Richard N. Frye, *The Golden Age of Persia: The Arabs in the East* (New York: Harper & Row, 1975). For a somewhat philosophical discussion of Islamic art that includes weaving, see Arthur U. Pope, *An Introduction to Persian Art Since the Seventh Century A.D.* (Westport, Conn.: Greenwood Press, 1972).

The best work on Persian textiles is Nancy Reath and Eleanor Sachs, *Persian Textiles and Their Technique from the Sixth to the Eighteenth Centuries Including a System for General Textile Classification* (New Haven: Yale University Press, 1937). It is logically and clearly written and has good illustrations of compound weaves. Carpets and Safavid textiles are covered briefly in Arthur U. Pope, *Masterpieces of Persian Art* (New York: The Dryden Press, 1945). A most important reference is Arthur Pope and Phyllis Ackerman, *Survey of Persian Art,* 13 vols. (London: Oxford University Press, 1965). Phyllis Ackerman, "Persian Textiles," *CIBA Review* 98 (June 1953) is a delightful survey. Two good studies for Sassanian silks can be found in "The Early History of Silk," *CIBA Review* 11 (July 1938); and Michael Meister, "The Pearl Roundel in Chinese Textile Design," *Ars Orientalis* 8 (1970):255-267.

For some technical aspects see Hans E. Wulff, *The Traditional Crafts of Persia, Their Development, Technology, and Influence on Eastern and Western Civilizations* (Cambridge, Mass.: The M.I.T. Press, 1966). Especially for the illustrations see: Rokuro Kamimura, ed., *Textiles of Iran* (Kyoto: Unsodo, 1962) with its short text in Japanese; Cyril Bunt, *Persian Fabrics* (Leigh-on-Sea, England: F. Lewis, 1963); A. F. Kendrick and Sir Thomas Arnold, "Persian Stuffs with Figure Subjects," *Burlington Magazine* 37 (1920):237-244; and Rahim Anavian and George Anavian, *Royal Persian and Kashmir Brocades* (Tokyo: Senshoku to Seikatsusha, 1975).

H. W. Haussig, *A History of Byzantine Civilization* (New York: Praeger Publishers, 1971) will give thorough background, and Rene Guerdan, *Byzantium: Its Triumphs and Tragedy* (New York: Capricorn Books, 1962) is a popularization good for economic and social aspects of Byzantine civilization. John Beckwith's important book, *Early Christian and Byzantine Art* (Baltimore: Penquin Books, 1970), includes textiles. Perhaps the best source on Byzantine textiles is "Byzantine Silks," *CIBA Review* 75 (August 1949), which has more information on the industry than any other readily available source. Cyril Bunt, *Byzantine Fabrics* (Leigh-on-Sea, England: F. Lewis, 1967) has three pages of rather general information and fifty-seven plates. Pauline Johnstone, *The Byzantine Tradition in Church Embroidery* (Chicago: Argonaut, 1967) is an important scholarly source.

In 1950 and 1951 the most important books on Turkish textiles were published. *Turkish Textiles and Velvets XIV-XVI Centuries* by Tahsin Oz, curator of the Topkapi Saray Museum, discusses the collections there and something of the early industry. The plates are outstanding. There is a second volume, published in 1951, but it has not been translated into English except for some short resumés about the later years of textile production. Agnes Geijer, *Oriental Textiles in Sweden* (Copenhagen: Rosenkilde and Bagger, 1951) includes a discussion of the Ottoman textiles found with those of the Far East and

Central Asia in Sweden. (Many were the products of Russian trade in the sixteenth and seventeenth centuries). More readily available is a good survey by Louise W. Mackie, *The Splendor of Turkish Weaving* (Washington, D.C.: The Textile Museum, 1973). This includes a catalog of The Textile Museum's Turkish collection. Water B. Denny, "Ottoman Turkish Textiles," *Textile Museum Journal* 3, No. 3 (December 1972):55-56 is also a very good general survey. See, too, A. J. B. Wace, "The Dating of Turkish Velvets," *Burlington Magazine* 64 (April 1934):164-171; and the Victoria and Albert Museum's *Brief Guide to Turkish Woven Fabrics* (London: Victoria and Albert Museum, 1950).

Many sources on carpets are available and include the books by Pope and Mackie already cited. Only a few will be given here. The Textile Museum in Washington, D.C. has a large collection of rugs, and its journal has carried many scholarly articles. A recent and comprehensive work is M. S. Dimand and Jean Mailey, *Oriental Rugs in The Metropolitan Museum* (New York: The Metropolitan Museum of Art, 1973).

Overviews are provided in Ignaz Schlosser, *The Book of Rugs: Oriental and European* (New York: Bonanza, 1963); Preben Liebetrau, *Oriental Rugs in Colour* (New York: Macmillan Co., 1963); and Michele Campana, *Oriental Carpets* (London and New York: Paul Hamlyn, 1969). The color plates in these three are very good. More detail on weaving centers and rug types is given by Walter A. Hawley, *Oriental Rugs: Antique and Modern* (1913; reprint ed., New York: Dover Publications, 1970). Ulrich Schurmann, *Oriental Carpets* (London: Paul Hamlyn, 1966) has excellent illustrations but a very brief text.

6. THE MEDIEVAL TEXTILE INDUSTRY IN SOUTHERN EUROPE

The Middle Ages in Europe extended from about 400 A.D. to about 1500 A.D.—that is, from the fall of Rome to the discovery of the New World. Textile historians are concerned with the later medieval period when there was an adequate agricultural surplus to support the aristocracy and specialized craftsmen necessary for luxury textile production. That production was also inspired in part by the Crusaders who had acquired a taste for Oriental silks.

Great textile centers were located in southern Europe by the Muslims who had conquered Spain in the eighth century and Sicily in the ninth. Christian sections of Spain, Italy, and then France learned the business, and the West was soon in competition with the East. European textiles, often very Oriental in flavor, were marketed in the Near East. It was logical for the first European patterned silks to be like the Oriental, because both the prototypes and the first European craftsmen came from the East. The woolen and linen industries, although certainly reaching into southern Europe in the medieval period, belonged more to northern Europe.

Technologically the West raced ahead of the East. Towns devoted to textile manufacture grew up, and widespread and complex guild systems developed with them. Task specialization became commonplace. As early as the tenth century water power was used to operate a fulling mill in Tuscany. The belt-driven spinning wheel, invented in India, was an important timesaving device. The throwing mill was an extremely important technical advance made in fourteenth century Italy. One mill could do the work of a hundred throwsters by twisting and winding silk simultaneously. It was so technically efficient that it did not need improvements for five hundred years. The above constitute a small industrial revolution; however, there was a difference between the employment of machines in the fourteenth century and in the eighteenth and nineteenth centuries. In Lucca, for example, a master throwster leased or owned one or two mills and employed

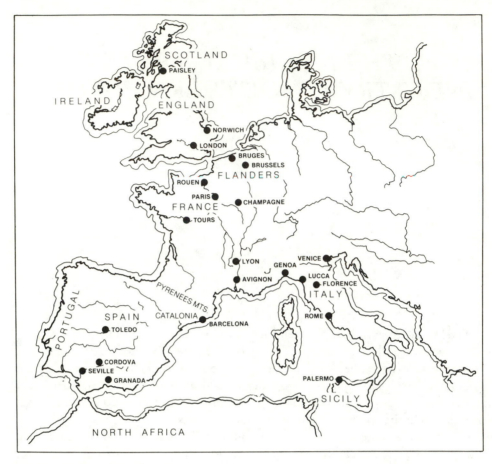

FIGURE 6.1 / Europe.

just a few workers; there was not the great concentration of workers and machines as in modern factories.

HISTORICAL OVERVIEW

Spain

The Iberian Peninsula in southwestern Europe was a melting pot since the days of Neanderthal. Greeks, Phoenicians, Carthaginians, Romans, Goths, Vandals, Celts, Moors, and Arabs—all these left imprints on Spanish and Portuguese culture. Catalonia, an autonomous state until the eighteenth century, was an important region for woolen and (later) cotton cloth production. Large numbers of sheep were raised in the valleys of the Pyrenees on Spain's northern border. Important textile centers were located at Seville, Barcelona, Cordova, Toledo, and Granada. (Figure 6.1).

Iberia, one of the most vigorous parts of the Roman Empire, was overrun by

Vandals and Visigoths in the fifth century. At the time, Iberia was Christian and had an opulent Byzantine court. Internal dissension enabled the Moors (North African Berbers and Arabs) to conquer much of the country in 712. The Muslims settled mostly in fertile Andalusia where they started sericulture, something new to Spain. By 756 the Umayyad Caliph, independent of the Eastern Abbabsids, ruled from Cordova, one of the greatest cultural centers of the Middle Ages. In the eleventh century ships were carrying textiles from Spain throughout the known world, and in the twelfth and thirteenth centuries a rise in population increased urbanization and manufacturing. Contact and trade with northern Europe expanded. The mid-fourteenth century brought the Black Death, decimation of the population, a decline in trade, and financial difficulties.

After the Muslim conquest some of the northern Spanish states remained Christian and embarked on a reconquest that was completed in 1492. That date marks not only the journey of Christopher Columbus, but also the peak of the Spanish Inquisition, instigated in 1478 under Isabella and Ferdinand to promote nationalism by enforcing Catholicism. The Jews, talented textile workers and merchants, could choose between baptism and expulsion. By 1502 the Muslims had one alternative to baptism—death. Those who did convert were called Moriscos.

Conquests in the New World made Spain a powerful nation, one that dominated Europe in the sixteenth century. But the Spanish squandered Mexican and Peruvian gold and silver on European wars and ostentatious display. They supplied their colonies with goods purchased in Italy and other countries rather than investing in their own productive capacity. In time Spain lost its economic and political advantage.

Spain's Philip II (1556-1598) was responsible for the rigorous persecutions of Protestants in the Netherlands during the sixteenth century—persecutions that drove skilled textile workers to England, Germany, France, and Switzerland. Philip III, too, was short-sighted and expelled the Moriscos, also skilled craftsmen, from Spain in the early seventeenth century. As a consequence the silk industry, which had been second to that of Italy, went into decline.

Sicily

Palermo was founded by the Phoenicians in the eighth century B.C. and was then taken over by the Carthaginians in the fifth. The Romans conquered it in 254 B.C. The Vandals came in the fifth century A.D. and the Byzantines in the sixth. The Muslims made Sicily the base for their western empire in 831 A.D. and built a textile trade. The Normans conquered the island in 1072; under Rogers I and II, the arts and crafts flourished until Palermo was taken over by the German Hohenstaufens in 1194. Economic decline set in under Frederick I, another unenlightened ruler who deported a minority group of skilled craftsmen and merchants (Arabs who had been settled on Sicily for nearly four hundred years). Frederick's grandson, Frederick II, undid some of the damage by patronizing the arts. In 1266 the French defeated the Hohenstaufens in Sicily and the textile industry was ruined in the subsequent turmoil.

Italy

Much of Italy is agriculturally poor land, and so, over time, its people have had to develop trading and manufacturing skills in order to survive. The Italian cities became small states in the medieval period, and rivalry among them was intense. During the thirteenth century there was a real commercial and artistic upsurge, inspired in part by the Crusades and the business they brought, and then by a rising interest in trade with the Near East once the threat of Arab pirates was reduced. The cosmopolitanism evident in medieval Italian cities was preparation for the Renaissance of the fifteenth century. Medieval textile centers included Lucca and Florence in Tuscany, Genoa on the northwest coast, and Venice, bordering on the Adriatic. Other Italian towns had their weavers, of course, but those four are usually given as proveniences for extant textiles.

Lucca reached a peak of prosperity in the ninth and tenth centuries, because it was located on the roads to Pisa, Florence, and Rome. Rich pilgrims going to Rome were a good market for luxury goods, especially fine linens and woolens. In the late tenth century Lucca lost its preeminence to Florence, although it remained a major market town and silk manufacturing center.

In the medieval period, Florence was dominated by monasteries where weaving shops were established to help supply the domestic market. Dyeing and finishing woolens from Flanders was an important industry in Florence. The city suffered much turmoil during the thirteenth and fourteenth centuries; in the fifteenth the Medici family commenced its rule. The Renaissance began in Florence—the city of Dante, Petrarch, Donatello, Michelangelo, and Leonardo.

Genoa grew to importance as a medieval commercial center and made good profits derived from the Crusaders. In the sixteenth century the Genoese were the principal bankers of southern Europe and controlled the Spanish trade by controlling the monetary and credit systems. By the late sixteenth century Genoa was an important lacemaking center.

Genoa's main rival was Venice, an important trading center as early as the ninth century, because it served as an intermediary between Constantinople and the areas in eastern Italy under its control. By the late eleventh century, Venice had a lively trade with Constantinople, and treaties gave Venetians commercial equality, relief from tariffs, and freedom of residence in Constantinople. In 1204 Venetians were able to turn the Fourth Crusade against Constantinople, and much of the loot from the sack ended up in Venice. Venice then controlled most of the routes to the Near East—and spices and silks. It was from Venice that Marco Polo set forth for China in the thirteenth century, returning with new goods and new ideas. The fifteenth and sixteenth centuries saw Venice lose its power relative to Western Europe as the sea discoveries opened the Americas and the Far East to European trade.

SPANISH TEXTILES

Very little is known about the Spanish textile industry prior to the thirteenth century. Early Spanish silks bore close resemblances to those of Byzantium, Persia, Syria, and Egypt with single or paired animals in roundels or banded patterns with Kufic lettering. One of the earliest extant fabrics (Plate 37) is a fragment from the tunic of the Infante Felipe, who lived in the latter part of the thirteenth century. The upper part of the textile shows typical interlacery worked into stars that enclose rosettes. Two of the three lower bands have Kufic script that repeats the term for blessing (*baraka*).[1]

Valuable textiles were preserved for many years and passed from one generation to the next. They were considered stores of wealth. A fifteenth century Spanish princess, given in alliance to a foreign king, might have filled three ships with her dowry. There might have been chests of *samit* with Sassanian animals, *sendal* (lightweight silk for linings and banners[2]), *ciclatoun* (heavy silk for mantles), and *camocan* (silk damask). Velvets, both cut (Plate 38) and uncut, some brocaded in gold, others made heavy for alcove curtains and wall hangings, may have shimmered in kermes red and polychromes. Heavy silks with brocaded loops in three different heights and rich brocades may have been destined as gifts for distant clergy. There may also have been chests of typical Hispano-Moresque (Hispano-Islamic) textiles with patterns of intertwined tracery (Plate 39), angular Kufic and cursive *Naskhi* lettering, geometric formations of stars, circles, squares, and rectangles, and many pieces of silk tissue with tiraz borders. Some beautiful Mudejar fabrics, made by Muslims living under Christian rule, may have combined the arabesque with Gothic castles and heraldic animals in the Italian mode. (Plate 40). In the bottom of one chest there may have been a very old silk tapestry, made in Spain by a Copt and long treasured for its bands of gold. Other striped fabrics may have given a chiaroscuro effect, that is, light bands with dark designs alternating with dark bands and light patterns. There may have been narrow bands made by tablet weaving, a noted Spanish skill, with large supplies of embroidery. Huge quantities of linens and woolens would have probably completed the cargo. Most of these textiles would have gone into storage rooms in the castle—perhaps along with the dowries of the two previous queens who died in childbirth—and to them the booty taken by the king in war would be added. He may have captured a huge pavilion tent made of gold and silver brocade and furnished with tapestries from Flanders and carpets from Persia. (The many brilliantly colored silk banners and pieces of brocade would have been divided among deserving nobles and the church treasuries.)

The Spanish silks have been preserved and studied, although fabrics of other fibers were manufactured in much greater quantitites. Since Roman times wool, flax, and hemp supplied domestic needs, and by the eleventh century there were small surpluses for trade. The wool industry, centered in Catalonia from the thirteenth to the fifteenth century, was by far the most productive of the peninsula's textile trades. Wool was brought from all over Spain and from England, and woolens were sent to northern Europe, Constantinople, and North Africa. Spain is supposed to have been the first European nation to weave cotton (when it was brought by the Moors), but there was little demand for it until Indian prints reached Spain via Portugal in the seventeenth century. The cotton industry flourished in Catalonia in the eighteenth and nineteenth centuries—using cotton from America.

SICILIAN SILKS

Probably many textiles attributed to Sicily were actually made elsewhere,[3] but there is no doubt that many fine silks were made there between the mid-twelfth and the late thirteenth centuries. Although it is not known whether silk weaving was introduced into Sicily by the Byzantines or by the Arabs, Roger I did find a royal tiraz in operation when he captured Palermo in the eleventh century. Roger II is generally given credit for the Sicilian silk industry, because in 1147, while on an expedition in Byzantine territory, he "invited" a large number of Greek weavers to go to Palermo. Here they were installed in the old tiraz, and they seemed to have worked in harmony with the Muslims. So, as in Spain, there was a blending of the Christian and Islamic in textile design. With some silk fabrics it is impossible to determine whether Spain or Sicily was the place of origin, although Sicilian color combinations are generally less harsh.

A weave closely associated with Palermo was *diasprum*,[4] the first western silk weave that showed a texture difference between the background and the design. A similar effect was first achieved in Seljuk Persia during the same period. Diasprum, later called lampas, was a compound weave with a tabby ground and a pattern formed with heavy weft using a binding system giving the effect of twill.

Sicilian design is characterized by vertical elements that unify horizontal bands of animals and trees (Plate 41). Red and green peacocks and griffons seem particularly common. Themes differ from those of Byzantium and the East, yet there is a similarity achieved by the use of tree of life motifs. Pomegranates and fantastic animals appear in twelfth century textiles. Thirteenth century textiles show the diversity of design needed to meet the demand from the royalty and clergy of Italy, France, and England.

Little is known about Sicilian silks after 1300, as they were largely replaced by textiles woven in the Italian cities. Most of the weavers fled when Sicily was taken over by the French in 1266. It was to Lucca in Tuscany that they went.

ITALIAN TEXTILES

Lucca

When the Palermo weavers went to Lucca they found an active textile industry that had been founded during the eleventh century by Jewish weavers from southern Italy. By that time sericulture was known in Lombardy, so the Jews may have woven the native silk. But the prominence earned by Lucchese silks has been credited to the Sicilians and to the shrewd Italian merchants who knew how to sell cloth abroad. Lucchese weavers could make almost every kind of silk fabric known in the Middle Ages and were able to present large displays at the Champagne fairs in the twelfth and thirteenth centuries and in Bruges and Paris in the fourteenth and fifteenth. Church inventories of the late thirteenth century list more sendals, samits, damasks, brocades, taffetas, and *baldachins* (heavy silks brocaded in gold and silver and embellished with precious stones) from Lucca than from any other place. In addition to great variety, Lucchese fabrics were noted for their high quality.

Diasprum (diasper, panne diasperati, lampas), first made in Sicily, was one of the most famous products of Lucca (Plate 41). The design was woven in thick, untwisted (and so, glossy) silk weft and was raised in relief from the duller background. At first the Lucchese wove diasprum in monochrome, then they used two color effects with some sections of gold. The weave was most popular in the fourteenth century.

Lucca was also a city of velvet, although it is not certain whether it originated there or in Florence or Venice. Business letters and inventories of the fourteenth century list velvets with two and three pile heights, both cut and uncut types, monochromes and polychromes, velvets brocaded in gold and silver, and some with satin grounds.

Very early Lucchese designs showed strong Islamic influence and the roundels and single animals of Persian and Byzantine origin. This changed in the twelfth century to a pairing and stylization of animals and birds. In the next century framing was completely eliminated, but the arrangement of motifs still gave a horizontal feeling. Gothic castles and hunting scenes began to appear, and by the fourteenth century a Lucchese textile was in agitated motion. The impact of the Chinese textiles that reached Italy in large quantities in the early fourteenth century freed the Lucchese silks from their old patterns, and fantastic animals— dogs, griffons, peacocks, and falcons—leaped or swooped among the castles, clouds, and trees (Plate 42). Rays of the sun, or streaks of rain, characterized Lucchese textiles from the thirteenth to the fifteenth century (Plate 43).

Venice

Preeminence passed to Venice in the early fourteenth century when weavers and merchants fled the political strife in Lucca. There already was a silk weavers' guild in Venice, and satin and damask had been made there since the late thirteenth century. The Lucchese arrived destitute, but they were given looms and a special quarter in the city by the Venetians, who welcomed the weaving secrets of the new immigrants.

Venetian fabrics were probably the most varied of all made in Italy, because Venice had the closest ties with the East. Early fabrics were strongly Byzantine and Persian in pattern, and Italian velvets made in the sixteenth century cannot always be distinguished from those of Turkey.[5] Although they took on the same kind of free movement seen in fourteenth century Lucchese designs, Venetian fabrics were more restrained. Ship and boat designs frequently identified a cloth from Venice.

Venice became a major velvet center in the mid-fifteenth century, because its designers shifted from the small figures of Gothic hunting scenes to large, simple floral patterns more suitable to velvet construction. Leaf panels with pomegranates or pine forms, bifurcating stems, and small blossoms were more appropriate to a three-dimensional pile surface (Plate 44). Many of these new velvets were no longer polychrome but sophisticated monochromatic masterpieces of maroon, ruby red, violet, or blue combined with gold.

Venice produced other fabrics as well—damasks, ribbed silks, brocades, and *drap d'or.* This *cloth of gold* was patterned with the background woven in gold thread from Sicily or Cyprus. Gold brocade, on the other hand, had the design woven with metallic thread. These rich textiles were frequently sent to eastern Europe, as well as to the north.

Florence

Florence, city of the lily, took the lead in the sixteenth century, because its designs were even more original than those of Venice, and because designers had learned to scale patterns down for costume. Florence had a silk industry in the thirteenth century that became famous for brilliantly dyed sendals used in dresses and linings. In the fourteenth century the city became a major center because of the Lucchese weavers who fled there and established shops.

The apex of Florentine weaving coincided with the development of the artichoke motif (probably derived from the pomegranate, which was in turn derived from the lotus). The artichoke was also known as the pineapple, love fruit of South America. It was combined with floral motifs and great serpentine curves (Plate 45). And, as the animals had disappeared in the fifteenth century, so did the birds vanish in the sixteenth.

Florence was also noted for its orphreys, ecclesiastical vestment bands illustrating sacred subjects (Plate 46). Woven orphreys were a substitute for more costly embroidered ones of the fourteenth century and were woven several bands wide, then cut into strips. Brocatelle construction, with silk and gold weft on linen warp, made the pattern stand out. The Annunciation, the Crucifixion, and the Nativity were the most common depictions.

Genoa

Genoa, too, came into prominence in the fifteenth and sixteenth centuries. Constant warfare had prevented the city from reaching its potential earlier. She was most famous for her velvets, *velours de Genes,* with large S curves flowing over voided grounds. Some velvets had satin or ribbed backgrounds, lighter in shade than the pattern and done in two pile heights to give an especially rich quality. *Jardiniere,* garden velvets, were popular for furnishing fabrics. Another specialty of Genoa was *ferronnerie,* the voided velvet with patterns that looked like wrought iron (Plate 47).

Italian Textiles in General

Often it is not possible to identify the Italian city where a particular fabric was woven. Designers, who were frequently painters, and weavers moved from place to place, and good designs were frequently pirated. All the cities were in competition for the same buyers—the clergy and nobility. In order to insure sales to those markets the guilds established rigid standards for each type of cloth, and deviations were severely punished. In the fifteenth century, however, social conditions allowed for greater organization of manufacturing and trade, giving rise to a middle class. The market moved down the social scale, and standards tended to slip as a greater quantity of luxury textiles was needed. Some weaving towns were too slow to change—or too reluctant to lower standards—and lost their positions of leadership. Some of the business went to French weavers, although Italians continued to weave some marvelous fabrics on into the eighteenth century. Sericulture remained an important industry, and Italy supplied the yarn for French and English looms.

MEDIEVAL GUILDS

It is not clear where or when guilds first appeared. They may have had their beginnings as organizations of the poorer classes in Byzantium or as associations of workers in northern Europe. It is thought that the Florentine guilds originated in corporations of merchants and artisans known in ancient Rome as *collegia* (schools or professions).[6] As a well-defined structure of society, like the manorial system, guilds belong to the late Middle Ages. Strongest in the freest city-states of Italy, Flanders, and Germany, guilds took different forms in various parts of Europe, but all operated under the principle that control of industry belonged to the producer.

There were two basic kinds of guilds. The Guild Merchant, the earlier of the two, held special privileges from the crown and trading rights that could not be abridged by the municipalities. The Merchant employed a species of the domestic system of manufacture: he purchased raw silk and gave it out to specialized workers who owned their own tools and were paid by the piece. They worked at home or in small workshops. After each stage of manufacture—throwing, winding bobbins, weaving—the goods were returned to the Merchant who passed them out to the next group of workers. Under this system weavers seldom acquired much capital and even had to rent looms from the Merchants because they were too poor to buy them. The Merchants reached their zenith in the twelfth century, then gave way to the second type, the Craft Guilds that reached their ascendancy in turn about the middle of the fifteenth century.

The Craft Guilds, associations of masters, journeymen, and apprentices, were usually small, each serving a specialized occupation—silk reelers, silk weavers, dyers of fast colors, dyers of fugitive colors, fullers, wool weavers, etc. Often there were associations of two or more related guilds. Goals of the guilds were economic, social and moral, and political.[7] The prestige and welfare of each craft was defended by regulating both production and conditions of sale, and even the *appearance* of fraud was not allowed. Detailed regulations prescribed qualities of materials, specifications for the finished article, and the price at which something could be sold. Methods of work and conditions of apprenticeship were regulated. The guild gave security in bad times and medical assistance during illness. Fraternal societies, affiliated with the guilds, maintained "chests" or funds to be given to the poor, the hospitals, and as dowries for the daughters of poor members. Each guild vied for the political favors of local and regional officials: the town magistrate, the prince, or the bishop. The guilds paid fees to these officials in return for certain privileges, such as reductions in tolls.

MEDIEVAL TRADE

Textiles were different from many other products of the early guilds, because they were traded in much more distant markets. Nonperishable and easy to transport, fabrics, yarns, and dyestuffs had been an important part of the Old World trader's pack since ancient times.

International trade was stimulated by growing populations and by the Crusaders, who not only brought back new products to Europe but also attained a certain worldliness not known in the early Middle Ages. The Crusades also freed the Mediterranean from Muslim pirates, opening it to the Italian trading ships that brought exotic goods from the East to be sent by caravan over the Alps into Northern Europe.

Trade fairs were held all over Europe, but the most famous were those of the Champagne region. (see Figure 6.1). The earliest was held in the fifth century, and major fairs were held yearly at Troyes, Lagny, Bar-sur-Aube, and Provins from the twelfth to the fourteenth century. Fairs were rotated throughout the year so that merchants could attend more than one. Because they were located midway between Flanders and the Mediterranean, the Champagne fairs drew the largest numbers of foreign merchants.[8]

A fair customarily lasted forty-six days. Its first period was devoted to the sale of cloth, the second to leather, and the third to other goods. The cloth period lasted ten days, seven for exhibition and three for sale. At the close of the sale period accounts were settled through a complex system of credits. The towns built storehouses and visitor accomodations, and supplied legal, banking, and protective services. The fairs also stimulated local cloth production, and some of the great market towns became renowned for their fabrics.

Protection for traveling merchants was very necessary to the success of the fairs. When traders could no longer travel safely overland to Champagne, they bypassed France and went by sea to Flanders and Germany. This happened in the late thirteenth century when Champagne lost its independence as a consequence of the marriage of Jeanne of Navarre to Philip the Fair. Philip increased taxes on sales, confiscated goods, promoted war, and generally ruined business. Another frustration was the repeated extraction of tolls and duties along the trade routes.[9]

MEDIEVAL AND RENAISSANCE FRENCH FABRICS

During the early Middle Ages textile production was often centered in the monasteries or carried out under the protection of a church that could also protect markets. In France linens and hempen cloths were usually produced at home, although some towns were, by the thirteenth century, quite famous for their fine shirt and undergarment fabrics. Rheims, an old Roman town, made *serges* and *etamines* (lightweight open weave wool) as well as linens for the Champagne fairs. France had a fairly important woolen industry. Rouen was weaving woolens in the thirteenth century, silks in the fifteenth. Toulouse, Avignon, Nimes, and Paris were other early weaving towns. Much linen was woven in Normandy and Brittany.

The Champagne fairs were a major stimulus to production, and weaving districts grew up around the market towns. Provins, where half the townspeople worked in textiles, produced the best *draps pleins* (whole color cloths). Most fabrics in the thirteenth century were tightly woven, but Provins made a cheap open weave called *vingtaines. Biffes*, plain-colored and striped, sold readily in Paris and Lyon. *Pers de Provins* exemplified the talents of the woad dyers.

Besides ruining the Champagne fairs, Philip the Fair seemed bent on destroying the whole of the French textile industry with his fiscal policies. The plague and the Hundred Years' War (1337-1453) also had devastating effects. The English pillaged and burned their way across France; warehouses and cloth halls were emptied and thousands of cartloads of cloth sent back across the English Channel. Markets were unstable, and there was little inspiration for fine work. The English and Dutch usurped what little French foreign trade there had been.

Louis XI (1461-1483), although not in the least interested in sumptuous attire, introduced silk weaving to Lyons. In 1466 he settled some Lucchese weavers there, much to the opposition of the merchants of Lyons who did not want a local industry interfering with their lucrative import business. In 1470 the Italians were moved on to Tours where they were granted special privileges in return for teaching French apprentices. Designs from Tours imitated the large, bold ones of Italy.

Francis I (1515-1547) is to be remembered for bringing the Renaissance to France. The building of Fontainbleau was one of his great achievements and he invested tremendous sums in luxurious furnishings. Francis was a dandy: his doublets were always jeweled, he liked satins and laces and ruffles of the finest linen batiste, his coats were of fur-lined velvet, and his hats were adorned with ostrich feathers. Women of his court were resplendent, immobilized by dresses heavy with gold. The event of the century took place in 1520 when Francis met Henry VIII of England at the Field of the Cloth of Gold near Calais. It was reported that even the sails on Henry's ships were of cloth of gold, and his enormous tents were hung with gold and silver brocades and rich tapestries. For two weeks the kings and their courts cavorted in fabulous finery, changing garments several times a day.

Francis realized that the economy of his kingdom suffered with the import of so many Spanish, Italian, and Flemish fabrics, and in 1536 he renewed his efforts to make Lyon a silk weaving center. This time Lyon was more receptive, because Tours had prospered by weaving silk. Francis gave grants and privileges to some Italians to start shops. Duties, high enough to discourage imports, were placed on oriental silks in order to protect the new industry. Francis I also tried to build up the French woolen industry and forbade the import of Flemish serge. By mid-century the city of Amiens was even inventing new kinds of cloth. But late in the sixteenth century slovenly work caused a decline in business, and the religious wars that swept France destroyed many budding industries.

The sixteenth century saw the Reformation and the beginnings of religious persecutions that had far-reaching effects on the textile industries of many countries. Europeans were more interdependent before the sixteenth century than after; the opening of the New World and the Far East brought a power struggle and heightened competition between countries as they vied for foreign trade. This competition for trade and the increase in foreign contacts caused Europeans to become more inventive with their textiles.

NOTES

1. Florence Lewis May, *Silk Textiles of Spain: Eighth to Fifteenth Century* (New York: The Hispanic Society of America, 1957), p. 93.

2. Ibid., p. 62. Sendal may have been a general term, used as we use silk.

3. Otto von Falke, *Decorative Silks,* 3rd ed. (New York: William Helburn, 1936), p. 23.

4. Adèle Weibel, *Two Thousand Years of Textiles* (New York: Pantheon, 1952), p. 57.

5. Nancy Andrews Reath, "Velvets of the Renaissance, From Europe and Asia Minor," *Burlington Magazine,* June 1927, pp. 298-304.

6. John Edgcumbe Staley, *The Guilds of Florence* (New York: Benjamin Blom, 1967), p. 33.

7. Georges Renard, *Guilds in the Middle Ages* (1918; reprint ed., New York: M. Kelley, 1968), p. 32.

8. H. Wescher, "The Cloth Trade and the Fairs of Champagne," *CIBA Review* 65 (March 1948):2368.

9. H. Wescher, "Swiss Fairs and Markets in the Middle Ages," *CIBA Review* 62 (November 1947), gives a good account of road conditions and travel hazards.

BIBLIOGRAPHY

There are few sources in English for Spanish textiles. The principal reference is Florence Lewis May, *Silk Textiles of Spain: Eighth to Fifteenth Century* (New York: The

Hispanic Society of America, 1957), which includes in the excellent bibliography a number of articles in old museum publications. May gives many detailed descriptions of specific textiles and good illustrations.

Both Otto von Falke, *Decorative Silks,* 3rd ed. (New York: William Helburn, 1936) and Adele Weibel, *Two Thousand Years of Textiles* (New York: Pantheon, 1952), have sections on Spanish textiles. Ethel Lewis, *Romance of Textiles* (New York: Macmillan Co., 1937) has a rather general summary. Cyril Bunt, *Hispano-Moresque Fabrics* (Leigh-on-Sea, England: F. Lewis, 1966) is very brief, but the plates are helpful. "The Development of the Textile Crafts in Spain," *CIBA Review* 20 (April 1939) is a good overview of the wool, silk, tapestry, and carpet industries. A brief discussion and photographs of later Spanish textiles can be found in Christa Charlotte Mayer, *Masterpieces of Western Textiles from The Art Institute of Chicago* (Chicago: The Art Institute, 1969).

Two old books are Leonard Williams, *The Arts and Crafts of Older Spain, Vol. 3. World of Art Series* (Edinburgh: T.N. Foules, 1907); and Mildred Stapley Byne, *Popular Weaving and Embroidery in Spain* (New York: Helburn, 1924), which is good for its vocabulary of household items.

For two economic studies see James C. La Force, "Royal Factories in Spain, 1700-1800," *The Journal of Economic History* 24, no. 3 (September 1964):337-363; and *Development of Spanish Textile Industry 1750-1800* (Los Angeles: University of California, 1965). "The Catalan Textile Industry," *CIBA Review* no. 3 (1963) discusses guilds, trade, and the wool and cotton industries.

Sicilian and Italian textiles are also included in von Falke, Weibel, Lewis, and Mayer. Three works edited by Cyril Bunt—*Sicilian and Lucchese Fabrics* (1961), *Venetian Fabrics* (1959), and *Florentine Fabrics* (1962)—in the series *World's Heritage of Woven Fabrics* published by F. Lewis at Leigh-on-Sea, England, give very brief overviews and numerous plates. Many of the textiles in the plates do not have verified proveniences, however. Much more accurate descriptions of many textiles, beautifully illustrated in color, are given in Antonio Santangelo, *Treasury of Great Italian Textiles* (New York: Harry N. Abrams, 1964). Santangelo also gives some good background information. *Textiles of the Italian Renaissance: Their History and Development*, written by John Kent Tilton and published by Scalamandre Silks, New York (n.d.), is very helpful for design.

John Edgcumbe Staley, *The Guilds of Florence* (New York: Benjamin Blom, 1967) has good information on the silk and wool industries and on dyeing. The Italian trade in English wool is covered in T. H. Lloyd, *The English Wool Trade in the Middle Ages* (Cambridge: Cambridge University Press, 1977). Some *CIBA Review* articles discuss manufacturing and economic and social conditions. They include "The Textile Trades in Medieval Florence," 27 (November 1939); "Venetian Silks," 29 (January 1940); and "Lucchese Silks," 80 (June 1950). A short, but interesting, article is Llena C. Di Sorio, "Velvets from Venice," in *Apollo* (September 1975), pp. 203-207.

The classic source in English on medieval French fabrics is Paul Rodier, *The Romance of French Weaving* (New York: Frederick A. Stokes Co, 1931). Rodier is a little difficult to follow, but his book is full of interesting stories. Lewis has a short chapter on the French Renaissance in *Romance of Textiles. CIBA Review* articles on France include "Silks of Lyons," 6 (February 1938); "Fashions and Textiles at the Court of Burgundy," 51 (July 1946), which tells how different fabrics were used in medieval Europe; "Textile Art in Sixteenth Century France," 69 (July 1948), with information on French fashion; and "Rouen—French Textile Center," 135 (December 1959). See chapter 8 for other references.

There is no definitive history of textile design, and the subject is complex. Four authors are fairly clear in their presentations and include medieval textiles. Alan S. Cole, *Ornament in European Silks* (London: Debenham and Freebody, 1899) is very good, although its classifications seem somewhat oversimplified. George Hunter, *Decorative Textiles* (Philadelphia: J.B. Lippincott, 1918) concentrates on furnishing fabrics. Richard Glazier, *Historic Textile Fabrics* (New York: Charles Scribner's Sons, 1923) reads easily. W. Born's "Textile Ornament," *CIBA Review* 37 (January 1941), relates ornament to technical processes.

7. *TEXTILES OF THE FAR EAST*

The Far East includes eastern Siberia, China, Japan, Korea, India, and the countries of Southeast Asia. There are as many differences between the peoples within the region as there are between Orientals and Occidentals. In studies of world history, art, or material culture, the disparities between East and West have often resulted in the Oriental being considered a separate entity, but with textiles, especially, this should not occur. Since ancient times, Indian and Chinese textiles have made a notable contribution to the development of Western textile design and technology. Conversely, Western ideas have influenced Oriental textiles. This was especially true after the seventeenth century, when European trading ships began to make regular trips to the Orient. By the eighteenth century some fabrics were being made in India and China to European specifications. However, little was known in the West about Japanese textiles until the nineteenth century, when Europeans and Americans began to appreciate fully the rich diversity among all Far Eastern textiles.

THE LANDS AND THE PEOPLES

India

The subcontinent of India is a huge triangle, about one-third the size of the United States, with a broad northern boundary formed by the Himalaya Mountains and a very narrow southern tip jutting into the Indian Ocean (Figure 7.1). The Himalayas, source of the main rivers of India, serve as a barrier against the cold winds of Tibet and Central Asia and cause the monsoons from the Indian Ocean to rise and cool enough so that rains fall on a lowland plain that is about two hundred miles wide and stretches from the desert in the west to Calcutta and the Bay of Bengal in the east. This is one of the most fertile regions in India, and large

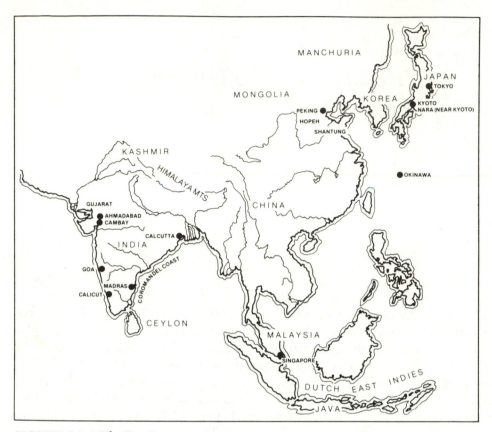

FIGURE 7.1 / The Far East.

quantities of jute are grown in the eastern part (now Bangladesh). To the south is the Deccan Plateau where the greatest amount of the world's cotton is grown, and at the very tip of India lie the southern coastal plains with their high fertility, high rainfall, and high population density. The arts and crafts of Ceylon, the large island off the south coast, and of Kashmir and Pakistan are closely allied to those of India.

Wave after wave of immigrants since the Stone Age has resulted in a population with quite diverse racial, linguistic, and religious characteristics. Most people still live in rural villages, although there are some very large cities in India, a few of which have been important textile centers for hundreds of years.

The largest number of Indians are Hindus. Hinduism is a religion, a philosophy, and a social system with rules for all aspects of daily life. It is one of the world's oldest religions; it has no one founder, no central authority, no ecclesiastical organization. The basic concepts of Hinduism were brought by the Aryan invaders in 1500 B.C. Only a person's body dies, his soul does not, but rather moves into the body of another living thing (reincarnation). A soul is reborn again and again in an effort to reach *moksha,* the final state of salvation and freedom from the life-death cycle. *Karma* is the belief that what one does in this life determines one's state in the next. Good deeds move one to a higher rank. *Dharma* is the path each must follow in performing his duties and obligations to the family and society. These beliefs made the Hindu concept of caste, with its rigid stratification of society, feasible. Four main castes developed, but within these there were thousands of divisions. A subcaste might follow occupational lines. In the textile world, silk weavers, spinners, and block printers formed separate subcastes. The indigo dyers were among the untouchable subcastes, possibly because they worked with urine. Occupational groups changed in composition and order of rank from time to time and place to place.

Embroidered and painted Hindu temple hangings depicted the legends of heroes and gods as well as peaceful rural scenes with animals and birds. The tiger hunt was a favorite motif.

A much smaller number of Indians are Muslims. Islam first reached India in the seventh century, but it was not a major religion until the thirteenth. Muslim beliefs have always contrasted strongly with Hindu beliefs, particularly in the matter of diet. Indian textiles owe a debt to Muslim designers who perfected floral patterns. Mogul textiles of the sixteenth and seventeenth centuries are medleys of roses, tulips, lilies, irises, poppies, and other garden blooms. The link to Safavid Persia is particularly evident in the floral metallic brocades woven by Muslims in India.

A minor, but wealthy, merchant class living in some western Indian cities follows the tenets of Jainism. The sect first formed in the sixth century B.C. in revolt against some Hindu practices. Jainist temple hangings exhibit rich iconography with goddesses and cosmic symbols. Jainists believe in nonviolence towards all living things. (Mahatma Gandhi, who spun on a charkha to symbolize a boycott against British rule and British goods in the 1920s and 1930s, held some of the same convictions, although he was not a Jainist.)

Other religions in India have smaller numbers of adherents. Buddhism developed in the sixth and fifth centuries B.C., and many of its doctrines were absorbed into Hinduism. Christianity, generally centered in southern India, probably started with the proselytizing of St. Thomas in the first century. Jesuits in the sixteenth century and Prostestant missionaries in the seventeenth century made many conversions. The Parsis, who live in the Bombay area, constitute another minor religious group. They are descendants of Zoroastrians who fled Muslim persecutions in Persia during the seventh and eighth centuries. It is, however, the Hindus and the Muslims who have had the greatest impact on textile development in India.

China

Over the Himalayas from India lies the country once called by its people the "Middle Kingdom"—the center of the world. It is now the largest of all Asian nations and the most populous nation in the world. China descends in steps from the Himalayas until it reaches the great river valleys where most of the Chinese have lived and farmed for thousands of years. China's size and number of rugged areas have made it difficult for anyone but a very strong leader to control all of the country. Instead, China has consisted of a number of warring states throughout most of its history.

China's population is more homogeneous than that of India. The vast majority of people are Mongoloids and call themselves the Han Chinese, although there are some fifty minority groups scattered about the country. The Chinese are noted for centuries of conservatism, during which traditional arts and crafts changed very little. Rapid industrialization and urbanization in China is, of course, changing this outlook.

The thought of Confucius, who lived in Shantung province from 551-479 B.C., has been the greatest single influence on the customs, manner, and outlook of the Chinese. Confucianism deeply influenced all aspects of Chinese life and even those people who embraced Taoism and Buddhism. Confucius taught that man was guided by the will of heaven and should act in accordance with that will, by showing reverence for the customs and traditions of the past. The solutions Confucius offered for the evils of his day do not seem unique—a return to virtue and a turning away from the pursuit of material profit. Confucianism really did not take hold until the second century B.C., when its teachings became the state philosophy of the Han dynasty and the basis for a "classical" education. Scroll, pearl, book, and leaf motifs in textiles symbolize the ancestor worship of Confucians. Cloud designs (Plate 55), which are rarely seen in non-Chinese textiles, belong to the same ancient tradition.

Taoism, founded in the sixth century B.C. by the sage Lao-tzu, complemented the austere, duty-conscious Confucianism with its reverence for past tradition by taking a more joyful and carefree attitude toward life. Taoism was both a philosophy (which became something of a diversion for the educated class) and a religion with an organized priesthood. Basically, Taoism endorsed a sort of yielding passivity and an absence of strife and coercion. Taoists spoke of the magical associations of man and the universe, depicting human functions (such as blood circulation in man) and the workings of the natural order (the flowings of rivers) in analogous relationships. Taoists regarded death as only one aspect of reality—one to be accepted with serenity. Taoist motifs include a variety of musical instruments and flowers, as well as cranes and stags (which symbolized longevity). From ancient Chinese tradition the Taoists took and enlarged upon the principles of Yin and Yang—illustrating the harmonious interplay of opposites in the universe (male and female, light and dark, etc.). Yin represented the female (the passive, dark, and absorbing), while Yang represented the male (the active, light, and penetrating). Earth was Yin, heaven Yang. As a popular religion, Taoism grew fastest during the Han dynasty (202 B.C.-220 A.D.), when it came into competition with Buddhism.

Buddhism, last of the three major teachings of Chinese tradition, reached China from India during the first century A.D. The Buddha (567-487 B.C.) was born to a noble family in a small Himalayan kingdom, and for thirty years his life was so sheltered he was not even aware of poverty and disease. When the Buddha finally saw harsh reality, he left his family to wander about the country in search of the meaning of life. The *Four Noble Truths* make up his understanding of it and are the principal teachings of Buddhism: life is full of pain and suffering; man causes them by his cravings; if man ends desire, he can end suffering; and craving can be ended by careful discipline and moral conduct. Like the Hindus, Buddhists believed in continued rebirth and eventual attainment of *nirvana (moksha)*. This was symbolized on textiles as the "endless knot." Other Buddhist emblems (Figure 7.2 and Plate 57) symbolized infinite changing (the wheel of the law), the appeal to wisdom (the conch shell), charity (the umbrella or parasol), spiritual authority (the canopy), purity (the lotus), ceremony (the vase), and tenacity (the fish).

Authors vary quite markedly in their interpretations of Chinese textile symbolism. Indeed, there is no total agreement on which motifs represent the ideas of individual religions.

Japan

Japan (Nippon) is comprised of four main islands and many small ones bounded on the east and south by the Pacific Ocean and on the west by the China Sea and the Sea of Japan. It is a land of mountains and volcanoes and steep ravines covered with contorted trees. The islands support a rich variety of plants—sources for both dyestuffs and design inspiration. Japanese textiles, more than those of any other country, reflect the need for and appreciation of nature that is experienced by so many humans. Japanese designers have been most adept in transmitting that feeling to textiles, and the traditional kimono is a perfect canvas for asymmetrically designed scenes and rhythmic arrangements of plant forms (Plate 63).

The dignified simplicity found in textile design had its origins in Shintoism, the most ancient of Japanese religions. The basic tenet of this polytheistic creed required the offering of thanksgiving and sacrifices to a multitude of natural spirits inhabiting stones, mountain tops, and graves. According to Shinto belief, the sun goddess gave imperial rank to her grandson Jimmu, the first emperor of Japan, sometime between 660 and 60 B.C. He ruled over a people now regarded as a single ethnic group of Mongoloids who had migrated from Manchuria and Korea to join the indigenous Ainu, a Caucasoid people who may be direct descendants of early Neolithic settlers.

Buddhism was introduced into Japan from Korea in the sixth century A.D. In the eighth century, it became the Japanese national religion, although over time there was some merging of Buddhism and Shintoism in everyday religious practices. The Buddhists brought the concept of rank by color from T'ang China. All people below the rank of prince had to wear certain colors according to their position in the royal hierarchy, and one did not wear a color assigned to a higher rank unless he was willing to face arrest.

The school of Zen Buddhism developed in Japan after the late twelfth century. Zen priests played an important role in furthering art and culture, including the Noh (No) dramas and the tea ceremony. The Noh dramas were the pantomimes and tales of ancient legends performed for court amusement and supposedly intelligible only to the aristocracy. Many silk brocades were imported to make the opulent costumes; there were no limits to boldness in color and design and few to the costume budget. Some of the magnificent fabrics were cut from worn costumes and made into robes for Buddhist priests. The tea ceremony, on the other hand, required fabrics of simple weave and pattern and restrained colors.

INDIAN TEXTILE HISTORY

The record of ancient and medieval Indian textiles exists mostly in literature and sculpture. There is archaeological evidence of a cotton textile industry at Mohenjo-Daro in the Indus Valley around 3000 B.C., and a few fragments survive from much later periods. Most of the extant textiles are dated after the seventeenth century, because the monsoon climate has been very destructive to early specimens. The Greeks with Alexander the Great wrote of the fine flowered muslins and robes embroidered in gold they had seen in India. They may also have seen the cotton fiber that grew on trees.

A handbook of administration, the *Arthasastra*, tentatively dated to the third century B.C.,[1] dealt with methods for distributing materials to spinners and weavers whether the workers were guild members or worked privately at home. At that time few occupations were open to women. Indeed, women who elected not to marry were not allowed to hold jobs. However, weaving was permitted to widows and retired prostitutes. The *Arthasastra* gave the penalties for fraudulent practices and listed the taxes to be paid by weavers. Among the textiles mentioned were white bark cloth from Bengal, linen from Banaras, cottons from south India, and several kinds of blankets, the best described as being slippery and soft.

In ancient and medieval India the textile industries were politically controlled, and if a ruler was favorably disposed towards the arts, weaving prospered. Differentiation was made between the rural textiles woven for the masses and those made in state workshops for royalty and the well-to-do in other countries (Plate 48). The best workmanship was found in the ritual hangings for temples, and even in modern times it has been considered preferable to destroy worn ones rather than allow them to fall into foreign hands.

Few good commentaries survive from the early medieval period (900–1200 A.D.) when terms were used inconsistently. Fabric names apparently represented the places where they were woven, and details about weaving techniques were scanty.

The Muslim period in India extended from around 1200 A.D. to 1760 when the British took over. A succession of sultans controlled most of India until Genghis Khan attacked early in the thirteenth century and Tammerlane invaded in the late fourteenth. Marco Polo left detailed accounts of the people and industries of the coastal regions of India in the late thirteenth century. He mentioned seeing on the Coromandel Coast the finest and most beautiful cloth in all the world—buckrams like the tissues of spider webs, and he observed dyeing with indigo in the great textile center of Cambay and spinning of cotton in Gujarat. Under the Sultan of Delhi (1325-1351) price controls for food, cloth, and other commodities were initiated to help fight inflation. A permit was required to buy silks, satins, and brocades, and only the well-to-do were allowed to have them. The sultan employed four thousand silk weavers who made robes of honor, hangings, and gifts of gold brocade for foreign dignitaries.

Babur, a descendant of Genghis Khan, founded a new and important dynasty, the Mogul, in 1526. A series of great rulers—the greatest Akbar who ruled for the second half of the sixteenth century—governed a glorious empire where the textile arts flourished until the late seventeenth century. Some of the best accounts of Indian textiles were written by European ambassadors to the Mogul courts. Fabulous horse and elephant trappings, as well as the apparel, pillows, and wall hangings, were remarked upon. A king always wore a garment but once. There were marvelous gold brocades called *kimhabs,* or *kincobs,* from Banaras. Writers proclaimed on the sheerness of Dacca muslins, called *evening dew, running water,* or *sweet-like-sherbert.* Seventy-three yards, a yard wide, weighed only one pound. By comparison, the finest Swiss cottons ever made were at best sixteen or seventeen yards to the pound.

European settlements appeared in India in the latter part of the Mogul period. Motivated by the desire to break the spice trade monopoly held by Venice and the Arabs, Vasco da Gama found the sea route to India by sailing around Africa in 1498, and by 1510 the Portuguese had jurisdiction in Goa on the west coast of India. For a short time they controlled the Asian trade by taking over the port of Malacca (near Singapore), where they met trading junks from China. The Portuguese carried *pintados* (painted cottons) east from India to trade for spices.

Indian textiles were more important to the Dutch and the English than to the Portuguese. The Dutch East India Company was chartered in 1597, the East India Company in 1600. Their ships went first to India with bullion to exchange for the cotton textiles that could be bartered for spices in the Malay Archipelago. Eventually, the Dutch gained a monopoly in Indonesia, with trade centered in Java, and the English withdrew to India to establish trading stations known as "factories." One of the intentions of the East India Company was to sell English woolens in Asia, but broadcloth was never more than a novelty in India. By 1649 the British were sending chintz (see chapter 4) and cheap cotton calico to England. Much was for reexport to America, the Near East, West Africa, and the slave plantations in the West Indies. A four-cornered trade developed. The East India Company shipped calicos to London where they were sold to the Royal Africa Company. The latter shipped them in turn to West Africa as *guinea-cloth* to be bartered for people. These slaves, and any remaining cloth, were shipped to the West Indies and exchanged for sugar, cotton, and tobacco—all cargoes bound back for England.

Contemporary Indian Textiles

Where tradition, not fashion, rules, concentration on the aesthetic can prevail instead of mere change. Indian textile heritage has been preserved by the woman's sari, which often exhibits fine weaving, delicate textures, beautiful colors, and rich patterns (Plate 49). A formal sari might be of silk (or a cotton called *jamdani),* brocaded in floral patterns formed with many tiny bobbins, each holding a different color. An everyday sari could be a simple striped or checked cotton or a solid made iridescent by having the warp of one color, the weft of another. Sometimes saris are exquisitely block printed with gold or silver floral sprays or show allover spot patterns of tie-dye. Ikat is used for traditional diamond or trellis patterns.

Embroidery is important in India and there are many regional styles. Sometimes it is the work of village women; other times it is done by male professionals. There is a vast difference between the work that reaches western markets and the fine embroidery, important for its symbolism, that was made for the courts and temples of old India.

Phulkari (flower work) is a specialty of Punjab embroiderers. Bright-colored floss silk is worked on cotton with a darning stitch (Plate 50). Phulkari is sometimes combined with the mirror work that originated when blue and green beetle backs were sewn onto wedding garments of the hill tribes of southern India. Orthodox Hindus disapproved the practice and so pieces of mica were substituted. Eventually the mica was replaced by bits of glass or mirrors.

A type of chain stitch is worked with a hook in Gujarat to make birds, animals, humans, and flowers in bold colors. In the valley of the Ganges plant designs are worked in white on soft fabrics using satin stitch, and near Bombay running stitches make delightful animal figures on loosely woven cotton. The cross stitch is popular all across India.

Carpets are still made in India, as they have been for hundreds of years. Most are made with knotted wool pile on a cotton back. Patterns are strongly Persian but show a preference for naturalistic plants and animals.

THE SHAWLS OF KASHMIR

In the nineteenth century a Kashmir shawl was one of the rarest and most beautiful gifts that could be offered to any woman (Plate 51). The romantic appeal was enhanced by descriptions of the Vale of Kashmir, known as one of the dream spots of the earth. Isolated by the Himalayas, too remote to be of much interest to the conquerors who passed back and forth across Asia, Kashmir served for hundreds of years as a resort for India's nobility.

Woolen blankets and shawls were woven and exported to the Roman Empire, but the Kashmir industry became famous after Zain-ul'Abidin (1420-1470 A.D.) brought in Turkestanni and Persian weavers. By the sixteenth century shawls were being hoarded as forms of wealth, and in the late seventeenth Western visitors reported seeing men wearing large decorative scarves across their shoulders. Toward the end of the eighteenth century European and New England ladies discovered "India" shawls; the soft fabric draped beautifully, the colors shimmered, and the pine patterns spoke of the mysterious East. Discerning ambassadors and sea captains carried them home, and a fashion took hold. Napoleon's officers in Egypt sent them to their French ladies around the turn of the century. Josephine owned three or four hundred Kashmirs.

Fibers and Yarns

The fiber, called *cashmere* (after the old spelling of Kashmir) or *pashmina* (derived from the Persian *pashm*), was combed from the undercoat of the Tibetan or Central Asian goat. The goats were not raised in Kashmir; the fiber was imported from nearby Tibet. Other fiber, molted from wild sheep and goats of the high Himalayas, was specially prized for so-called "ring shawls," so fine they could be drawn through finger rings. Women picked and sorted the pashmina, then spun it into 2,500 yard lengths on crude charkhas (see Figure 2.5). The yarn went to the dyers who used some 300 tints in Mogul times, but only about sixty by the beginning of the nineteenth century, when indigo, logwood, carthemus, saffron, and cochineal were among the dyes identified by Western visitors. The delicate colors were made fast by the special waters of Dal Lake.

Making the Shawls

By the beginning of the nineteenth century, shawl weaving involved several specialists. The warp maker cut the yarns into three and one-half-yard lengths and plied them. Then the warp dresser sized the yarns with rice water and the warp threader prepared the loom. The pattern designer made the design in black and white, and he and the colorist dictated the colors and numbers of threads to be used to a scribe who wrote it down in a kind of shorthand.[2] The weavers wound their weft yarns on many bobbins, small pieces of wood with ends charred so as not to damage the weaving.

Tilikar (or *kani*) shawls were made in interlocking twill tapestry, a technique that probably originated in central or western Asia. Each shawl was woven very slowly, face down on a single horizontal loom by one, two, or three weavers. As demand grew, several looms and weavers were employed to make one shawl, a patchwork, easily identified because it would not lie flat (Plate 51).

After weaving, the shawl was turned over to the cleaner who cut loose threads, and then it went to the mender, the *rafugar*, who touched up with needlework. The shawl was registered and a tax assessed. Then it was washed, stretched, and packed for export. Prices could be as high as several thousand dollars if the shawl were large and intricately woven. The brokers and the tax collectors, not the weavers, made the profits; the weaver was often the first to die in a famine.

In 1803, an enterprising Armenian representing a Turkish firm in Constantinople introduced the *amli* (embroidered) shawl. One could be produced at a third the cost of a kani and at first they were not taxed. The early ones were exquisitely worked, but by the late nineteenth century embroidery degenerated into cheap and coarse chain stitch designs on rough cloth.

Shawl Design

There are several stories giving the origin of the cone design associated with Kashmir shawls (Plate 51). It is at least as old as sixth century Egypt and Sassanian Persia, where it appeared as a curled leaf motif, and it is very common today. One theory is that it derived from the cone of the date palm and symbolized fertility and renewal of life in ancient Chaldea. Another theory dates the motif to the Mogul Emperor Babur who wore in his turban a jeweled ornament, almond shaped with an aigrette of feathers.[3] A weaver purportedly copied it and started a fad. The motif has been said to represent the picturesque windings of the Jhelum River, the side impression of a fist (fist palm), a little onion (in Venice), the Persian sacred flame, the wind-blown cypress, a mango (Hindu Kairy), a butha (or buta, a general Indian name for flower), and a cone or a pine. In the West it is called a paisley.

Kashmir shawl designs were mostly floral until the middle of the eighteenth century, when they began to take on the characteristic cone arrangements. Cones were rather short and fat until the 1830s, when they became elongated with slender tips. By the 1850s they were almost abstract scrolls. Many shawl designs originated in Europe, and at one time Frenchmen went to Kashmir with the purpose of improving the patterns.

Famine struck Kashmir periodically, but never devastated the weavers as completely as in the 1870s when the Franco-Prussian War closed the French market and the fashion for Kashmir shawls died.

CHINESE TEXTILE HISTORY

Chinese chronology divides into dynasties, or periods of rule by members of the same family. Although no fabrics survive from the Shang dynasty (1523-1028 B.C.), pseudomorphs of textiles used to wrap elaborately cast bronzes have yielded some information about fibers and weaves. The pseudomorphs are the result of the organic structure of the textiles being replaced by the products of bronze corrosion.[4] The Chou dynasty (1122-256 B.C.) is important in that it coincided with the Scythian period in Central Asia. Chinese figured silks and embroideries were found in Scythian graves, indicating the extent of Chinese trade at that time.

Han Silks

The Han dynasty (202 B.C.-220 A.D.) is one of the most important for textile historians. It was a period of great political and social change, and one of the great periods in Chinese history when the arts were highly advanced. This has been demonstrated by the 1968 excavation near Peking of the tomb of a Han prince and his consort. Her funeral suit was made of over two thousand jade tablets stitched together with gold wire.

Sir Marc Aurel Stein, an early twentieth century archaeologist, was responsible

PLATE 46 / A Florentine orphrey (a band on a religious garment) of
brocatelle construction depicting the Assumption, circa fifteenth century.
42½" x 9¼". (Courtesy of The Detroit Institute of Arts. City Purchase)

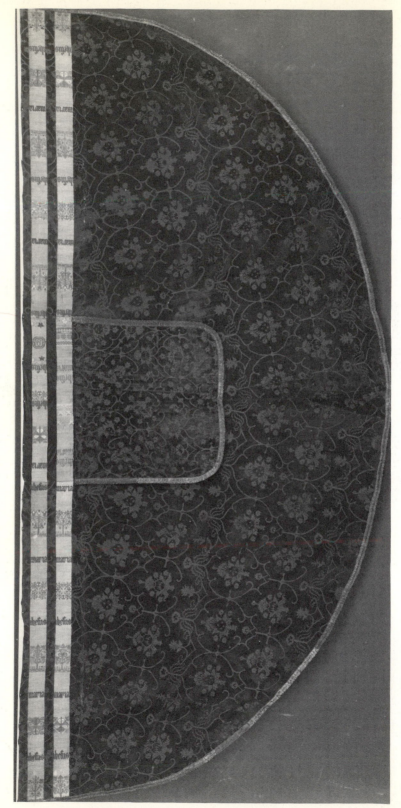

PLATE 47 / Late fifteenth century Italian cope. 111″ x 51½″. (Courtesy of The Detroit Institute of Arts. Gift of Mr. and Mrs. Edsel B. Ford)

PLATE 48 (*above*) / An Indian weaving shop, from Gilroy's *History of Silk, Cotton, Linen, Wool, and Other Fibrous Substances* (1845).

PLATE 49 (*right*) / Indian brocade from the *Journal of Indian Textile History*.

PLATE 50 (*below*) / Phulkari embroidery from the *Journal of Indian Art and Industry*.

PLATE 51a (*left*) / Kashmir shawl.

PLATE 51b (*right*) / Detail of the Kashmir shawl.

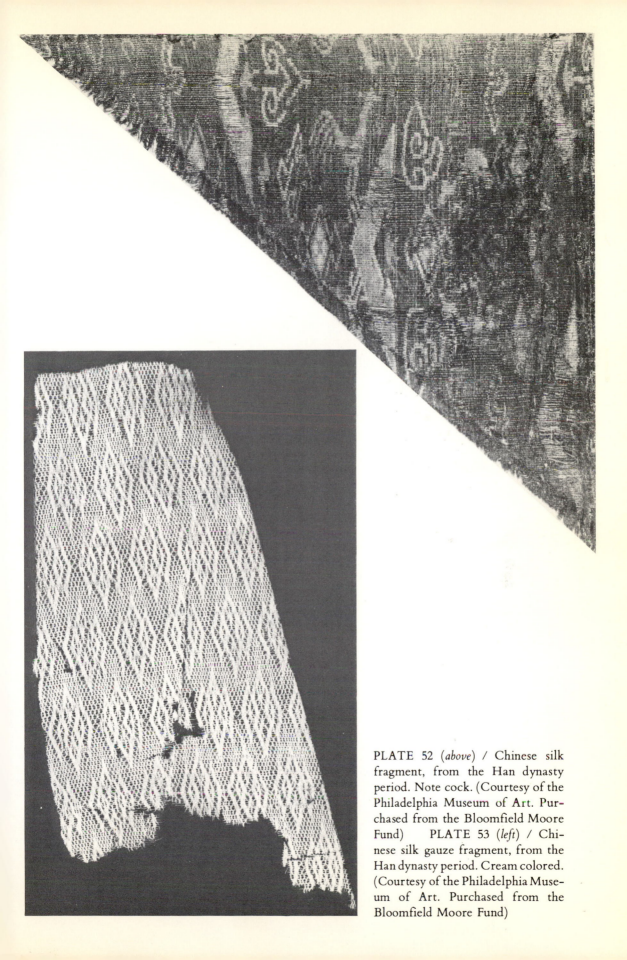

PLATE 52 (*above*) / Chinese silk fragment, from the Han dynasty period. Note cock. (Courtesy of the Philadelphia Museum of Art. Purchased from the Bloomfield Moore Fund)   PLATE 53 (*left*) / Chinese silk gauze fragment, from the Han dynasty period. Cream colored. (Courtesy of the Philadelphia Museum of Art. Purchased from the Bloomfield Moore Fund)

PLATE 54a (*above*) / "Cock on Drum Calling the Faithful to Prayer," from an eighteenth century Japanese tsuzure-ori in the Ming style. PLATE 54b (*below*) / A detail from the Japanese tsuzure-ori showing the slit tapestry construction also characteristic of Chinese k'o-ssu.

PLATE 55 / Chinese velvet hanging. (Crown Copyright. Victoria and Albert Museum)

PLATE 56 (*above*) / Seventeenth century Chinese damask. (Crown Copyright. Victoria and Albert Museum)   PLATE 57 (*below*) / Ming dynasty silk. Yellow ground with blue, red, green, pink, and white design, and gold thread. (Courtesy of The Metropolitan Museum of Art, Fletcher Fund, 1934)

PLATE 58 / Ch'ing embroidery.

PLATE 59 (*above*) / Seventeenth or eighteenth century Chinese dragon roundel and diaper silk. (Courtesy of The Metropolitan Museum of Art, Gift of Mrs. Nellie B. Hussey, 1942)
PLATE 60 (*below*) / Detail of a seventeenth century Japanese priest's robe in gold brocade from the Nishijin Looms, Kyoto. (Courtesy of the Metropolitan Museum of Art, Purchase, Pulitzer Bequest, 1919)

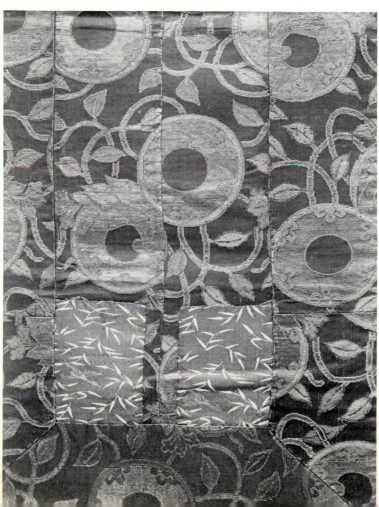

PLATE 61 / Detail of a seventeenth century Japanese Noh-dance robe in a gold brocade called *kara-ori*. (Courtesy of The Metropolitan Museum of Art, Rogers Fund, 1919)

PLATE 62 / A nineteenth century Japanese brocade. (Courtesy of The Metropolitan Museum of Art, Gift of Mr. and Mrs. H. O. Havemeyer, 1896)

PLATE 63 / Silk kimono from the first half of the eighteenth century. Red rinsu (crepe) damask with pattern of orchids and chrysanthemums of fret ground and embroidery. (Courtesy of the Royal Ontario Museum, Toronto. Gift of Mrs. Edgar J. Stone)

PLATE 64 / Boy's kimono with samurai arms and armor, showing Yuzen dyeing and embroidery. (Courtesy of The Textile Museum, Washington, D.C. T.M. 1973.18.5 Gift from Mrs. Marcia T. Lystad)

PLATE 65 / One of the pagan heroes, Julius Caesar, from The Heroes Tapestries of Paris, last quarter of the fourteenth century. (Courtesy of The Metropolitan Museum of Art, The Cloisters Collection, Gift of John D. Rockefeller, Jr., 1947)

PLATE 66 / The Unicorn in Captivity from The Hunt of the Unicorn, VII. Wool and silk
with metal threads. A French or Flemish work of the late fifteenth century, from the
Chateau of Verteuil. (Courtesy of The Metropolitan Museum of Art, the Cloisters
Collection, Gift of John D. Rockefeller, Jr., 1937)

for the major collections of Han textiles now found outside China.[5] Stein excavated along the Silk Road and provided vivid descriptions of the terrible Tarim Basin (see Figure 2.16), Lou Lan (the City of the Dead), and the magnificent figured silks, embroideries, tapestries, and gauzes that had been on their way to Rome (Plates 52, 53). Some of the walled outposts, once manned by prisoners and outcasts from Chinese society, have yielded an amazing variety of textile fragments. These specimens seem to prove that the Chinese mastered pattern weaving long before the West.

The outstanding weave of the Han dynasty, and a weave unequaled in later periods, is best described as a compound warp-faced tabby. It is a rep construction (more warp than weft) and the patterns were made by floating pattern warps. Because similar patterns were later made in Damascus, these Han silks came to be called damasks even though they were polychrome—not monochrome as damask usually is. They were probably woven on a pattern rod loom not a drawloom.[6] Patterns of lozenges, birds, trees, and animals integrated by cloud bands or scrolls were common.

Gauze weave was probably an innovation of the Han dynasty. Made with a special device to move the warp, the leno construction gave firmness to low count, lacy fabrics, which were patterned with lozenges. Gauze continued to be woven into the twentieth century and was used for summer robes that were frequently embroidered.

T'ang Textiles

All through the Six Dynasties, a period of internal disunity and strife, the Han textile techniques were preserved and then were carried on into the T'ang dynasty (618-906 A.D.) The T'ang was another great period in Chinese history, marked by prosperity and an expansion of the empire. Trade with India was developed. A money economy replaced a barter economy when the government lost control of the major silk producing center in Hopeh. Prior to that rolls of silk were used as the means of exchange or for storing wealth. A network of small rural markets fed the larger centers, and exports increased until the Central Asian routes were closed by the barbarians.

Weft-faced compound twills are associated with the T'ang dynasty. They are known today from fragments found along the Silk Road and from textiles in the Shosoin, an eighth century repository in Nara, Japan. This weave may have developed in the Near East and spread eastward with the drawloom, but textile historians have no conclusive proof. The patterns on T'ang figured fabrics are quite different from those on the warp-faced Han textiles. Motifs reflect the adoption of Buddhist, Indian, Sassanian, and Hellenistic elements. Animals are arranged symmetrically, usually facing each other (affronté). Vines and rosette medallions are characteristic.

It was during the T'ang dynasty that *k'o-ssu,* the most highly prized fabric of China (and indeed the entire world), was first woven. It is likely that the tapestry technique used in k'o-ssu originated in Syrian wool weaving. When adapted to silk, it made superlative document covers, hangings, and robes that sometimes cannot be distinguished from paintings. The word k'o-ssu meant broken or cracked silk and referred to the tiny slits formed along the design edges giving a clever three-dimensional effect (Plate 54).

The imperial families of other dynasties encouraged silk tapestry weaving. During the fifteenth century some of the finest k'o-ssu was made when the famous weavers of South China were assembled in Peking to reproduce the great pictures of the T'ang dynasty. A weaver might spend his entire lifetime on one commemorative hanging or imperial robe. K'o-ssu was the single fabric too highly esteemed by the Chinese to be included among their exports.

Sung Silks

The China of the Sung dynasty (960-1279 A.D.) was far ahead of its contemporary states. Agricultural innovations (including cotton cultivation) and advanced manufacturing techniques raised the standard of living. Transportation facilities improved and sea trade expanded. Literacy and education spread with the development of block printing. Paradoxically, sex segregation increased and the practice of foot binding, which effectively crippled women, became widespread.

Satin, which may have originated in Zatun, was important during the Sung dynasty. Genghis Khan probably introduced satin to Europe in the thirteenth century; it made wondrous banners. Sung weavers made elaborate brocaded satins.

The earliest extant brocades come from the Sung dynasty, although the weave was probably known in China as early as the Han period. Over fifty T'ang brocade patterns were recorded in a Sung book, two of them named "dragon coiling through a hundred flowers" and "wild geese flying into clouds." Yarns of strap gold—gilded leather strips—were used for brocade wefts.

Yuan and Ming Textiles

The Yuan dynasty (1279-1368 A.D.) was founded by Kublai Khan in completing the Mongol conquest of China. It was in Kublai Khan's court that Marco Polo spent seventeen years as an advisor of privileged position. During the Yuan dynasty the Asian trade routes, formerly closed by the barbarians, reopened.

The Ming (1368-1644 A.D.) drove out the Mongols and closed China to the rest of the world, bringing a stable period when the arts were patronized on a large scale and standards were high. The period is probably most famous for the fine quality porcelains sent to Europe in the seventeenth century.

Velvet was probably woven in China for the first time when the Portuguese brought Spanish velvets in the late sixteenth century, although it is also possible that the technique reached China from Persia via Central Asia during the Yuan dynasty. There was a limited number of velvet weaving centers, and it was strictly a luxury fabric (Plate 55). The Chinese became adept at both painting and embroidering it. A variety of other weaves can also be seen in the Yuan and Ming textiles dispersed around the world. Some of the most intricate are found in European churches where they have been carefully preserved. Because silk is a very perishable fiber, especially with continued exposure to light, many hangings have disintegrated. (Plates 56 and 57).

The Ming were famous for embroidery. The technique, very adaptable for the rendering of symbolic motifs, predated the Han dynasty. (Stein found chain stitch embroidery in Han graves.) Later, embroidery was combined with painting and worked on figured cloth, making design upon design.

Just as in early America, every Chinese girl learned to embroider. Peasants did a cross stitch with indigo yarn on homespun cotton and grass cloth for bed hangings and squares to pin on dress fronts. The embroidery told stories or offered felicitations. More sophisticated silks were done in satin, stem, long and short, and Peking stitches. The last, actually a French knot, was known as "the forbidden stitch," because it eventually was banned when women went blind doing it. Couching, especially with gold thread, and appliqué were common.

Purely Chinese were the Mandarin squares (pectorals) embroidered with animals and other symbols used to identify the ranks of various officials. The squares were worn front and back on the full robes of Chinese dignitaries. When the Manchus came to power the emblems of the Ming were rendered obsolete and sold off in the West.

Ch'ing Design

The Ch'ing dynasty (1644–1912 A.D.) was the period of rule by the Manchus, ancestors of the present-day Manchurians. The crafts were most important during the eighteenth century when the largest amount of Chinese fabric was exported to Europe. There were several large textile centers with factory-type operations making textiles for export, while fabrics for home consumption and the Chinese court were made in smaller workshops. Embroidery was delightful (Plate 58). Ch'ing textiles also reflected many centuries of symbolism.

Some of the oldest motifs were the "twelve ornaments" that represented authority and power. The emperor wore all twelve. Buddhists used the "Eight Emblems of Happy Augury" (Figure 7.2), and Confucians the "Eight Precious Things" (Figure 7.3). The Taoists used the "Eight Emblems of the Immortals" (Figure 7.4). In later periods there was a tendency to mix all the figures, especially on exports.

The *feng-huang,* a gaily colored bird with long fluttering tail feathers and a two-horned crest, had character. His appearance was modified from time to time, and in later years he was known as the phoenix, symbol of peace and prosperity, yang and yin. The *duck* spoke of felicity and married love, and the *khi-lin,* a sort of antelope with an ox tail, or little scaly horse with horns, brought good luck. The *dragon,* of course, was China (Plates 55 and 59).

Dragons lived in rivers, the sea, and the sky. They had families, just like

FIGURE 7.2 / Buddhist Emblems (from Hackmack, 1973).

mortals, and they loved them in the same way. Dragons controlled the winds, the thunder, the rains, and the rising flood waters. Usually Chinese dragons were benevolent—unless provoked. There were two kinds: The *lung,* with five claws, horns, scales, and a moustache—worn by the emperor and his close family; and the *mang,* more serpent-like with four toes or claws, worn by nobles of lesser rank. There were lots of rules concerning who could wear what kind and how many dragons on his robes until the revolution in 1911.

JAPANESE TEXTILE HISTORY

Very little is known about the history of Japan before the eighth century. The early Japanese made cloth from hemp, ramie, mulberry, and wisteria vine fiber. Silk was not known until the second century A.D., when the Chinese sent silkworm eggs and woven silk was imported from Korea. In the fourth and fifth centuries Chinese and Korean weavers emigrated to Japan where they were given land and titles in exchange for their knowledge.

Nara Textiles

The Nara period (710-785 A.D.) was a brief but golden time in Japanese history.

FIGURE 7.3 / Confucian Emblems (from Hackmack, 1973).

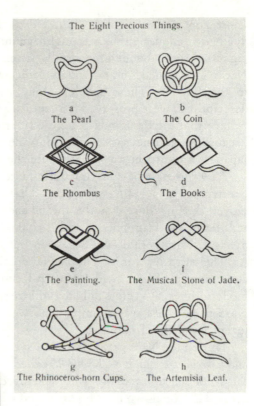

The Eight Precious Things.

a	b
The Pearl	The Coin
c	d
The Rhombus	The Books
e	f
The Painting.	The Musical Stone of Jade.
g	h
The Rhinoceros-horn Cups.	The Artemisia Leaf.

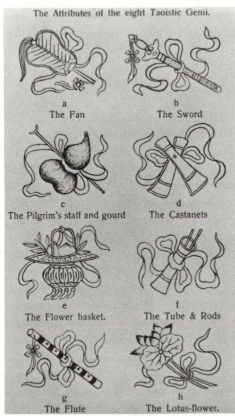

The Attributes of the eight Taoistic Genii.

a	b
The Fan	The Sword
c	d
The Pilgrim's staff and gourd	The Castanets
e	f
The Flower basket.	The Tube & Rods
g	h
The Flute	The Lotus-flower.

FIGURE 7.4 / Taoist Emblems (from Hackmack, 1973).

Close contact with T'ang China led to the development of many weaving and dyeing techniques. In the mid–eighth century, the Emperor Shomu commissioned a gigantic bronze Buddha for installation in the Shosoin, the imperial repository at Nara. Shomu died, and his widow dedicated his art treasures and household goods to the Buddha. These articles, along with dedicatory records giving detailed descriptions, were preserved for centuries in the sealed building. Western scholars believe that the thousands of textile fragments came mostly from China and Iran, because the Japanese were not using the drawloom in the eighth century. Some Japanese authors, however, attribute the textiles to their own weavers.

Nishiki is an important, if indefinite, term. It has been used as a name for several constructions, including brocade, and has come to mean any textile with a colorful woven design. More exactly, the Japanese use *tate nishiki* for the warp-patterned textiles of the Han dynasty and *nuki nishiki* for weft-patterned silks of the T'ang dynasty, Nara period, and Sassanian Persia.[7]

The word *aya* was used in the Nara period to denote a patterned fabric made by combining plain and twill, or warp-faced and weft-faced twill (like damask). In modern times, aya refers only to twill weave. Gauze fabrics were also woven in the Nara period. *Sha* was a simple leno weave, while *ra* was stiffer and had woven lozenge and floral patterns.

During the Nara period Japanese dyers were adept at *rokechi* (wax resist dyeing) and *kokechi* (tie and dye). *Kyokechi,* called jam dyeing, reached Japan from China in the sixth century and was well developed by the Nara period. Folded cloth was pressed between two boards perforated with designs. The dye entered through the holes.

Heian and Kamakura Textiles

During the Heian period (785-1185 A.D.) Japan turned inward to a life of luxury, overrefinement in ceremonies, and a flourishing textile industry. Costume was voluminous; a lady might wear a dozen layers, with colors delicately coordinated. There are no extant fabrics from this period, but Lady Murasaki's *The Tale of Genji* describes some of the court costumes in detail. The ladies gave up the multitudinous layers for the *kosode,* the small-sleeved kimono, in the *Kamakura* period (1185-1333). Life became more practical; the military controlled the government, and resources were consumed in fending off the Mongols.

During the late Heian period the first real brocade was made in Japan after students brought it back from China. The new fabric was called *kinran* (Plate 60) after its gold threads. An overlay of gold foil was applied to fine tough paper made from mulberry fiber, and the paper was cut into strips for weft. In the Kamakura period, brocading, painting, and embroidery were used to put the *Mon,* or family crest, on textiles. The designs were used to identify a certain lord, his family, and his servants.

Muromachi and Momoyama Textiles

The *Muromachi* (Ashikaga) period (1334-1573 A.D.) was a time of continued warfare and the flowering of the arts. Almost contemporary with the Ming dynasty, the Muromachi period coincided with two centuries of strife and change in Europe. The Ashikaga moved the capital to Kyoto, a major weaving and embroidery center since the eighth century. Magnificent fabrics were woven for costumes worn in the newly popular Noh dramas. Japan was united in the Momoyama period (1573-1615 A.D.) and industry prospered. Each year trading ships carried Japanese goods to southeast Asian ports, and soon Europeans were in Nagasaki seeking Japanese silks.

Seigo, a stiff silk that made trousers stand straight out sideways and *yukata,* a soft cotton crepe weave made with irregular floats, were two quite contrasting Muramachi fabrics. Cotton was also used for warp in a silk tapestry called *tsuzure nishiki.* The Japanese called it "fingernail tapestry," because the weavers battened the weft with long, specially grooved nails. Tsuzure nishiki was a development of *tsuzure-ori* (linked weaving), copied from and nearly identical to Chinese k'o-ssu (Plate 54).

Brocades were important during the Muramachi and Momoyama periods, when Ming imports were copied. A most sumptuous gold brocade, *kara-ori* (Plate 61) was woven with satin design on a twill ground and had elaborate plant, animal, and bird designs (Plate 62).

Velvet *(birodo)* belongs to the late Momoyama and early Edo periods. Several stories were told about how the Japanese first learned to make it—one that a Chinese weaver happened to leave in one of the wires used to hold up the pile warp. The Japanese invented a method for resist dyeing velvets woven with delicate floral patterns.

Edo Dyeing

During the *Edo* (Tokugawa) period (1615-1867 A.D.) Japan closed its doors to the outside world and artistic extravagance was patronized in courts set up at Edo (Tokyo) to occupy the feudal lords. Although some trade with the Dutch continued, the quantity of textiles that reached the West was small until Commodore Perry opened Japan to American trade in 1854.

Thus, Edo fabrics were made for the Japanese alone, and as the period advanced textile artists turned to age-old dyeing techniques and used them with a perfection unrivaled anywhere. Ikat (Kasuri), tie-dyeing (Plate 63), jam dyeing, and block printing were well developed.

A famous fabric of the Edo period, and one still popular for the ceremonial kimono, is *Yuzen* work (Plate 64). A seventeenth century fan painter, Miyazaki Yuzen, perfected an old method for applying resist paste with sharpened sticks in order to retain very precise design outlines. He was also adept at "twilight dyeing"—one color shaded off into an entirely different one. Yuzen published a catalog of kimono designs for which his dealers took orders. Many individual designs were available, bamboo and plum blossoms ranking highest. Ideographs telling messages such as "I like a fight" remind us of the screen-printed T-shirts of the 1970s. The beautiful stencils used to apply resist paste have been collected as art objects. Very thin paper layers are reinforced with webs of hair, so fine as not to hinder the work.

Japanese design is a combination of native and Chinese motifs. Stories of filial affection, Chinese legend, Japanese mythology, tales of chivalry, fantastic creatures, plants both naturalistic and symbolic have all been represented on Japanese textiles. During the second half of the nineteenth century Japanese design had a particularly strong influence on Western art and interior decoration, giving rise to a style called Japonaiserie.

NOTES

1. Romila Thapar, "State Weaving-Shops of the Mauryan Period," *Journal of Indian Textile History* 5 (1960):51.

2. Luther Hooper, *Hand-Loom Weaving: Plain and Ornamental* (London: Sir Isaac Pitman & Sons, 1910), pp. 157-158.

3. Mita K. Parekh, "Identification of Nineteen Shawls from the Drexel Historic Costume Collection" (Master's thesis, Drexel Institute of Technology, 1961), p. 28.

4. John Vollmer, "Textile Pseudomorphs on Chinese Bronzes," in *Irene Emery Roundtable on Museum Textiles 1974 Proceedings: Archaeological Textiles,* ed. Patricia L. Fiske (Washington, D. C.: The Textile Museum, 1975), pp. 170-174.

5. Marc Aurel Stein wrote several books including *Serinda* (Oxford: Clarendon Press, 1921); *Innermost Asia* (Oxford: Clarendon Press, 1928); and *On Ancient Central-Asian Tracks* (London: Macmillan, 1933).

6. Krishna Riboud, "Techniques and Problems Encountered in Certain Han and T'ang Specimens," in *Irene Emery Roundtable.* p. 156.

7. Shosoin Office, ed., *Treasures of the Shosoin* (Tokyo: Asahi Shimbun Publishing Co., 1965), p. 90.

BIBLIOGRAPHY

Textile study should not be divorced from costume study, and this is particularly true of India. Jamila B. Bhushan, *Costume and Textiles of India* (Bombay: Taraporevala Sons & Co., 1958) is one of the classic sources and has excellent illustrations. Another is Moti Chandra, *Costumes, Textiles, Cosmetics and Coiffure in Ancient and Mediaeval India* (Delhi: Oriental Publishers, 1973). Chandra also has two important articles in the *Journal of Indian Textile History:* "Indian Costumes and Textiles from the Eighth to the Twelfth Century," no. 5 (1960):1-41; and "Costumes and Textiles in the Sultanate Period," no. 7 (1967):5-61. See

CIBA Review 36 (November 1940) for "Indian Textiles in Indian Costumes."

Rustam J. Mehta, *Masterpieces of Indian Textiles* (Bombay: Taraporevala Sons & Co., 1970) is a very good overview and is helpful for terms. *Textiles and Ornaments of India* (New York: Museum of Modern Art, 1956) has a chapter by Pupul Jayakar ("Indian Fabrics in Indian Life") that is thought provoking, and another chapter by John Irwin ("Indian Textiles in Historical Perspective") that helps relate textiles to Indian traditions. One of their references was John Forbes Watson's several volumes on India written in the 1860s and 1870s. See Watson, *Collection of Specimens and Illustrations of the Textile Manufactures of India,* 4 vols. (London, 1873-1880); and *Textile Manufactures and Costumes of the People of India* (London: India Office, 1866).

Very detailed information on fibers can be found in Jogesh Chandra Ray, "Textile Industry in Ancient India," *Journal of Bihar and Orissa Research Society* 3, pt. 2 (1917):179-245. Romilar Thapar, "State Weaving-Shops of the Mauryan Period," *Journal of Indian Textile History* no. 5 (1960):51-59 has some of the same information and is easier to locate. For an understanding of the craftsman's relation to society see "India, Its Dyers and Its Color Symbolism," *CIBA Review* 2 (October 1937); and Purushattam Jain, *Labor in Ancient India* (New Delhi: Sterling Publishers, 1971).

Vilhelm Slomann, *Bizarre Designs in Silks: Trade and Traditions* (Copenhagen: Ny Carlsberg Foundation, 1953) offers some good background on Mogul textiles. See also the bibliography for painted and printed textiles in chapter 4. Best for trade textiles are John Irwin and Katharine Brett, *Origins of Chintz* (London: Her Majesty's Stationery Office, 1970); and Alice Beer, *Trade Goods* (Washington, D.C.: Smithsonian Institution Press, 1970). John Irwin and P. R. Schwartz, *Studies in Indo-European Textile History* (Ahmedabad, India: Calico Museum of Textiles, 1966) is a superior discussion of trade and includes a glossary of textile terms. The same information is covered by Irwin in a series entitled "Indian Textile Trade in the Seventeenth Century." See the *Journal of Indian Textile History* no. 1 (1955):5-30; no. 2 (1956):24-42; and no. 3 (1957):59-72.

Joan Erikson, *Mātā Nī Pachedi, a Book on the Temple Cloth of the Mother Goddess* (Ahmedabad, India: National Institute of Design, 1968) is a short picture book showing the whole process of block printing. Also useful is Ajit Mookerjee, ed., *Banaras Brocades* (New Delhi: Crafts Museum, 1966).

A major work is John Irwin and Margaret Hall, *Indian Embroideries Vol. 2 Historic Textiles of India at the Calico Museum* (Ahmedabad: The Calico Museum, 1973). It covers court, trade, temple, and folk embroidery and includes a valuable glossary of stitches and terms. "Embroidery in India," *CIBA—GEIGY Review* no. 3 (1972) is outstanding for its colored illustrations.

Various books on oriental carpets have sections on Indian rugs. See the bibliography to chapter 5. Kamaladevi Chattopadhyaya, *Carpets and Floor Coverings of India* (Bombay: Taraporevala Sons & Co., 1969) is comprehensive.

John Irwin is the major authority of Kashmir shawls. The Victoria and Albert Museum (London: Her Majesty's Stationery Office) published his *Shawls: A Study in Indo-European Influences* in 1955 and *The Kashmir Shawl* in 1973. Much of his information came from the manuscripts of an early nineteenth century English traveler to India and Kashmir, William Moorcroft.

A helpful review and catalog, *The Kashmir Shawl,* was published in New Haven, Connecticut in 1975 by the Yale University Art Gallery. Rustam Mehta, *Masterpieces of Indian Textiles,* has a brief overview on shawls, and Thomas W. Leavitt, "Fashion, Commerce and Technology in the Nineteenth Century: The Shawl Trade," *Textile History* 3

(December 1972):51–63 is an overview of Indian (Kashmir), European, and American shawls. Another survey can be found in Katherine Lester and Bess Oerke, *Accessories of Dress* (Peoria, Illinois: Manual Arts Press, 1940), pp. 224–236. An old source, good for terminology, is Margaret King, *Cashmere Shawls* (1892: reprint ed., Cincinnati: The Cincinnati Museum, 1921).

Good for background and interesting general reading on travel in India is Ruth Gallup Armstrong, *Sisters Under the Sari* (Ames, Iowa: The Iowa State University Press, 1964). With a view towards preserving the old craft, Nelly Sethna did an exquisite little book entitled *Shal: Weaves and Embroideries of Kashmir* (New Delhi: Wiley Eastern Private Ltd., 1973) that will be of special interest to designers. Note also the bibliography for Paisley shawls in chapter 8.

Several books on Chinese art include sections on textiles: Martin Feddersen, *Chinese Decorative Art* (New York: Thomas Yoseloff, 1961); Judith and Arthur Hart Burling, *Chinese Art* (New York: The Viking Press, 1953); Stephen W. Bushell, *Chinese Art,* vol. 2 (London: Victoria and Albert Museum, 1924), which is somewhat outdated; and Margaret Jourdain and R. Soame Jenyns, *Chinese Export Art in the Eighteenth Century* (London: Spring Books, 1967).

A classic work is Alan Priest and Pauline Simmons, *Chinese Textiles* (New York: Metropolitan Museum of Art, 1934). This is now available from University Microfilms, Ann Arbor, Michigan. A more recent overview that includes textiles and costume is a booklet by Ernest E. Leavitt, *The Silkworm and the Dragon* (Tucson: Arizona State Museum, 1968). Other good references on costume include Alan Priest, *Costumes from the Forbidden City* (New York: The Metropolitan Museum of Art, 1945); A. C. Scott, *Chinese Costume in Transition* (New York: Theatre Art Books, 1960); and Edmund Capon, *Chinese Court Robes in the Victoria and Albert Museum,* a booklet reprinted from the Museum's *Bulletin* 4, no. 1 (January 1968). (Dragons are usually found in the costume books.)

Han and T'ang textiles have received considerable attention since the explorations of Sir Marc Aurel Stein. His biography, *Sir Aurel Stein: Archeological Explorer* has been written by Jeanette Mirsky (Chicago: The University of Chicago Press, 1977). Frederick H. Andrews described and drew the textiles found by Stein in "Ancient Chinese Figured Silks Excavated by Sir Aurel Stein," *Burlington Magazine* 37 (July 1920):3–10; (August 1920):71–77; (September 1920):147–152. Han and T'ang silks are also discussed and illustrated in "Early Chinese Silks," *CIBA Review* no. 2 (1963). Another important study is Vivi Sylwan, *Woollen Textiles of the Lou-lan People: Reports from the Scientific Expedition to the North-Western Provinces of China* (Stockholm: Tryckeri Aktiebolaget Thule, 1941).

The Stein textiles stored in India have been given close study by Krishna Riboud who wrote several scholarly articles including "Procedures and Results of A Study: Sir Aurel Stein Textile Collection at the National Museum, New Delhi," *Bulletin De Liaison Du Centre International D'Etude Des Textiles Anciens* (CIETA *Bulletin*) no. 2 (1970):24–74, an important source; "Further Indication of Changing Techniques in Figured Silks of the Post-Han Period (A.D. 4th to 6th Century)" in CIETA *Bulletin* (1975), pp. 13–39; and "Techniques and Problems encountered in Certain Han and T'ang Specimens," *Irene Emery Roundtable on Museum Textiles, 1974 Proceedings: Archaeological Textiles,* ed. Patricia L. Fiske (Washington, D.C.: The Textile Museum, 1975), pp. 153–159. Chinese archaeological textiles have been updated in two pieces in Veronika Gervers, ed., *Studies in Textile History* (Toronto: Royal Ontario Museum, 1977): Krishna Riboud, "A Closer View of Early Chinese Silks," pp. 252–280 has excellent photographs; and Hsio-Yen Shih, "Textile Finds in the Peoples' Republic of China," pp. 305–331 is a very detailed listing of various discoveries.

Jean Mailey, *Chinese Silk Tapestry: K'o-ssu from Private and Museum Collections* (New York: China Institute in America, 1971) is an important catalog. K'o-ssu is also covered by Madeleine Jarry, *World Tapestry from its Origins to the Present* (New York: G.P. Putnam's Sons, 1969); and by Kax Wilson in a very short article entitled "K'o-ssu," *Handweaver and Craftsman* 24, no. 4 (August 1973):42.

One general Chinese history that is especially good, because it shows China in its relations with foreigners, is Nigel Cameron, *Barbarians and Mandarins: Thirteen Centuries of Western Travelers in China* (New York and Tokyo: Walker/Weatherhill, 1970). Marco Polo and the textiles he saw are written about in Muriel J. Hughes, "Marco Polo and Medieval Silk," *Textile History* 6 (1975):118-131. Another story about the first Europeans in China, as well as technical analyses of several fabrics, can be found in Harold Burnham, *Chinese Velvets: A Technical Study,* Art and Archaeology Division Royal Ontario Museum Occasional Paper 2 (Toronto: University of Toronto Press, 1959). An interesting account of the Spanish trade with China via Manila is Schuyler Cammann, "Chinese Influence in Colonial Peruvian Tapestries," *Textile Museum Journal* 1, no. 3 (1964):21-34. Another article by Cammann, "A Chinese Textile in Seventeenth Century Spain," *Textile Museum Journal* 1, no. 4 (1965):57-62, has good information about mandarin squares.

Several books on oriental carpets have sections on Chinese rugs; note the bibliography for chapter 5. Others specific to China are Gordon Leitch, *Chinese Rugs* (New York: Dodd, Mead and Co., 1935); Tiffany Studios, *Antique Chinese Rugs* (Rutland, Vermont: Charles Tuttle, 1969); H. A. Lorentz, *A View of Chinese Rugs from the Seventeenth to the Twentieth Century* (London and Boston: Routledge & Kegan Paul, 1972), an excellent study; and Adolf Hackmack, *Chinese Carpets and Rugs* (1924; reprint ed., New York: Dover Publications, 1973). Hackmack is good for design.

Information on design and symbolism can also be found in Otto von Falke, *Decorative Silks* (New York: William Helburn, 1936); Priest, *Chinese Textiles;* Leavitt, *The Silkworm and the Dragon;* "Animal Motifs on Fabrics," *CIBA Review* no. 1 (1967); and Michael Meister's "The Pearl Roundel in Chinese Textile Design," *Ars Orientalis* 8 (1970):255-267. Pauline Simmons, *Chinese Patterned Silks* (New York: The Metropolitan Museum of Art, 1948) is an excellent discussion of design development. A book that includes the symbolism of Chinese ritual robes and k'o-ssu is Bernard Vuilleumier, *The Art of Silk Weaving in China* (London: The China Institute, 1939). Check, too, C. A. S. Williams, *Outlines of Chinese Symbolism and Art Motives* (1931; reprint ed., New York: Dover Publications, 1977).

Helen Benton Minnich, *Japanese Costume and the Makers of its Elegant Tradition* (Rutland, Vermont and Tokyo: Charles E. Tuttle Co., 1963) is excellent, because it clarifies many of the nomenclature problems that have arisen in Japanese textile research. (The Westerner's lack of ability to read Japanese is a principal factor). Minnich also employs superior illustrations. Another very good reference, especially for plates of kimonos and Noh robes, is Seiroku Noma, *Japanese Costume and Textile Arts* (New York: Weatherhill, 1974). Helen Cowan Gunsaulus, *Japanese Textiles* (New York: Japanese Society of America, 1941) is a valuable book with splendid plates; she concentrates on Noh robes. Two small books were published by Charles E. Tuttle in Rutland, Vermont: *Textiles and Lacquer: Pageant of Japanese Art* by the Tokyo National Museum staff (1953); and Tomoyuki Yamanobe, *Textiles* (1957). One of the F. Lewis series, published at Leigh-on-Sea, England in 1958, is Katsutoshi Nomachi, *Japanese Textiles.* The text is short, the illustrations numerous. In 1920 the Victoria and Albert Museum published its *Guide to the Japanese Textiles,* by A. P. H. Smith and Albert Koop.

Several books on Japanese art have sections on textiles. See H. Batterson Boger, *The*

Traditional Arts of Japan (Garden City, N.Y.: Doubleday and Co., 1964), pp. 277-286; Martin Feddersen, *Japanese Decorative Art* (New York: Thomas Yoseloff, 1962), pp. 208-218, good for dating, iconography, and bibliography; and Alex Newman and Egerton Ryerson, *Japanese Art: A Collector's Guide* (New York: A. S. Barnes and Co., 1966) with a good glossary of costume and textile terms.

For exceptional color plates and descriptions of the Nara textiles see the Shosoin Office, ed., *Treasures of the Shosoin* (Tokyo: Asahi Shimbun Publishing Co., 1965). Mosataha Ogawa, *The Enduring Crafts of Japan* (New York and Tokyo: Walker/Weatherhill, 1968) is a fascinating study of elder craftsmen who were designated living national treasures, because they studied and preserved the traditional methods. The photographs in this book are important documents.

An old reference, Shojiro Nomura, *An Historical Sketch of Nishiki and Kinran Brocades* (Boston, 1914) includes a catalog of 120 rare brocades dating from the fifteenth to the nineteenth century. Mr. Nomura, who served as Helen Minnich's mentor, also published a small booklet by the same title in Kyoto. Ikats are covered in *Japanese Country Textiles,* a booklet by the Royal Ontario Museum (Toronto, 1965); and in Toshio and Reiko Tanaka, *A Study of Okinawan Textile Fabrics* (Tokyo: Meiji-Shobo, 1952). There is a brief introduction in English and a good set of color plates. See *CIBA Review* no. 4 (1967) for "Japanese Resist-dyeing Techniques." Stencil dyeing is covered in detail in Frances Blakemore, *Japanese Design through Textile Patterns* (New York and Tokyo: Weatherhill, 1978).

An interesting account of the Asian textile trade is given in Tamezo Osumi, *Printed Cottons of Asia: The Romance of Trade Textiles* (Rutland, Vermont: Charles E. Tuttle Co., 1963). This book has very good plates. See also Katharine B. Brett, "The Japanese Style in Indian Chintz Design," *Journal of Indian Textile History* no. 5 (1960):42-50.

8. TEXTILES IN NORTHERN EUROPE

The focus on cloth production shifted northward from Spain and Italy after the sixteenth century. During the early modern period change in the textile industries was most pronounced in the British Isles, although France, Switzerland, and the Low Countries also witnessed many innovations in cloth making. Increasing populations created not only larger markets for textiles but also labor surpluses and attendant social problems.

TEXTILE PRODUCTION

Decline of the Guilds

Changes in the guild system began to occur in the mid-fifteenth century. States became more powerful, and individual cities and guilds lost ground to them in regulating wages and working hours. Internal problems of narrow traditionalism, bickering between crafts, lack of solidarity in the hierarchy, and corruption by money and family interests reduced guild effectiveness. Decay became more rapid in the sixteenth century. Surplus journeymen moved to the suburbs of London, Paris, and other towns, where they could escape jurisdiction of city council and guild leaders. There, they set up as small masters. Cloth production was to spread farther into the country giving rise to the domestic, or putting-out, system. Clothiers bought raw wool for distribution to spinners, then sent the yarn out to weavers. The domestic system served to accelerate the concentration of capital within the merchant classes.

The sixteenth century brought other changes. Fashion change accelerated with the rising affluence and expectations of the middle class. In England there was increased demand for imports. The Dutch introduced the *new draperies*, lightweight drapable fabrics with worsted warp and woolen weft. A variety of patterns could now be woven in wool. Soon the new draperies were being woven in Lancashire and Norwich (Figure 6.1) by immigrants from the Low Countries. As England became an exporter of woolens and worsteds, money and power were further concentrated with the merchants who gathered cloth for shipment abroad. Guild methods were no longer appropriate, and by the eighteenth century the craft guilds were reduced to being mere professional societies.

New Working Conditions

Meanwhile, labor legislation at a national level increased, especially under the English Tudors. Ostensibly, laws were enacted to protect the poor working class. But more often than not this was not the result. The rural putting-out system spread at an unprecedented rate throughout Europe. It was the ideal system for utilizing household labor, which was relatively low in cost. Gradually, small independent producers were cut off from supplies of raw materials by a growing class of capitalists, the enterpreneur-manufacturers, who tended to control those supplies. Wages were brought down because the guilds had weakened and the working-class population had increased. The cheapest labor was probably that of the inmates of the poorhouses and the many vagrants who roamed the country. Sometimes these people were gathered into large buildings, often unused monasteries, where they were induced to work medieval equipment.

Economic Policies

The seventeenth century saw the start of national economic policies as the great European monarchies gained power. Of real interest is the mercantile system, most highly developed under the guidance of Jean-Baptist Colbert, comptroller general of finances under Louis XIV (1643-1715). Mercantilism (as an economic theory) advocated government regulation of a nation's production and foreign trade in order to increase political power. The balance of trade should be favorable—exports greater than imports. Colonies were to be suppliers of raw materials and consumers of manufactured goods. A strong nation should have a large population of workers to produce goods and soldiers to expand and hold overseas markets. Domestic consumption of imported luxuries should be kept to a minimum, and thrift practiced in order to develop capital. Under the mercantile system production was regulated; there were ordinances specifying lengths and widths for pieces of cloth, dyeing, and finishing methods. Colbert put the textile industry under guild jurisdiction, but red tape and corruption flourished.

England, too, followed a mercantilist policy, although the British monarchy did not have the powers of control held by Louis XIV. The Dutch reached the peak of their glory in the seventeenth century by the pursuit of mercantilist policies. The system seems to have been conducive to innovation, because the seventeenth century saw the production of many new textiles. Frequently, they were substitutes for luxury textiles, for example, new woolens with the gloss of silk.

From about the mid-eighteenth to the late nineteenth century, both France and

England generally subscribed to a policy of laissez-faire. It was now assumed that society would benefit most if individuals were left to pursue their own ends without government interference. Mercantilism gave way to "liberal" economics, and the factory system developed under that doctrine.

The Factory

In the modern sense a factory is defined as a single, permanent site where machines, utilizing power other than human, are tended by large numbers of operators. Considerable amounts of capital are needed for plant and equipment, and rigid organization and specialization are essential for efficiency. Manufacturies, not true factories because there was no central power system, had been known since Roman times. Certainly, fulleries and dyeing establishments were almost factories, and a Muslim tiraz was a place where large numbers of workers gathered and practiced a limited amount of specialization. Many medieval textile workshops fell into the same category.

The advent of the factory system is associated with the Industrial Revolution, which very broadly means the period from about 1760 to the First World War, when industry shifted from a largely rural handicraft system to an urban one dominated by the machine. More narrowly defined, and of greater interest to textile historians, the Industrial Revolution refers to the period of very rapid change in Great Britain (from about 1770 to 1850), when textile production shifted from the home to the factory. Domestic production could no longer supply the demand; it was becoming too expensive to distribute and collect materials from the number of weavers necessary. The increased pilferage of raw materials by workers who needed extra pay was another problem.

The Industrial Revolution doomed many weavers in Britain to a standard of living below the subsistence level. It was the cotton industry that was first to industrialize, but the putting-out system continued in the linen, woolen, and silk industries well into the 1840s. Labor was in such surplus during this period, when large numbers of people were forced to leave agriculture and move to the cities, that many found themselves in the cotton mills. Now there was no home garden or cow to fall back on; housing was crowded and unemployment chronic. For many it was psychologically impossible to adapt to a long regimented day.[1] Factory managers generally considered their workers immoral, uncooperative, and shiftless, and paid the lowest possible wages on that account.

Women and children who had always worked at preparing the fiber and spinning at home went off to the factories for thirteen hour days where they worked for even less than the men earned. One short passage from a report on the condition of the weavers at Spitalfields about 1836 sums up the feelings of a weaver giving testimony on his earnings and those of his wife:

> Q. Have you any children?—A. No; I had two, but they are both dead, thanks be to God!
> Do you express satisfaction at the death of your children?—I do; I thank God

for it. I am relieved from the burden of maintaining them, and they, poor dear creatures, are relieved from the troubles of this mortal life.[2]

The sufferings of textile workers in this period were well described by Charles Dickens and Karl Marx.

The Inventions

Three major factors are said to have been responsible for the Industrial Revolution: the discovery that iron could be smelted by using coke, the invention of the steam engine by James Watt in 1770, and the invention of textile machinery.

The first textile invention of importance was John Kay's flying shuttle (Figure 8.1). In 1733 Kay contrived a very simple arrangement with pulleys and cords and a box at each end of the shuttle race to catch the bobbin. The weaver alternately pulled a handle with one hand and beat up the weft with the other, thus doubling or tripling his weaving speed, sometimes to twenty yards a day. Two weavers were no longer needed to make wide cloth (Figure 8.2). The flying shuttle was quickly adopted, but the industry refused to pay Kay any royalties. He lost most of his money in lawsuits trying to protect his patent and died in poverty in France.

The flying shuttle gave the handweaver a short period of ease. He could earn what he needed with less work; he did not weave more because the spinners could not keep up with him. The beginning of the solution to that problem came with the invention of the spinning jenny by James Hargreaves in 1767 (Figure 8.3). Hargreaves was a poor and uneducated spinner, and according to one story his daughter Jenny knocked over his wheel and the idea of using multiple vertical spindles came to him (the spindle is horizontal in the traditional spinning wheel). Basically, the jenny consisted of a frame holding two racks of spindles, one for partially spun roving and the other for the finished yarn. The operator turned a wheel and a carriage moved out, drawing the roving and imparting twist as the spindles revolved. When the carriage returned, the yarn was wound on the spindles. The jenny worked on the same principle as that of the wool wheel— intermittent spinning—and it could be used at home. Hargreaves made several jennies and sold them. At one stage, a mob of handspinners, fearing loss of their livelihoods, broke into his house and destroyed many of the machines. Eventually Hargreaves died on a poor farm. His jenny increased the supply of weft but was not suitable for making yarn strong enough to be used for warp.

Arkwright's water frame could make warp. Richard Arkwright was a poor barber who traveled widely buying hair for wigs. He heard of the jenny, took over the idea, and worked up a water powered spinning machine with drafting rollers (Figure 8.4). A series of rollers operating at different speeds attenuated the roving while a flyer spindle twisted it. The water frame operated on the same principle as that of the Saxony wheel—continuous spinning. Arkwright is remembered as the father of the Industrial Revolution, because he opened factories where large numbers of his water frames were installed. By 1782 his mills employed 5,000, and

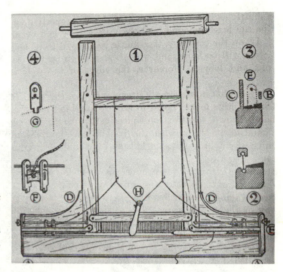

FIGURE 8.1 *(right)* / Flying Shuttle
(from Hooper, 1914). *FIGURE
8.2 (below)* / Weaving Wide Cloth
on a French Broadloom (from Marsden, 1895).

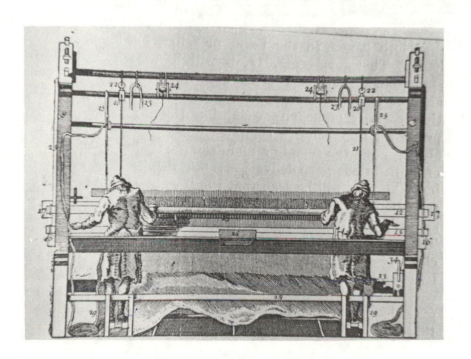

FIGURE 8.3 (*above*) / Spinning
Jenny (from Kissel, 1918).

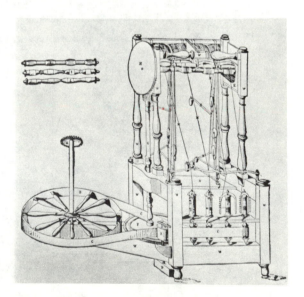

FIGURE 8.4 (*right*) / Arkwright's
Water Frame.

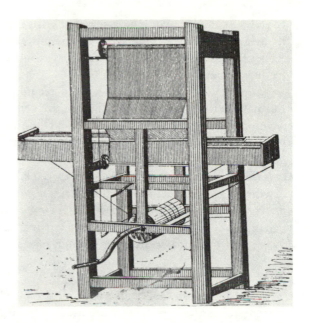

FIGURE 8.5 / Cartwright's
Power Loom (from Kissel, 1918).

Arkwright had become rich.

In 1779 Samuel Crompton carried Arkwright's invention even further and invented the cotton mule, named so because it was a cross between the vertical spindles and the traveling carriage of the jenny and the drafting rollers of the water frame. Very fine yarn could be made quickly, because one spinner could oversee a thousand spindles simultaneously. Crompton was a quiet, introspective man, unfit for business. He gave his machine to the public to avoid its being destroyed and because he could not afford a patent.

Now there was a surplus of yarn. One day in the early 1780s, Edmund Cartwright, a minister and poet, overheard two merchants discussing the problem and asked himself, "Why not harness the loom to power?" Supposedly, Cartwright had never seen a loom, but he was able to build a crude prototype of the modern power loom (Figure 8.5). A major problem with the early models was that they had to be stopped frequently to size the warp or else have two operators in attendance. The invention of the dressing machine in the early nineteenth century made the power loom practical.

There was now too much fabric to be washed, dyed, and finished; and the chemists and engineers were challenged. Eventually, in the 1830s machines and processes came into synchronization, more or less, and home textile crafts declined ever more rapidly.

NORTHERN EUROPEAN TEXTILES

Tapestries

In the opinion of many the machine age brought decadence. The middle class could now demand, and get, cheap art. One ardent enemy of the machine, William

Morris, an Englishman long associated with the arts and crafts movement, helped to bring one ancient craft into the twentieth century by founding the Merton Abbey Tapestry Works in 1881. Tapestry is one textile that continues to be made by medieval methods.

Tapestry construction was an old technique when it was first practiced in Europe (perhaps as early as the eighth century), and it reached its greatest development between the fourteenth and the eighteenth centuries. Tapestries were huge reproductions of paintings (usually made in sets), often to specific measurements so as to fit definite spaces. Nobles had them woven to order for certain residences but would frequently pack them up for a move to a new estate or when they went off to war. Tapestries served as wallpaper, insulation, walls and doors, curtains for cozy alcoves, tributes, and bribes. They were hung from balconies during feast days and served as royal carpets for troops of nobles' horses. Tapestries told stories after the fashion of stained glass windows.

Materials and Weaving

Most European tapestries had wool warp and weft, although some linen, silk, cotton, gold, or silver wefts were used for detail. Silk was especially important in the eighteenth century. Wool took the natural dyestuffs well, and the range of shades increased from about twenty in Gothic tapestries to almost two thousand in eighteenth century weavings. Many of the beautiful colors have since faded, leaving the woad and indigo blues, madder reds, and weld-over-woad greens that now seem to predominate.

Tapestry is the weave that utilizes so many more weft than warp that the warps are completely covered by the wefts. Ribs form in the warp direction; the fewer and coarser the warp, the more prominent the rib. This effect, called *grain*, became finer over the centuries as thread counts increased.

Pattern is formed by discontinuous wefts that interlock, or do not and form slits (see Figure 3.18). Many of the slits are sewn up after the fabric is taken off the loom. *Hachure*, the blending of two different colored wefts, shades and molds figures. *Eccentric* wefts (Plate 115), battened as curves or packed more tightly in some areas than in others, enhance realism.

An outstanding feature of European tapestries is that they are woven with design verticals parallel to the weft. Tapestries are hung with the warp going crosswise. This method of weaving makes it possible to make larger copies of paintings, usually wider than high, and the horizontal ribs create shadows that help round and blend figures into continuous scenes. Unfortunately, the tapestry is less durable hung this way, especially when slits pull apart.

Two kinds of looms are used. The older, perhaps a descendant of the warp-weighted loom, is called the *high-warp* (or *haute-lisse*), and is simply a very heavy two bar loom (Figure 8.6). The *low-warp* (or *basse-lisse*) is a heavy version of the horizontal treadle loom. More accurate work is attributed to the high-warp loom, although weaving on the low-warp is faster. The weaver works from a cartoon, an enlarged color-coded drawing of the design. This hangs on the wall behind the

FIGURE 8.6 / High-Warp
Loom (from Diderot's
encyclopedia).

high-warp weaver and is laid under the warp on the low-warp loom.

In the Middle Ages the weavers wove directly from models, the artists' paintings, and made some of their own adaptations. Next, artists made cartoons by drawing out the designs on canvas the same size as the tapestry. Often several tapestries were woven from the same cartoon, with some variations in borders or details. Thus, tapestry making was the work of two distinct groups, the artists and the weavers, with their tasks spelled out in the guild regulations.

Historical Overview

Although we have documentary evidence of northern European tapestries back to the eighth century, the oldest one extant was made in Cologne early in the eleventh century. It depicts bulls and griffons in medallions, patterns strongly reminiscent of the Syrian and Byzantine. At least three tapestries (two with religious themes) were woven for the Halberstadt Cathedral in the Rhineland in the late twelfth century.

French inventories and a few surviving tapestries give a better picture of the fourteenth century, when the industry was centered in Paris and Flanders. From Paris came the most famous work of the fourteenth century, the Angers *Apocalypse*, woven for the Duke of Anjou by Nicolas Batille in the 1370s. Seven pieces, each a little over sixteen feet high and up to eighty feet in length, made up the original set illustrating the Revelations to St. John.[3] Also famous is the French *Nine Heroes* set, housed in the Cloisters in New York. Both are chivalric in theme (Plate 65).

Arras, in Flanders, was such an important center that its name became synonymous with tapestry: the high-warp luxury tapestry industry was specially promoted there. Arras retained its supremacy in the fifteenth century as the Paris workshops declined in importance, and it was particularly prosperous because of patronage from the dukes of Burgundy. The Burgundians covered their walls with classical mythology, chivalrous romances, and instructive allegories.[4] They owned so many tapestries that they hung them in layers, and Duke Philip the Good had a special building in Arras to house his collection.

Tournai, which made huge tapestries, and Brussels, famous for its reproductions of religious paintings, next took the lead. France again became important, its provincial centers more so than Paris. Tapestries of the fifteenth century are especially rich sources of costume information. They have also been used for botanical research; about one hundred different kinds of plants have been identified in the six large tapestries and fragments that comprise the *Unicorn* set in the Cloisters in New York.[5] These represent the *Millefleur Tapestries*, made in Brussels and in France (Plate 66).

Brussels led the industry in the sixteenth century, because it had the patronage of the papacy and the royal houses of Spain and Austria. The work was controlled by the rich merchants in Brussels, and many regulations were issued to prevent the frauds and forgeries now becoming prevalent. For the first time marks identifying the maker were woven into the tapestries. Designs were monumental.

The rest of the Flemish industry was broken up by the religious persecutions, causing a diffusion of skills; itinerant Flemish masters set up shops in Italy, England, and Germany. The seventeenth century marks a definite shift back to France, because Henry IV, a promoter of arts and crafts, established workshops in the Louvre and encouraged immigration of Flemish weavers. In 1662 Gobelins was established as the royal maufactory under orders of Colbert. The first director was Charles Le Brun, a painter who designed the *Story of Alexander, Life of Louis XIV,* and other famous sets. Gobelin was another word used synonymously with tapestry. Shortly after Gobelins was opened, the workshop at Beauvais was established as a private enterprise administered by Flemings (Plate 67). It was state-subsidized and made tapestries for the nobility and rich bourgeoise. Beauvais was noted for *verdures*, landscapes with vegetation, and *grotesques*, decorative architectural compositions with small figures. The Aubusson workshops opened in 1683 and wove genre scenes and exotic themes depicting India, China, South America, and Africa.

In the eighteenth century French tapestry lost its magnificence and became merely decorative—adapted for the smaller salon. Contemporary military themes and pastoral scenes were popular; religion was out of fashion. Toward the end of the century there was a return to classicism, then the art went into a decline until its revival in the latter part of the nineteenth century.

The Silks of Lyons and Spitalfields

The poor weaver's livelihood depended upon the moods of royalty or the caprices of fashion. A period of mourning could bring famine—a royal wedding, feast. In the seventeenth and eighteenth centuries fashion was more apt to change the fabric—not the cut—of costume, and pirates were always ready to steal a good design and ruin its value by overexposure.

The silk industry had been firmly established in Lyon during the sixteenth century, and the economic policies of Colbert enabled the city to take the lead away from Italian centers in the seventeenth century, at the same time the French tapestry industry was besting that of Flanders. Throughout most of the seventeenth and eighteenth centuries Lyons was the leading producer of drawloom patterned silks in Europe because of the technical skills of her craftsmen and talents of great designers such as Jean Revel (born 1684), Philippe de Lasalle (born 1723), and Jean Pillement (born 1728).

Seventeenth century silk patterns were large and bold, woven on the scale of baroque furniture. Brocades and damasks showed formal floral motifs. Later in the century patterns smaller in scale, but still florals, made their appearance. Around 1700 a number of silks termed "bizarre" were woven (Plate 68). The source of these unusual patterns has not been definitely determined, and there is some interesting controversy about them.[6] Lace-like patterns were popular about this time (Plate 69), then gave way to large naturalistic floral patterns (Plate 70). Popular in the mid-eighteenth century were the chinoiserie patterns showing happy Chinese doing whimsical things. (Note Plates 67 and 74.) The chinoiserie of the seventeenth century had been just as inaccurate in depicting life in the mysterious East. Eighteenth century chinoiserie harmonized with the growing feeling of lightness and delicate charm of rococo pattern. The period of Louis XVI at the end of the eighteenth century brought very dainty textiles with refined floral patterns. Classic motifs, based on the stimulation to designers provided by the excavations at Pompeii and Herculaneum, were woven during this period just before the French Revolution.

In the eighteenth century Lyons had only one serious rival—Spitalfields of England. It was a district outside London, and the site of a twelfth century hospital and house for the needy. So, at one time, the area was known as "hospital fields."[7] Spitalfields and nearby Bethnal Green were settled by French Protestants and Walloons in the 1560s, and populations swelled when many refugees fled to England after the revocation of the Edict of Nantes in 1685.

For the most part the silks woven in Spitalfields were copies of French silks. The only designs unique to Spitalfields were some brocaded florals on light grounds woven in the mid-eighteenth century (Plate 71). Many were *lustrings* (taffetas). Silk was more expensive for the English than for the French, and the best time for the industry in Spitalfields came during the Seven Years' War (1758-1763), when French overseas trade was blocked by English ships.

Spitalfields and Lyons, as well as other European silk weaving centers, were hurt severely by the changes in fashion that brought a preference for cotton fabrics. Many protectionist acts were passed in England, but conditions in Spitalfields continued to worsen until the industry ended there in 1860. Lyons weavers were more prosperous, because they were patronized by Napoleon after the fashion of eighteenth century royalty, and because later they were able to weave new jacquard patterns that appealed to the rich. (Plate 72).

Competition from cotton was not confined to the nineteenth century. The silk weavers had been fighting against cotton since the late seventeenth century.

Printed Linens and Cottons

French Prints

Some of the first painted Indian fabrics to arrive in France were shown at the Saint-Germain fair in 1658. Instantly popular, they were used for furniture covers and draperies, then for dressing gowns. As early as 1675 *indiennes*, inexpensive, poor quality copies of Indian chintz, were being printed in France with wood blocks in fugitive colors.

Alarmed at the competition, silk and tapestry makers prevailed on the comptroller-general of finance, Claude Lepeletier, to issue the October 1686 edict ordering destruction of all blocks and prohibiting the sale of all *toiles peintes* (cloth painted or colored), whether Indian or French, after December 1687. The penalty for disobedience was a heavy fine and having one's shop burned down. At the same time Huguenot printers were leaving for England, Holland, Switzerland, and Germany. The demand for *indiennes* only increased, and there was continued smuggling. Often government agents looked the other way, but at times the ban was enforced. Gowns were ripped from ladies strolling along the boulevard or apartments were invaded and the bed curtains torn away, the owners fined.

From about 1745 on, enforcement was relaxed and printworks began to spring up in France at Mulhouse, Marseilles, Angers, Rouen. In 1759 all restrictions were removed. Of the many new printworks that opened, one of the most important was at Jouy. The term *toiles de Jouy* has become synonymous for monochrome prints showing the typical delightful scenes printed at Jouy (although many of them were printed elsewhere).

The story of Jouy is the story of Christophe-Philippe Oberkampf. His grandfather was a dyer in Wurtemberg, and his father, also a dyer, traveled extensively to learn *indienne* techniques. He discovered the method for printing blue on a white ground and eventually opened a printworks in Wiesenbach, where Christophe was born in 1738. Young Oberkampf started his printing apprenticeship at age eleven, and in 1753 father and son migrated to Switzerland where the father remained.

By 1758 Christophe Oberkampf was in Paris, well-skilled in printing fast colors, *bon teint*, and ready to set up shop the moment it became legal. A site, Jouy-en-Josas (on the Bièvre near Versailles) was chosen, and Oberkampf settled into a tiny home workshop where he was designer, block cutter, printer, and dyer. A series of partners financed the enterprise, and by 1763 it was deemed a success. Favored by queens and countesses, Jouy was granted the special privileges of a Royal Manufactory in 1783.

For over fifty years, until his death in 1815, Oberkampf remained at Jouy, ringing twice daily the bell that summoned and dismissed hundreds of workers. He was an enlightened employer who ran an efficient, paternalistic business and an alert manager willing to adopt new methods. His political dexterity must have been remarkable. After catering to the royal court, he was still able to obtain protection from the Committee of Public Safety by switching to patriotic motifs. As money depreciated during the revolution, he bought cloth and stored it along with the printed goods made by the workers he was reluctant to let go, even though the market was depressed. Later, Oberkampf was able to earn Napolean's favor and the Legion of Honor when Jouy patterns were changed to the classical style.

Oberkampf was successful because he attended to quality. Output was limited to colorfast dyes; each piece stamped *bon teint* meant it could be washed with ease, although perhaps it did not offer the wider range of colors printed by less quality-conscious shops. Oberkampf also attended to design. He hired his own designers (the most outstanding was J. B. Huet) and was an originator, not a copier like so many of his contemporaries. The most characteristic toiles de Jouy were genre scenes showing people, animals, and buildings—subjects, scenes from mythology and folk tales, the manufactory at Jouy (Plate 73), commemorative scenes such as ones showing Joan of Arc, or the discovery of the New World. Chinoiserie was popular (Plate 74), and designs showing the "Four Parts of the World" and the "Four Seasons" became famous.

In 1770 Oberkampf initiated copperplate printing and in 1797 roller printing, a method which unfortunately limited color and design. An important invention of Jouy was solid green in 1809. The secret was traded to English printers in return for information about roller printing and cotton spinning. The English, too, had been printing linens and cottons (Plate 75).

English Prints

Calico printing began near London in 1676 and prospered until around 1700, when the wool and silk industries became alarmed at the competition from both imported Indian chintz and domestic copies. Then, as in France, there followed a period of prohibitions and denunciations.

The Spittlefields Ballads
or
The Weaver's Complaint Against the Callico Madams

> Our trade is so bad
> That the weavers run mad
> Through the want of both work and provisions,
> That some hungry poor rogues
> Feed on grains like our hogs,
> They're reduced to such wretched conditions,
> Then well may they tayre
> What our ladies now wear

And as foes to our country upbraid 'em,
Till none shall be thought a more scandalous slut
Than a tawdry Callico Madam.

When our trade was in wealth
Our women had health,
We silks, rich embroideries and satins,
Fine stuffs and good crapes
For each ord'nary trapes
That is destin'd to hobble in pattins;
But now we've a Chince
For the wife of a prince,
And a butterfly gown for a gay dame,
Thin painted old sheets
For each trull in the streets
To appear like a Callico Madam.[8]

In 1736 the cotton interests were able to force passage of the Manchester Act, which allowed the printing of cloth made with linen warp and cotton weft. Then, in 1774, the prohibitions against printing all-cotton cloth were removed—testimony to the growing power of Arkwright. Soon the leadership passed from London printers to firms established near Lancashire cotton mills.

It is frequently difficult to distinguish an English print from a French one. The French have been much better documented, and it is possible that many prints attributed to French centers are actually English. One sure mark of English manufacture between 1774 and 1811 is the presence of three blue threads in the selvage of cotton cloth. These enabled the printer to claim a lower excise rate than if he had printed imported cotton calico.

Early eighteenth century prints were adaptations of Indian chintz (frequently designed by Europeans), the large exotic florals in reds, purples, and browns obtained from mordant printing and dyeing with madder (see chapter 4). Then, in the 1730s, an important discovery was made. It had not been previously possible to get a blue design on cloth without using the resist method. The addition of orpiment (arsenic trisulphide) to a cold ferrous sulphate indigo vat made it possible to delay oxidation long enough to *pencil* (brush) the blue onto the cloth. The process was known as *English blue*, and *pencil blue*. The oxidation occurred so quickly that only fine lines or dabs of blue were possible, but the process lent itself to sprigged floral patterns. Later, around 1780, the *China blue* process was developed. This involved printing undissolved indigo in a paste of copperas (ferrous sulphate) and gum onto the cloth. Then the cloth was dipped in ferrous sulphate to reduce the indigo, then into lime to dissolve it. China blue was used with copperplates.

The English made some very fine copperplate prints between 1760 and 1790 (Plate 76). These were monochromes, although colored details were sometimes applied by block or hand. Copperplate printing lost ground to roller printing.

Block printing continued to be used well into the nineteenth century.

Developments in dye chemistry came with the growth of roller printing in England. Edward Bancroft's 1785 discovery of a fast yellow made from quercitron was of great importance. Quercitron, bark of the black oak, was an important American export. The yellow dye was good for all fibers and was preferred for silk and wool even after aniline dyes were introduced. Until about 1810, if one wanted a fabric printed with fast colors the choice was madder, indigo, or quercitron. In the period between 1810 and about 1840 a whole series of new colors, all natural dyestuffs, were developed. There were browns and oranges from manganese, chrome, and antimony minerals, pinks from cochineal, Prussian blue made from prussiate of potash and iron salts.

The Shawls of Nineteenth Century Europe

The marvelous shawls of Kashmir were popular in Europe from the last quarter of the eighteenth century until the 1870s. Kashmir shawls were very expensive, and European manufacturers realized they would have a good market if the shawls could be imitated. At first this was done by embroidery. Then in 1784 at Norwich in England, designs were block printed onto cotton neckerchiefs. In 1792 a Norwich weaver, using the flying shuttle, wove a single piece of cloth four yards square to be used for an embroidered shawl.

The earliest woven Kashmir-type shawls were probably made in Edinburgh on damask looms, then in Norwich on drawlooms called harness looms, because they possessed pattern harnesses in addition to regular harnesses. Norwich and Edinburgh continued as shawl centers, but Paisley in Scotland eventually became the leader. By 1820 Paisley was actually shipping imitation Kashmir shawls to India and Persia. The French started weaving shawls in 1804 and later were to become the best designers for jacquard shawls.

More information has survived from Paisley than from the other centers. Paisley, near Glasgow, was an old textile town, a center for manufacture of linen lawn, silk gauze, and thread. The thread business started as one supplying silk heddles for looms and expanded to become a leading industry. Paisley was also a dyeing and bleaching town. The shawl industry gave the town a reprieve from the Industrial Revolution, because the work was very specialized. Life was reported as being nearly ideal with hard-working, cultivated people living in close proximity to nature. Depression did strike Paisley from time to time and eventually the power loom took over, but conditions there were better than in many other places.

Fiber

It was much too expensive to import the soft cashmere wool that gave Kashmir shawls their lovely soft drape. Various attempts were made to raise the goats in Europe, but only the French were successful when they crossed the Russian and Angora species. So, several different kinds of yarn were used in European shawls.

The finest, called cashmere, was made in Amiens with a silk core wound with goat fiber. Often silk warp and a weft of a fine grade of sheep's wool were used. Fine Botany worsted was imported from Australia, and after the 1830s the terms *Botany* and *Thibet* (falsely implying cashmere) were used synonymously. Some machine spun cotton was used in Paisley shawls, but its use is generally associated with the decline of the industry.

Weaving

The so-called harness shawl of Paisley was an imitation of the intricately woven twill tapestry of Kashmir, but it was a masterpiece in its own right. The shawls were woven in a variety of sizes and shapes. In contrast to the Kashmirs, which were patchwork, Paisley shawls were each woven in one piece. (Plate 77).

The preparation of the warp might be called a sort of ikat process. Yarns were measured out onto a frame with slides that could be screwed down tightly to block horizontal and vertical sections from a particular dyebath. Thus it was possible to simulate the multicolored sections of a patchwork Kashmir. The next trick was to weave the shawl with exactly the right number of weft per inch so that the pattern would come out correctly. The technique, called *fillover* because the fabric was woven face down, was most like continuous brocading. The warp were fine, the pattern weft heavier, and a very fine binder weft secured the weave. The pattern weft, of several colors, floated on the back when not needed in the pattern. In order to reduce the weight of the shawl, the floats were clipped, first by hand, later by a rotary shearing machine. Thus, other ways of identifying a Paisley shawl are by its fuzzy back and the short pieces of pattern weft that sometimes come out from a low count shawl. Drawlooms were used in Paisley until about 1845 when the jacquard came into general use.

Color and Design

The color schemes in Paisleys are similar to those of Kashmirs, although a bit more somber and generally not as varied. Red and black predominate with additions of oranges, greens, blues, and white.

Designs were taken from Kashmir shawls, although many were original and sometimes quite un-Kashmir in aspect. The elongated pine was the usual motif, and designs could get quite complex (Plate 78). Pirating was common and much complained about until a system for registering designs was developed. The mixing of Kashmir and European shawl design was as common as the mixing of Indian and European printed design had been. There is one example of a French design being copied in Paisley ten years before that same design, intended for the East, was woven in Kashmir. Perhaps that same Kashmir shawl then served as "oriental inspiration" for a new Paisley shawl back in Europe.

The peak of the fashion for shawls was reached in the 1850s and 1860s when Abraham Lincoln and other men wore them. Cheapening by printing and power weaving put the product into the hands of the great mass of people, and a fashion that had lasted a hundred years, turned to lace and embroidery. The Paisley weavers migrated to America in hopes of continuing their old way of life.

NOTES

1. Sidney Pollard, "Factory Discipline in the Industrial Revolution," *The Economic History Review*, 2nd ser., 16, no. 2 (1963):254-271.

2. *British Parliamentary Papers, Industrial Revolution: Textiles,* 10 vols. (Shannon, Ireland: Irish University Press, 1968), 9:250.

3. Madeleine Jarry, *World Tapestry* (New York: G. P. Putnam's Sons, 1969), p. 30.

4. H. Wescher, "Fashions and Textiles at the Court of Burgundy," *CIBA Review* 51 (July 1946):1859.

5. E. J. Alexander and Carol H. Woodward, *The Flora of the Unicorn Tapestries* (New York: The New York Botanical Garden, 1974), p. 2. This is a reprint of articles in the *Journal of The New York Botanical Garden* (May and June 1941).

6. Vilhelm Slomann, *Bizarre Designs in Silks, Trade and Traditions* (Copenhagen: Ny Carlsberg Foundation, 1953) is the classic source now refuted by some scholars.

7. *Parliamentary Papers*, 9:231.

8. Arthur Hayden, *Chats on Cottage and Farmhouse Furniture* (New York: Stokes, 1917), pp. 326-329.

BIBLIOGRAPHY

Good for a survey of the textile trade in the sixteenth century is "Fashions and Textiles of Queen Elizabeth's Reign," *CIBA Review* 78 (February 1950). An important book based on extensive primary sources is George Unwin, *Industrial Organization in the Sixteenth and Seventeenth Centuries* (New York: A. M. Kelley, 1963). Both Thomas Ellison, *The Cotton Trade of Great Britain* (1886; reprinted, New York: M. Kelley, 1968) and Hugh Bodey, *Textiles: Past-into-Present Series* (London: B. T. Batsford, 1976) link the English and Flemish industries. Note also the entries under flax, cotton, and wool in the bibliography for chapter 2.

The putting-out system is elucidated in Alfred P. Wadsworth and Julia de Lacy Mann, *The Cotton Trade and Industrial Lancashire, 1600-1780* (Manchester, England: Manchester University Press, 1965) and by Unwin, *Industrial Organization*. Two sources on mercantilism include "Colbert and the French Wool Manufacture," *CIBA Review* 67 (May 1948) and Charles Woolsey Cole, *French Mercantilism 1683-1700* (New York: Octagon Books, 1965). Cole cites many textile regulations enacted under the system.

There are, of course, many accounts of the Industrial Revolution. One that is short and easily read is John Addy, *The Textile Revolution* (London and New York: Longman, 1976). "The Evolution of Mills and Factories," *CIBA Review* no. 1 (1968) considers economic aspects of the factory system. Friedrich Klemm, *A History of Western Technology* (Cambridge, Mass.: M.I.T. Press, 1964) is a good general history. S. D. Chapman, *The Cotton Industry in the Industrial Revolution* (New York: Macmillan, 1972) is concise and illustrates the variety of living conditions experienced during the period. The social historian would find a tremendous amount of material about life in Britain during the early nineteenth century in the ten volumes of the *British Parliamentary Papers, Industrial Revolution: Textiles* (Shannon, Ireland: Irish University Press, 1968). These are the reports of committees appointed to investigate the problems of the day.

The Industrial Revolution in England had its impact on India and America. See Arthur Silver, *Manchester Men and India Cotton, 1847-1872* (Manchester, England: Manchester

University Press, 1966); and James A. Mann, *The Cotton Trade of Great Britain: Its Rise, Progress, and Present Extent* (1860; reprint ed., New York: Augustus M. Kelley, 1968).

Studies on individual manufacturers are always interesting for insight into everyday life. One of many is Alfred Plummer and Richard E. Early, *The Blanket Makers 1669-1969* (New York: Augustus M. Kelley, 1969). It is the story of the company that makes the famous Hudson Bay blankets. Shorter studies can be found in the English journal *Textile History*.

Encyclopedias are good for information on the textile inventions. Also, Walter English, *The Textile Industry: An Account of the Early Invention of Spinning, Weaving, and Knitting Machines* (London: Longmans, Green and Co., 1969) is excellent for explanations of machinery. English also wrote "A Technical Assessment of Lewis Paul's Spinning Machine," *Textile History* 4 (1973):68-83. Harold Catling, *The Spinning Mule* (Newton Abbot, England: David and Charles, 1970) is fairly technical, as is Richard L. Hills, *Power in the Industrial Revolution* (New York: Augustus M. Kelley, 1970). George Unwin, *Samuel Oldknow and the Arkwrights: The Industrial Revolution at Stockport and Marple* (New York: Augustus M. Kelley, 1968) is another interesting specialized study. The Merrimack Valley Textile Museum in North Andover, Massachusetts published an exhibition catalog in 1965 entitled *Wool Technology and the Industrial Revolution* with good illustrations of machinery. Note also the bibliography in chapter 10.

A good place to begin a study of tapestry is Madeleine Jarry, *World Tapestry* (New York: G. P. Putnam's Sons, 1969). The illustrations are very good but unfortunately there is no general index. Joseph Jobé, ed., *Great Tapestries: The Web of History from the 12th to the 20th Century* (Lausanne, Switzerland: Edita S. A., 1965) also is difficult to use for reference because it lacks an index. But the illustrations are magnificent, the text well written, and the technical information presented clearly. A good overview in a little paperback can be found in W. S. Sevensma, *Tapestries* (New York: Universe Books, 1965) and in Adolph Cavallo, *Tapestries of Europe and of Colonial Peru in the Museum of Fine Arts, Boston*, 2 vols. (Boston: Boston Museum of Fine Arts, 1968). "Tapestry," *CIBA Review* 5 (January 1938) is another brief survey, and "Tapestries," *CIBA-GEIGY Review* no. 3 (1973) gives an excellent discussion of cartoon making and other technical aspects of twentieth century tapestries.

There are many older books on tapestries. As a rule they describe individual tapestries in detail (with fewer illustrations than is common in more recent works). One of the classics is Phyllis Ackerman, *Tapestry: The Mirror of Civilization* (1933; reprint ed., New York: AMS Press, 1970). Ackerman discusses tapestries of the whole world in an interesting style. See also George Leland Hunter, *Tapestries: Their Origin, History, and Renaissance* (New York: John Lane Co., 1913), which has an interesting section on prices; W. G. Thomson, *A History of Tapestry from the Earliest Times Until the Present Day* (London: Hodder and Stoughton, 1906); and Helen Candee, *The Tapestry Book* (New York: Tudor Publishing Co., 1935), which gives a table of the major tapestry periods.

Other references are quite specialized. Roger-A. D'Hulst, *Flemish Tapestries from the Fifteenth to the Eighteenth Century* (New York: Universe Books, 1967) is beautifully illustrated and gives the stories of individual tapestries. An excellent source of biographical information on tapestry weavers is Roger-Armand Weigert, *French Tapestry* (London: Faber and Faber, 1962). A very detailed study, Dorothy Shepherd, "Three Tapestries from Chaumont," *The Bulletin of the Cleveland Museum of Art* 48, no. 7 (September 1961):158-177, relates what little is known about the French industry in the Loire Valley. H. C. Maillier wrote three books on English tapestry, all published in London: *History of the Merton Abbey*

Tapestry Works (Constable, 1927); *English Tapestries of the Eighteenth Century* (Medici Society, 1930); and *The Tapestries at Hampton Court* (Ministry of Public Buildings and Works, 1951). English military tapestries are discussed in detail in Alan Wace, *The Marlborough Tapestries at Blenheim Palace* (London and New York: Phaidon, 1968). Alan Haynes, "The Mortlake Tapestry Factory 1619-1703," *History Today* 24 (January 1974):32-40, helps to fit tapestry weaving into the total European textile industry picture. Margaret B. Freeman, *The Unicorn Tapestries* (New York: The Metropolitan Museum of Art, 1974) is a delightful booklet. Freeman's book, with the same title and publisher, was issued in 1976. Both have superb illustrations.

Two works will help decipher tapestries: E. S. Whittlesey, *Symbols and Legends in Western Art: A Museum Guide* (New York: Charles Scribner's Sons, 1972); and Jack Franses, *Tapestries and their Mythology* (New York: Drake Publishers, 1975). This includes more current prices than Hunter's *Tapestries*.

The definitive work on European silks is Peter Thornton, *Baroque and Rococo Silks* (New York: Taplinger Publishing Co., 1965). He discusses the silk weaving centers and the development of design. A complement to Thornton's study is Santina M. Levey, "Lace and Lace-Patterned Silks: Some Comparative Illustrations," in *Studies in Textile History*, ed. Veronika Gervers (Toronto: Royal Ontario Museum, 1977), pp. 184-201.

Two surveys can be found in "Silks of Lyons," *CIBA Review* 6 (February 1938) and Cyril Bunt, *The Silks of Lyons* (Leigh-on-Sea, England: F. Lewis, 1960), which is mainly plates. Short, but interesting, are J. F. Flanagan, *Spitalfields Silks of the 18th and 19th Centuries* (Leigh-on-Sea, England: F. Lewis, 1954) and A. K. Sabin, *The Silk Weavers of Spitalfields and Bethnal Green with a Catalogue and Illustrations of Spitalfields Silks* (London: Board of Education, 1931). Natalie Rothstein, "A History of British Textile Design," *An Illustrated Guide to the Textile Collections of the World, Volume 2 United Kingdom-Ireland* (New York: Van Nostrand Reinhold, Co., 1976), pp. 53-64, shows the relationships between the English and French industries.

Roger-Armand Weigert, *Textiles en Europe Sous Louis XV* (Fribourg: Office Du Livre, 1964) has an English summary and good color plates. *Two Hundred Years of Textile Designs: Comprising France, England and America in the 18th and 19th Centuries* (New York: Scalamandre Museum of Textiles, n.d.) is helpful for design development.

The classic source for printing in France is Henri Clouzot, *Painted and Printed Fabrics* (New York: Metropolitan Museum of Art, 1927). It also includes Frances Morris, "Notes on the History of Cotton Printing Especially in England and America." See also the following in *CIBA Review:* "Medieval Cloth Printing in Europe," 26 (October 1939); "Textile Printing in 18th Century France," 31 (March 1940); and "Textile Printing in Switzerland," 105 (August 1954).

The English cotton and linen printing industry is covered by "English Chintz," *CIBA Review* no. 1 (1961). Mainly for the illustrations, see two booklets from the Victoria and Albert Museum (London: Her Majesty's Stationery Office): *English Chintz* (1955); and *English Printed Textiles, 1720-1836* (1960). An authoritative work with excellent bibliography is Florence Montgomery, *Printed Textiles: English and American Cottons and Linens 1700-1850* (New York: Viking Press, 1970). F. Lewis at Leigh-on-Sea, England published Frank Lewis, *English Chintz: A History of Printed Fabrics from Earliest Times Until the Present Day* (1942); and Cyril Bunt and Ernest Rose, *Two Centuries of English Chintz 1750-1950* (1957). Both have numerous plates. Some scholarly articles dealing with chintz design are John Irwin, "Origins of 'Oriental' Chintz Designs," *Antiques*, January 1959, pp. 84-87, and two by Barbara Morris: "The Classical Taste in English Wood-Block Chintzes," *The*

Connoisseur, April 1958, and "The Indian Taste in English Wood-Block Chintzes," *The Connoisseur*, March 1959.

Printing was, of course, dependent on the dyestuff industry. Note some of the entries for dyeing in the bibliography for chapter 4. See also Susan Fairlie's scholarly article "Dyestuffs in the Eighteenth Century," *The Economic History Review*, 2d ser., 17, no. 3 (April 1965):488–510.

Three references listed in chapter 7 for Kashmir shawls also have good information on European shawls: John Irwin, *Shawls: A Study in Indo-European Influences* (London: Her Majesty's Stationery Office, 1955); Katherine Lester and Bess Oerke, *Accessories of Dress* (Peoria, Illinois: Manual Arts Press, 1940); and Thomas Levitt, "Fashion, Commerce and Technology in the Nineteenth Century: The Shawl Trade," *Textile History* 3 (December 1972):51–63.

The classic work is Matthew Blair, *The Paisley Shawl and the Men Who Produced It* (Paisley, Scotland: Alexander Gardner, 1904). Blair's account of life in Paisley is glowing and makes us suspect his objectivity, but his details of drawloom operation are excellent. Similar in tone, but less reliable, is A. M. Stewart, *The History and Romance of the Paisley Shawl* (Paisley, 1946), originally a series of articles in the *Paisley Daily Express*. In 1966, the Paisley Museum published C. H. Rock, *Paisley Shawls*, which has good photos. Pamela Clabburn's four page information sheet, *Norwich Shawls* (Norwich: Norwich Museums Service, 1975), is a helpful piece of research. Information about early shawl printing can be found in Francina Irwin, "Scottish Eighteenth-Century Chintz and its Design—II" *Burlington Magazine* 107, no. 751 (October 1965): pp. 510–513.

PLATE 67 / The Chinese Fair, a French tapestry from the period of Louis XV. The
design is by Francois Boucher, 1743, the cartoon by Jean Joseph Dumont. (Courtesy of
The Cleveland Museum of Art. The Elisabeth Severance Prentiss Collection)

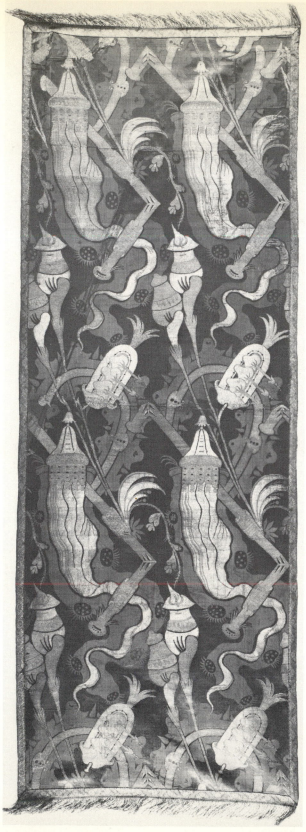

PLATE 68 / French bizarre silk from about 1710. Green damask, brocaded with silver and silver-gilt thread, and with pink silk details. (Crown Copyright. Victoria and Albert Museum)

PLATE 69 / Brocaded silk from Lyons in the period 1720-1725. Crimson with silver thread. (Crown Copyright. Victoria and Albert Museum)

PLATE 71 (*above*) / Brocaded silk from Spitalfields, mid-eighteenth century. (Crown Copyright. Victoria and Albert Museum)

PLATE 70 (*facing page*) / Brocaded silk from Lyons, *circa* 1770. (Crown Copyright. Victoria and Albert Museum)

PLATE 72 / French silk tissue from the Empire period (1800-1815). (Crown Copyright. Victoria and Albert Museum)

PLATE 73 / Printing Toiles at Oberkampf Factory at Jouy, France. A cotton textile, 1783, designed by Jean Baptiste Huet. (Courtesy of The Art Institute of Chicago. Gift of Mrs. Potter Palmer, 1953.306)

PLATE 74 (*above*) / Chinoiserie, plate-printed in blue, circa 1770-1780. (Courtesy of The Henry Francis du Pont Winterthur Museum)   PLATE 75 (*below*) / Block-printed linen from about 1780. (Crown Copyright. Victoria and Albert Museum)

PLATE 76 / Hangings in an arborescent pattern, plate-printed in indigo blue. Mahogany bed made in Massachusetts between 1760 and 1775. (Courtesy of The Henry Francis du Pont Winterthur Museum)

PLATE 77 / A Paisley shawl.

PLATE 78 (*above*) / Pine motif from the Paisley shawl.   PLATE 79 (*below*) / Blue resist. (Courtesy of The Henry Francis du Pont Winterthur Museum)

PLATE 80 / Handwoven check.

PLATE 81 (*facing page*) / Eighteenth century figured fabrics (watermarked 1801), from a textile sample book, by Booth and Theobald, Norwich, England. (Courtesy of The Henry Francis du Pont Winterthur Museum)

PLATE 82 / English wool calamanco quilt, from 1780-1800. (Courtesy of The Henry Francis du Pont Winterthur Museum)

PLATE 83 / A pieced homespun quilt from Ontario, circa 1865. Homespuns mainly tabbies, predominantly red in color. (Courtesy of the Royal Ontario Museum, Toronto)

PLATE 84 / Cotton bedspread printed by John Hewson, circa 1780–1800. (Courtesy of The Henry Francis du Pont Winterthur Museum)

9. TEXTILES AND INDEPENDENCE IN COLONIAL AMERICA

Imports supplied most of America's textile needs, both for utilitarian and decorative purposes, until about 1750, when the movement toward self-sufficiency in fabric production became serious. It is that movement that ought to interest Americans, because it can be correlated to the events leading to independence. A "homespun heritage" developed when imports became unavailable or too expensive. Fabrics made in America between 1640 and 1780 were plain and functional and matched the colonial way of living.

COLONIAL AMERICA

Colonial America included the area of North America that eventually became the original thirteen states. There had been Spanish settlements in the New World for some time, but the landing at Jamestown in 1607 was the beginning of permanent colonies.

In general, the colonies north of Maryland were to be the commercial ones—highly dependent on trade in timber, molasses, and slaves. By 1700 the American merchant fleet, operating mainly in the northern colonies, numbered about fifteen hundred vessels, and its trade routes covered half the world. The colonies to the south were agricultural—dependent on the rice, tobacco, and cotton that was traded with England. (South Carolinians grew indigo and Georgians silk.)

To the middle colonies came the Dutch, spinners and weavers in those colonies from an early date in spite of a prohibition against textile manufacture made by the Dutch West Indian Company, owners of "New Netherland." Pennsylvania was a haven for many English, Welch, Scots, Irish, Dutch, and Germans, as well as for Quakers. The colony was to enjoy rapid economic growth with Philadelphia and Germantown becoming early centers for textile manufacturing. The professional

234

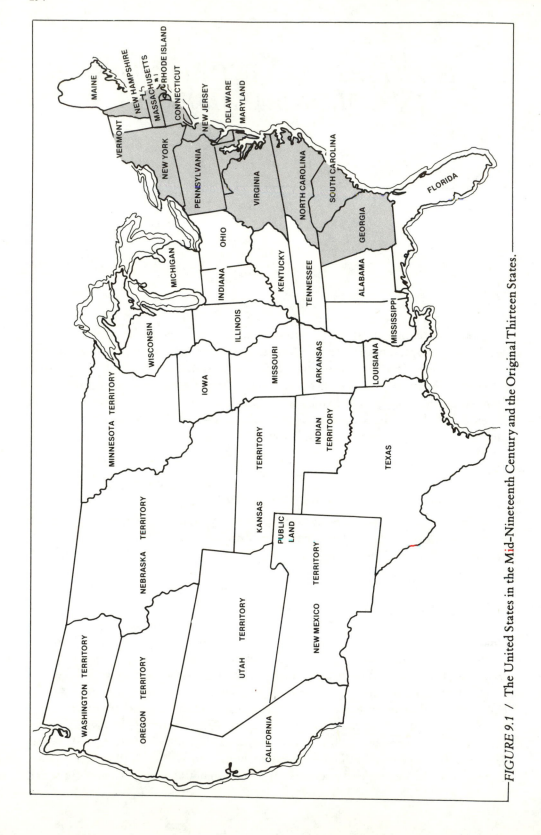

FIGURE 9.1 / The United States in the Mid-Nineteenth Century and the Original Thirteen States.

weaver was most welcome and was often given land as inducement to settle in a community.

At first the colonists brought their clothing and bedding with them and received additional supplies from England whenever a ship brought new settlers. There was little thought of making fabics until supplies became short.

For each man at Jamestown the company supplied suits of canvas, frieze, and broadcloth, but the Pilgrims in 1620 had a more difficult time because they did not have clothing suitable to the severe climate. Later, more knowledgeable, the Massachusetts Bay Company stocked extra suits of Hampshire kersey, green cotton waistcoats, and blankets of Welch cotton, and soon, their store was selling all kinds of fabrics. Ships crossed the Atlantic frequently, and by the late 1630s the Massachusetts General Court, the colonial legislative body, found it necessary to pass sumptuary laws against the use of elaborate textiles—including lace—because Puritans were becoming much too interested in worldly goods. Wills and inventories listed numerous fabrics, which formed a relatively large portion of an estate at that time.

By 1640 the story was different. Because of improved political conditions in England, there was a marked decline in new colonists as well as fewer ships bringing goods. The decrease in settlers also depressed prices for the farm commodities that colonists had been selling to new arrivals. New Englanders no longer had the means to buy as many imported textiles. The Massachusetts General Court began to study the colony's potential for textile production by counting weavers (who were offered subsidies), spinners, and amounts of available seed. (Flax and hemp seed were considered valuable enough to be used for legal tender.) In Connecticut the General Court ordered that hemp and flax be sown by each family and cotton be imported. In 1645 the Massachusetts General Court passed the following order.

> Forasmuch as wollen cloth is so useful a commodity without which wee can not so comfortably subsist in these parts, by reason of the cold winters, it being also, at present, very scarce and deare amongst us, and likely shortly to be so in parts from whence we can expect it, by reason of ye wars in Europe destroying in a great measure the flocks of sheepe amongst them, and also ye trade and means it selfe of making woolen cloaths and stuffs, by ye killing and otherwise hindering of such persons, whose skill and labor tended to that end; and whereas, through the want of woolen cloaths and stuffs, many pore people have suffered much could and hardship, to ye impairing of their healths, and ye hazarding of some of their lives, and such who have bene able to provide for their children cloathing of cotton cloth, (not being able to get other) have, by that means, had some of their children much scorched with fire, yea, divers burnt to death; this Court, therefore, (taking into consideration our present condition in this particular, as also having an eye to the good of posterity, knowing how usefull and necessary wollen cloths & stufs would be for our more comfortable cloathing, & how profitable a merchandize it is like to be, to transport to other parts) doth hereby desire all ye towns in general, and every one in particular within the jurisdiction, seriously to weigh the

premises, and accordingly that you will carefully indeavour the preservation and increase of such sheope as they have already, as also to procure more with all convenient speed into their several towns by all such lawful wayes and means as God shall put into their hands, & for the better effecting hereof we thinke meete it be propounded to each several town, being called to assemble together, to know who will buy ewe sheope at the rate of forty shillings apiece, under 3 years ould, & how many they wilbe bound to buy, & in what they will make payment, that so there may be some course taken for the sending for them into other parts abroad; and that each towne would appoint one of themselves who shall take a note of the names of such as are willing to further ye worke, together with ye number of ye sheope they will buy and ye nature of their pay, & shall return ye several notes to Maior Gibon, his house in Boston, at or before ye first of ye 7th month next; and, further, it is desired that such as have an opportunity to write to their friends in England who are minded to come to us, to advize them to bring as many sheope as conveniently they can, which being carefully indeavoured, we leave the succease to God.[1]

In 1656 the Massachusetts General Court decided that all idle hands should be put to spinning, and local selectmen assessed families for a quarter, a half, or a whole spinner and imposed fines of twelve shillings for every pound short that a family might be. The equivalent of a whole spinner was three pounds of cotton, wool, or flax spun every week for thirty weeks.

In theory, manufacturing was not allowed in the colonies, because, under the English mercantile policy, they were to serve as suppliers of raw materials and consumers of British manufactured goods. In addition to shortages, yet another condition contributed to the movement toward home production of textiles. Increasing competition from Dutch traders resulted in the enactment of the British Navigation Act of 1651. Intended to confine English commerce to English ships, it stipulated that goods brought to England from Europe could be carried in English or country of origin ships, but goods brought from Asia, Africa, or America must go to England, Ireland, or an English colony only in British or colonial ships. In 1660 a restrictive addition stated that no merchandise could be imported into the colonies except in English ships navigated by Englishmen. For example, cotton fabrics coming from India to America had to be landed in England first. Certain American exports including cotton, indigo, and dyewoods could be shipped only to England, and so markets for some colonial products were curtailed. In 1663 another provision added duties to colonial imports and made cloth even more expensive. Colonists were forced to buy only English goods. But there was considerable smuggling, and in spite of English restrictions against textile manufacture, there were reports from New York of "everyone" making his own linen and a large part of his woolens.

By 1690 the British had become aware of the potential for textile manufacture possessed in the colonies, which exported some wool to France in exchange for silk textiles in 1698. In 1699 the English passed the Wool Act in order to protect their wool industry. It stated that:

No Wool, Woolfells, Shortlings, Morlings, Wool Flocks, Worsted, Bay or Woolen Yarn, Cloath, Serge, Bays, Kerseys, Says, Frizes, Druggets, Cloath Serges, Shalloons or any other Drapery, Stuffs or Woollen Manufactures whatsoever, made or mixed with Wool or Wool Flocks, being of the Product or Manufacture of any of the English Plantations in America shall be laden on any Ship or Vessel.[2]

It was also illegal to transport woolens between colonies or out of the king's dominions under penalty of forfeiture and fine of £500.

Lord Cornbury, governor of New York, reported the following to the British Board of Trade in 1705.

Besides, the want of wherewithal to make returns to England sets men's wits to work, and that has put them upon a trade which, I am sure, will hurt England in a little time; for I am well informed that upon Long Island and Connecticut they are setting upon a woolen manufacture, and I myself have seen serge, made upon Long Island, that any man may wear. Now, if they begin to make serge, they will, in time, make coarse cloth and then fine. How far this will be for the service of England, I submit to better judgments; but, however, I hope I may be pardoned if I declare my opinion to be that all these Colloneys, which are but twigs belonging to the main tree—England—ought to be kept entirely dependent upon and subservient to England, and that can never be if they are suffered to go on in the notions they have that, as they are Englishmen, soe they may set up their same manufactures here as people may do in England; for the consequence will be, if once they can see they can cloathe themselves, not only comfortably but handsomely too, without the help of England, they, who are not very fond of submitting to government, would soon think of putting in execution designs they had long harboured in their breasts. This will not seem strange, when you consider what sort of people this country is inhabited by.[3]

The colonists found it prudent to produce their own essential clothing, but for luxuries—the brocades and damasks—Americans still had to rely on Europe.

By the middle of the eighteenth century public funds were being used in Boston and Philadelphia to promote textile manufacturing. Many small factories, employing the poor, were established, and this small manufacturing capability was highly valued when trade was restricted during the French and Indian Wars. Housewives also rallied to make clothing for the soldiers. When the wars ended in 1763, there was a large increase in textile imports, but this was soon followed by a severe economic depression. Depression also hit the English textile workers when the colonists, irritated by the strict orders given to English ship captains to stop smuggling, refused to pay trade debts (American importers were heavy users of credit).

The restrictive legislation passed by England to help pay for the wars was, no doubt, a major reason for the American movement towards independence. The 1764 Sugar Act, which levied duties on molasses primarily, also included silk, Bengals and stuffs mixed with the silk of Persia, China, or East India, as well as callicoes, cambric, and French lawns. In answer to this, the men of Philadelphia resolved to wear only American made woolens. Home production increased, and so did smuggling from Holland and France.

Another boycott ensued when the Stamp Act was passed. On 4 March 1766 at Providence, Rhode Island, a group of prominent young ladies formed "The Daughters of Liberty" and spent the whole day spinning. Other such groups were formed with the resolve not to purchase any British manufactures until the Stamp Act was repealed. In 1768 the senior class at Harvard voted to take their degrees dressed only in American made garments, and Yale followed the next year with a vote to wear homespun at commencement so that every one would be in fashion. Much of the woolen cloth came from a manufactory in East Hartford, a company that made seventeen thousand yards of excellent woolen cloth in 1767.

The ten years of agitation that preceded the American Revolution did much to prepare people for home manufacture, and the colonies went into the war with some capacity for textile production. There had also been a westward movement after the French and Indian Wars, and as people went farther from the seaports (often to regions away from rivers and roads), there was an increase in household manufacture and self-sufficiency.

During the revolution many at home deprived themselves in order to send supplies to the army, but fiber, equipment, and workers were inadequate, and the soldiers seldom had sufficient clothing and blankets. Not all imports were cut off by the war; at times New York, the Carolinas, and Georgia received almost a normal supply of English cloth. The colonists also traded with other countries, and privateering supplied many goods, although they were expensive.

After the war there was a sudden decline of interest in household manufacture, and floods of foreign finery were landed even before the Treaty of Paris was signed. This brief respite for the ladies ended when Americans realized that they would have to maintain their industrial as well as political independence. Specie was in very short supply, and it was recognized that home production of textiles was needed to keep money from flowing out of the country.

COLONIAL TEXTILES

Among colonial textiles there were bays and says, lustrings and perpetuanas, tammies and druggets, fearnaughts and cherryderries—all of them names we don't hear anymore. There were serges and calicoes, chintzes and Osnaburgs, lawns and flannels—fabrics we still use. And there were some fabrics—dimity, broadcloth, frize—with names that are still familiar, but which were much different in colonial times.

Spellings of the hundreds of fabric names were often unique, phonetically inspired, and so varied as to lead researchers to think there were more kinds of fabrics than was actually the case. Many textiles were named for the places where they were made, and so two identical ones might have different names. Sometimes a name indictated a width, a color, or a finish. The fiber content reported was not always accurate, especially with regard to cotton. Mixtures were often reported as being of a single fiber, and whether a fabric was a woolen or a worsted was not always clear.

Still, the number of different textiles available to the colonists was large. Inventories, order letters, advertisements, and account books indicate this. There is no doubt that most of the fabrics came from Great Britain; they were imported by merchants in Boston, New York, and Philadelphia and then transferred to other centers throughout the colonies.

The common colonial textiles could have been imported or made in America after about 1640. Although fabrics of complex weave can most surely be identified as being imports, others, including the vast array of simple fabrics—bedding, table linens, everyday clothing fabrics—could have been made on either side of the Atlantic, since the materials and equipment were the same. In fact, homespun made today in the United States can be identical to homespun made in England in the seventeenth century. Then too, many of the basic fabrics could, at times, be imported more cheaply than they could be made at home, and immigrants brought large supplies of household linens—a practice that continued into the nineteenth century. Without having some documentation it would be difficult to identify a fabric as positively being made in colonial America.

Not many colonial fabrics have survived the wear, moths, and sunlight—and being made over several times—to end up as pieces in a treasured quilt. Large amounts of colonial rags went into paper, which was always in short supply in those days. Some garments and furnishing fabrics, carefully stored in museums, and some old swatch books will give an idea of what was used. However, most information comes in written records that are sometimes difficult to interpret.

In the seventeenth and eighteenth centuries, fabrics formed a much greater portion of the total value of a family's goods than they do today, and a higher portion of income was spent on clothing relative to the amount spent on housing. Fabrics were also used more then as status symbols; bed furniture (curtains, valances, and covers), which consumed many yards of cloth, may serve as an example.

Fibers

The dominant fibers used during the colonial period were hemp, flax, wool, some cotton, and some silk. In addition, there were some reports of nettle (a bast fiber used in a fabric called *Scotch cloth*) and hair (dog, buffalo, rabbit, and goat) being used. This was more likely on the frontier where the common fibers might be scarce.

Hemp has always grown wild in many parts of the world, and when New Englanders first arrived they found the indians using it for cordage and nets. A somewhat better quality was found in Virginia, and some hempen fabrics were fine enough to be used for apparel as well as for bed and table linens.

Flax was the principal fiber used in America from the time of the earliest settlements. Almost every farmer grew some, and the whole family took part in the processing. It took almost a year from the time the flax was planted until the yarn was ready for weaving. Home production persisted into the nineteenth century, but as a fiber, flax became less and less important as methods for cotton production improved and factory-made textiles superseded homespun.

Wool was the other major fiber, but its production got off to a much slower start than did flax growing. Wolves, indians, and colonists liked to eat sheep, and winters were hard in New England. But by 1664 there were some 100,000 sheep in Massachusetts, and it has already been noted that the British were alarmed by the possibility of competition with their own growing industry, an alarm that culminated in the Wool Act.

American woolens could not compete with British fabrics when quality was important. Sheep raised in America before the revolution were coarse wool types, and neither weaving nor finishing techniques were well advanced. Wool was spun in the grease (the sheep were washed before shearing), and the wool not scoured as it is now. Carding was done at home, combing by professionals.

Cotton was a minor fiber in colonial America; it was hard to get and difficult to spin. Most cotton fabrics were imports from England that originated in India. The first report of cotton being imported into New England was of 110 pounds brought to Wethersfield, 90 to Windsor, and 200 to Hartford in 1643. The General Court of Connecticut had dispatched a ship to Barbados for supplies of cotton needed to carry out a 1640 edict promoting home textile manufacture.

Cotton was to become more important as a raw material for the mills of England. Early in the eighteenth century most of the cotton imported by England came from the Near East or the West Indies, but in 1764 about 800 pounds were sent from the Carolinas. From then on, American exports to England gradually increased. The market for the South's cotton was relatively small, however, until Eli Whitney invented his gin in 1793. Then, as the machinery for spinning cotton was improved and as yarn could be purchased for home weaving, its use was greatly increased.

Typical American fabrics were not made of silk. Numerous attempts were made to establish the silk industry in various colonies (especially in Virginia and Georgia), but in most places the aim was to supply raw material for England's luxury fabric industry. Silk cultivation started in Jamestown in 1620 after James I sent silkworms, and bounties offered by the colonial government kept the industry going in a modest way until the 1660s when tobacco proved to be a much more profitable crop. Some silk was grown in the Carolinas and Georgia in the early eighteenth century, and the peak in Georgia was reached in 1759 when 10,000 pounds were exported.[4]

The silks produced in colonial America were generally of poor quality, because the process of making yarn (reeling and throwing) was not understood. Weaving and finishing were not skillfully done, so fabrics were stiff, fuzzy, and lacking in the luster and color-fastness of English silks. Imported silks were expensive. Records of their use as bed furniture are scanty—wool and cotton were the furnishing fibers. The peak for imports of dress fabrics, elegant figured silks from Spitalfields (Plate 71), came in the 1760s. Later, a change in fashion as well as the revolution caused a sharp decline in the demand for luxury textiles.

Colonial Spinning Wheels

Two basic types of spinning wheels were used in colonial America. The first, the great (or wool) wheel—high or long wheel in Ireland—was used to spin woolen yarn (see Figure 2.6). The spinner held the carded roll of fiber in her left hand, attached some fiber to the spindle, turned the wheel by hand or with a little wooden "finger," walked backward to attenuate the strand and allow the twist to be put in, and then, turning the wheel in the opposite direction, walked forward to wind the yarn on the spindle. It was time consuming, but good exercise, and it showed off the spinster's figure. These wheels were easy and cheap to make. Many can be seen today in the hill country of Kentucky and North Carolina. Cotton and silk waste were also spun on the great wheel.

The second type, on which both worsted and linen yarns were spun, was the so-called Saxony or flax wheel (see Figure 2.7). This was a small wheel on which yarn could be spun continuously, because there was a flyer, the U-shaped device that wound the yarn onto the spindle without having to stop the wheel and reverse directions. Spinning was faster on this one, and the spinner could sit and operate the treadle with her feet.

There was always a shortage of yarn. It has been said that it took at least four spinners to keep one weaver in yarn. One visualizes the colonial woman as being permanently attached to her spinning wheel—and she was not to be free of it until well into the nineteenth century.

Colonial Looms

The horizontal frame loom brought to America by the settlers was the same one that had been used in Europe for hundreds of years (see Figure 3.8). Most often the loom was made at home, although some of the parts came from Europe. There were many slight variations; however, most probably had four harnesses. Usually multiple harness looms were owned by professional weavers, but there were some farm women who could weave patterned linens and coverlets on them.

There were always fewer looms than spinning wheels. Several people in the family worked on the same loom, even on the same piece of cloth or rug. Variations in weaving skill can often be noted on surviving fabrics. Many yards of warp were put on the loom and several items woven; variations could be achieved by changing the weft or treadling sequence. Drafts of favorite weaves were treasured, then passed down to the next generation. The loom was often placed in a separate building in warm climates, perhaps in the loft or small addition in chilly New England.

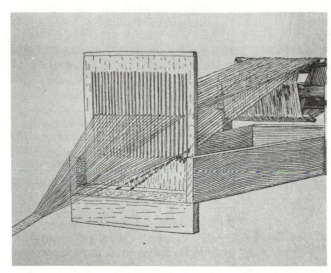

FIGURE 9.2 / Tape Loom
(from Mason, 1899).

Easy to move from place to place, perhaps taken on a visit to friends, was the toy-like tape loom. A rigid heddle, a padle shaped board with alternating slots and holes, was attached to a box or frame or used alone (Figure 9.2). The tape loom was used to weave all sorts of narrow fabrics: ties for clothing, loops for hanging curtains, wicks for oil lamps, and decorative edgings.

Finishing and Coloring

Fabric finishing was limited in the seventeenth and eighteenth centuries, because skilled workers as well as equipment were in short supply. This was a primary reason why English fabrics were preferred; their variety was much greater than that of American fabrics. Old newspaper advertisements, though, tell us that as early as 1722 in Boston linen could be made into buckram (sized with gum), calendered, watered (moiréd), and dyed in Boston, and that in 1731 another Bostonian could dye and glaze fine chintz. And from the *Boston Gazette* of 14 May 1754:

> Alexander Fleming, Dyer, lately from Great Britain, has set up said Business in Boston, in a House of Mr. Arthen's near Dr. Gardner's in Marlborough Street, on the same side of the Way, who can dye all sorts of Colours, after the best Manner and Cheapest Rate, viz. Scarletts, Crimsons, Pinks, Purples, Straws, Wine Colours, Sea-Greens, Saxon ditto, common Blues, shearing, dressing and watering of clothes: Also he can dye linen Yarn either red, blue, green, yellow or cloth colours, and all Colours on silks, and cleaning of Cloths.[5]

William Simmons used the *Virginia Gazette* of 13 January 1774 to inform the public that he could full cloth and also fill, dye, and dress it. He would even weave, and give instruction as to the preparation of yarn for weaving.[6]

Fulling mills were the first finishing establishments in America: the mill at Rowley, Massachusetts was built in 1643. By the late seventeenth century there were many water-powered fulling mills in the colonies. If one wasn't nearby, the housewife could always have a fulling bee. Everyone in the neighborhood came, sat on chairs arranged in a circle, and stamped the wet, soaped cloth laid out on the floor.

It is not known how much dyeing was actually done at home in colonial times.[7] Women traded recipes for the use of common plants, and the indigo, madder, and dyewoods that could be purchased. Dye plants were certainly grown in colonial gardens. The stereotype is of a colonial woman continually stirring a kettle of simmering yarn, probably dyeing it butternut brown. But it is very likely she utilized the services of the local professional dyer whenever possible.

Printing was a textile craft not well developed in colonial America. In fact, it was not practiced to any extent in Europe until the last quarter of the seventeenth century. A few printers in America did, however, advertise in the eighteenth century papers, and some people probably block-printed linen as a sideline at home.

With so few textiles being printed in America, it is no wonder that the ladies of Boston, New York, and Newport avidly awaited announcement in the local newspaper of the arrival of a cargo of Indian or English prints. Extant samples with amazingly clear colors can be seen in old business papers and order books.

There is one group of textiles peculiar to the Connecticut River valley and eastern New York state, about which controversey has swirled for many years. These, known as "American blue resist prints," were probably dyed with indigo. Because they have very large floral and leaf designs of blue on a white ground, it is not certain what method was used (Plate 79).[8] This, of course, is just the reverse of traditional resist patterns (see chapter 4).

Much research still needs to be done in the early coloring and finishing methods, if indeed the sources can be found. The late colonial period was the time when many new developments in industrial methods of textile production were being made in Europe.

Fabrics

As we have noted, fabrics made of flax and wool requiring a minimum of finishing were apt to have been made in the colonies, with amounts and types increasing as the skilled population increased. Others were imported. Silks and cottons, with only a few exceptions, were imported. Sometimes the same fabric type was made in both Europe and America. *Cloth* and *stuff* both became general terms for a piece of fabric.

Linens

Linens were both coarse and finely woven. *Tow cloth*, made from the short flax fibers, was the coarsest plain weave (most linens were plain weave), and it was used for men's clothing, sacks, and wrapping cloths. Another coarse linen was called *duffel.* Duffel was also recorded as a woolen, and it may have been a combination fabric. It had a thick nap and was used for dressing gowns and bags.

Osnaburg, a staple cotton fabric today, was most commonly an unfinished linen that had originated in the German city of Osnabruck. Also reported as being made of wool and cotton, it was used for clothing as well as for sacks. *Dowlas* was a similar fabric that originated in Daoulas, Brittany. Dowlas might be spelled *dolas, doulas, doulace* or *dowlace*—another problem for the researcher. Another similar fabric, but one made of tow, was called *Tecklenburg,* because it came from a town of that name in Westphalia. In the same weight group was *Virginia cloth,* made of tow and cotton for mid-eighteenth century servants' clothing.

From England George Washington ordered *buckram,* a linen stiffened with a gum or paste. In the 1770s *cambric,* a lightweight linen slightly narrower than lawn, was in heavy demand. Made first in Cambrai, France, it was later a specialty of Scotland and Ireland. Many kinds of *lawn* were imported during the eighteenth century: long, spotted, broad, clear, fine, and superfine. Some were listed as having flowers, and so were probably printed. Both cambric and lawn were later to be made of cotton. *Holland,* a closely woven cloth for sheets and shirts, was frequently mentioned in inventories. Brown Holland was unbleached. *Huswife's cloth* was a middle-grade, all-purpose linen.

Linen *checks* (Plate 80) were popular, because they didn't show the dirt and were easy to weave. Also made in the colonies were the figured weaves, or *fancies,* with patterns called "double diamonds," "honeycomb," "rings and chains," "Ms and Os."

Mentioned often in the literature, perhaps because of its rhythmic name, is *linsey-woolsey.* It was made with a linen warp (flax could be spun into good strong yarn) and a wool weft (a more scant supply of wool could be extended this way). The wool gave warmth and flame retardancy to many colonial petticoats, which often had weft stripes of home dyed colors.

Lots of linsey-woolsey was made in America and the records of George Washington's 1767 weaving establishment list "Lindsay Woolsey" with "Lindsay-plaided, Linsey, and Linnen."[9] So it is likely that there was at least one other fabric, "Linsey," or some version of the name, that was all linen. It may have been made originally in the English village of Linsey in Suffolk, or the name may have been a corruption of the French *linsel,* meaning linen cloth. Linsey-woolsey was made for a long time. Soldiers went to the Civil War in it, but by then it had a cotton warp.[10]

Wool Textiles

The variety of wool fabrics used in colonial America was very great. One of the first to be brought to the New World (it was traded to the indians by the first fishermen and explorers) was *shag.* Shag was a coarse, long napped woolen; it was also known as *duffel.* It may have been like *baise,* or *bay,* a plain weave, napped flannel, which was eventually called bayeta and used in Navajo blankets. *Flannel* was very common and easily made at home, then taken to a fulling mill to be finished. A thick white flannel blanketing was given the name *swanskin.* And try to visualize *fearnaught,* a heavy coating that stood against the worst winter storm.

> Ye weavers, all your shuttles throw,
> And bid broad-cloaths and serges grow.[11]

Serge, a worsted twill, was very popular for bed curtains in the seventeenth century; *say,* or *saye,* resembled it. When *serge de Nimes,* black or blue in 1770, was made of cotton, it became denim. *Lasting,* or *everlasting,* was probably another worsted twill, and *perpetuana,* a durable woolen made in England since the sixteenth century. *Broadcloth,* a wide imported wool fabric, was made by two weavers at first (see Figure 8.2.) and later with the fly (or flying) shuttle (see Figure 8.1). *Kersey* was a coarse, napped, narrow wool cloth made at an early date in America.

Shalloon, a worsted wool lining fabric, was sometimes embossed with small figures; *anteloons* were related. Wool texiles with woven figures included *duroy, floretta, Mecklenburg, Battavia,* and *barlicorn* (Plate 81).

There was a large group of wool fabrics with ribs, described as "having grain" because of the prominent crosswise rib effect (seen in poplin and taffeta). There was *camlet* (chamylyt, chamlett, camelot, etc.), *cambleteen* (an inferior grade of camlet), *harrateen* and *moreen* (both moiréd), and *cheney* (called china). These were finished to imitate fine silk taffetas and moirés. Patterns could be stamped with hot molds or carved rollers to give the effect of woven damask. Large quantities were imported to furnish the homes of New England.

Another very important textile was *calamanco* (with the appearance of heavy cotton chintz) used for dress goods, utility cloths, but especially for bed furniture (Plate 82). There are several calamanco quilts to be seen in New England's historic houses. Definitions vary greatly, but in colonial times calamanco was most likely a wool satin, sometimes figured. It came in bright colors, was often striped, and had a heavy glaze. *Durant, tammy,* and *russel* were similar.

Cotton Textiles

Coarse cotton textiles were made in America, or they were imported from England, but the fine ones came from India. *Fustian,* made with linen warp and cotton weft, was popular in America. *Velveret* and *thickset* were similar and also used for heavy work clothing. But for lovely soft clothing and hanging textiles, India was the source. Here the nomenclature becomes fantastic—*allejars, brawls, allibanies, coffies, gurras, guzzies,* and *cherryderry* (American for charadaries, or carridaries, meaning a striped or checked cloth). *Hum-hum* started out as the Arabic *humman,* meaning "a Turkish bath."

In the eighteenth century *calico* meant a plain weave cotton fabric resembling the linens of the time. It came from Calicut, on the Malabar Coast of India. Now calico is printed with small, brightly colored flowers, but in the seventeenth century it was often plain colored or even white, although it could be printed or painted. *Guinea hen,* having a blue background with white spots or flowers, was only one variety. *Muslin* was another, and in 1678 there was a printed calico called *calmendar.* Calico lived on into the nineteenth century to become a cheap cotton turned out in the mills of New England and a cloth indispensable to the ladies of covered wagon trains. Today, an imitation of flowered calico is seen in polyester double knits.

Chintz in the eighteenth century meant the dress and furnishing fabrics that were made in India by the mordant and resist-dyeing technique (see chapter 4). To the English it was a variety of calico. The brilliant and fast colors were highly valued in both Europe and America.

A cotton fabric that has changed significantly since colonial times is *dimity.* Now it is a sheer corded, striped, or checked white cotton. Then, it was heavy, sometimes a twill, sometimes figured, and at first an Indian import and later a staple, home-loomed cloth.

George Washington and many other gentlemen wore breeches of *nankeen,* a yellow cotton twill. In his day it was probably made in Manchester, England, but it was originally woven in the orient of a particular type of yellow cotton grown in China.

Silks

The silk textiles found in colonial America were usually heavy, but became lighter when they needed to meet competition from cottons. They came from all over the world. *Bengal,* a stripe for woman's apparel, was imported from India. *Sarcanet,* a firm but thin lining for cloaks and hoods, came from Persia and *Mantua* from Italy (mantua was also a general term meaning a silk fabric)). *Padusoy* (padaway), a strong ribbed silk used for waistcoats, also came from Italy. France sent gorgeous examples of *brocatelle, lampas, damask,* and *brocade*—all drawloom figured fabrics.

Many of the silks were ribbed and related to *taffety* (taffeta), a very old fabric from Persia. *Lustring (lutestring)* was a glossy variety with a soft hand and *alamode,* a lightweight black lustring. *Peeling* was light weight and crisp. There was also a wide variety of *satins* from various places, and *satinesco,* an inferior quality of satin used in the seventeenth century. It should be noted that many satins were made of wool. Today, the satin weave is not used for wool fabrics.

These are only a few of the many fabrics known in the seventeenth and eighteenth centuries. Many came and went with fashion changes, as fabrics do now. Others became the staples of many years' standing.

Needlework and Rugs

Although they became more important in the nineteenth century, needlework and rugs are also part of the textiles of colonial America. As leisure increased, and there were more servants to do their chores, ladies turned to lace making and embroidery.

Wealthy Pilgrims indulged in lace wearing, but the poor could not. In 1634 an edict was passed prohibiting both the making and the wearing of lace.[12] The Huguenots were especially famed for their pillow lace, but there was no industry in America like the one in Europe.

The term *wrought* meant needlework. Embroidery had been a common pastime in England, and so, even the earliest colonists were making samplers. Very small girls were taught to work little verses on linen. Chair and table covers, and especially bed furniture, were frequently wrought. Colonial crewel work, usually lighter in scale and feeling than Jacobean work, its English counterpart, is well known and fine examples remain. Crewel was used on petticoats (the fashions of the period displayed the petticoat), on pockets that were tied around the waist under a skirt, and for pictures.

Early colonial rugs went on the table instead of the floor—floors might be sanded or covered with a painted canvas floor cloth. Oriental carpets, called "Turkey carpets," were imported by the very rich and imitated by those less well-to-do. Colonial women did *Turkey-work* by sewing yarns into a coarse cloth and knotting them into loops that were cut to form a fairly dense pile. By about the middle of the eighteenth century, the English were manufacturing Turkey-fashion carpets. Several girls worked together to knot yarns on wide warps crossed by weft between the rows of knots.

Other types of woven carpets were made in England about the same time but were not manufactured in America until the nineteenth century. *English* (Kidderminster, ingrain, or Scotch) was a double weave construction without pile. Brussels and Wilton were both pile weaves, while Axminster was a pile carpet made by hand knotting. *List carpets,* woven of strips of cloth (usually selvage), were made in America, however. Even these were not used commonly in pre-revolutionary days.

Another kind of rug belongs to the eighteenth and early nineteenth centuries and was pretty much confined to New England. *Bed ruggs* were made by sewing wool yarns into a background fabric leaving loops (which were sometimes cut) to make a heavy warm bedcover. There is a definite difference between the running stitch sewing techniques used for bed ruggs and the method used to hook rugs.[13] Bed ruggs were the products of people from relatively isolated areas and might perhaps be compared to the colcha embroideries of New Mexico—also good examples of folk art.

NOTES

1. William R. Bagnall, *The Textile Industries of the United States, Volume I, 1639-1810* (1893; reprint ed., New York: A. M. Kelley, 1971), pp. 6-7.

2. William B. Weeden, *Economic and Social History of New England: 1620-1789,* 2 vols. (1890; reprint ed., New York: Hillary House Publishers, 1963), p. 388. (Note: Woolfells were skins from which the wool had not been sheared or pulled; flock, inferior fibers added to low-grade fabrics to make them heavier. According to Samuel Johnson, *A Dictionary of the*

English Language, 2 vols. (London, 1755), shortling meant the felt or skin of a sheep shorn, and morling (or mortling) meant wool plucked from a dead sheep. Bay yarn was "a denomination sometimes used promiscuously with woolen yarn.")

3. Bagnall, *Textile Industries,* p. 12.

4. Little gives an interesting account of this period in Georgia. Frances Little, *Early American Textiles* (New York: The Century Co., 1931), pp. 132-139.

5. George Francis Dow, *Every Day Life in the Massachusetts Bay Colony* (Boston: The Society for the Preservation of New England Antiquities, 1935), pp. 128-129.

6. John R. Commons, ed., *A Documentary History of American Industrial Society,* 10 vols. (Cleveland: The Arthur H. Clark, Co., 1910) 2:326-327.

7. Rita J. Adrosko, *Natural Dyes in the United States* (Washington: Smithsonian Institution Press, 1968), p. 8.

8. Florence H. Pettit, *America's Indigo Blues: Resist-printed and Dyed Textiles of the Eighteenth Century* (New York: Hastings House, 1974).

9. Commons, *Documentary,* 2:324.

10. Johnson, *Dictionary* s.v. "linsey-woolsey." Linsey-woolsey is defined as "vile, mean, of different and unsuitable parts; a lawless linsey woolsie brother." (Note: Harold and Dorothy Burnham, *'Keep me warm one night' Early handweaving in eastern Canada* (Toronto: University of Toronto Press, 1972), p. 62, suggests that linsey-woolsey was a derogatory name for drugget, because it was not "all wool and a yard wide.")

11. Johnson, *Dictionary,* s.v. serge.

12. Francis Morris, *Notes on Laces of the American Colonists* (New York: Needle and Bobbin Club, 1926), p. 1-4.

13. William L. Warren, *Bed Ruggs/1722-1833* (Hartford: Wadsworth Atheneum, 1972), p. 23.

BIBLIOGRAPHY

Primary sources for colonial American textile information include wills and inventories, diaries and personal letters, merchants' order and account books, and old newspaper advertisements. Contemporary travel books and old dictionaries are also useful.

The two older books that cover the subject most completely are William R. Bagnall, *The Textile Industries of the United States, Vol. I, 1639-1810* (1893; reprint ed., New York: A. M. Kelley, 1971); and Frances Little, *Early American Textiles* (New York: The Century Co., 1931). Bagnall is especially detailed with biographical information but does not cite many references, nor is there an index. The preface, however, attests to his labors in making the work accurate, a task that took several years of verifying dates and facts. Frances Little also used primary sources but did not cite references. The book has an extensive bibliography. Another excellent work, which explains the system of manufacturing and the changes that occurred, is Rolla Milton Tryon, *Household Manufactures in the United States, 1640-1860* (The University of Chicago Press, 1917), originally a doctoral dissertation. Woman's work is thoroughly discussed in Edith Abbot, *Women in Industry* (1910; reprint ed., New York: Source Book Press, 1970).

Good for background are William B. Weeden's *Economic and Social History of New England: 1620-1789,* 2 vols. (1890; reprint ed., New York: Hillary House Publishers, 1963); Bernard Bailyn, *The New England Merchants in the Seventeenth Century* (Cambridge: Harvard University Press, 1955); and John R. Commons, ed. *A Documentary History of American*

Industrial Society, 10 vols. (Cleveland: The Arthur H. Clark Co., 1910), Volumes I and II cover the colonial period. See also Victor S. Clark, *History of Manufactures in the United States, Volume I, 1607-1860* (New York: McGraw Hill, 1929), and Arthur M. Schlesinger, *The Colonial Merchants and the American Revolution, 1763-1776* (New York: F. Ungar, 1957).

Alice Morse Earle's books, especially *Customs and Fashions in Old England* (1893; reprint ed., Detroit: Singing Tree Press, 1968), and *Colonial Days in Old New York* (New York: Charles Scribner's Sons, 1897) have interesting odd bits of information. Her *Home Life in Colonial Days* (1898; reprint ed., Stockbridge, Mass.: The Berkshire Traveler Press, 1974) is good for fiber processing and weaving information.

Two very helpful theses are Ruth Yvonne Cox, "Textiles Used in Philadelphia 1760-1775" (Master's thesis, University of Delaware, 1960) and Susan C. Finlay, "Textile Availability, Use and Significance in Essex County, Massachusetts, 1628-1686 (Master's thesis, University of New York College at Oneonta, Cooperstown Graduate Program, 1974).

Helpful and well done is a little book by D. Pennington and M. Taylor, *A Pictorial Guide to American Spinning Wheels* (Sabbathday Lake, Maine: The Shaker Press, 1975). It is the result of five years' study and collecting. See, too, Marion L. Channing, *The Magic of Spinning* (1966) and *The Textile Tools of Colonial Homes* (1971), both published by the author in Marion, Massachusetts.

Printing is covered by Florence M. Montgomery, *Printed Textiles: English and American Cottons and Linens 1700-1850* (New York: Viking Press, 1970); and Florence H. Pettit, *America's Printed & Painted Fabrics 1600-1900* (New York: Hastings House, 1970). Rita Adrosko, *Natural Dyes in the United States* (Washington, D. C.: Smithsonian Institution Press, 1968), is best for dyeing.

Fabric names and descriptions are given in Abbot Lowell Cummings, *Bed Hangings: A Treatise on Fabrics and Styles in the Curtaining of Beds, 1650-1850* (Boston: The Society for the Preservation of New England Antiquities, 1961); George Francis Dow, *Every Day Life in the Massachusetts Bay Colony* (Boston: The Society for the Preservation of New England Antiquities, 1935); and George Cole, *Encyclopedia of Dry Goods* (Chicago: Cole, 1900). See also several articles in *Antiques* magazine by Hazel E. Cummin: "Colonial Dimities, Checked and Diapered," September 1940; "What Was Dimity in 1790?," July 1940; "Moreen—A Forgotten Fabric," December 1940; "Calamanco," April 1941; "Tammies and Durants," September 1941; and "Camlet," December 1942. Other articles in *Antiques* include Cedric Larsen, "Cloth of Colonial America," January 1941; Anna Brightman, "Woolen Window Curtains—Luxury in Colonial Boston and Salem," December 1964; and Florence M. Montgomery, "Furnishing Textiles at the John Brown House, Providence, Rhode Island," March 1972.

One of the few references on eighteenth century American imports is Natalie Rothstein, "Silks for the American Market," *The Connoisseur*, October and November 1967. Very important is Philip White, ed., *Beekman Mercantile Papers, 1746-1799*, 3 vols. (New York: New York Historial Society, 1956). Research by noted museum curators can be found in Patricia L. Fiske, ed., *Irene Emery Roundtable on Museum Textiles, 1975 Proceedings* (Washington D. C.: The Textile Museum, 1976).

See Nancy Dick Bogonoff, *Handwoven Textiles of Early New England* (Harrisburg, Pa.: Stackpole Books, 1975) for both good photographs of American textiles and diagrams of bedding and window curtains. Excellent photos are also found in Francis Morris, *Notes on Laces of the American Colonists* (New York: Needle and Bobbin Club, 1926). Georgiana Brown Harbeson, *American Needlework* (New York: Bonanza Books, 1938) gives a good overview of colonial embroidery, and Ethel Bolton and Eva Coe, *American Samplers* (1921;

reprint ed., New York: Dover, 1973) is quite complete. The two important works on floor coverings are Rodis Roth, *Floor Coverings in 18th Century America,* United States National Museum Bulletin 250 (Washington, D. C.: Smithsonian Press, 1967); and Nina Fletcher Little, *Floor Coverings in New England Before 1850* (Sturbridge, Mass.: Old Sturbridge, Inc., 1967).

10. INDUSTRIALIZATION AND TEXTILES IN NINETEENTH CENTURY AMERICA

For textile study the American nineteenth century can be considered to extend from the end of the revolution to the time between the two world wars. During this period textile manufacture was completely industrialized. The shift of cloth production from the home to the factory was made at different rates across the country, and for a long time the two systems coexisted. The nineteenth was the cotton century and also the century that witnessed the birth of man-made fibers.

NINETEENTH CENTURY AMERICA

When the revolutionary war ended in 1781, the new nation was faced with many problems, including a severe shortage of both skilled labor and capital. Currency was thoroughly depreciated, and there was no way to raise public revenues. The country was flooded with European goods that often stayed on merchants' shelves because money was scarce. Household manufacture had shown a sharp, temporary decline, and many small businesses, such as those for silk manufacture, had failed during the war.

Prominent leaders recognized the need for economic independence, especially in textile production, and numerous societies for the encouragement of manufactures were formed. In Philadelphia, New York, Boston, and other places, these societies raised money to start factories, employ the poor, increase agricultural knowledge, and bring order to commerce. Some societies operated warehouses where goods could be sold—there was no marketing system of wholesalers and retailers. Alexander Hamilton helped by urging protective tariffs and subsidies to new industries in his 1791 report to Congress on the state of manufactures.

There was, however, much public resistance to the idea of the United States as a manufacturing nation. Most of the population farmed and saw no reason for transferring labor to manufacturing. There was also a strong feeling that the growth of factories would degrade workers, as had happened in England. It was in part this popular opinion that forced the early mill owners to a position of paternalistic concern for their operatives—an attitude that changed about mid-century when immigrants flooded into the country.

One of the heroes of nineteenth century America was the Englishman Samuel Slater, named "The Father of American Manufactures" by Andrew Jackson. In 1782, on the death of his father, the fourteen year old Slater apprenticed himself to Jedediah Strutt, partner of Richard Arkwright (inventor of the water frame for spinning). At the end of his six-and-a-half-year indenture, Slater decided to emigrate in response to American advertisements for mechanics. Because of English restrictions against the emigration of skilled people, he left secretly (disguised as a farmer), not even daring to bid his mother farewell.

He went to New York, then to Providence, where, under the sponsorship of the wealthy Quaker merchant Moses Brown, he formed a partnership with Smith Brown and William Almy. Slater agreed to build Arkwright machines from plans only in his head. He was to operate them for a dollar a day and share one-half the profits of the business.

The mill in Pawtucket started spinning in December 1790 and was so successful that the other partners were hard pressed to sell all the cotton yarn. At first it was put out to local weavers, but eventually a number of agents along the East Coast were engaged to sell it.

To Hannah Wilkinson, Slater's first wife, is given the credit for the invention of cotton sewing thread. In 1793 she took some of his yarn spun from long staple Surinam cotton and plied it on her spinning wheel. It proved to be stronger than the linen thread in use at the time, and a new industry was born.

Another nineteenth century hero, Eli Whitney, held the title "Father of Mass Production." This he earned as a musket manufacturer. Born in Westboro, Massachusetts in 1765, Whitney grew up helping his father make hoe and axe blades in their small shop. By teaching in a neighborhood school he earned enough to put himself through Yale and on graduation went south to teach.

Whitney invented the cotton gin in 1793 while recuperating from smallpox at the Georgia home of the widow of the famous revolutionary general Nathanael Greene. Eli could fix anything. So, after he had repaired the children's toys and her embroidery frame, Mrs. Greene suggested he figure out a way to separate seeds from cotton. Some old style gins had been in use in the South, but they were not good enough, nor was hand labor fast enough, to enable farmers to meet the growing demand for cotton.

Some accounts say Whitney got his idea from watching the chickens clawing through the fence for grain, others say it came from observing the slave women using their long fingernails to clean the cotton. At any rate, his gin had rollers with teeth that drew the fibers through an iron mesh and left the seeds behind. Whitney and a partner set up a ginning business, but several planters infringed on his patent and copied his machine. The business failed, and he turned to gun making.

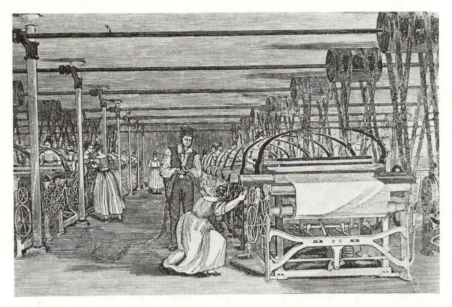

FIGURE 10.1 / Power Weaving (from White, 1836).

Industrial progress was slow. Many small mills sprang up, but at first they only spun yarn, and a curious half-home, half-factory system of production ensued. For example, the cotton for Slater's mill was cleaned at home, spun at the mill, sent to other homes to be woven, then was taken back to the mill for bleaching and dyeing. It was an inefficient system that took two or three years to turn fiber into finished cloth.

The Embargo Act of 1807, passed to avoid conflict with both England and France, forbade nearly all foreign-bound merchant ships from leaving American ports, all exports, even over land, and some imports from Britain. It nearly ruined the New England textile industry by destroying the purchasing power of the commercial population in the coast towns.[1] Then war with England from 1812 to 1815 brought increased demands for domestic cloth, and there was a rush to build new mills. Dumping of English goods on American markets after the war ruined many firms, but the war led to the passage of protective tariffs and a new determination to develop an American textile industry.

Power weaving, first introduced around 1815, brought all operations into the cotton factory. Only plain types of coarse cloth could be made, but it was the demand for these goods, a demand that grew with the movement west, that made the industry grow. Foreign markets were found. The China trade, opened in 1784, became important in the 1830s (Figure 10.1).

In the 1830s and 1840s the cotton mills of Lowell, northwest of Boston, employed a labor force recruited from the farms of New Hampshire and Maine. Young girls of good education went to Lowell to work thirteen-hour days, six days a week for $1.80 to $3.15 a week. One dollar and twenty-five cents of that went to a boarding house where four to six girls shared a room. Reports conflict about the conditions under which these girls lived and worked. The most glowing, which extolled the virtues of working in the mills, were published in the *Lowell Offering*, a magazine written and edited by the mill girls with the endorsement of the company. Newspapers portrayed something much different: "poor girls when they can toil no longer, go home to die. Average working life of girls is only three years. Few of them ever marry: fewer still ever return to their native places with reputations unimpaired."[2] It was said that the windows in the mills were nailed down, the boarding houses overcrowded and full of sick girls.

By the 1830s child labor was common in many factories and it usually meant a ten- to twelve-hour day. Children, being small, were especially adept at crawling under the spinning jennies and other machines. Work was generally not hard, nor even continuous, but conditions were unhealthy, and there was no time for school. In America it was common practice to hire children out at a very early age (even three or four). Sometimes work, such as the cleaning of cotton, was brought to the home for them to do.

New Englanders had been moving west in search of better farm lands since the revolution, and they started the textile industry in New York state. The first mills in Oneida County were incorporated in 1810. Power looms were introduced in 1818. The cotton industry, and later knitting mills, spread west along the Mohawk Valley. Many cities and towns in central and western New York had some textile industry by the time the Erie Canal was finished in 1825 and goods could be shipped easily. Small mills opened in Ohio and Indiana also, mostly to serve only a local area.

Some of the religious groups that lived in segregated communities were closely associated with fabric production. These groups—the Moravians, the Mormons, the Amana Society, and others—were all characterized by their industry and desire to be self-sufficient. The Shakers were a group especially noted for their textiles. They grew flax and raised sheep, and some communities raised silk worms. They made all of their equipment and produced the cloth needed for their communities and extra to sell. Their cottons and woolens were called "Shaker Goods," and after 1850 that name was given to imitations woven in outside mills.

The inmates of the early prisons made up another segregated group. It was common practice to put women to spinning and men to weaving. Records indicate that weaving and clothing manufacture for prison needs was frequent. In 1828 the agent and keeper of the state prison in Auburn, New York, reported to the legislature on the advantages of the Auburn ("Silent") System.[3] Absolute silence was enforced at all times. The men were kept in separate cells (3½' x 7' x 7' cages) at night, and during the day they worked in various shops. The shops had double walls; tourists (at twenty-five cents each) and the guards could walk between them and look through peepholes at the convicts, whose labor had been contracted to a local carpet, coverlet, and tweed manufacturer (see Plate 88). Local residents complained about being deprived of jobs while the contractor exploited prison labor.

Prior to the Civil War most migration to the West was to the Pacific Coast—California and Oregon—and to the Mormon settlements in the Utah Territory. The mountain states were not settled to any degree before the great mining booms of the 1870s, although there were settlements there in the 1850s. The mountain states became sheep producers; wool was their principal contribution to the American textile industry (see Figure 9.1).

California, Oregon, and Utah were settled early enough, and the distance from the East was great enough, to make some textile manufacture worthwhile. The Mormons were given credit for the first woolen mill in the West—opened in 1853 at West Jordan, Utah—to make satinets. The first mill in Oregon (at Willamette) was opened in 1857, but it did not realize a profit until the Civil War brought a large demand for army blankets. In 1858 Californians opened their first woolen mill at Black Point, where quality flannel for shirts was made. The Pendleton mill in Oregon started as a scouring plant in 1893, and after 1900 the still famous jacquard "indian" blankets were made there.

Meanwhile, in the South, cotton had become "King." The economy depended on it—and on slavery. There were a few mills in the South at an early date, most of them associated with plantations, but there was no real industry until the 1870s.[4] The Reconstruction brought New Englanders into the South to utilize the large labor pool of emancipated slaves and poor whites. Former plantation owners became mill managers. Few immigrants went South, because they were not interested in competing for the low wages that stayed low and were a major factor in the general movement of the New England textile industry into the South during the twentieth century.

NINETEENTH CENTURY TEXTILES

Many of the basic fabrics of colonial America were still produced in the nineteenth century (Plate 83), although they sometimes changed in fiber content, and the consumption of yardage per capita increased—most notably for the well-to-do lady whose costume, by mid-century, could use up a hundred yards of cloth. Ladies felt that their large purchases helped provide jobs for poor mill workers. Many Americans still had to be very thrifty; clothing was made over several times, and mending was almost a venerated activity. The introduction of the sewing machine at mid-century increased fabric consumption and paved the way for the ready-to-wear industry. Fashion change accelerated after the Civil War and fabric manufacturers enlarged their selections.

Fibers

Flax and Wool

The position of flax as a major textile fiber was reversed during the early nineteenth century as cotton production took hold. Some was still grown on the farms of New York and Vermont, but gradually the quality of the flax grown in America deteriorated, until, by the end of the century, it was grown only for seed.

The woolen industry was slower than the cotton industry to reach maturity for a number of reasons. It was difficult to work poor quality fiber, and the resulting fabrics could not compete with English woolens. Household manufacture of woolens, unlike that of cotton fabrics, was well established. The equipment for processing wool was more complex, and it was harder to find skilled labor to build and operate it. The transition to power weaving was made later for wool than for cotton.

Poor quality raw material was at the heart of the problem. American sheep were of the coarse, long wool types, haphazardly bred and generally neglected. It had long been recognized that American sheep needed to be improved by breeding with the fine-wooled Merinos, sheep difficult to obtain from foreign countries reluctant to sell them. There are a number of claims for "first" imports of Spanish Merinos, but it is agreed that the very first two, brought to Boston in 1793, were eaten by mistake. Another of the "firsts" was Don Pedro, brought to Delaware in 1807 by Messrs. Du Pont de Nemours and Delessert, who had the largest flock in the state in 1812 and were soon to become important woolen manufacturers. Merino shipments from Portugal began in 1810.

In the 1820s a craze for Saxony sheep started. Everyone who could afford the exorbitant price had to have a ram of this extraordinary fine-wooled breed, which was descended from the Spanish Merino and had been raised with special care in Germany since 1765.

Several societies for the improvement of wool were formed. There was a large increase in the sheep population between 1814 and 1831, especially in Pennsylvania, New York, and Vermont. By the 1830s medium-grade wool, suitable for manufacturing, was being sent east from New York state and the Midwest. The sheep industry moved continuously westward, and ever since the transcontinental railroads were finished in the late 1860s and 1870s the Rocky Mountain and Pacific Coast states and Texas have supplied the New England mills with wool.

Carding, so necessary in preparing the wool for spinning, had always been a tedious job with the old teasel cards. In 1784 a machine for bending wire for cards was invented, and women and children could pick up the wires and pieces of leather at a factory and spend their spare time inserting the wires by hand. It was a good activity to do while visiting, and some children even took pans of wires to school.

The carding machine was a better solution. The first one was patented in England in 1748 by Louis Paul, but it did not prove practical until about 1772, when the mechanism that fed fibers into the machine was invented. There were several early attempts to make carding machines in America, but it was the British type, introduced by the Scholfield brothers who immigrated in 1793, that was successful. In Old Sturbridge Village in Massachusetts there is an original Scholfield carding machine run by water power (at a rather relaxing, quiet, slow, rhythmic rate) (Plate 4). The carding machine proved to be a great stimulus for the home weaving of woolens.

The woolen industry matured around the time of the Civil War and stood twenty years behind the cotton industry. Factories were greatly enlarged to meet demand for uniforms and blankets—even to the point where there was a glut after the war. Some home weaving continued, especially in the South and Midwest during the war when cloth was scarce; but by the 1870s it was a thing of the past.

Cotton

In the days before agricultural colleges, letters describing experiments with cultivation of different kinds of cotton were exchanged between planters. There was a frequent exchange of both information and seed with the West Indies, islands that produced a lot of cotton for English mills. Geographically the South was more closely linked with the West Indies than to the North.

The finest grade of American cotton was *Sea Island*, a long-staple fiber grown principally on islands located between Charleston and Savannah. According to one story it was discovered by accident. A planter had been sent some cotton seed by a friend in Jamaica, but he needed the sacks for something and dumped the seed out on the dung pile. They grew so well during the wet season that he was able to transplant two acres of cotton. Sea Island cotton was seldom ginned with Whitney's machines; the much older fluted roller gin was used.

Upland was the other major variety, and much larger quantities of it were grown. Of medium-staple length, Upland was well suited for general grades of machine woven fabrics. It was grown principally in North and South Carolina, Virginia, and Georgia. Variations were developed in New Orleans, Alabama, Mississippi, etc., and were so named.[5] In 1834 *Nankeen cotton*, the yellow-tinged fiber from China, was successfully grown in Alabama.[6]

Silk

If ever there was an American dream, it was that any common man could get rich by raising silk. In 1814 Tench Coxe was uncertain about what should be done about the industry and thought the most interesting and essential use for silk was boulting cloth for flour mills.[7] Then, in the 1830s horticulturists discovered a variety of Chinese mulberry that would grow rapidly, would produce large leaves, and would live in the United States—at least long enough for speculators to realize fantastic profits. When the Cheney Brothers of Connecticut started business in 1834, seedling mulberry trees were $4 a hundred. By 1836 the price had jumped to $30. Rare among many, the Cheney company stayed with the silk business and became renowned weavers, although they had to use imported raw silk.

Pamphlets (probably it was the "how-to-do-it" writers who made the most money) touted silk cultivation as the ideal home activity. It was an industry that could be adapted to the resources of any family, they said, and a family could retain its independence, become wealthy, keep its girls at home, and help the nation.[8] All over the East housewives had silkworms spinning in the parlor, and they often produced enough fiber for a pair of stocking or gloves.

The fad moved across prairies and mountains. Brigham Young saw possibilities and in 1855 ordered a supply of mulberry seed and silkworms from France. Many Mormon women managed to get enough silk to make dresses, and some very fine silk textiles were woven in Utah. One woman, however, had no luck at all in 1875—her silkworms died of fright during a thunder storm.[9]

Man-made fibers

The nineteenth century witnessed the birth of man-made fibers, more than two hundred years after Robert Hooke first suggested the possibility. Eighteen eighty-four is given as the date for the first successful nitrocellulose textile filament.[10] It was about the turn of the century when the viscose process was developed. The process for acetate came somewhat later. In 1914 William Dooley had little to say about artificial silk except that the manufacturing process was explosive and that the fiber lacked tensile strength and elasticity.[11] By 1925 Cassie Small had more information about rayon (called wood fiber, fiber silk, or glos), and she mentioned that in the early days (ten or fifteen years before) a woman had better not let herself be caught out in the rain if she was wearing a dress of the new fiber.[12]

Advances in Spinning

Americans were inventive and made many adaptations and improvements for the old spinning wheel. It was still so useful an item in the 1860s that thousands were being manufactured. But it was machine spinning that was most important in the nineteenth century. The jenny was the first spinning machine in use in America. Then Samuel Slater brought Arkwright's water frame, which could be used to spin coarse cotton warp.

Wool was spun on the jenny until about 1830 when the *jack* was invented (Figure 10.2). The jack was the first water powered wool spinning machine, and it was patterned after Crompton's mule. After a "self-actor" device was added in 1870, the jack became known as a mule, and it was used well into the twentieth century for spinning wool.[13]

Ring spinning, invented about 1830, became the chief method for spinning cotton. The machine was vertical with rollers to draw out the fiber. The spindles were located under the rollers. Each spindle had a steel ring around it, and on each ring was a wire (called a traveler) through which the yarn passed to the bobbin on the spindle. As the spindle revolved the traveler was drawn around the ring. Because the traveler went more slowly than the bobbin, twist was put into the yarn.

Nineteenth Century Looms

The major innovations of the nineteenth century were the jacquard mechanism and the power loom. Other inventions such as the dandy loom that moved the cloth automatically (1802) and the dobby pattern loom (as well as many American and English improvements) speeded total mechanization of the textile industry. The knitting industry also grew steadily, mainly in the Middle Atlantic states.

FIGURE 10.2 / Spinning Jack (from White, 1836).

Invented in France at the beginning of the century, the jacquard device reached America in the 1820s. Early models were attached to handlooms and used mostly for coverlet and carpet weaving (see Figure 3.14). Adoption of the jacquard resulted in a more rapid change in dress fabric patterns. Thus, it was not quite as easy as it had been to remake old dresses and stay in fashion.

The two different types of power looms came to be associated with different systems of manufacturing, the *Waltham* and the *Rhode Island*. The Waltham loom, developed by Francis Cabot Lowell in 1816 after a trip to England and Scotland, was a complex and expensive machine. The labor system associated with the Waltham loom was Lowell's as well. Single persons, mostly female, lived in boarding houses, and the company took charge of their lives. Wages were paid in cash, and for women they were a bit higher than those paid in the Rhode Island system.

The Rhode Island system was associated with the Gilmour or Scotch loom, introduced to America in 1815 by the Scot William Gilmour, who made the inexpensive power loom available to all who were interested in copying it. The Rhode Island mills using Gilmour looms employed whole families and often made wages payable in goods at the company store.

Developments in Finishing and Coloring

Discoveries and advancements in chemistry paralleled spinning and weaving inventions. There was a kind of chain reaction—the improvement in one phase of production necessitated advancements in other phases. During the nineteenth century finishing was generally moved out of the mill into specialized converting establishments. A large number of improvements were made in the last half of the century, and then finishing practices did not change much until the advent of man-made fibers.

An important contribution to the textile industry was the "American System" for bleaching cotton. Dr. Samuel Dana's 1837 discovery for using muriatic (hydrochloric) acid after a lime boil, and following that with two caustic soda boils, rather than the customary four alkali boils, brought significant savings in labor, time, and chemicals.[14]

There were advances in American woolen finishing as well. In 1792 Samuel Dorr of Albany produced a shearing machine that employed a number of cutting blades on the cylinder—like an old hand powered lawn mower. The gig mill, a cylindrical machine for napping, was invented in 1797. It still used the teasels that had been used for a very long time to raise the nap of woolens. (Teasels for the woolen industry were grown around Skaneateles in New York state from 1832 until the mid-twentieth century. Teasels were used in preference to bent wires for finishing better woolens, because the barbs would break off rather than damage the fabric when a burr or entanglement of fibers was encountered.)

Americans did not make any significant contributions to the world dye industry apart from the development of synthetic fiber dyes in the twentieth century. Up to 1860 dyeing operated at the medieval level, although dyers were aided by handbooks such as *The Country Dyer's Assistant* (1798) and *The Dyer's Companion* (1806). Many such recipe books were brought from Europe.

There was no commercial production of natural dyestuffs in the United States, with the exception of the indigo that was grown in South Carolina. Some housewives grew small plots of dye plants and were aided in their dyeing endeavors by printed recipes. Many dyes were readily purchased, madder and indigo most commonly. The chamber pot method (utilizing urine) was the way of the nineteenth century. Dyeing wool (most home dyeing) and dyeing cotton (industry dyeing) required different methods. In fact, cotton fabrics were more generally printed than dyed.

Wood block printing was the method commonly used in early America; copperplate printing never reached the level attained in Europe (see Chapter 8). Most printing establishments were small and often did dyeing and refurbishing of dirty and faded garments as well.

John Hewson of Philadelphia was the most famous American block printer. Ten pieces of his work are extant (Plate 84).[15] Hewson was trained in England and came to America in 1773 on invitation from Benjamin Franklin. He opened a bleach yard and print works soon after arrival and, except for a wartime stint in the Continental Army and a British prison, continued printing until 1810 when he turned the business over to his son. Among the fabrics Hewson printed were handkerchiefs, dress goods, men's waistcoats, and bedspreads. The members of the Pennsylvania Society for the Encouragement of Manufacturing of the Useful Arts were so impressed with his work they awarded him a gold medal.[16]

Roller printing (see Figure 4.3) started in the United States about 1810 and was well established in 1825. The machine has not changed significantly since its invention, except for an increase in the number of rollers. By 1876 a duplex machine that could print eight colors simultaneously on both sides of the cloth was in operation.

Fabrics

A survey of different localities and time periods will give an idea of the textiles commonly in use during the nineteenth century.

The 1820s

About 1820, a period when home manufacture was still quite important, a typical American family lived on a small farm in New England and would have been able to raise enough flax to weave the usual bed sheets, table linens, and towels. Possibly a woman in the household would have been able to operate a multiharness loom, but it is more likely that her diaper figured table linens were woven by a professional weaver. Beds often had covers of checked linen, blue and white or red and white; Indian chintz might still be in use for bed curtains. Factory made cotton ticking for the straw mattresses could be purchased for around fifty-five cents a yard, coarse cotton sheeting for thirty-five cents. Blankets were still being woven at home, of wool grown on the farm. Many women did needlework or made lace (Plate 85).

A great variety of dress fabric was available. Sheer muslins from India had been very popular since 1800, and many accounts were written about the idiocy of wearing the light, white cotton in the New England winter, even with invisible lamb's wool underwear. *Sprigged* (design penciled on), *spotted*, and *jaconet* (cross bar) *muslins* were bought. It is doubtful that muslins sheer enough for the fashion could have been made in New England mills at that time. Ginghams were made by handweavers—a power loom for making them was not perfected until much later. Calico, considered disgusting by the rich, could have been cylinder printed in the United States by 1820. Satin, damask, and linen cambric were probably imported, as were *crepe* (spelled *crape* in England) and *bombazine* (a corded cotton and silk), both worn for mourning. American-made nankeen was used for women's apparel.

Men's clothing was made of nankeen, corduroy, jersey (knitted wool), serge, and linsey-woolsey. Wool broadcloth and *cassimere* (Kerseymere), two of the earliest fabrics to be made in American mills, were used for outer wear. Flannel was a basic. Men's waistcoats were made of some of the most interesting textiles: embroidered satin, *velveret* (a ribbed cotton), striped *Marseilles* (a raised weave cotton from Beverly, Massachusetts).

A somewhat novel use of factory woven canvas was made in the early years of the century. Strips were sewn together, given several coats of paint, and then stenciled with designs. These *floor cloths* were used in place of expensive carpets. They could be painted to look like ingrain or Brussels, or be quite original. They were made in factories and at home in the attic or barn, because the paint took a very long time to dry.

Farther west, in Ontario County of New York, household production was of even greater importance. We are told that in 1822 the Seth Jones family of Bristol produced

> 319 yards of linen cloth, 25 of kersey for bags, 32 of shirting, 35 of diaper, 52 of cotton and linen, 199 of woolen cloth, 16 of kersey for blankets, 24 of plain flannel for blankets, 28 of cotton and wool, 34 of cotton, 22 of worsted, 30 pairs of socks, 7 pairs of stockings, 3 pairs of mittens, 5 bed quilts, 1 carpet, 27 pairs of pantaloons, 23 frocks, 2 surtouts, 4 coats, 4 sailor coats, 12 aprons, 1 bed tick, 7 blankets, 10 flannel sheets, 20 linen sheets, 30 shirts, 5 vests and 12 kersey bags.[17]

The Seth Jones family was awarded a premium by the Ontario County Agricultural Society for their year's accomplishment.

The 1840s

By 1840 a typical American family would be living farther west, perhaps in Indiana, still on a farm where some weaving and spinning was going on, but the majority of the staple fabrics would have been purchased, unless the family was very poor. Most textiles came from New England mills, a few from local producers, and a few from abroad.

Cassimere, basic in style and medium in price as were most of the cottons made in American mills, was by then one of the staple products of the woolen industry. Another staple was *satinet*, woven with a cotton warp and wool weft in sateen weave and finished as a woolen. Kentucky jean was also a mixture with cotton warp and wool weft, but it was woven in twill. More expensive *cashmere,* a soft woolen or worsted twill, had the same twill weave as the center of a Kashmir shawl. Other woolens, *merino* (a twill) and *delaine* (plain weave) were popular for house dresses and sometimes were printed. For more formal occasions women had dresses of *gros de Naples,* a silk ribbed fabric; *barege*, a gauzy silk and wool cloth from France; and *Pekin stripe*, silk with contrasting lengthwise stripes of satin and grosgrain. Handmade lace was popular.

American coverlets were at a peak of popularity in the 1840s. Great numbers were made by the thousands of handweavers who came to the United States in the early decades of the nineteenth century. In England, Ireland, Scotland, and Germany they had been trained for an occupation that was rapidly becoming extinct, so they bought small acreages in New York, Pennsylvania, Kentucky, Ohio, or Indiana where they could farm and weave. Rarely is coverlet weaving associated with New England, although many of the immigrant weavers spent some time working in the mills before they headed west. Some became itinerant weavers, often using their clients' looms. Coverlets were much in vogue in country areas, and the fad went west with the population; women needed warm and attractive bed covers, and coverlets could be made relatively inexpensively from homegrown wool. Weaving costs ranged from two or three dollars for a single weave to ten or twelve dollars for a double-woven jacquard.

The overshot is the oldest type of coverlet (Plate 86). Made in America during the last quarter of the eighteenth century, overshot coverlets could be woven by nonprofessionals on four-harness looms, but they were more frequently made by immigrant Scotch weavers. These coverlets show a foundation of plain weave with warp and two sets of filling that switch from one face of the cloth to the other at the supplementary pattern weft of wool (see chapter 3). Drafts were passed down from one generation to the next and carried traditional names: chariot wheels, blazing star, trailing vine, Whig Rose—patterns based mostly on circles and squares. Some designs are so intricate they have a tendency to vibrate (Plate 87). More coverlets were made in overshot construction than in any other, and more overshot coverlets were made in the mid-Atlantic states than anywhere else.

Much less common are the summer and winter coverlets. Their construction is similar to overshot in that there is a plain weave ground and a supplemental pattern weft. They are different in that the float length is never longer than three, and snagging is not the problem that it is with overshot. Summer and winter designs are small geometric figures in dark and light. The coverlets are reversible, with one side predominately dark (winter) and the other predominately light (summer). They have a somewhat flecked appearance and are fairly heavy. They should not be confused with double cloth construction, which is also reversible.

The double woven coverlet is a third type. It is characterized by two sets of warp and two sets of filling that switch from one face of the cloth to the other at the edges of the pattern figures, making reversible patterns (Plate 88). Sometimes they were made on multishaft looms, but after 1825 the handloom with a jacquard attachment was generally used. Coverlets made with the jacquard became popular rapidly, because complex and varied designs could be woven. Most weavers had a selection of patterns to choose from, and they had sets of prepunched cards. The end borders could be individualized with the owner's name and the date of weaving, or the weaver's name and identifying motif, and it is the kind of coverlet that is especially valuable to historians (Plate 89). As with the other types of coverlets, the early jacquards were woven in two pieces that were seamed together. Eventually the flying shuttle was adopted and looms made wider. Probably because they cost more than single coverlets, jacquards were better preserved. There are many around today. A family may own one that has been passed down with the erroneous tale that a great, great grandmother or aunt wove it. It is very unlikely that a jacquard loom was ever operated by anyone but a professional weaver. It is also unlikely that the jacquard weavers were itinerants. The loom was just too bulky, and delicately balanced, to be moved easily, although weavers did travel to take orders. It is probable, however, that an ancestor raised the wool and spun it at home (and maybe dyed it indigo blue or madder red), then sent it to be woven.

Handweaving of coverlets ended with the Civil War. Many weavers joined the army or were quite old by that time. Attention was given to more necessary weaving, and the demand died. There was a brief revival for the American centennial in 1876, but the machine loomed coverlets with their commemorative designs were of poor quality, lightweight, and the colors were not fast.

The 1850s and 1860s

By the late 1850s and early 1860s a wide variety of fabrics was available to those who could pay the price. Brocades, *matelassé* (a kind of silk double cloth with a raised, puckery pattern), pique, poplin, moiré, taffeta, and *doeskin* (a broadcloth with a soft, lustrous finish) were especially popular. Velvet was used in quantity. The choice of woolens was large and included merino, *camel's hair* made from sheep's wool, broadcloth, cashmere, *challis* (a soft woolen printed with tiny flowers), and *albatross*, a fine, soft plain weave. *Alpaca*, made in Liverpool of alpaca fiber weft on cotton warp and popular because it defied dust, and *mohair,* a stiff wiry cloth made from Angora goat fiber warp and cotton, wool, or silk weft, were similar to *brilliantine* and *Sicilian.* Worsted yarns were used to make *bunting* (soft, lightweight, plain weave, dyed in solid colors) and serge, the old favorite twill. Homespun (Plate 83) was still in use.

In the South the gentry still bought many luxurious fabrics from abroad. The slaves wore their owners' hand-me-downs on Sunday and *Negro cloth* (calico, nankeen, osnaburg, linsey-woolsey) for everyday. When wartime blockades closed the ports, some Southerners were humiliated when, in church at least, they found themselves more shabbily dressed than their slaves. The Civil War brought extreme shortages to the South; people remade, wove their own, and used fabrics they had never used before. They tore up mattresses to get wool or used cow hair for the weft in jean (a twill with cotton warp and wool weft). The price for calico jumped to twenty-five dollars a yard, then soared to fifty.

A Texan, Isaac Newton Stubblefield, served in the Texas Militia, then joined the Union Army, and finally went to Mexico where he was serving with the Federals when the war ended. He was concerned about his family and wrote the following letter.

Brownsville June 16th/65

Dear Wife & Children,

I wrote you a letter yesturday I thought then I would get to go over to Matamoros to day & bring the goods over that I bought yesterday but it was soe that I could not goe   I have not got the Bill   Consequently I cant give you all the articles I will get it and send it to you with the goods   Yalanie has promised he will take them as far as Houstin   Christian talks of going with him   I will give you a bill from memory about 100 yds Calico of the best quality I could get   40 yds Bleached Domestic   30 yds worsted also 6 yds worsted damaged but I got it cheap   11 pairs Shoes   3 hooped Skirts   24 yds of heavy flannel goods for under Skirts of the Mexican style maid a purpos So [I] got it at less then cost one dollar per yard . . .

Goods are very cheap here & I think they will be high for a time in Texas   I have laid them in so that you can sell what you don't want but you had better Keep all you want or may want for the next year.[18]

The End of the Century

For many Americans times were hard in the 1870s, too. Some headed west in old

PLATE 85 / Lace, embroidery on net, made by Miss Catherine Skinner of Wethersfield, Connecticut, in 1813. (Courtesy of Mrs. William Griswold)

PLATE 86 / An overshot coverlet. (Courtesy of Mrs. Richard Bowen)

PLATE 87 / An overshot coverlet. (Courtesy of The Denver Art Museum)

PLATE 88a (*above*) / Jacquard coverlet made at Auburn Prison, New York State.
PLATE 88b (*below*) / Detail of the jacquard coverlet.

PLATE 89 / Jacquard coverlet made by "A. Davidson, Fancy Weaver," around 1830. (Courtesy of The Denver Art Museum. Gift of James Economos)

PLATE 90 *(above)* / Twine-plaited shirt from Tonto Monument (1200-1400 A.D.). Length 26″. (Arizona State Museum, The University of Arizona. Photo by E. B. Sayles)   PLATE 91 *(below)* / A Breech cloth from Gourd Cave, woven in double-weft twill. (Arizona State Museum, The University of Arizona. Photo by E. B. Sayles)

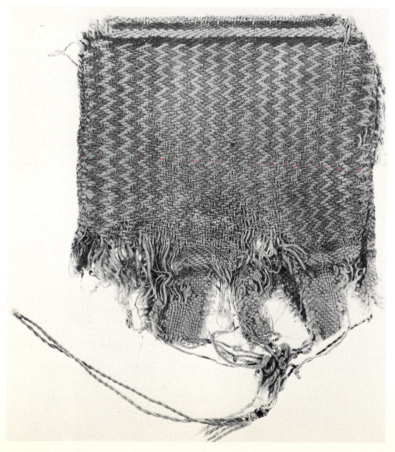

PLATE 92 (*above*) / Hopi maiden's shawl of cotton and wool.   PLATE 93 (*below*) / Hopi ceremonial sash. (Courtesy of The Denver Art Museum)

PLATE 97 (*top*) / Navajo rug illustrating diamond twill.　　PLATE 98 (*bottom*) / Navajo rug illustrating tufting with mohair.

(*Facing page*)
PLATE 94 (*top*) / Navajo chief blanket.　　PLATE 95 (*center*) / Navajo rug illustrating beading.　　PLATE 96 (*bottom*) / Navajo blanket illustrating reclining twill.

PLATE 100 / Navajo dress.

PLATE 99 *(facing page)* / Two Grey Hills rug.

PLATE 103 / Chimayo rug. Detail 2′ x 3′.

(*Facing page*)
PLATE 101 (*top*) / Detail of a Germantown rug showing
outlining and "lazy lines."   PLATE 102 (*bottom*) Jerga.
(Courtesy of the Museum of New Mexico, photo by Arthur
L. Olivas)

PLATE 105 / Colcha embroidery. (Courtesy of the Museum of New Mexico, photo by Arthur L. Olivas)

PLATE 104 (*facing page*) / A Rio Grande blanket reflecting the influence of Mexican Saltillo serape. (Courtesy of the Museum of New Mexico, photo by Arthur L. Olivas)

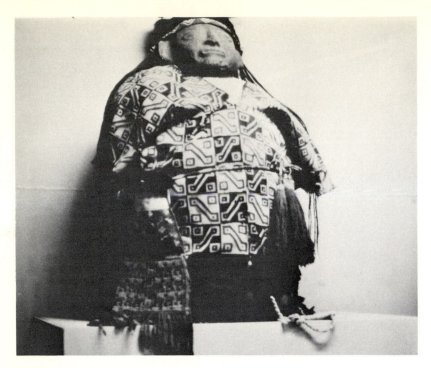

PLATE 106 (*above*) / Peruvian mummy bundle.   PLATE 107 (*below*) / The burying
ground at Paracas.

army uniforms, linsey-woolsey, and calico. Children wore underwear made from cotton flour sacks. In fact, flour sacking became a very practical textile in the mining camps and sod houses. It was used extensively for patching (printed advertising included), for hooked rugs, for quilts, and for just about anything. Heavier grain sacks were converted into men's trousers; old tent canvas made nightgowns. Anne Ellis wrote of the good old days in the mining camps.

> Our clothes were not a problem then, as they are today. A new dress twice a year, Christmas and the Fourth of July, Mama usually making them out of three yards of calico, purchased with a quarter you had "boned" one of the boys for.[19]

Some struck it rich and wore *ladycloth*, a fine quality flannel; *tarlatan*, a variety of crisp muslin, rather coarse, and so low in count as to be almost transparent; cashmere for wedding dresses; velvet; and *astrakam,* mohair fabric with closely curled pile, resembling karakul. During the summer the rich wore *grenadine*, a gauze weave; *foulard,* a lightweight silk, often printed; *cambric,* a plain weave cotton glazed on one side; *organdy*; and *crepe de Chine*, a lightweight silk. *Percale*, introduced in 1865, was often made into dresses. It was a closely woven cotton of better quality than calico, often printed with small geometric figures.

Delineator magazines for the 1890s list a great variety, including many of the staples from previous years. Ribbed fabrics were important: *gros de Londres*, a lustrous dress silk similar to *epringle* made of silk and wool; *gros de Tours*, heavy for mourning; and *grosgrain*, a fine ribbed silk like *faille. Prunella,* plum colored, was a rich satin-weave worsted used for clergymen's gowns and ladies' dresses. *Henrietta* was a soft worsted filling-faced twill, similar to cashmere. Many of these fabrics continued to be used during the early part of the twentieth century.

NOTES

1. Caroline F. Ware, *The Early New England Cotton Manufacture: A Study in Industrial Beginnings* (New York: Russell and Russell, 1966), p. 39.

2. Elisha Bartlett, M.D., *A Vindication of the Character and Condition of the Females Employed in The Lowell Mills, Against The Charges Contained in The Boston Times, and The Boston Quarterly Review* (Lowell, Mass.: Leonard Huntress, Printer, 1841).

3. *Report of Gershom Powers, Agent and Keeper of The State Prison, at Auburn. Made to The Legislature, Jan. 7, 1828* (Albany, 1828), p. 110.

4. Some suggested readings include Kenneth M. Stampp, *The Peculiar Institution: Slavery in the Ante-bellum South* (New York: Alfred A. Knopf, 1968); Broadus Mitchell, *The Rise of Cotton Mills in The South* (1921; reprint ed., New York: Da Capo Press, 1968); and Ernest M. Lander, *The Textile Industry in Antebellum South Carolina* (Baton Rouge: Louisiana State University Press, 1969).

5. George S. White, *Memoir of Samuel Slater* (1836; reprinted., New York: A. M. Kelley, 1967), p. 365.

6. Ibid., p. 382.

7. Tench Coxe, *A Statement of the Arts and Manufactures of the United States of America for the Year 1810* (Philadelphia, 1814), p. xiv.

8. Citizen of Mansfield, Connecticut, *Practical Hints on the Culture of the Mulberry Tree, Together with the Art of Raising Silk Worms in the Best Manner, with the Cheapest and Most Simple Furniture and Fixtures* (Hartford: Gurdon Robins, Jr., 1839).

9. Daughters of Utah Pioneers, *Heart Throbs of the West*, compiled by Mrs. Kate B. Carter, 10 vols. (Salt Lake City: Daughters of Utah Pioneers, 1939) 1:299.

10. Williams Haynes, *Cellulose The Chemical That Grows* (Garden City, New York: Doubleday & Co., 1953), p. 20.

11. William H. Dooley, *Textiles*, rev. ed. (New York: D. C. Heath and Co., 1914), p. 230.

12. Cassie Paine Small, *How To Know Textiles* (Boston: Ginn and Co., 1925), pp. 313-315.

13. Merrimack Valley Textile Museum, *Wool Technology and The Industrial Revolution: An Exhibition* (North Andover, Massachusetts: Merrimack Valley Textile Museum, 1965).

14. Bernard K. Easton, "The Origin of Bleaching," *CIBA-GEIGY Review* no. 3 (1971), p. 5.

15. Florence M. Montgomery, *Printed Textiles: English and American Cottons and Linens 1700-1850* (New York: Viking Press, 1970), p. 92.

16. Harrold E. Gillingham, "Calico and Linen Printing in Philadelphia," *The Pennsylvania Magazine of History and Biography* 52, no. 2 (1928):104.

17. Alexander C. Flick, *History of the State of New York,* 10 vols. (New York: Columbia University Press, 1934), 6:194.

18. Unpublished letter, courtesy of Mrs. Howard D. Funk and Mrs. Robert E. Barnard (Jean Stubblefield).

19. Anne Ellis, *The Life of An Ordinary Woman* (Boston: Houghton Mifflin Co., 1929), p. 86.

BIBLIOGRAPHY

Primary sources are numerous: many archives hold business records, diaries, and letters. Old mail order catalogs can be used. Nineteenth century magazines and newspapers are readily available in many libraries.

Books are plentiful; many listed in the bibliography of chapter 9 can be used for the nineteenth century also. Of these, the following are especially helpful: Little, *Early American Textiles;* Bagnall, *The Textile Industries of the United States;* Tryon, *Household Manufactures in the United States;* Commons, *A Documentary History of American Industrial Society;* Clark, *History of Manufactures in the United States;* Montgomery, *Printed Textiles;* Pettit, *America's Printed & Painted Fabrics;* Roth, *Floor Coverings;* Little, *Floor Coverings in New England;* Burnham, *'Keep me warm one night';* and Cole's *Encyclopedia of Dry Goods.*

Tench Coxe, *A Statement of the Arts and Manufactures of the United States of America for the year 1810* (Philadelphia, 1814) is full of all sorts of information and opinions. It has been reprinted and should be available in libraries holding U.S. Documents. chapter 1 of Melvin T. Copeland, *The Cotton Manufacturing Industry of the United States* (1917; reprint ed., New York.: A. M. Kelley, 1966), presents an excellent brief overview of the early textile industry and the conditions that either encouraged or discouraged its growth. Copeland has some helpful information on finishing. John

Brown, ed., *Lamb's Textile Industries of the United States* (Boston: James H. Lamb Company, 1911) gives a good overview of both men and business however, references are not cited. Another general survey is Perry Walton, *The Story of Textiles* (New York: Tudor Publishing Co., 1925). Walton only lists his sources and does not cite them. The introduction to *Manufactures of The United States in 1860 Compiled from the Original Returns of the Eighth Census, under the Direction of the Secretary of the Interior* (Washington: Government Printing Office, 1865) is good for the history of cotton goods, woolens, worsteds, and carpets. A book that is similar in style to the Alice Morse Earle works is Mrs. Ella Shannon Bowles, *Homespun Handicrafts* (Philadelphia: J. P. Lippincott, 1931).

Specific to the cotton industry is Caroline Ware's classic, *The Early New England Cotton Manufacture* (1931; reprinted., New York: Russell and Russell, 1966). Its approach gives the reader a good conception of conditions during the period between the revolution and 1846. Paul F. McGouldrick continues the cotton story from 1836 to 1886 in the very detailed study, *New England Textiles in the Nineteenth Century: Profits and Investments* (Cambridge: Harvard University Press, 1968). Another profound study is Jacob Burgy, *New England Cotton Textile Industry: A Study in Industrial Geography* (Baltimore: Waverly Press, Inc., 1932).

The classic work on the wool industry is probably Arthur Harrison Cole, *The American Wool Manufacture*, 2 vols. (Cambridge: Harvard University Press, 1926). It is quite complete, and much technical information about spinning and weaving is included. A well written, easy-to-read book is Norman L. Crockett, *The Woolen Industry of the Midwest* (Lexington: The University Press of Kentucky, 1970). John Borden Armstrong has been most thorough in his research for *Factory Under the Elms* (Cambridge: M.I.T. Press for the Merrimack Valley Textile Museum, 1962) and has written, in this book, a fascinating history of the small textile town of Harrisville, New Hampshire.

George S. White, *Memoir of Samuel Slater* (1836; reprint ed., New York: A. M. Kelley, 1967) is the authority, but it is inconvenient to use because it has no index. E. H. Cameron, *Samuel Slater: Father of American Manufactures* (Freeport, Maine: Bond Wheelwright Co., 1954) is much more readable and includes an extensive bibliography. The life of the inventor of the cotton gin is covered best by Jeannette Mirsky and Allan Nevins, *The World of Eli Whitney* (New York: The Macmillan Co., 1952). More difficult to read is Constance McL. Green, *Eli Whitney and the Birth of American Technology* (Boston: Little, Brown and Co., 1956). Nathan Appleton, *Introduction of the Power Loom and Origin of Lowell* (1858) and Samuel Batchelder, *Introduction and Early Progress of the Cotton Manufacture in the United States* (1863) have been combined and edited by George Rogers Taylor under the title *The Early Development of the American Cotton Textile Industry* (New York: Harper and Row, 1969). The reader will get a feeling for the personalities of Appleton and Batchelder, early textile enterpreneurs. Many textile companies have published their histories, often commemorating a centennial. One is Dane Yorke, *The Men and Times of Pepperell* (Boston, 1945).

The source on the Lowell mill girls that is easiest to obtain and quite quick to read is Harriet H. Robinson, *Loom and Spindle, or Life Among the Early Mill Girls*. It was written in 1898 but has been reprinted (Kailua, Hawaii: Press Pacifica, 1976). Margaret H. Koehler wrote a good article, "Two Miles of Girls," for the June 1972 issue of *Yankee*. In *Women in Industry* (1910; reprint ed., New York: Source Book

Press, 1970), Edith Abbott explains why machinery was viewed with disfavor in New England.

For a brief history of immigration to the United States see John F. Kennedy, *A Nation of Immigrants* (New York: Harper & Row, 1964). Donald B. Cole, *Immigrant City: Lawrence, Massachusetts, 1845-1921* (Chapel Hill: The University of North Carolina Press, 1963) tells the complete story of the labor forces in that textile city. The English immigrants are discussed in chapter 3 ("Spindle and Shuttle") of Rowland Tappan Berthoff, *British Immigrants in Industrial America 1790-1950* (Cambridge: Harvard University Press, 1953) and by Herbert Heaton, "The Industrial Immigrant in the United States, 1783-1812," *Proceedings of the American Philosophical Society* 95 (October 1951):519-527.

Grace Rogers Cooper researched two prominent New England families for *Scholfield Wool-carding Machines,* U.S. National Museum Bulletin No. 218 (Washington, D.C.: Smithsonian Institution, 1959) and *The Copp Family Textiles* (Washington, D.C.: Smithsonian Institution Press, 1971). A book that gives much personal detail about a family engaged in woolen manufacture in eastern New York is Thomas W. Leavitt, *The Hollingsworth Letters* (Cambridge: Society for the History of Technology and the M.I.T. Press, 1969).

American handweaving is the topic of Constance D. Gallagher, *Linen Heirlooms* (Newton Center, Massachusetts: Charles T. Branford Co., 1968). She includes directions for weaving early patterns. Allen H. Eaton, *Handicrafts of the Southern Highlands* (1937; reprint ed., New York: Dover Publications, Inc., 1973), shows how these early handcrafts have moved into the twentieth century. A good start on the study of quilting—which interests the textile historian because it is a craft that preserved old fabrics—can be made with Patsy and Myron Orlofsky, *Quilts in America* (New York: McGraw-Hill Book Co., 1974). Its bibliography is extensive.

For a study of the technology of machine weaving there are a number of manuals available, many dating from the end of the nineteenth century. Even those from the early twentieth can be helpful. Two are Emanuel A. Posselt, *Technology of Textile Design* (Philadelphia Textile Publishing Co., n.d.) and Alfred Spitzli, *A Manual for Managers, Designers, Weavers, and All Others Connected with the Manufacture of Textile Fabrics, Containing Definitions, Derivations and Explanations of Technical Terms; The Use Made of Many Substances* (West Troy, New York: A. and A. F. Spitzli, Publishers, 1881). (Very long titles generally identify late nineteenth century books.) A sort of "how-to-do-it" book for textile designers is R. T. Lord, *Decorative and Fancy Textile Fabrics* (London: Scott Greenwood, 1898). Somewhat biased toward the United States is John Lord Hayes, *American Textile Machinery: its early history, characteristics . . . relations to other industries, and claims for national recognition* (Cambridge: Cambridge University Press, J. Wilson and Son, 1879).

Some of the sources above have information on finishing, but see also Harry Bischoff Weiss, *The Early Fulling Mills of New Jersey* (Trenton: New Jersey Agricultural Society, 1957), and Frederick H. Greene, *Practice in Finishing* (Philadelphia: The Textile Record, 1886), a handbook for finishing woolens and worsteds. Some information on dyeing in America can be found in *Dye Plants and Dyeing—a Handbook* published by the Brooklyn Botanic Gardens in 1964 and in Franco Brunello, *The Art of Dyeing in the History of Mankind* (Cleveland: Phoenix Dye Works, 1973), a translation of the 1968 Italian edition. Rita J. Adrosko, *Natural Dyes in the United States* (Washington, D.C.: Smithsonian Institution Press, 1968) is the definitive work. Of interest are Elijah Bemis, *The Dyer's Companion: With a New Introduction by Rita J. Adrosco* (1815; reprint ed., New York: Dover Publications, 1973), and J. and R. Bronson, *The Domestic Manufacturer's Assistant, and Family Directory in the Arts of Weaving and Dyeing* (1817; reprinted., Newton Centre, Massachusetts: Charles T. Branford Co., 1949).

For the story of early printing see H. E. Gillingham, "Calico and Linen Printing in Philadelphia," *The Pennsylvania Magazine of History and Biography* 52, no. 2 (1928):97-110. Ian Quimby and Polly Anne Earl, eds., *Technological Innovation and the Decorative Arts, Winterthur Conference Report 1973* (Charlottesville: University of Virginia Press, 1974), published for The Henry Francis du Pont Winterthur Museum, has a good chapter on roller printing written by Theodore Z. Penn. White's *Memoir of Samuel Slater* also has a chapter on calico printing. Paula Preston's booklet, *Printed Cottons at Old Sturbridge Village* (Sturbridge, Massachusetts, 1969) is still available. Joyce Storey, *Van Nostrand Reinhold Manual of Textile Printing* (New York: Van Nostrand Reinhold, 1974) contains the history of various printing methods but is particularly specific about cylinder engraving methods. See Florence M. Montgomery, *Printed Textiles: English and American Cottons and Linens 1700-1850* (New York: Viking Press, 1970) for additional references.

Two booklets, both by Catherine Fennelly, have been published by Old Sturbridge Village: *Textiles in New England, 1790-1840* (1961) and *The Garb of Country New Englanders 1790-1840* (1966). Costume books such as Elizabeth McClellan, *History of American Costume* (1904; reprint ed., New York: Tudor Publishing Co., 1969), and Blanche Payne, *History of Costume* (New York: Harper & Row, 1965) give some information on fabrics used during different periods.

Sources on coverlets are plentiful. Three very good ones are Mildred Davison and Christa C. Mayer-Thurman, *A Handbook on the Collection of Woven Coverlets in The Art Institute of Chicago* (Chicago: The Art Institute, 1973); Pauline Montgomery, *Indiana Coverlet Weavers and Their Coverlets* (Indianapolis: Hoosier Heritage Press, 1974); and Virginia D. Parslow "James Alexander, weaver," *Antiques*, April 1956. A recent museum catalog is *American Coverlets of the Nineteenth Century from the Helen Louise Allen Textile Collection* (Madison, Wisc.: Elvehjem Art Center, University of Wisconsin, 1974). An older and well-known book is Eliza Calvert Hall, *A Book of Hand-Woven Coverlets* (1912; reprinted, Rutland, Vermont: Charles E. Tuttle Co., 1966). Coverlets are often combined with quilts and other bed coverings. Books that do this include Florence Petro, *American Quilts and Coverlets* (New York: Chanticleer Press, 1949); Charleton L. Safford and Robert Bishop, *America's Quilts and Coverlets* (New York: Weathervane Books, 1974); and Imelda G. DeGraw, *Quilts and Coverlets* (Denver: The Denver Art Museum, 1974).

There are many dictionaries and encyclopedias for fabric definitions. Cole's *Encyclopedia of Dry Goods* is good and so are two by Eliza B. Thompson: *The Silk Department* (1918) and *The Cotton and Linen Departments* (1917), both published by the Ronald Press Company in New York. Others include George and Daniel Bible, *Pocket Dictionary of Dry-Goods, Etc.* (New York: The Trade Printing and Publishing Co., 1896), and C. Brown, *Scissors and Yardstick; or All about dry goods* (Hartford, Conn.: C. M. Brown and F. W. Jaqua, 1872). Most textile textbooks have glossaries of fabric names—and the conflicts among definitions can be frustrating. Do not overlook general dictionaries.

11. FABRICS OF THE AMERICAN SOUTHWEST

A study of the American Southwest offers a good opportunity to compare the textiles of three distinct cultures within one small geographical area. The Basketmaker (later Pueblo) indians, Spanish settlers, and Navajo indians have produced enormous quantities of clothing, blankets, and rugs. Fabrics made over a thousand years ago and preserved by the very dry climate can be found exhibited next to something woven just yesterday.

Most of the important studies of Southwestern textiles have been made by archaeologists and anthropologists, and often the terminology is unique to those disciplines. Southwestern textiles exhibit the changes effected by the use of materials introduced by both conquerors and traders, as well as changes in quality resulting from different reasons for production.

THE REGION AND ITS HISTORY

For purposes of textile study, the Southwest includes the area that is presently New Mexico and Arizona as well as adjacent parts of Utah, Nevada, Texas, Colorado, and Mexico. The Colorado, the Rio Grande, and the San Juan are the important rivers of the area. They drain a land of many scenic contrasts—pine clad mountains and plateaus cut by steep canyons, towering buttes and spires that rise dramatically from desert valley floors, vivid coloring in the bright blue skies, red sandstone, and blue-green pinon. Much of it is harsh land, with extremes of temperature—and vast distances between sparsely settled places. But it is a land with magnetic appeal.

The Rio Grande valley was for hundreds of years the main route into the northern part of the region where most of the Pueblo Indian and Spanish settlements were clustered. The Navajo roamed the thousands of square miles in northern New Mexico, Arizona, and southern Utah, all the territory of the ancient Anasazi.

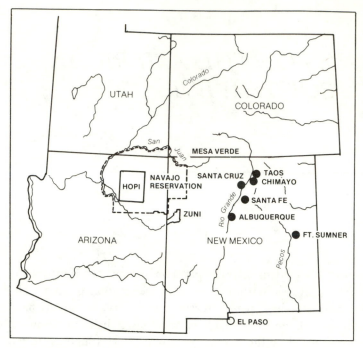

FIGURE 11.1 / The Southwest.

The Southwesterners

Man was living in the Southwest at least twenty-five thousand years ago. In the early centuries A.D., there were several distinct groups. Most is known about the textiles of the Anasazi people of the northern plateau. Fortunately for archaeologists the Anasazi believed in life after death and buried their dead fully clothed and accompanied by items they believed were necessary in the next world. Burials were made in caves, and fabrics and bodies (erroneously known as mummies) were preserved by desiccation. Anasazi culture is divided into two periods (or horizons): the Basketmaker, ending about 700 A.D. (a beginning date has not been established), and the Pueblo, extending from 700 A.D. to the present.

Named Basketmakers because their bodies were found with many baskets, or had baskets over their heads, these early people were small Mongoloids with straight black hair and medium to dark brown skin. The men were about five feet tall, the women somewhat shorter. At first they were hunters and gatherers, eventually they farmed. At night, or in bad weather, they took shelter in caves and shallow recesses that wind and water had cut into the sandstone cliffs. Sometimes they built crude pit houses, little hollows in the ground covered with domes of wood and clay.

Pueblo (Spanish for their dwellings) refers to the same people—although it is possible that there was an infusion of some new blood—after 700 A.D., when their manner of living changed. They began to build groups of jacal houses (made of upright poles chinked with mud) on the mesa tops and became serious farmers. Eventually they learned to build with stone and constructed great apartment complexes. The ruins of these are now major tourist attractions. Essentially, the Pueblos were a peaceful people who lived in harmony with their environment.[1]

The second group to be considered are the Navajo indians—the most noted Southwestern weavers today. Quite different linguistically and anthropometrically from the Anasazi, they descended from the Athaspascan groups of northwestern Canada. They may have entered the Southwest along with the Apache as early as 1000 A.D., although archaeologists do not have evidence of their being there before 1500.[2] The Navajo accepted much of the culture of the Pueblo, including weaving, although their ceremonials remained distinct. They continued to live a semi-nomadic life in small bands and never formed the large population centers typical of the Pueblos.

A third group of Southwesterners arrived in the sixteenth century. These were the Spaniards in search of gold and converts for Christianity. Some sent back to Spain for their ladies, but most married Indians and settled into a somewhat medieval life in Santa Fe and the villages nearby. The pure-blooded rich, who were never really very rich, lived in the Spanish manner as best they could on small haciendas, and some of the ladies spent their days doing needlework. The poor had their adobe villages, and their lives largely revolved around the Catholic church. For well over two hundred years the Hispanos lived in extreme isolation and had few material goods. Sometimes it was two years between visits of the freighters from Veracruz. The distinctive Hispano folk art reflects both the influence of religion and the passive simplicity of life by the Rio Grande.

Historical Overview

The Anasazi

Southwestern chronology begins with 300 A.D., marking the beginning of the Basketmaker II period or phase (Basketmaker I is a slot that has been left open by archaeologists for further discoveries and possible links to previous cultures).[3] Evidence indicates that these people grew corn and squash and hunted extensively. Their baskets were well developed, but they had no pottery. They had no loom-woven textiles but knew weft-twining, looping, and braiding techniques.

Basketmaker III, 500-700 A.D. (Kent) or 400-700 A.D. (Willey) called Modified Basketmaker by Wormington,[4] marks a stage when pit houses were grouped into villages and a few surface houses were built. Pottery was made by coiling clay and firing, and sandal making was at an advanced level. Examples of tapestry weave have been found dating from this period, although it is not certain that a loom was used to make them. While there is some evidence to the contrary,[5] it is assumed by archaeologists that cotton cultivation and the true loom (with heddles and two bars) moved northward from Mesoamerica together and reached the Anasazi about 700 A.D. The inception of cotton weaving is more generally associated with the Pueblo period.

Five culture periods are commonly used for the Pueblos: 1,700-900 A.D.; II, 900-1100 A.D.; III, 1100-1300 A.D.; IV, 1300-1500 A.D.; and V, 1550 to the present.[6] The first two periods are sometimes combined and called Developmental Pueblo, a period marked by life in small villages on the mesa tops.

Pueblo III is known as the Great-Pueblo or Classic Period. The well-known cliff dwellers of Mesa Verde belong to this period that marked the height of communal living. Enormous multistoried buildings with over a hundred rooms were erected on mesa tops, valley floors, or in large caves. Community living fostered the arts and religion. Specialization was possible, and weaving techniques were greatly advanced. Perhaps this was the "golden age" for weaving. Perhaps it only seems so, because the greatest variety of fabrics has been preserved from this period.

Toward the end of Pueblo III there was a mysterious and sudden abandonment of the northern sites. Various theories have accounted for it: severe drought, persistent marauding enemies, or abduction by space ships. Therefore, Pueblo IV (1300-1550) is called the Regressive Period, because it was a time of instability and migrations. Population centers shifted to the valleys of the Little Colorado and the Rio Grande. About thirty thousand people were living in thirty to seventy towns along the Rio Grande when the Spanish arrived in 1540 at the beginning of Pueblo V.[7] During Pueblo V there was a significant change in the textiles, because the Spanish introduced both sheep and a forced labor system.

The Spanish

Coronado brought the first sheep as part of his food supply; they were Churro, a scrawny, hardy breed with long straight wool. The indians called them "little blacke beastes with wooll and hornes" and thus recognized a source of black for their textiles.

Coronado captured the Pueblos at Zuni (supposed to be the Seven Golden Cities of Cibola) in July of 1540 and spent the next winter near the Rio Grande. His men, in need of clothing, went through twelve of the pueblos collecting some three hundred pieces of cloth (cotton mantas), and the natives even had to surrender the garments they were wearing.[8] The Indians were spared more contact with the Spanish, except for a few friars and adventurous soldiers, until Juan de Onate was given contracts for settlements. In 1598 he marched into New Mexico with four hundred people, more sheep, and a glorious wardrobe of Italian velvet suits trimmed with gold passementerie, shirts of satin, and stockings of silk.[9]

Relations with the indians were less than ideal. The Spaniards took over whole pueblos, and the indians were taxed, enslaved, and tortured. When Sante Fe was founded in 1610, it appeared the Europeans were there to stay. The Pueblos labored under *encomienda,* a system whereby a certain number of Indians (after baptism) were entrusted to a Spanish settler who was to instruct, protect, and pay them in return for tributes and labor. Weaving was part of both of the latter; there was a yearly levy of one *vara* (thirty-three inches) of cotton cloth per family, and it is thought that there were weaving workshops in the missions.

In 1680 the indians united and revolted, forcing all the Spaniards—except the ones they massacred—down the Rio Grande to El Paso, where they remained for twelve years. The Spanish returned in force and captured Santa Fe by the same tactic the indians had used against them in 1680—cutting off the water supply. Presumably this was the time when the Navajos learned to weave, as many of the Pueblos fled to Navajo country to avoid Spanish reprisals.

The Navajo

When Coronado entered New Mexico in 1540, the Navajo were living in small seminomadic groups in the country west of the Rio Grande pueblos. Some farmed peacefully near the pueblos and the name Navajo was acquired from the Tewa word "Navahu," which signified a large area of cultivated fields. The Spanish, who did not go into Navajo territory until the early eighteenth century, named them *Apaches de Navajo* about 1626 and generally did not differentiate them from the Apaches.

The Eighteenth and Nineteenth Centuries

The eighteenth century was relatively tranquil except for the forays of the Navajo, Apache, and Comanche who raided the haciendas for slaves and sheep. By mid-century there were around ten thousand Hispanos in New Mexico. Half lived in haciendas and half in Santa Fe, Albuquerque, El Paso, and Santa Cruz.[10] The European handloom had been introduced by then, but only fourteen were listed in Spanish New Mexican inventories for the fifty years prior to 1800.[11] There seems to have been a sharp drop in weaving by the Pueblos during the eighteenth century,[12] and the first Spanish reference to Navajo weaving was made in 1780.[13]

In the early nineteenth century New Mexico saw its first Americans. Traders from Missouri reached Santa Fe in 1812 with $30,000 worth of merchandise that sold rapidly. The year that Mexico gained independence from Spain (1821) was the same year the wagon route from Independence, Missouri was opened. The Santa Fe Trail was to bring New England textiles to the Southwest in quantity. The mountain men, in New Mexico to trap furs and hold rendezvous at Taos in the 1830s, were the first Americans to have contact with the Navajo. The latter were famous at that time for sarapes so tightly woven as to be waterproof.

When the United States took possession of New Mexico in 1846, the Navajos were busy raiding. They boasted that they let the Mexicans live only because they were useful as shepherds for the tribe. Each spring they sued for peace so they could grow their crops undisturbed. In the fall they resumed raiding. American soldiers found Navajo blankets especially suitable for placing between the ground and their bedding. During a military reconnaissance mission in 1849 James Simpson wrote: "It seems anomalous to me that a nation living in such miserably constructed mud lodges should, at the same time, be capable of making, probably, the best blankets in the world."[14]

New Mexico was the scene of a small amount of military action during the Civil War, but the indians caused much more havoc. After years of unrestrained marauding, the Navajo were literally rounded up in 1863 by the first New Mexico Volunteers under the command of Kit Carson and marched to Fort Sumner, a concentration camp, in the hot Pecos Valley of eastern New Mexico. After five years they were allowed to return to their homeland, by then a reservation under control of the United States government. Indian life came under the influence of the trader and indian agent. In the 1880s the railroad brought tourists who purchased rugs in the Albuquerque station from indians no longer wearing traditional attire. Velvet, calico, and denim were now "indian."

ANASAZI FABRICS

The Basketmakers had small wardrobes and mainly wore blankets of rabbit fur strips twined with cords. For modesty the women had little aprons of fringe hanging from a band, one worn fore, one aft. Sandals were common, very necessary, and made by several techniques of weaving and braiding. The Basketmakers made belts, bags, and trump lines. Prehistoric Pueblo accumulations were somewhat larger; there were socks, shirts, leggings, kilts, caps, and quivers.

Fibers and Spinning

Yucca, the tough, bayonet-leaved plant so common in the Southwest, supplied the greatest amount of fiber for sandals, cordage, and bags. Leaves were soaked in water, then pounded to release the hemp-like fibers. These may have been hackled by drawing through the teeth. They were eventually twisted into yarn by rolling on the thigh.

Another vegetable fiber, apocynum, was the bast of Indian hemp. It was softer than yucca, and items made from it were more pliable. Juniper bark was shredded for diapers, menstrual pads, and women's aprons. Women hacked off their own hair or used the undercoat from pet dogs to make cordage and sashes. Hair from bison, deer, mountain goat, and other animals was spun on cross bar spindles.

By Pueblo II, cotton had replaced bast in woven textiles, and it is believed that *Gossypium hopi* was the variety used prehistorically, because it had a short growing season and could be raised at fairly high altitudes. Probably, the prehistoric Pueblo indians cultivated cotton and prepared it for spinning by the same methods as those used historically by the Hopi. Cotton was planted in holes made with digging sticks in the fields at the mouths of arroyos where flood waters would spread out. Bolls were picked before maturity and ripened by sun drying. The seeds were then picked out by hand and the fiber beaten with slender rods until fluffy, or the unginned fiber was folded into a blanket that was beaten until the seeds came loose and adhered to it. Cotton was spun on spindles with clay or wooden whorls.

Anasazi Constructions

The prehistoric Anasazi used an amazing number of construction methods. Many nonloom techniques were well developed by Basketmaker III (500-700) and continued in use after the Pueblos started weaving.

Nonloom Techniques

Warp-twining was used to make narrow bands and trump lines. By counter-pairing, or twisting the pairs of warp toward or away from each other between picks, a plaited effect was achieved. It could be done with warps hanging free, anchored between two sticks, or passed continually around two sticks. Weft-twining, just the opposite and a very common technique outside the Southwest, was used to make trump lines, flexible containers with yucca warp and apocynum weft, and blankets of either strips of rabbit fur or turkey feathers wrapped around yucca cord.

Other nonloom methods, looping, netting, and braiding, employed single sets of elements (see chapter 3). Bags and socks were made by looping; a seamless and shaped article could be formed by varying the size of the loops. Generally cotton yarn was used, but looped fabrics of apocynum and human hair have been found. Feathers might be inserted into the loops to provide warmth. Knotting, a netting technique, was used for snares and bags. Belts, sashes, trump lines, and shirts (Plate 90) were braided and plaited.[15]

Weaving

Three types of primitive looms were used in the Southwest: the belt, or backstrap loom for narrow items; the horizontal loom, used more in Arizona; and the vertical loom, the basic type in use by the Anasazi after 1100 A.D. Anchor loops found in ruins indicate that it was set up in the kiva (ceremonial room) and in the house.

Many kinds of cotton textiles were woven, but plain weave cloth was made most often. The simple variation of plain weave, the use of warp or weft stripes, or plaids and checks, was not as common as it came to be with the historic Pueblo. Some examples of half or semi-basket weave have been found; in these either two warp or two filling were used as one. Plain weave was varied at times by the use of heavy strings or rags (every bit of cloth must have been utilized in some way) in the weft.

Twill (Plate 91) was second in importance to plain weave. Regular and broken (herringbone and diamond) twills were known, and some distinctive ones combined colored warp and weft in striped and plaid twill blankets. Intricate patterns were worked out in both twill tapestry and twill brocade, generally in narrow widths for bands, bags, knife cases, and quivers. Some pieces showed negative design of thin white lines on dark ground. Tapestry (unbalanced, weft-faced, plain or twill weave) was monochrome with no design, interlocking with different colored weft looped around each other at the edges of designs, or slit. Brocaded textiles had alternating base and decorative wefts. Brocading was a technique that developed rather late and was largely replaced by embroidery.

Lace-like textiles were made either by weft-wrap openwork or gauze weave. Weft-wrap was a technique in which certain filling yarns were not carried the full width of the cloth but were wrapped tightly around certain warps and previously inserted fillings in order to draw them apart and form open spaces. Various patterns, usually on oblique lines, were built from units of holes. Gauze weave (see Figure 3.30) produced more horizontal and vertical design arrangements by using open units made by crossing adjoining warps between picks. Heddles can be set up to do this, but it is not known if the Anasazi knew how.

The Pueblos could also shape textiles on the loom. Warps might be drawn closer together by subsequent picks, or a filling yarn could be broken off and replaced by a warp. An edge warp might be carried into the textile a short distance and then broken off, or it could be twisted into the selvage for a few turns and then broken off.

Design and Color

Both structural and applied design was based on small geometric units—mainly triangles, terraced figures, rectangles, and squares—placed along horizontal, vertical, or oblique lines to make allover patterns. Painted textiles showed angled and sawtooth hooks—designs unusual for woven cloths. Circles (more like rounded squares) could be achieved by tie-dyeing.

Most Anasazi cloth, especially the nonloom kind, was not dyed. Dyeing was usually done at the yarn stage and in a number of colors. The sources of the vegetal colors are not known, but inorganic dyes have been identified as red hematite, yellow ochre, and blue-green copper sulphate.

Embroidery was known, but it was not nearly as important as it was with the historic Pueblo. Needles used for embroidery, crude sewing, and darning were made from small bones, cactus spines, or the tips of yucca leaves.

HISTORIC PUEBLO TEXTILES

Many Anasazi textile techniques had already died out by the time the Spanish arrived, and there was an even more rapid decline when the Indians were put to weaving utilitarian fabrics for their masters. No examples of seventeenth and eighteenth century textiles survive, although Pueblo men continued to weave dresses, blankets, shirts, sashes, and garters into the twentieth century. The best examples of traditional textiles were collected in the nineteenth century.

Cotton Textiles

The Spanish wrote of great fields of cotton at Zuni, and it must have been an important crop in the seventeenth century while the wool industry was becoming established. The Rio Grande Pueblos stopped growing cotton in the late 1700s and the others in the 1850s, when they could get cotton batting or string from the traders. Cotton was spun on a fairly long spindle with the whorl partly up the shaft. The tip was rested on the ground and the spindle rolled against the thigh. There is no evidence of the indians ever having used a spinning wheel.

One of the most interesting cotton weavings was the bride's dress. Her husband-to-be wove a plain white robe, or *manta,* and during the first year of marriage he embroidered it with rainclouds, flowers, and butterfly designs. The woman wore the garment for ceremonies, and it served as her burial shroud. Maiden shawls were also made of white cotton but had borders twilled in blue or red wool (Plate 92). Cotton was traditionally used to make sashes—braided, woven in coarse twill, or crocheted. (The latter technique was learned from the Spanish.) Cotton sashes, made to be worn around the hips of male dancers in many Pueblo ceremonies, were brocaded with red, green, and black wool in a traditional design that was a conventionalization of the mask of a broad-faced Kachina (Plate 93).[16] Pueblo woven cotton was also intended for breechclouts and dance kilts, which were embroidered. Commercial cotton cloth was seldom used as a base for embroidery.

Wool Textiles

The old type sheep had relatively greaseless wool that was suited to the same carding and spinning methods used for cotton. It did not have to be scoured in a country where water was scarce, although sometimes it was cleaned with suds made from yucca roots. Wool eventually replaced cotton for most everyday Pueblo clothing. A typical woman's garment was a dress about 50" by 60" having a black or brown (natural colors) center with broad bands of indigo blue diamond twill. Blankets were made in checked and plaid patterns or stripes (some similar to Navajo designs) and in varied sizes. Shirts of heavy blue wool, and narrow belts and garters in red, green, black, and white wool were typical.

Embroidery

The Pueblos became famous for their embroidery. Although known prehistorically, it probably did not become important until wool—more easily dyed in a wider range of colors than cotton—was available. Embroidery could be used to make patterns much faster than brocading, the technique that produced nearly identical results. A type of back stitch unique to Pueblo embroidery was used to fill spaces solidly. At least a two-ply yarn was needed so the needle could be brought up between the strands. Then the whole yarn was carried forward a short distance for the next stitch.[17] Negative design—the white background forming part of the pattern—was prominent in Pueblo embroidery.[18]

Weaving and embroidery have just about ended among the Pueblo indians: only the tourist market is left.

NAVAJO TEXTILES

Weaving Periods

Navajo textiles are classified into five distinct periods based on intended use, materials, construction techniques, and design and color. Navajo women have been weaving for over two hundred and fifty years, and during that time some aspects of the craft have changed markedly.

Very few textiles remain from the *Early Period* (1700-1850), and little is known except that the Navajo learned weaving from the Pueblo, probably sometime after 1680—the date of the Pueblo uprising against the Spanish. The earliest dated fragments come from Massacre Cave, the site of a Spanish punitive raid in 1804 or 1805. These were striped and had some bayeta (yarns raveled from trade cloth), indications that weaving was well established. Early Period textiles were woven primarily for clothing—serapes, women's dresses (two identical blankets joined together), shoulder or "chief" blankets (with longer dimension crosswire, Plate 94), and belts and sashes were made on narrow looms. Saddle blankets and throws were made for both Navajo use and trade.

During the *Classic Period* (1850-1875) as well, textiles were used mainly for clothing or bedding, but they were distinguished by excellent design and tight, smooth, uniform weaving. They were essentially indian products for indian use, and they were worn by many western tribes. Navajo weavers took special pride in their work during this period.

The *Transition Period* (1875-1890) marked the beginning of the indian product made for the white market. When the Navajo returned to their reservation from Fort Sumner, they adopted Anglo costume. The influence of gaudy trading post merchandise lowered design standards. Machine spun cotton and wool yarn as well as aniline dyes became available. The blanket, which was not to be made much after 1890, changed into a floor rug for the white man's home. Anglo traders were responsible for the switch in product; they encouraged the women to weave and supplied many materials and design ideas. More importantly, they were the marketing agents.

Degeneration set in during the *Rug Period* (1890-1920). Rugs were low count with coarse yarns of wool from poor grade sheep, and designs were badly executed in garish aniline colors. Traders bought by the pound, so the Indians loaded rugs with sand. Faced with the loss of their market because so many rugs were inferior, several traders instigated a craft revival in the 1920s, the beginning of the *Contemporary Period.* Navajos were encouraged to handspin fine yarns in natural wool colors or to dye with native materials. Premiums were paid for well-designed and well-woven rugs, and a high quality Navajo textile was soon to be considered a piece of art.

Distinguishing Materials

Classic blankets have seldom been surpassed in quality, because they were made from the fine, soft inner coat wool of the old Navajo sheep. Most of these sheep were killed by the soldiers who rounded up the Navajo in 1863, and the other sheep introduced to the reservation were never as well suited to native cleaning and spinning. The women spun their yarn several times, working it down to a very fine, strong yarn for warp (Figure 11.2).

The Navajo raised goats, because they were hardy and able to forage on land not fit for sheep. But goats were responsible for much erosion when they ate the grass to such low levels that it could never recover. Mohair fiber was easy to card but difficult to spin, because it was smoother, straighter, and more wiry than wool. Very often it was mixed with wool. Warp made of mohair was practically indestructible.

An old Navajo legend told of Spider Man using cotton for warp, and some cotton may have been used in the Early Period. It was of no importance, however, until machine spun yarn was obtained from the traders during the Transition Period. Since it was weaker than handspun wool, its use for warp was generally discouraged, even though some excellent quality rugs were woven with it. Cotton was not used for weft.

The most prestigious material in Early and Classic Period blankets was bayeta, yarn raveled from a type of heavy flannel trade cloth similar to that cherished by all North American indians. This coarse woolen, probably with worsted warp and a long nap, had been introduced into England in the sixteenth century by the Huguenots. Subsequently, Manchester became an important baise weaving center. *Bayeta* is the Spanish word for the English *baise,* or *bays,* derived in turn from the French *baie,* meaning berry. Bayeta was originally dyed a red-brown with Avignon berries. The cloth that reached the Navajo was piece dyed with cochineal most often, and sometimes with logwood, Brazil wood, indigo, or fustic. Bayeta cloth was traded by the English to the Spanish, who in turn brought it to New Mexico by way of the Rio Grande route from Mexico. Eventually a kind made in Manchester came in through East Coast cities, and some was manufactured in New England. The real story of bayeta is clouded over by years of ambiguous reporting. Some dealers now sell as genuine bayeta any blanket with raveled cloth, be it old cochineal dyed bayeta or American red flannel underwear. In the narrowest sense it was an imported cloth traded to the indians, who raveled and respun it in order to get red for their blankets. Sometimes it can be identified by tiny white spots, the undyed areas that were the result of piece dyeing with incomplete penetration

FIGURE 11.2 / Navajo Spinning (from Matthews, 1884).

where the yarns originally crossed. Bayeta is associated with the high quality weaving of the Classic Period.[19]

Commercially spun yarn was used as both a shortcut and to get good colors easily. Saxony, also called zephyr, was a silky three-ply machine spun wool yarn used in late Classic and early Transition blankets. A four-ply machine spun wool yarn that was commonly used during the Transition Period and early Rug Period was called *Germantown* after the town in Pennsylvania known for its wool spinning, even though much was spun elsewhere. Germantown yarn was dyed in brilliant aniline colors that usually faded, and it was often woven onto cotton twine warp.

FIGURE 11.3 / Navajo Vertical
Loom (from Matthews, 1884).

Rugs frequently had tassels, and some were known as "eye dazzlers" because of their patterns. Most of the time they were tightly woven.

A heavy machine spun wool carpet yarn was used for a short time in the Rug Period, but rugs made from it were very coarse. In the 1870s and 1880s, some rugs had weft that were half-inch strips torn from bolt cloth; these were not of high quality.

Weaving

Looms

Historians say that the Navajo adopted the loom in entirety from the Pueblos, but legend says that Spider Woman taught the women how to weave on a loom that Spider Man told the men how to make. Perhaps it was this extra boost from the underworld that made it possible for the Navajo to accomplish so much on her loom.

Two types of looms were used—the large vertical blanket or rug loom (Figure 11.3), by far the more important, and the belt or waist (backstrap) loom used to make narrow textiles (Figure 11.4). The vertical, and movable, loom was set into a permanent loom frame constructed of two posts set solidly into the earth (or perhaps two trees that grew close together) with cross pieces set at top and bottom. Some were in the hogan, others outside, perhaps in a rudely constructed brush shelter. The baby's cradle board could be propped up near mama.

FIGURE 11.4 / Navajo Belt
Loom (from Matthews, 1884).

Men were more apt to weave on the belt loom. In direct opposition to the
textiles made on the common vertical loom, the textiles made on the belt loom
were warp-faced; the warp showed on the surface of the finished sash, garter, or
belt.

Weaves

In the Early Period plain weave, filling-faced, was the most common
construction. It could be varied by changing the weft colors to make horizontal
stripes, or by beading, using two colors with alternate wefts different, to form
vertical stripes (Plate 95). The latter was less frequent. During the Classic Period
the weaver's repertoire was extended by the introduction of true tapestry weave—
the use of discontinuous wefts to make patterns. By interlocking wefts between
warp, or taking alternate colors around a single warp, vertical lines were formed;
these could be used to build terraced figures. Twill, which had probably been
known in the Early Period, was used to some extent in the Classic Period (Plate 96).

The Transition Period saw the development of acute angles in tapestry weave,
and design possibilities were vastly increased. Herringbone (reversing twill)
became common, and diamond (goose eye) twill developed (Plate 97). Two very
rare techniques, two-faced construction (one set of warp, two sets of weft forming
different patterns on either face of the rug) and pulled warp (wedge weave) were

initiated during the Transition Period. (The latter gave the rug a scalloped edge.)

Only one new technique, tufting, was used in the Rug Period. Extra strands, usually mohair, were suspended around warp, tied to the warps, or interwoven a short distance within a rug woven in plain or twill weave (Plate 98). All previously used techniques were employed during the Contemporary Period, and some complex figured twill developed. However, plain weave tapestry continued to be the most important.

Design and Color

Navajo textile design is angular. Few circles, arches, or rounded corners were used until very recently, when some rugs depicting sunsets, Christmas trees, and other nontraditional patterns have turned up showing the use of eccentric, or curved, wefts. The weaving process, of course, put limitations on design possibilities: Navajo patterns were based on one or more of four possible elements: horizontal stripes, vertical stripes, angles of about forty degrees (achieved by the advancement of a single colored weft by one warp with each pick), and steeper angles of about fifty-two degrees (made by weaving two successive weft of the same color on the same advancement by one plan).

It is generally agreed that no religious symbolism can be attributed to Navajo weaving.[20] Objects made for everyday use—clothing and blankets—are seldom symbolic. Weaving did not originate with the Navajo, and since weaving was mostly for Pueblo, Spanish, and American markets, there was no reason to incorporate symbolism. The Navajo did have names for design figures though,[21] and some people have been able to read celestial meaning into them.

One of the amazing feats of the Navajo weaver was the ability to carry the design in her mind and convert it correctly into woven form—there were no weave diagrams or cartoons to follow. Designs came from many sources, many of them often found at the trading post, and design types developed within the spheres of certain traders' influence. One example, the Ganado (or Hubbell) rug, with red background and a predominance of cross-shaped or diamond elements, became an easily identified type. Another, the famous Two Grey Hills style, emerged around 1911 as the result of efforts by J. B. Moore to encourage fine weaving. These rugs were eventually identified by fine handspun natural colored yarns, high yarn counts, and complex geometric designs enclosed in solid or figured borders (Plate 99).

Rugs can be dated by design; each period had a characteristic or dominant style. Any early style could be, and was, copied, but certain designs can be no older than specific periods. In the Early Period (1700-1850) continuous horizontal stripes, with some grouping or zoning, constituted most patterns. In the Classic Period (1850-1875) beading was used somewhat more, although it was never especially common. Important to Classic design was the introduction of the right-angled terraced figures often used to make small geometric forms on the borders of women's dresses (Plate 100). Horizontal stripes were sometimes discontinuous and grouped, or they were made to form the background for more complex patterns in shoulder blankets.

The Transition Period (1875-1890) is important for the introduction of serrate or diamond design. No Navajo textile with acute angled patterns can be dated earlier. Outlining, or tracing a contour in a thin line of a contrasting color, was an outgrowth of the serrate design. It is associated with aniline dyes, Germantown yarn, and generally good quality weaving (Plate 101). The first pictorial rugs, depicting Santa Fe trains, animals, and all sorts of other things, were woven during the Transition Period.

The important characteristic of Rug Period (1890-1910) design is the border. With borders came a change in design concept—frames were woven for designs that usually had predominant central figures. In older rugs and blankets design was continuous, as if the textile had been cut from a bolt, and isolated figures were rare. Once in a while one sees a single weft from the center area of the rug, cutting through the border "to let the weaver's spirit out." The Rug Period also saw the beginning of the so-called ceremonial or Yei weavings showing Navajo divinities. The first ones shocked the Navajo.[22] Now, in the Contemporary Period, they are standard tourist items.

Color as well can be used to date Navajo textiles. In the Early and Classic Periods, most color came from the natural wool—white, black, brown. Sometimes these were blended in carding to get greys and tans. Indigo came from Mexico; reds came as bayeta to be raveled. There was only occasional use of inorganic coloring agents (blue clay, red hematite, yellow ochre) and vegetal dyes (rabbit brush, sumac, mountain mahogany).

The real change came in the 1880s when aniline dyes reached the reservation. Color burst forth; envelopes of dye and mordant were easy to get and easy to use, but the colors were seldom fast. Restraint did not come until the 1920s, when, in conjunction with the revival of old designs and quality weaving, the indians were encouraged to use some of the old vegetal dyes and find new ones. Now, some new commercial dyes can be used to reproduce the soft muted native colors.

To briefly sum up, Navajo textiles have always been made chiefly from wool, but the sources of that fiber have changed. Different breeds of sheep have been raised by the Navajo, and sometimes the yarn, and even the unspun wool, have come from outside the reservation. Hand and texture of the textiles have varied during different periods because of the kinds of fibers and yarns used.

Technology has changed very little over two hundred and fifty years; the old Pueblo loom and spindle have been the best possible tools for use in a primitive, seminomadic culture, and surely any maintenance problems could be easily solved.

The reason for production, although always aimed at trading, shifted radically around 1870 from clothing to rugs. Another rationale, though, may be the real reason why the Navajo have continued to weave. Weaving has been an integral part of the woman's life. There were special ceremonies for overwork, and maidens were kept from weaving before marriage lest they overdo. Even in the mid-twentieth century the family kept the oldest girl at home and raised her in the old traditions, which included weaving. Knowing how to weave gave prestige; even when there was no economic benefit, there still was a psychological lift.

RIO GRANDE TEXTILES

Two different names, Rio Grande and Chimayo, have been given to the blankets and rugs woven by the Spanish New Mexicans (known also as Hispanos, Mexicans, and Spanish Americans). Rio Grande is the better term because it is inclusive. Chimayo refers more to blankets woven since the late nineteenth century in a few villages north of Santa Fe and in the San Luis Valley of Colorado, an area settled by New Mexicans after 1851. The craft continues to this day in Chimayo and Truchas, New Mexico, where foot powered looms are operated in small weaving shops by local weavers who make blankets, rugs, jackets, neckties, purses, and other small items.

Little is known about Rio Grande weaving prior to 1800. Due to the great isolation, however, it is logical to assume that there was at least some attempt at production of household fabrics at an early date. A trade invoice for a shipment from Santa Fe to Chihuahua in 1638 did include nineteen pieces of *sayal* (coarse woolen for dress goods) each a hundred varas long (a vara was equal to about thirty-three inches), as well as thirty-two small mantas (shawls). Apparently, there was a small surplus at that time.[23] The fact that each piece of sayal was over ninety yards in length makes it probable that the horizontal loom with a warp beam capable of holding many yards was in use at that time, although it was not documented until the mid-eighteenth century.

Trade from New Mexico to Mexico remains to be researched, but we know that in 1805 the quality of the textiles exported was very poor. The government in Mexico City hired two professional weavers, Ignacio and Juan Bazan, to take good equipment to Santa Fe and teach weaving for a period of six years. The Bazans were concerned mostly with improving the basic wool fabrics that were produced in New Mexico then: bayeta (or *sabanilla*), *jerga* (gerga), and *fresada*. Bayeta and sabanilla were terms used for the plain weave homespun made for clothing and mattress covers. When the English fabric reached New Mexico, bayeta referred to that, and sabanilla meant homespun. Twill weave jerga was woven with very thick yarns and was used for carpet, coarse clothing, and sacks (Plate 102). Fresada was blanket or poncho cloth. As the work was presumably a corruption of the English *frieze*,[24] it was probably napped. Loosely woven and coarse in texture best describe the early fabrics of Spanish New Mexico.

Early American accounts describe rooms of adobe houses as having earthen benches covered with blankets or quilts called *colchons*. The walls behind the benches were covered with Dutch cotton (later American calico) to protect the shoulders from the whitewash. Floors were covered with jerga, worth about thirty cents a yard at that time. People slept on the floor, and clothes were kept in carved wooden chests. Some of the first Americans to reach Santa Fe found the attire of the women especially provocative, because short jerga or bayeta "petticoats" displayed the ankles. Also, the linen or cotton chamisas exposed bosoms and arms— and the ladies wore no underwear.[25]

Weaving Materials and Equipment

Wool was the primary fiber used in Rio Grande textiles. Sheep raising was an important industry in New Mexico, although the animals were used mainly for food. Cotton was not raised by the early Spanish colonists, and the Pueblos gradually stopped growing it. The Bazans may have tried to reintroduce cotton, but it was more usual in the early nineteenth century for New Mexicans to import English and French cottons via Mexico. The climate was not suitable for raising flax, and there is no evidence of silk culture in New Mexico. The Hispanos, as did the Navajo, used Saxony and Germantown yarn and cotton warp in the late nineteenth century. They did not need to ravel cloth for color, because dyes were readily available. Now, weavers of Chimayo buy their yarn from eastern mills, where it is specially spun as single ply.

The Hispanos used the Indian spindle and continued to spin fine yarn with it even after a crude, short, fat version of the wool wheel was introduced sometime around 1800. The Saxony wheel was not popular in New Mexico.

The Spanish did not use the vertical indian loom but wove on a massive adaptation of the medieval frame type. Its supports were cut from tree trunks, heddles were made of narrow strips of rawhide with holes punched for the warps to go through, the reed formed from very thin branches of dried sagebrush, and the shuttles hand carved from fruitwoods. The modern weaver at Chimayo still prefers his old smoothly worn apricot wood shuttle.

Because the horizontal looms were relatively narrow, blankets were made in two pieces and seamed. These seams are one of the identifying characteristics of Rio Grande blankets. A sort of tubular weave was sometimes used to make wide blankets without seams, but these had double warps in the center (Plate 103).

Many yards of crosswise stripes were woven as well as checked and plaid twill jerga. Beading was used as were some small geometric motifs in blankets. After the third decade of the nineteenth century, elaborate designs of lozenges and medallions were copied from the famous Saltillo serapes of Mexico (Plate 104).

In the days before aniline dyes, the Spanish New Mexicans were more likely than the indians to use commercial dyes such as indigo, Brazilwood, logwood, and cochineal. They also grew a few dye and medicinal plants and gathered others including mountain mahogany, chokecherry, chamiso (rabbit bush), and other yellow flowers. Wool was dyed at the yarn stage, and there are a few examples of indigo ikat dyeing, probably introduced by the Bazans.[26]

Sometimes it is difficult to distinguish a Rio Grande textile from a Pueblo or a Navajo one, especially if it is woven with horizontal stripes. However, there are some clues. Rio Grande blankets may have the center seams mentioned above. These are never seen in Pueblo or Navajo textiles. At the selvage, Rio Grande textiles show pairs of warp (Plate 103), Pueblos and Navajos singles. The Navajos, and sometimes Pueblos, have edge cords for reinforcement. A distinguishing feature of Navajo weaving is the diagonal *lazy line* (Plate 101) formed by a weaver who sat in one spot, wove a section, then moved and wove another area that was joined to the first. She did not always carry a weft the full width of the rug, even if no change in color was necessary to make the pattern.

Additional questions are raised by the textiles woven by the Navajo specifically for the Mexican trade in designs borrowed from them, or by rugs woven by captive Navajo women who might copy Mexican serapes on their own upright looms or introduce Navajo techniques to horizontal Mexican looms. There was also a mingling of material, technique, and design between the Pueblos and the Navajos.

Embroidery

Quite in tune with other softly colorful and unsophisticated forms of New Mexican folk art are the *colcha* embroideries (Plate 105). Some are reminiscent of Connecticut bed ruggs in texture and design, although they are made differently, and others resemble crewel work. Colcha work consumed a lot of yarn, because the relatively long stitches were laid close together. The needle was taken to the underside and brought up and down again to do a sort of couching stitch that held a long strand in place near its center. It is thought that women copied the stitches used in the Chinese silk embroideries that reached New Mexico in the eighteenth century. The earliest pieces of colcha work were used in churches, but bedcovers and wall hangings were soon to be done in colcha work. Twentieth century embroiderers have worked up some items of tourist art with flower, leaf, animal, and human figure motifs.

NOTES

1. For an enchanting novel about life in Tyuonyi Pueblo (now in Bandelier National Monument) based on ethnological and archaeological studies, read Adolph F. Bandelier, *The Delight Makers* (New York: Dodd, Mead and Co., 1916).

2. Gordon R. Willey, *An Introduction to American Archaeology: Volume One, North and Middle America* (Englewood Cliffs, New Jersey: Prentice-Hall, 1966), p. 232.

3. Kate Peck Kent, "The Cultivation and Weaving of Cotton in the Prehistoric Southwestern United States," *Transactions of the American Philosophical Society*, n.s., 47, pt. 3 (1957):658.

4. Ibid., p. 465; Willey, *Introduction*, p. 202; and H. M. Wormington, *Prehistoric Indians of the Southwest* (Denver: The Denver Museum of Natural History, 1956), p. 49.

5. Kent, "Cultivation and Weaving," pp. 491, 658.

6. Ibid., p. 465.

7. Paul Horgan, *Great River: The Rio Grande in North American History* (New York: Holt, Rinehart and Winston, 1954), p. 60.

8. Adolph F. Bandelier, "Documentary History of the Rio Grande Pueblos, New Mexico," *New Mexico Historical Review* 4, no. 4 (October 1929):303-334.

9. Ralph Emerson Twitchell, *Old Santa Fe: The Story of New Mexico's Ancient Capital* (1925; reprint ed., Chicago: The Rio Grande Press, Inc., 1963), p. 27.

10. Horgan, *Great River,* p. 348.

11. Harry P. Mera, "Spanish Colonial Blanketry" (manuscript in Laboratory of Anthropology, Santa Fe), p. 21.

12. Ibid., p. 20.

13. Charles Avery Amsden, *Navajo Weaving: Its Technic and History* (1934; reprint ed., Glorieta, New Mexico: Rio Grande Press, 1972), p. 130.

14. J. H. Simpson, *Navaho Expedition: Journal of a Military Reconnaissance from Santa Fe, New Mexico to the Navaho Country Made in 1849,* ed. Frank McNitt (Norman: University of Oklahoma Press, 1964), p. 96.

15. Kent, "Cultivation and Weaving," p. 593; and Irene Emery, *The Primary Structures of Fabrics* (Washington, D. C.: The Textile Museum, 1966), p. 60.

16. Emery, *Primary Structures,* p. 220 gives an exact description of this particular technique.

17. H. P. Mera, *Pueblo Indian Embroidery* (1943; reprint ed., Santa Fe: William Gannon, 1975). Published as *Memoirs of the Laboratory of Anthropology,* vol. 4, p. 8.

18. Ibid., p. 9.

19. For a discussion on bayeta see Amsden, *Navajo Weaving;* and George Wharton James, *Indian Blankets and Their Makers* (1914; reprint ed., Chicago: A. C. McClurg, 1927).

20. James, *Indian Blankets,* has the most information on symbolism.

21. Ibid., pp. 126-129.

22. Ibid., pp. 139-140.

23. Lansing B. Bloom, "A Trade Invoice of 1638," *New Mexico Historical Review* 10, no. 3 (July 1935):242.

24. E. Boyd, *Popular Arts of Spanish New Mexico* (Santa Fe: Museum of New Mexico Press, 1974), p. 182.

25. James M. Lacy, "New Mexico Women in Early American Writings," *New Mexico Historical Review* 34, no. 1 (January 1959):41-51.

26. Boyd, *Popular Arts,* pp. 202, 204.

BIBLIOGRAPHY

For background on the prehistoric Southwest see Gordon R. Willey, *An Introduction to American Archaeology, Volume One, North and Middle America* (Englewood Cliffs, New Jersey: Prentice Hall, 1966); H. M. Wormington, *Prehistoric Indians of the Southwest* (Denver: The Denver Museum of Natural History, 1956); and Charles Avery Amsden, *Prehistoric Southwesterners from Basketmaker to Pueblo* (1949; reprint ed., Los Angeles: Southwest Museum, 1964). The latter has an extensive bibliography. In *Navajo Weaving: Its Technic and its History* (1934; reprint ed., Glorieta, New Mexico: Rio Grande Press, 1972) Charles Avery Amsden has a good chapter on finger weaving and one on loom development in America.

The major source on prehistoric Southwestern textiles is Kate Peck Kent's outstanding work, "The Cultivation and Weaving of Cotton in the Prehistoric Southwestern United States," *Transactions of the American Philosophical Society,* n.s., 47, pt. 3 (1957):457-732. Other works by Kent are "Montezuma Castle Archaeology, Part 2: Textiles," *Southwestern Monuments Association Technical Series* 3, no. 2 (Globe, Arizona: Southwestern Monuments Association, 1954):1-103, and "Archeological Studies at Tonto National Monument, Arizona," *Southwestern Monuments Association Technical Series* 2 (1962):115-168, with other authors (C. R. Steen, L. M. Pierson, V. L. Bohrer). Of related interest is Patricia L. Fiske, ed., *Archaeological Textiles: Irene Emery Roundtable on Museum Textiles, 1974 Proceedings* (Washington, D. C.: The Textile Museum, 1975).

Original Spanish descriptions of the indians and their attire were published by George Parker Winship in "The Coronado Expedition, 1540-42," *Fourteenth Annual Report of the Bureau of Ethnology, 1892/93* (Washington, D.C.: Government Printing Office, 1896), pp. 329-613, and by Adolph F. Bandelier in "Documentary History of the Rio Grande Pueblos, New Mexico," *New Mexico Historical Review* 4, no. 4 (October 1929):303-334.

Amsden gives some background on the Spanish and the Pueblos in his *Navajo Weaving*. Sources on the Hopi are plentiful, and one especially good one is a little book, Ruth De ETTE Simpson, *The Hopi Indians* (Los Angeles: Southwest Museum, 1953), which includes a helpful bibliography. For color see Mary-Russell Ferrell Colton, *Hopi Dyes* (Flagstaff: Museum of Northern Arizona, 1965). An interesting work by a controversial pioneer ethnologist is Frank H. Cushing, *My Adventures in Zuni* (Palmer Lake, Colorado: Filter Press, 1967), a reprint of a three part series in volumes 25 and 26 of *The Century Magazine*, 1882-1883. Leslie Spier, "Zuni Weaving Technique," *American Anthropologist* 26, no. 1 (January-March 1924):64-85 is helpful. Especially admirable for its drawings is Virginia More Roediger, *Ceremonial Costumes of the Pueblo Indians* (Berkeley and Los Angeles: University of California Press, 1961). There are many design ideas and good information in H. P. Mera's classic, *Pueblo Indian Embroidery* (Santa Fe: William Gannon, 1975).

The Denver Art Museum has published and reprinted, from time to time since the 1930s, a series of leaflets on indian art that is still available at nominal cost. Most of the information was originally compiled by Frederick H. Douglas, who was in large part responsible for the outstanding collection of American indian textiles (and other indian art) in the Denver Art Museum. For Pueblo textiles see *Pueblo Indian Clothing* (No. 4); *Main Types of Pueblo Cotton Textiles* (No. 92-93); *Main Types of Pueblo Woolen Textiles* (No. 94-95); *Zuni Weaving* (No. 9697); *Acoma Pueblo Weaving and Embroidery* (No. 89); *Weaving in the Tewa Pueblos* (No. 90); *Weaving of the Keres Pueblos and Weaving of the Tiwa Pueblos and Jemez* (No. 91); and *Hopi Indian Weaving* (No. 18). For the Navajo see *Navaho Spinning, Dyeing and Weaving* (No. 3), and *Navaho Wearing Blankets* (No. 113). See also *Southwestern Weaving Materials* (No. 116), *Indian Vegetable Dyes* Part I (No. 63), and Part II (No. 71). These are all short, but concise.

To date there is no equal on the subject to Amsden's *Navajo Weaving*, written in 1934. This is the best place to begin study. Other important, but older, sources are Washington Matthews, "Navajo Weavers," *Third Annual Report of the Bureau of Ethnology, 1881/83* (Washington, D. C.: Government Printing Office, 1884), pp. 371-391, reprinted by Filter Press in Palmer Lake, Colorado, 1968, and "Navajo Dye Stuffs," *Annual Report of the Board of Regents of the Smithsonian Institution to July 1891* (Washington: Government Printing Office, 1893). Dr. Matthews was an army surgeon stationed on the indian reservations. U. S. Hollister, *The Navajo and His Blanket* (Denver, 1903) has been reprinted in Chicago by Rio Grande Press, 1974) as has George Wharton James, *Indian Blankets and Their Makers* (1914; reprint ed., Chicago: A. C. McClurg, 1927). James is one of the classics (but is quite romantic in tone) and is best read in conjunction with Amsden, who has many comments about it.

In the 1930s anthropologist Gladys A. Reichard lived with the Navajo and learned to weave. The reader who is interested in trying a rug should see her *Spider Woman: A Story of Navajo Weavers and Chanters* (New York: Macmillan, 1934) and especially her *Navajo Shepherd and Weaver* (1936; reprint ed., Chicago: Rio Grande Press, 1968). The best works of the 1940s are Nonabah G. Bryan, *Navajo Native Dyes: Their Preparation and Use* (Washington, D. C.: Bureau of Indian Affairs, 1940), and H. P. Mera, *Navajo Textile Arts* (Santa Fe: Laboratory of Anthropology, n.d.). Short works that contain information on contemporary weaving as well as history are Kate Peck Kent, *The Story of Navajo Weaving* (Phoenix: The Heard Museum of Anthropology and Primitive Art, 1961); Gilbert S. Maxwell, *Navajo Rugs—past, present, and future* (Palm Desert, California: Best-West Publications, 1963); and Bertha Dutton, *Navajo Weaving Today* (Santa Fe: Museum of New Mexico Press, 1961). Anthony Berlant and Mary Hunt Kahlenberg, *Walk in Beauty* (Boston: New York Graphic Society, 1977) is an expert presentation of the history of Navajo weaving. Many periodicals, such as *Arizona Highways, El Palacio,* and *Southwestern Art*, have published recent articles on this very popular subject; one needs only to check their indexes. By now the reader is aware that no decision has yet been made in the literature on whether the word is spelled Navajo (Spanish origin) or Navaho (by English pronunciation).

For the personal story of the first American woman to reach Santa Fe read Susan Shelby Magoffin, *Down the Santa Fe Trail and Into Mexico, 1846-47* (1926; reprint ed., New Haven: Yale University Press, 1962). Some other nineteenth century accounts include Josiah Gregg, *Commerce of the Prairies: The Journal of a Santa Fe Trader 1831-39,* 2 vols. (1884; reprint ed., Philadelphia: J. B. Lippincott, 1962), several other reprints of which are available; George W. Kendall, *Across the Great Southwestern Prairies,* 2 vols. (Ann Arbor: University Microfilms, 1966), written in 1844; and W. W. H. Davis, *El Gringo: Or, New Mexico and Her People, 1857* (Chicago: The Rio Grande Press, 1962). Other books good for background are Paul Horgan, *Great River: The Rio Grande in North American History* (New York: Holt, Rinehart and Winston, 1954), and *The Centuries of Santa Fe* (New York: E. P. Dutton & Co., 1956); and David J. Weber, *The Taos Trappers: The Fur Trade in the Far Southwest, 1540-1846* (Norman, Okla.: University of Oklahoma Press, 1971). Edward H. Spicer and Raymond H. Tompson, eds., *Plural Society in the Southwest* (New York: Interbook, Inc., 1972) is a thoughtful, sociologically oriented work.

The best current source on Rio Grande weaving is E. Boyd, *Popular Arts of Spanish New Mexico* (Sante Fe: Museum of New Mexico Press, 1974). Only a portion is devoted to textiles, but study of the whole book will help show their relationship to the rest of Spanish New Mexican art. Roland F. Dickey, *New Mexico Village Arts* (Albuquerque: University of New Mexico Press, 1949) also presents a total picture. In 1949 the San Vicente Foundation, Inc. published H. P. Mera, *The Alfred I. Barton Collection of Southwestern Textiles* about Pueblo, Navajo, and Rio Grande weaving. In 1977, the University of New Mexico Press published Marion E. Rodee, *Southwestern Weaving,* a catalog of the Maxwell Museum of Anthropology collections, which include the three principal types. Good articles in *The New Mexico Historical Review* are Lansing B. Bloom, "Early Weaving in New Mexico," 2, no. 3 (1927):228-238, and Arnold L. Rodriquez, "New Mexico in Transition," 24, no. 8 (1949):184-222. Designers should see Nellie Dunton, *The Spanish Colonial Ornament and the Motifs Depicted in the Textiles of the Period in the American Southwest,* 2 pts. (Philadelphia: H. C. Perleberg, 1935). Embroidery students should see the *Bulletin of The Needle and Bobbin Club* 16, no. 2 (1932):19-26 for Mary Cabot Wheelwright, "Some Embroideries from New Mexico." Costume and textiles are discussed in Carmen Espinosa, *Shawls, Crinolines, Filigree* (El Paso: Texas Western Press, 1970).

12. FABRICS OF SOUTH AND MIDDLE AMERICA

The textile arts are very old in Peru and the other countries along the west coast of South America and in Mesoamerica—Mexico, Guatemala, El Salvador, and Honduras (Figure 12.1). Mesoamerica, Nicaragua, Costa Rica, and Panama comprise Middle America.

The historical record of Peru is written in its textiles and ceramics, as there was no writing prior to the Spanish Conquest. Fortunately, great quantities of textiles have been preserved in arid burying grounds. Weaving may be as old in Mesoamerica, but the damp tropical climate has destroyed the evidence. Records are carved on stone slabs or found on painted vases or in Aztec picture writing.

Scientists do not know where the indians of South and Middle America originated nor when they first came to the New World. Physical anthropologists generally believe the Americas were peopled by Homo sapiens who came from northeast Asia via the Bering Strait land bridge 20,000 to 40,000 years ago.[1] It is possible that Southeast Asians crossed the Pacific on rafts, and North Africans the Atlantic. Other theories include a land bridge from the lost continent of Atlantis, visits by Phoenicians, and a migration of Israelites across the South Pacific. The multitude of linguistic groups in South and Middle America suggests several places of origin, and study of the textiles and their similarities to Old World fabrics adds to the speculation.

Agriculture was completely developed in both areas by 2000 B.C., although some plant cultivation had begun much earlier. Cotton, for instance, was probably cultivated by 3000 B.C. The textile arts evolved with the increased leisure permitted by a more certain food supply. There is evidence that weaving was known in Peru almost as early as 6000 B.C., although 2500 B.C. is generally given for the beginning of twining, with weaving starting a few hundred years later.[2]

FIGURE 12.1 / South and Middle America.

PERUVIAN FABRICS

The Peruvians prepared their dead carefully for life in the next world. A corpse was usually dressed in its best clothing, then fixed in a squatting position and wrapped with many layers of cloth, forming a great egg-shaped bundle.[3] Tools, jewelry, and other items were buried with the mummy bundles deep in the sand, in rocky niches, or in adobe vaults. The bundle of an important person might be clothed in a specially woven shirt, have a false head mounted on top, and be placed in a temple wall recess where it could be worshipped (Plate 106).

Many burying grounds were used for centuries. In spite of a great loss of information from years of looting, archaeologists, working since the late nineteenth century, have been able to establish a cultural history for Peru by studying the textiles and ceramics.

The Textile Chronology

Archaeologists divide pre-Conquest Peruvian history into three time periods (horizons), each with characteristic ceramic and textile styles. The periods between horizons are called intermediate periods. The sequence is Early Horizon (1400–400 B.C.), Early Intermediate Period (400 B.C.–550 A.D.), Middle Horizon (550–900 A.D.), Late Intermediate Period (900–1450 A.D.), and Late Horizon (1450–1530 A.D.).[4]

There are three very different geographical areas in Peru: the coastal region—North Coast, Central Coast, and South Coast; the Highlands of the Andes Mountains; and the jungle region of eastern Peru. Most of the extant pre-Conquest textiles have come from the desert burying grounds on the coast, where it seldom rains (Plate 107). Weaving was just as important in the Highlands, and it continues there today. Indeed, more clothing was necessary in the colder climate. Thus, another way to study textile chronology is by division into cultures that were more or less specific to certain geographical areas but overlapped in time.[5]

The *Chavin* (1500–300 B.C.) was the first widespread cultural style. It originated on the North Coast, dominated the Central Highlands, and had influence on the South Coast. Religious cults were represented in fine stone carving and ceramics by the feline, or puma, and other anthropomorphic figures. Plain weave cotton fabrics were tie-dyed or painted with animal or plant forms. The cotton plant seemed to be a design unique to textiles.

The *Paracas* culture (900–100 B.C.), covering the end of the Early Horizon and the beginning of the Early Intermediate Period, is noted for its textiles. The culture was centered on the Paracas Peninsula and at other sites on the South Coast. The textiles of the first phase (900–500 B.C.) show a strong Chavin influence (Plate 108). A new religious cult appeared in the Paracas Cavernas phase (550–300 B.C.) and was represented on embroidered and painted fabrics by the Oculate Being, a fantastic creature with appendages and huge staring eyes (Plate 109). The presence of trophy heads suggests a warlike society. Paracas Necropolis (300–100 B.C.) textiles show even greater elaboration of the Oculate Being, then a more naturalistic representation of plants and animals.

Nazca (100 B.C.–700 A.D.) was another important South Coast culture. Fabrics were embroidered and painted with naturalistic motifs symbolizing bountiful harvests. Almost all the major weaving techniques ever practiced in Peru were known in the Nazca period. Tapestry with geometric motifs became important.

Tiahuanaco (700–110 A.D.) was a pan-Peruvian culture centered on Lake Titicaca in Bolivia and at Wari in the Central Highlands. There was a well-developed highway system to the lowlands. The most characteristic Tiahuanaco textile is fine tapestry worked into frets and spiral patterns as well as feline figures and human faces. A few tapestry shirts survive. Brocading, double cloth, and featherwork were well developed.

From about 1100 to 1400 A.D. in the Late Intermediate Period, outstanding textiles were produced on the coast by three closely associated cultures: *Chimu* on the North Coast, *Chancay* on the Central Coast, and *Ica* on the South Coast. Most textiles extant come from this period, although they represent earlier techniques and designs. Birds and fish are common.

The best documented culture, the *Inca*, was very short (1438-1530). The Incas, headquartered in Cuzco, were responsible for a phenomenal expansion of a "socialistic" empire unique in world history. Forts and administrative centers were built along the coast from Chile to Ecuador and throughout the Highlands.

The most flawless textiles were woven by Virgins of the Sun, Inca women who led lives of seclusion in the temples. They were chosen by an official selection process. Government administrators classified all girls at the age of ten and selected the most intelligent, skillful, or beautiful for special educations or, on certain occasions for sacrifice. After school was completed, the girls were again classified for various duties, including service to the Sun, Inca gods, or imperial mummies.

The Inca period ended with the Spanish Conquest. Between 1531 and 1533 Francisco Pizzaro, by playing the warring Inca factions against each other, was able to take over the rule with a mere handful of Spanish soldiers.

Pre-Conquest Textiles

Peruvian costume was simple and made of loomed pieces (with four finished edges) sewn together. Fabrics were not cut and tailored. Concentration was on pattern and color, which were often used to designate the wearer's home region or rank.

A man wore a breechcloth, a wrap-around skirt, and a shirt that could be either knee or waist length. A mantle, worn over the shoulders and knotted in front or on one shoulder, and the addition of a distinctive headdress and sandals completed the costume.

A woman wore a one-piece robe wrapped around her body and tied with a decorative belt. The mantle was held together in front by a large pin, called a tupu, often elaborately decorated. She would also wear a head band and sandals. Both sexes used intricately woven bags for coca (a narcotic) and personal items.

It appears that fabrics were woven specifically for funerary purposes as well as to be burned as sacrifices. Taxes and tributes were paid in cloth, so weaving was a full time activity for many Peruvians, male and female.

Fibers and Spinning

The first Peruvian fabrics were twined from the leaf and bast fibers of local plants. These fibers continued to be used in relatively small quantities for nets, bags, and some apparel. They were probably twisted by hand without benefit of a spindle.

PLATE 108 (*above*) / Detail of a Paracas painted mantle. (Courtesy of The Cleveland Museum of Art. The Norweb Collection)   PLATE 109 (*below*) / Paracas embroidery showing an oculate being.

PLATE 110a (*above*) / Picking the seeds and impurities from cotton on the south coast of Peru near Ica.   PLATE 110b (*below*) / Net from the south coast of Peru.

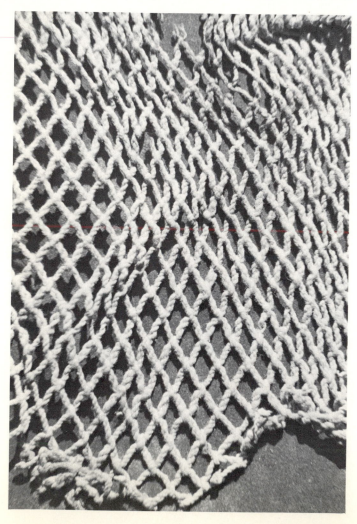

PLATE 111 (*above*) / Needle knitting. Length of parrot, 2″.   PLATE 112 (*below*) / Peruvian twined fabric.

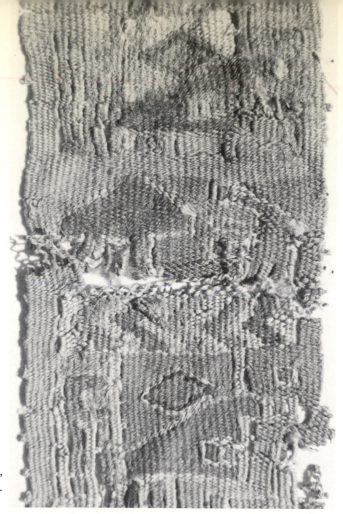

PLATE 113 / Peruvian tapestry, possibly from the Nazca period. Width, 1½″.

PLATE 114 / Peruvian tapestry, sewn to plain weave, possibly from the Chancay period. Width of bird, ½″.

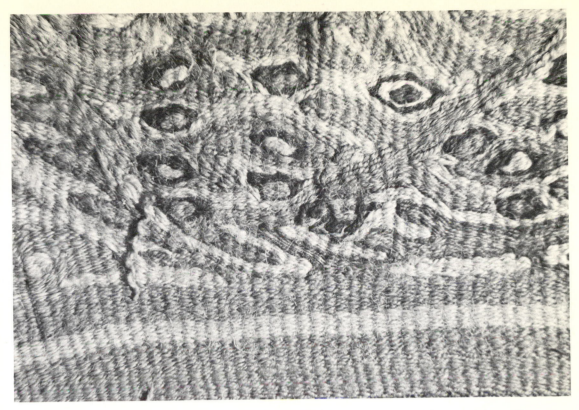

PLATE 115 (*above*) / Late Horizon (1450–1530 A.D.) tapestry with eccentric wefts.
PLATE 116 (*below*) / Peruvian gauze with embroidery.

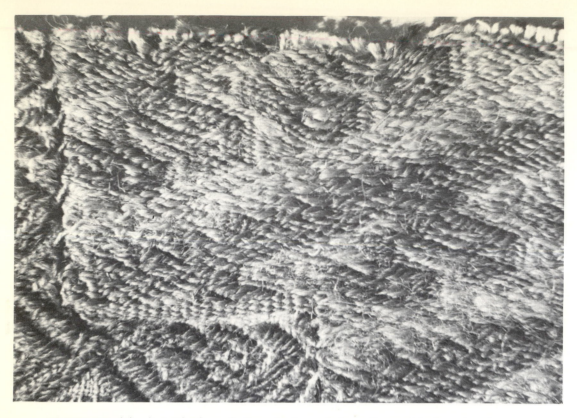

PLATE 117a (*above*) / The face of a Peruvian brocaded textile, possibly from the Chancay period.   PLATE 117b (*below*) / The reverse of the Peruvian brocaded textile.

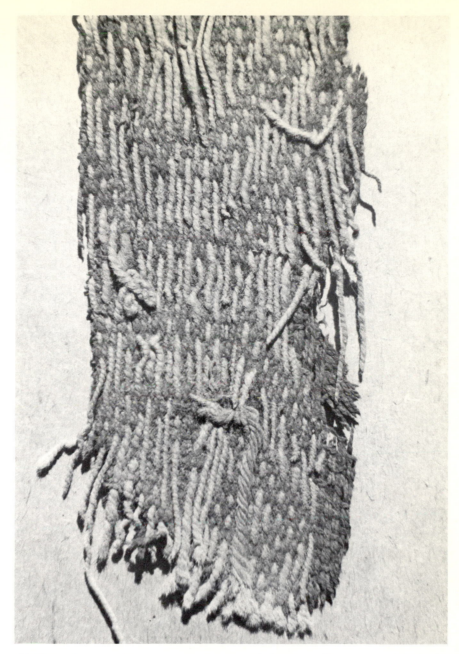

PLATE 118 / A Peruvian warp patterned fragment from the north coast. Width, 1″.

PLATE 119 (*above*) / Detail of a Peruvian warp patterned fabric. PLATE 120 (*below*) / Inca bag showing double weave below and tapestry above.

PLATE 121 (*above*) / A Peruvian painted textile.
PLATE 122 (*below*) / Peruvian embroidery from the
central coast. Width of bird, 3″.

PLATE 123 / Detail of a Late Intermediate Period (900-145 A.D.) feather tunic. Plain weave cotton with applied feathers. (Courtesy of The Textile Museum, Washington, D.C. 91.395)

PLATE 124 (*facing page*) / A Peruvian colonial tapestry. (Courtesy of The Denver Art Museum. Neusteter Institute Purchase)

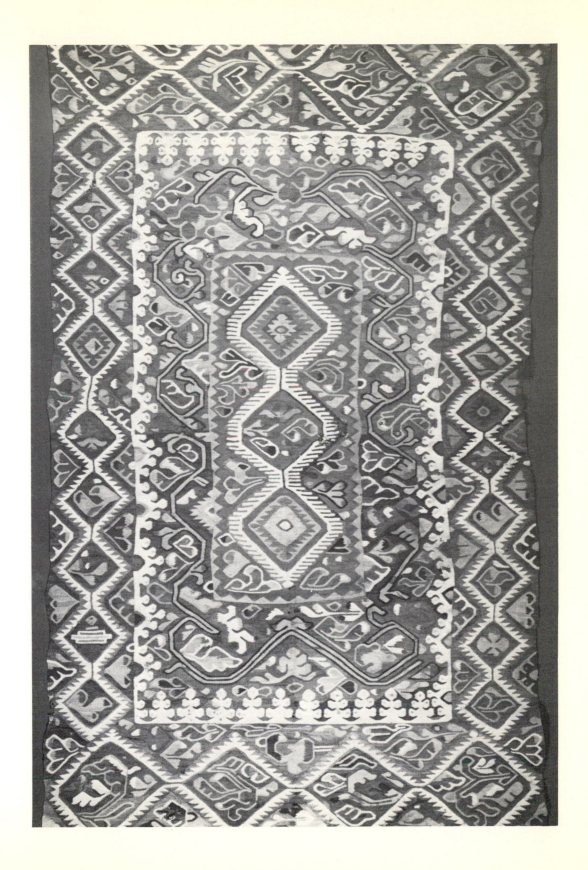

PLATE 125 / A Shipibo painted cotton.

PLATE 126 (*facing page*) / Detail of a Huipil from the Department Oaxaca, Mexico; probably made in the 1930s. It is a plain weave with guaze and weft-warp openwork. Cotton, 14½″ x10″ (area shown). (Courtesy of The Textile Museum, Washington, D.C. 1966.43.1)

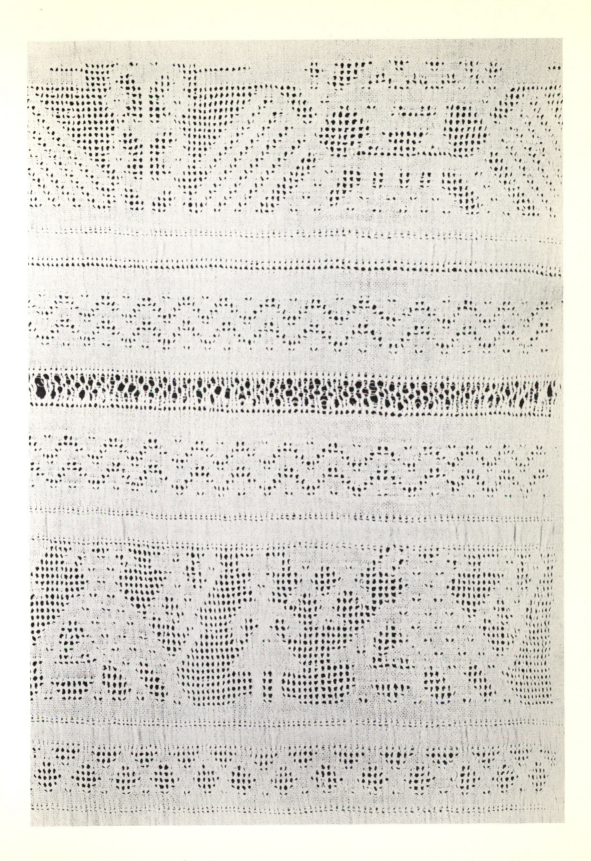

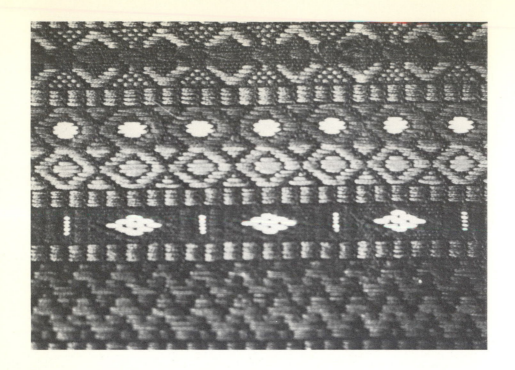

PLATE 127 (*above*) / Modern Guatemalan brocade. (Courtesy of Dr. Jacqueline Dupont)   PLATE 128 (*below*) / Modern embroidery from southern Mexico.

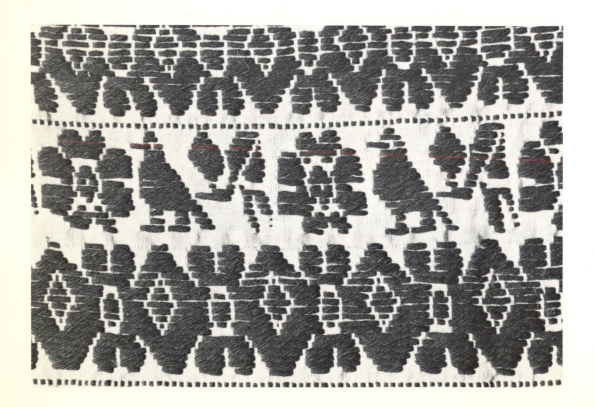

PLATE 129 / Weaver at a Guatemalan hotel, circa 1973. (Courtesy of Dr. Jacqueline Dupont)

PLATE 130 / A mola from Panama.

Cotton was the principal fiber used in pre-Conquest Peru. It was cultivated as early as 3000 B.C., although wild varieties would have been used earlier. Cotton grew in a range of shades from white to brown, and the darker shades were valued because they required no dyeing. The seeds and impurities were picked from the lint by hand (Plate 110a). Some little combs found in graves may have been used for carding. Cotton was spun on a slender spindle pointed at both ends and having a ring of baked clay in the center. The spindle was supported on the ground or in a small gourd. Newly spun yarn could be wound onto the spindle and the whole thing used as a shuttle in weaving. Yarns were very finely spun and were often plied. Sometimes there was deliberate overtwisting in order to produce crepe yarn.

The other major pre-Conquest fiber was wool from the highland cameloids—the llama, alpaca, and vicuna (see chapter 2). Alpaca was used most often in garments for it was soft and lustrous, while llama was generally too harsh to be worn next to the body. The fine, silky fiber on the vicuna was reserved to nobility. Wool was probably washed, carded, and spun on a drop spindle like the one still being used in Peru (usually to ply or respin commercial yarn). In most coastal fabrics, wool was used in sparing amounts, indicating its rarity. Contrary to mixtures woven in early modern Europe, Peruvian textiles had warps of cotton and wefts of wool.

Construction

Today, Peru is a paradise for textile technologists and handweavers. Thus, it is not surprising that almost all the textile techniques known anywhere were known in pre-Conquest Peru. Peruvian textiles are noted not only for their diversity but also for their technical excellence.

Several methods of looping and knotting single yarns or cords were employed in making bags, wigs, and fishnets (Plate 110b). Patterns and changes in texture could be achieved by varying the length of the loops and making arrangements of different sized loops. Most patterns were simple geometric designs, and there was complete development of looping techniques by 1500 B.C.

Peru has become quite famous for its looped, or knitted, fringes (Plate 111). Generally called *needle knitting* or *crossed knitting* (see chapter 3), the technique was perfected by the Nazca period.[6] Intricate arrangements of tiny animals, birds, and other figures were made with frequent color changes within each piece. Some authors describe it as an embroidery technique because of its similarity to buttonhole stitch.

Knotting was developed to the point where ornamental yarns were tied into the meshwork and cut to make what has been called imitation velvet. It was used to make little square caps. Feathers were also worked into knotted meshworks.

Braiding (diagonal interlacing) and plaiting (diagonal interlinking) were used in all periods for slings, cords, flat bands, and bags. The use of different colored yarns produced structural patterns. Sprang (loom plaiting) reached its zenith during the Nazca period. Intricate patterns were made by varying the arrangements of open spaces.

FIGURE 12.2 / Peruvian Loom (from a Spanish chronicle).

Large quantities of twined fabrics (see chapter 3) have been found in very ancient Peruvian graves (Plate 112). By varying the crossings, simple motifs like birds and serpents were obtained. Twining was replaced by weaving when the heddle loom was devised.

The loom of old Peru was the same simple backstrap or waist loom still in use throughout Central and South America (Figure 12.2 and Plate 129). The textiles were usually woven to the size needed, even if for a tiny grave doll, and were seldom cut. Pieces could be shaped during weaving by adding or subtracting warps or wefts or by other methods such as adjusting the loom bars so that one side was shorter than the other.[7]

Because the horizontal ground loom is still in use in the Andes and was not a type introduced by the Spanish, textile experts presume it was employed to weave wide cloths in pre-Conquest Peru. Vertical frame looms were probably used also.

The utilitarian fabrics were made in plain weave. All weights were woven, some thin and light enough to be folded for head cloths, others heavy and coarse for outer wrappings for mummies. Plaids and stripes were common. Rep construction,

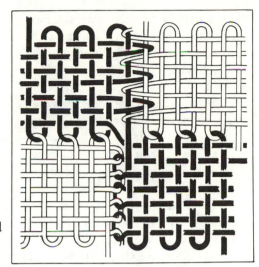

FIGURE 12.3 / Discontinuous Warp and Weft (adapted from d'Harcourt, 1962, Fig. 7).

often forming stripes of plain color used in conjunction with warp patterns, was woven. Basket weaves were also used.

Tapestry evolved around 900 B.C., and it could be made on a loom without heddles. It was all cotton or had cotton warp and wool weft. In some instances tapestry was very finely woven, with as many as two hundred weft per inch. Both interlocking and slit techniques were used (Plates 113 and 114). Sometimes the slits were arranged in stair steps to make grid patterns, or used to make intricate fringes. Eccentric wefts, not at right angles to the warp (Plate 115), were used to make curved figures. One type of tapestry had underfloats of weft carried from one motif to another, although generally tapestry was reversible and both faces were finished.

Not only narrow bands but also rather wide pieces of tapestry were woven. Some outstanding Tiahuanaco and Inca shirts have been studied, and it seems that the tapestry patterns were used to signify rank. Tapestry *(Qompi)* was an especially prestigious material for the Incas.

Tapestry is recognized by its discontinuous weft (see chapter 3), and the Peruvians knew a weave that employed discontinuous warps as well (Figure 12.3). The construction is known as *discontinuous warp and weft,* or *interlocking warp and weft*, and it made a double change of color, resulting in checkerboard patterns, feasible. A system of scaffold wefts was used.[8] The technique was sophisticated enough during the Nazca period to make curved and diagonal lines possible. Discontinuous warp and weft weaving might be related to the precision mending done by the Peruvians; fabrics were put back on the loom or were stretched on frames and carefully repaired by reweaving.

Delicate gauzes were made by a variety of techniques using fine regular and crepe spun cotton yarns. Some elaborate patterns were worked out by crossing warp yarns between picks, a variation of leno (see Figure 3.30). In other examples, the warps were spaced with interwoven wefts, perhaps weaving an over two, under two tapestry in adjacent sections (Plate 116). Warps or wefts could be omitted to make checked openwork. Gauzes were also made by *weft-wrap weaving,* in which weft were wrapped around warp and other weft to form patterns of holes (Plate 126).

The brocaded fabrics of Peru were as advanced as other weaves. Warp and weft were of cotton, while the supplementary weft was of wool. (Note the difference between the two faces of the brocaded textile in Plate 117). It was a technique adaptable to a wide range of patterns.

Complementary warp structures are very old (Plates 118 and 119). There are two sets of coequal warp of different color. During the weaving certain warp are picked up with the fingers or small sticks, while the weft is interlaced. The patterns are warp-faced and the pattern produced by the warp floats. The possibilities for design variation are almost limitless. Today in the Highlands of Peru and Bolivia patterns relate to individual regions and range from simple geometric designs to complex animal figures.

Double cloth, too, is very old. It is a combined weave structure using two sets of warp and two sets of weft. Patterns were angular and the same motifs appeared on both faces although they were reversed in color. Most was used for heavy bands or bags (Plate 120).

Dyeing and Painting

Peruvian dyes are being analyzed by researchers attempting to determine old trade routes. The wide range of hues known in old fabrics indicates widespread sources for dyestuffs.[9] In general, reds, browns, and golds seem to predominate in extant textiles, although many colors have changed with time.

Natural shades of cotton, alpaca, and llama were well utilized. Red came from a madder-like plant and from the cochineal insect (see chapter 4). Indigo blue and the purple from a mollusk (see Mesoamerican dyes, p. 336) have been identified. Many native plants supplied yellow. Soot was used for brown and black. Little is known about mordants except that they were used. Wool could be dyed in a much wider range of colors than cotton, and this is probably a major reason why it was preferred for weft.

Tie-dyeing and painting plain weave cotton cloths were fairly common in all periods beginning with Chavin (Plate 121). Some ikat, resist dyeing of warp before weaving, was known in pre-Conquest Peru, but it was fairly rare.[10]

Surface Decoration

Embroidery probably preceded many weaving techniques. It was at a peak in the Paracas and Nazca periods, although it was used in all periods. Several stitches have been identified: stem, buttonhole, satin, and loop. Late work especially tends to show the stitches following the horizontal of the weft, and it is difficult to distinguish it from brocading (Plates 116 and 122). Motifs were generally the same as woven ones. Both cotton and wool embroidery yarns were used. Needles were of bone, cactus and yucca spines, and pounded metal.

Featherwork links Peru and Mesoamerica with New Zealand, Tahiti, and Hawaii where the art was highly advanced.[11] Feathers came from brilliantly colored tropical birds: toucans, macaws (parrots), scarlet tanagers, blue jays, and hummingbirds. Application was done by several methods, but usually a cord was tied to several quills in turn and then was sewn to a base cloth. Layers of feathers were attached like shingles on a roof. Magnificent ceremonial cloaks of blue and yellow parrot feathers and tiny caps patterned of hummingbird feathers have been preserved (Plate 123).

Tufts, tassles, and metal sequins were used to decorate Peruvian textiles. What might seem to be the ultimate in textile decoration is housed in a Lima museum: thin plates of gold, cut to match the design shapes of the underlying textile, have been carefully stitched to the surface.

Colonial Textiles

Weaving continued after the conquest by Pizarro and his conquistadores in the 1530s. Natives still wore their traditional attire, and the Spanish had need for textiles. Each city in the Viceroyalty of Peru, which extended from Panama to Chile in the sixteenth century, had its own weaving workshops. Ecclesiastical and house furnishing fabrics (the latter somewhat later than the former) were woven expressly for the Spanish.

The Spanish introduced sheep's wool, linen, silk, and metallic yarns. They encouraged certain techniques, like tapestry and embroidery, and seem to have discouraged others, like featherwork, needle-knitting, and double cloth.

Some, although not many, colonial tapestries have survived (Plate 124). They exhibit a carry-over of high quality Incan weaving mixed with European design influence. Colonial tapestries are not pictorial but rather show the combination of many small designs: floral motifs, animals, armorial patterns, two-headed Hapsburg eagles, crowns, and various Christian symbols. Some show strong Hispano-Moresque influence (see chapter 6).

That the Peruvians drew on many sources for design is illustrated by some seventeenth century tapestries with Chinese motifs.[12] For more than two centuries, beginning in the late sixteenth, the Spanish sailed the "Manila galleons" between Mexico and the Philippines. The ships transported large quantities of Chinese silks that were then carried across Mexico and shipped on to Spain or sent to other parts of the New World. Briefly in the late sixteenth century, ships sailed directly from Lima to Manila for silks.

Textiles of Eastern Peru

Life is lived simply by the Shipibo and Conibo Indians in villages along the Ucayali River in the upper Amazon basin. Houses are open sided with overhanging palm leaf roofs. Women gather wild cotton and spin it on palm wood spindles with clay whorls and weave the plain cloth on backstrap or horizontal looms, or they purchase commercial cotton cloth.

A main activity is the painting of cotton cloth with "maze-like" designs (Plate 125). The original meaning of the designs, composed of straight lines and step frets, has been lost.[13] They have, however, widespread use among the indians. The same patterns are found on women's skirts, men's cushmas (shirts), trinket bags, pottery, paddles, spears, houses, and faces. Women embroider as well as paint the designs, and all colors are used, although brown and black tend to predominate. Many of these trademarks of the jungle indians are sold in tourist shops throughout Peru.

MESOAMERICAN TEXTILES

A few archaeological textiles, stone carvings, figurines, paintings, and picture writing with costume details, make it seem probable that most of the textile techniques used in Peru were also known in pre-Conquest Mesoamerica. The Mesoamericans, however, did not have alpaca and llama wool but used only cotton and other vegetable fibers.

Chronology

The *Preclassic Period* (2000 B.C.-300 A.D.) saw the development of village agriculture, pottery, and weaving.[14] The Olmec civilization began on the Yucatan Peninsula about 800 B.C. and was to be a base for other Mesoamerican cultures. Common social patterns and religious practices started to take shape when the Olmecs expanded over Mesoamerica. Great stone heads and carved jaguars testify to more than a mere subsistence society.

Two major civilizations reached prominence during the *Classic Period* (300-900 A.D.). During the early part of the period all Mesoamerica was dominated by the Teotihuacans from their huge city (near present-day Mexico City) in the Valley of Mexico. They used picture writing and a 260 day ceremonial calendar. Large pyramids were built for tombs and ceremonial centers. Teotihuacan civilization declined around 600 A.D.

The Lowland Maya reached their zenith in the latter part of the Classic Period after a long development in Guatemala. They used hieroglyphic inscriptions and made books, or codices, from bark fiber paper. Vividly painted pottery depicted multicolored ceremonial textiles, possibly of featherwork. The Maya made outstanding stone sculpture and murals. Stylized serpents, humans, jaguars, birds, and fantastic god representations typified Mayan art. Decline set in around 800 A.D. for unknown reasons. Although the Maya no longer controlled most of Mesoamerica, their civilization continued and experienced a revival in Yucatan between 1000 and 1200. A few textile scraps have been recovered from the Mayan sacred well at Chichen Itza in Yucatan.

The Classic Period ended with upheaval and strife throughout Mesoamerica, caused perhaps by desert peoples pressing in on the cities from the north. One such group was the Toltecs who moved into central Mexico and became an important military power.

The Aztecs rose to power about the middle of the *Postclassic Period* (900–1520 A.D.). Like the Inca in Peru they ruled for only a short period before the Conquest, but their civilization has been much better documented than the preceding ones. The great city of Tenochtitlan, built on an island in Lake Texcoco, was the capital of an empire that extended from coast to coast and from the Valley of Mexico in the north to Guatemala in the south. Hernan Cortes came to this city in 1519 and was able to defeat the emperor Montezuma and destroy Aztec civilization, partly because the indians believed he was the god Quetzalcoatl returning to claim his lost realm.

The textiles were destroyed—by man or by time—but the records remained. The Aztecs used picture writing with ideograms (a blazing temple represented defeat) and phonograms (objects represented sounds) for histories, tribute lists, genealogies, religious tracts, and piles of bureaucratic records. After the Conquest the Aztecs were quick to recognize the advantages of writing in the Latin characters of the Spanish and transcribed some of their old books. Most important to textile historians is the *Codex Mendoza,* drawn by the natives on command of the Viceroy de Mendoza to be sent to Charles V. It was seized at sea by the French and is now in the Oxford library. Other codices, written and drawn by the Spanish, also depict Aztec costume and craftwork.

Aztec Fabrics

Thus, there are records describing life in Tenochtitlan on the eve of the Spanish Conquest (about 1500). At the same time in Europe, the Muslims were being expelled from Spain, Henry VIII would very soon succeed to the English throne, and the Protestant Reformation would soon begin. It was the middle of the Ming dynasty in China, the Muromachi period in Japan, and the beginning of the Safavid in Persia.

Tenochtitlan was a beautiful city of white flat-roofed houses, some terraced, and most turned inward to little courtyards where the family work was done. There were towers, chapels, and huge pyramids where the sacrifices were made. Flowers grew everywhere. It is thought that as many as a million people lived in the city and surrounding area.[15] Outlying farms, some only rafts with soil piled on, supplied a city bustling with craftsmen and merchants. Canals were used as streets.

Luxury goods from all over the empire flowed into the city as tribute, and the markets abounded in fine textiles. Lengths of cloth were used as money. The cloth, piled high in the stalls or hung for easy examination, represented the culmination of traditional weaving.

Thousands of people attended the market, and each person's station in life was proclaimed by his wardrobe. The common man wore only a loin cloth, the *maxtlatl,* and a mantle, the *tilmatli* (a large rectangle worn over the left arm and tied on the right shoulder). This he shifted to cover his front when he sat down. The tilmatli was also his bedding. Priests sometimes wore short tunics under the tilmatlis, and soldiers had special close-fitting tunics and ankle length trousers to wear to war.

The woman's basic garment was the wraparound skirt tied at the waist with an embroidered belt. Lower-class ladies went topless or wore a *huipil* made of three narrow strips sewn together, then folded in half and formed into a tunic. Upper class women wore in addition the *quechquemitl*, a triangular cape without any opening except for the head. It was made from straight pieces of cloth, as were all other Aztec garments, and could be very decorative. Some women in Mexico still wear these traditional garments.

Cotton was brought to Tenochtitlan as tribute from the hot lands to the southeast. Both white and yellow varieties were native to Mexico, and extensive irrigation systems were developed for its cultivation. The fine, soft textiles made from cotton were reserved to the rich merchants and priests. The common folk used fibers from plants of the agave (Ixtle) family—sisal, maguey, and yucca. Agave fibers were spun into fairly fine yarns with a simple hand spindle called a *malacate* in Mexico. For very fine fiber like cotton, a smaller sized spindle was used and supported in a clay dish or gourd. The small amounts of hair fibers that were spun came from humans, rabbits, and dogs.

Women might weave on their backstrap looms as they sat in the market waiting to sell their cloth. They were watched over by the goddess of the arts, Xochiquetzal, who purportedly invented spinning and weaving. Tapestry, twill, gauze, checks, stripes, warp patterning, and brocade were all important. Weft-warp openwork was also known (Plate 126).[16]

Feathers for the priests' capes and headdresses might be on view in the market. The Aztecs bred exotic birds and periodically pulled the feathers. More common feathers were used to construct blankets and mats. Featherwork was to continue after the Conquest, but it was to take a different form. Bits of feathers were glued to backgrounds to make Christian religious illustrations.

Numerous natural dyestuffs were available. Cochineal was cultivated in individual households, indigo was common, and several dyewoods were indigenous. The indians on the west coast gathered the large Purpura shellfish and blew on them to cause a discharge of milky fluid that was dabbed on cotton yarn. As with Tyrian purple (see chapter 4), the color developed in sunlight. In Mesoamerica, however, the shellfish were large enough to be milked and returned to the rocks to be used another time.[17] Richly dyed yarns were sold for weaving and for embroidering sumptuous cloaks for the priests and holiday attire for the rich.

The designs used by the Aztecs were based in their religion. Essentially they believed in two supreme beings, the Lord and Lady of the Duality, who had produced all the other gods and humans. It was the lesser gods who were worshipped. One, the Sun God, had to be fed with human blood every day in order that darkness would not overtake the world. So the Aztecs offered human sacrifices. Religious beliefs also prescribed cremation of corpses wrapped in fine textiles and the burning of sacrificial victims on occasion.

Pre-Conquest Mesoamericans used stylized plant and animal patterns and geometric designs that were easily adapted to weaving and embroidery. Monkeys were popular, and stepped frets and triangles were common. Another ancient symbol was the "blue worm," a standing or reclining S said to represent the seven stars in the Little Bear.[18] The two-headed eagle, used commonly in modern Mesoamerican textiles, was associated in pre-Conquest Mexico with the god of fire and retained this meaning for the natives even after the Spanish had it woven to represent the Hapsburg Empire.

After the Conquest there were new motifs and an intermingling of the new with the old until most symbolism was lost. Certain patterns and colors came to represent different villages until commercial clothing became widely popular. The Spanish changed more than design: they brought new materials and new equipment. An anthropologist sitting in a Guatemalan market today would recognize the old Spanish influences and note the beginnings of new changes as well.

Modern Guatemalan Textiles

The market for fine textiles was eliminated with the Spanish Conquest: most Indian nobles were either killed or reduced to slavery. The rich Spanish imported their luxury textiles from Europe or the Far East, so pattern weaving became, for the most part, folk art made for local wear. As in other areas of the New World, the natives were put to weaving utilitarian goods for the Spanish.

The Spanish brought sheep, and the wool industry became important in the highlands. The wool was sheared, washed in cold water, and taken to market in small lots. Weavers bought what they needed and took it home for carding with the European-style hand cards set with metal teeth. Spinning was done with a short, fat version of the European Jersey wheel or on drop spindles. Commercially spun wool became readily available after World War II.

The Spanish also introduced silk to Mesoamerica, although it is possible that some wild kinds were already known. Sericulture flourished in Mexico in the late sixteenth century, and it was predicted that New Spain would soon become the greatest silk producer in the world and keep European looms well supplied. This did not happen because the Manila trade developed, and mulberry silk raising was extinct by the end of the eighteenth century. A small domestic oak silk industry continued to supply fiber for accenting woven designs and embroidery. In the nineteenth century, American floss silk and, in the twentieth century, rayon yarn were imported for the same purpose.

Flax growing and linen weaving were promoted by the Spanish, but flax could never compete with cotton. In the late eighteenth century some very high quality linens were woven in Guatemala.

It seems that the man's life changed more radically than the woman's after the Conquest. She continued to weave for her family on the backstrap loom, while he learned to use the European treadle loom. His wardrobe changed more, too. Men adopted the shirt and trousers of the Spanish and added a serape woven of wool. It was both a plain rectangle and a poncho-like garment with a slit for the head, woven in tapestry on the treadle loom (Plate 104). Very popular in the nineteenth century, the serape is now worn mostly for fiesta.

Women continued to wear the huipil, quechquemitl, and skirt. Their post-Conquest wardrobe addition was the *rebozo*, a long rectangle elaborately woven or embroidered, sometimes having intricately knotted fringes. Rebozos serve as shawls, blankets, baby carriers, and for many other purposes. Ikat dyeing, called *jaspe* in Guatemala, is frequently seen in cotton rebozos.

The modern tourist is apt to buy a *tzute*, a small square or rectangle used as a utility cloth for wrapping small items or as a head covering. Most likely the patterns would have been made by brocading, the most commonly used pattern weave in Guatemala.

Most of the design units in modern Guatemalan textiles, brocaded and embroidered, are simple stylized and abstract animals, birds, plants, and geometric forms. Motifs can be adapted to brocading (Plate 127) or to counted thread embroidery (Plate 128). An exception is seen in the involved floral embroidery worked on transfer patterns stamped on cotton muslin.

TOURIST TEXTILES

Since World War II machine made textiles have been distributed to all parts of the world, and in only a few places do people continue to wear home woven garments. Even though they are changing rapidly in character, these handcrafted fabrics continue to be of interest to textile historians, because they retain vestiges of old techniques (Plate 129).

Tourism has been one of the forces responsible for changes in textiles, but it has also been responsible for preserving some textile crafts from extinction. Craft workers have moved into the cities to weave full time in workshops. No longer do women integrate their weaving with household tasks. Patterns have become generalized and no longer represent particular villages or districts; they tend to be regarded as "typical." Low priced, poor quality textiles sell readily, so there is no reason to weave better ones.

The introduction of machine spun yarn has caused the loss of dyeing and spinning skills. Synthetic yarns have eliminated the need to grow cotton or wool. The aniline dyed yarns have resulted in some very nontraditional color combinations. Some of the lost skills are now being taught by outsiders interested in either preserving old techniques or starting new industries.

Meanwhile, many regions have been "mined" of most old textiles by collectors and merchants, some planning to make the textiles into garments suitable for western wear. Motifs from the handcrafted textiles of South and Middle America, Africa, Southeast Asia, and other regions are frequently used on commercially made fabrics. And it is not unusual for those fabrics to be found in the areas that served for their inspiration. But is this not all just a twentieth century version of history repeating itself?

MOLAS OF THE SAN BLAS ISLANDS

The Cuna indians, who live on some forty of the San Blas Islands near the coast of Panama, are making records of the twentieth century in textile form. These textiles are the molas constructed of commercially woven cotton cloth purchased from trading boats that ply the islands. Molas originally served, and still serve, as blouse fronts and backs. They are also now highly valued as wall hangings (Plate 130).

Cuna women started making molas about a hundred years ago, possibly as a replacement for body painting. The traditional method was essentially *repliqué*, or reverse appliqué, work. Several layers of different colored cloth were laid on top of one another. The major design figures were cut away from the first layers, smaller details within the main figures were then cut away from succeeding layers, and raw edges were folded back and carefully stitched down. Small pieces might be appliquéd to the surface and touches of embroidery used to complete the design. More recent molas are just appliqué work, and some are being made with sewing machines.

In the past, designs were religious and mythological or derived from island and ocean flora and fauna. More recently, current events, political figures, magazine advertisements, canned foods, and other examples of western material culture have served as design inspiration. There is a blending of old symbolism with modern science—one mola depicts a space vehicle as a giant bat with a reclining astronaut inside.

NOTES

1. Gordon R. Willey, *An Introduction to American Archaeology Volume One, North and Middle America* and *Volume Two, South America* (Englewood Cliffs, New Jersey: Prentice-Hall, 1966 and 1971), 1:13 and 2:9.

2. William J. Conklin, "An Introduction to South American Archaeological Textiles with Emphasis on Materials and Techniques of Peruvian Tapestry," *Irene Emery Roundtable on Museum Textiles 1974 Proceedings: Archaeological Textiles,* ed. Patricia L. Fiske (Washington D.C.: The Textile Museum, 1975) p. 23.

3. Ephraim George Squier, "A Plain Man's Tomb in Peru," in *Peruvian Archaeology: Selected Readings*, ed. John Howland Rowe and Dorothy Menzel (Palo Alto, California: Peek Publications, 1967), pp. 210-218.

4. Rowe and Menzel, *Peruvian Archaeology*, Introduction.

5. Mary Elizabeth King, *Ancient Peruvian Textiles from the Collections of The Textile Museum, Washington, D.C. and The Museum of Primitive Art, New York* (Greenwich, Connecticut: New York Graphic Society, 1965).

6. Lila M. O'Neale, "Peruvian Needleknitting," *American Anthropologist* 36 (1934):405-430; and Dorothy K. Burnham, "Coptic Knitting: An Ancient Technique," *Textile History* 3 (December 1972):116-124.

7. Mary Elizabeth King, *A Preliminary Study of a Shaped Textile from Peru, Workshop Notes*, The Textile Museum Paper No. 13 (Washington, D.C.: The Textile Museum, April 1956); and Junius B. Bird, "Shaped Tapestry Bags from the Nazca-Ica Area of Peru," *Textile Museum Journal* 1, no. 3 (1964):2-7.

8. Ann Pollard Rowe, "Interlocking Warp and Weft in the Nasca 2 Style," *Textile Museum Journal* 3, no. 3 (1972):70.

9. The principal methods used for dye analysis are infrared spectophotometry and thin layer chromatography.

10. Mary Elizabeth King, *A New Type of Peruvian Ikat, Workshop Notes*, The Textile Museum Paper No. 17 (Washington D.C.: The Textile Museum, June 1958).

11. Te Rangi Hiroa (Peter H. Buck), *Arts and Crafts of Hawaii, Section V Clothing* (1957; reprint ed., Honolulu: Bishop Museum Press, 1964), pp. 215-231.

12. Schuyler Cammann, "Chinese Influence in Colonial Peruvian Tapestries," *Textile Museum Journal* 1, no. 3 (1964):21-34.

13. William Curtis Farabee, "Indian Tribes of Eastern Peru," *Papers of the Peabody Museum of American Archaeology and Ethnology, Harvard University* 10 (1922):100.

14. Willey, *North and Middle America,* p. 93.

15. Jacques Soustelle, *Daily Life of the Aztecs on the Eve of the Spanish Conquest* (New York: Macmillan, 1961), p. 9.

16. Irmgard Weitlaner Johnson, "Weft-Wrap Openwork Techniques in Archaeological and Contemporary Textiles of Mexico," *Textile Museum Journal* 4, no. 3 (1976):63-74.

17. Wolfgang Born, "The Use of Purple Among the Indians of Central America," *CIBA Review* 4 (December 1937):124-129.

18. Donald and Dorothy Cordry, *Mexican Indian Costumes* (Austin: University of Texas Press, 1968), p. 177.

BIBLIOGRAPHY

Some references are useful for both South and Middle America. Gordon R. Willey's *An Introduction to American Archaeology: Volume One, North and Middle America* and *Volume Two, South America* (Englewood Cliffs, New Jersey: Prentice-Hall, 1966 and 1971) are major texts. Of a more popular vein are two works by Pal Keleman: *Medieval American Art* (New York: Macmillan, 1943), reprinted in two volumes by Dover (in 1969 with the textiles in volume 2), and *Art of the Americas: Ancient and Hispanic* (New York: Bonanza Books, 1969). Keleman treats textiles in the same context as other arts. Phyllis Ackerman, *Tapestry: The Mirror of Civilization* (1933; reprint ed., New York: AMS Press, 1970) has a chapter on Peru and Mexico that concentrates on design. Very important for bibliographies and specialized studies is Irene Emery and Patricia L. Fiske, eds., *Ethnographic Textiles of the Western Hemisphere: Irene Emery Roundtable on Museum Textiles, 1976 Proceedings* (Washington, D.C.: The Textile Museum, 1977).

Sources on Peru are extensive. One of the best for general background is J. Alden Mason, *The Ancient Civilizations of Peru* (Baltimore: Penguin Books, 1973). Mason includes a chapter on textiles and an extensive bibliography that is keyed by subject. Wendell C. Bennett and Junius B. Bird, *Andean Culture History,* 2nd ed. (Garden City, New

York: Natural History Press, 1964) contains a good introduction to Peruvian textiles. An important book, *The Peoples and Culture of Ancient Peru* (1969) by Luis Lumbreras, a noted Peruvian archaeologist, has been translated by Betty J. Meggers (Washington, D.C.: Smithsonian Institution Press, 1974). Edward Lanning, *Peru Before the Incas* (Englewood Cliffs, New Jersey: Prentice-Hall, 1967) is another authoritative source, as is Phillip A. Means, *Ancient Civilizations of the Andes* (New York: Scribners, 1931), with its chapter on textiles. Two recent popular articles describe archaeological work at some pre-Inca sites. Michael Moseley and Carol Mackey wrote "Chan Chan, Peru's Ancient City of Kings," for the *National Geographic*, March 1973; and Michael Moseley wrote "Secrets of Peru's Ancient Walls," for *Natural History*, January 1975. These help the layman understand some of the problems experienced by archaeologists.

There are two classics about the Incas and the Spanish. Garcilaso de la Vega, born of an Inca princess and a Spanish father, wrote *The Royal Commentaries of the Inca* when he was an old man, using notes taken in Peru before he left at age twenty-one. One of several available editions is *The Incas, The Royal Commentaries of the Inca Garcilaso de la Vega* (New York: Avon Books, 1964). Using Spanish chronicles, William H. Prescott wrote the *History of the Conquest of Peru* in 1847. Among many editions of Prescott's works is *History of the Conquest of Mexico and History of the Conquest of Peru* (New York: The Modern Library, 1936).

The best reference for costume is Gösta Montell, *Dress and Ornaments in Ancient Peru* (Goteburg, Sweden: Elanders boktryckeri aktiebolag, 1929). Ceramics served as the primary source material in Montell's researches. A much briefer but more readily available source is Nathalie H. Zimmern, *Introduction to Peruvian Costume* (Brooklyn: Brooklyn Institute of Arts and Sciences, 1949). Zimmern includes a review of the important early Spanish literature on Peru. See also John V. Murra, "Cloth and Its Functions in the Inca State," *American Anthropologist* 64 (1962):710-728.

The oldest work devoted just to textiles is William H. Holmes, "Textile Fabrics of Ancient Peru," *Bureau of American Ethnology, Bulletin 7* (Washington, D.C.: Government Printing Office, 1889), pp. 1-17. An earlier work by Holmes uses Peruvian textiles as part of a discussion of design and structure in different art forms. See "A Study of the Textile Art in Its Relation to the Development of Form and Ornament," in *Bureau of American Ethnology Sixth Annual Report 1884/5* (Washington, D.C.: Government Printing Office, 1888), pp. 189-252.

Other early studies include M. D. C. Crawford, "Peruvian Fabrics," *Anthropological Papers of the American Museum of Natural History* 12, pt. 3 (1915):52-104, and 12, pt. 4 (1916):105-191; and Philip Ainsworth Means, *A Study of Peruvian Textiles* (Boston: Museum of Fine Arts, 1932). This was a catalog for the museum's collection. Lila O'Neale was another researcher active in the 1930s. With A. L. Krober she wrote a survey of the periods and the textiles that were common in each. Of course, much has been learned since then, but see "Textile Periods in Ancient Peru: I," *University of California Publications in American Archaeology and Ethnology* 28, no. 2 (1930):23-54, with 48 plates.

There are two short surveys available, both illustrating museum collections. See Mary Elizabeth King, *Ancient Peruvian Textiles from the Collections of The Textile Museum, Washington, D.C. and The Museum of Primitive Art, New York* (Greenwich, Connecticut: New York Graphic Society, 1965), and Nora Fisher, *1500 Years of Andean Weaving* (Santa Fe: Museum of New Mexico, 1972). A well-written survey with concentration on mummy bundles is James Vreeland, "Ancient Andean Textiles: Clothes for the Dead," *Archaeology* 30, no. 3 (May 1977):166-178.

The most complete book on Peruvian textile construction is Raoul d'Harcourt, *Textiles of Ancient Peru and Their Techniques* (1962; reprint ed., Seattle: University of Washington Press, 1974). An article by d'Harcourt and some of his excellent diagrams can be found in *CIBA Review* 136 (February 1960). A very clearly presented survey of techniques is Junius B. Bird, "Technology and Art in Peruvian Textiles," in *Technique and Personality,* ed. Margaret Mead, Junius B. Bird, and Hans Himmelheber (New York: The Museum of Primitive Art, 1963), pp. 45-77. See also Ina Van Stan, *Problems in Pre-Columbian Textile Classification* (Tallahassee: Florida State University, 1958).

A number of specialized studies have been made by textile historians. An important one is Junius B. Bird and Louisa Bellinger, *Paracas Fabrics and Nazca Needlework* (Washington, D.C.: The Textile Museum, 1954). Alan R. Sawyer published "Tiahuanaco Tapestry Design," simultaneously in *The Textile Museum Journal* 1, no. 2 (1963):27-38, and as a booklet from The Museum of Primitive Art (New York, 1963). Ina Van Stan, *Textiles from Beneath the Temple of Pachacamac, Peru* (Philadelphia: University of Pennsylvania Museum, 1967) is a detailed study of one of Peru's most popular tourist sites.

The best readily available study of colonial tapestry is Part V of Adolph Cavallo, *Tapestries of Europe and of Colonial Peru* (Boston: Boston Museum of Fine Arts, 1968). His principal source was Nathalie Zimmern, "The Tapestries of Colonial Peru," *Brooklyn Museum Journal,* 1943-1944, pp. 27-52.

Studies of contemporary weaving include three by Ann Pollard Rowe: "Weaving Processes in the Cuzco Area of Peru," *Textile Museum Journal* 4, no. 2 (1975):30-46; *Warp-Patterned Weaves of the Andes* (Washington, D.C.: The Textile Museum, 1977); and "Andean Warp-Patterned Weaves," *Craft Horizons*, December 1977, pp. 38-40. Some of these same weaves are explained with instructions for making them in Marjorie Cason and Adele Cahlander, *The Art of Bolivian Highland Weaving* (New York: Watson-Guptill, 1976). Weaving in modern Bolivia is also the subject of Grace Goodell, "The cloth of the Quechuas," *Natural History*, December 1969, which relates textiles and weaving to modern life there. Goodell also wrote "A Study of Andean Spinning in the Cuzco Region," *The Textile Museum Journal* 2, no. 3 (1968):2-8. In the same journal, Junius B. Bird has calculated the time required for completing a poncho (around 500 hours). See "Handspun Yarn Production Rates in the Cuzco Region of Peru," *The Textile Museum Journal* 2, no. 3 (1968):9-16.

Miguel Covarrubias wrote two books that give general background on Mexico: *Mexico South: The Isthmus of Tehuantepec* (New York: Alfred A. Knopf, 1946), with a chapter on costume, and *Indian Art of Mexico and Central America* (New York: Alfred A. Knopf, 1957). Jacques Soustelle, *Daily Life of the Aztecs on the Eve of the Spanish Conquest* is a very readable account of Mexico-Tenochtitlan.

The major reference on Mexican textiles (and costume) is Donald and Dorothy Cordry, *Mexican Indian Costumes* (Austin, Texas: University of Texas Press, 1968). It is a photographic documentary of native costume and includes a brief historical overview of textiles and a comprehensive bibliography. Earlier work by the Cordrys was published as the following *Southwest Museum Papers* by the Southwest Museum in Los Angeles: "Costumes and Textiles of the Aztec Indians of the Cuetzalan Region," no. 14 (1940; reprint ed., 1964); and "Costumes and Weaving of the Zoque Indians of Chiapas, Mexico," no. 15 (1941).

Lila M. O'Neale, "Textiles of Pre-Columbian Chihuahua," in *Contributions to American Anthropology and History*, vol. 9, no. 45, Carnegie Institution of Washington Publication 574 (Richmond, Virginia: The William Byrd Press, 1948):95-162 is an important reference on archaeological textiles. "Textile Art in Ancient Mexico," *CIBA Review* 70 (September

1948) is a general history that pretty well covers what is known about pre-Hispanic Mexican textiles. Joy Mahler, "Garments and Textiles of the Maya Lowlands," in *Handbook of the Middle American Indians*, ed. Robert Wauchope, 16 vols. (Austin: University of Texas Press, 1965), 3:581-593 is a good discussion of the problems of costume study using art objects as the sources of information. A. H. Gayton, "Textiles and Costumes," in *Handbook of the Middle American Indians* (1967), 6:138-157 is a brief overview with black and white illustrations and helpful references on both Mexican and Guatemalan fabrics.

There are two principal authors on Guatemalan textiles and costume, Lilly De Jongh Osborne and Lila O'Neale. With Vera Kelsey, Osborne wrote *Four Keys to Guatemala* (New York and London: Funk and Wagnalls, Co., 1939), a good general study of the country with sections on costume and textiles. Osborne published *Guatemalan Textiles*, Middle American Research Series Publication No. 6 (New Orleans: The Tulane University of Lousiana, 1935), and *Indian Crafts of Guatemala and El Salvador* (Norman: University of Oklahoma Press, 1965), with most of the latter book devoted to textiles, costumes, and related crafts. In 1966 Lilly de Jongh Osborne and Josephine Wood published a very detailed study of costume, *Indian Costumes of Guatemala* (Graz, Austria: Akademische Druck—u. Verlagsanstalt, 1966).

Lila M. O'Neale's major work is *Textiles of Highland Guatemala*, Carnegie Institution of Washington Publication 567, 1945 (New York: Johnson Reprint Corp., 1966). It is a detailed study of the costume from various villages and includes a section on the basics of Guatemalan materials and techniques, as well as an interesting chapter on trade textiles. See also Lena Bjerregaard, *Techniques of Guatemalan Weaving* (Florence, Kentucky: Van Nostrand Reinhold, 1977).

Ann Parker and Avon Neal, *Molas: Folk Art of the Cuna Indians* (New York: Clarkson N. Potter, 1977) is beautifully illustrated with Ann Parker's photographs. More of her work can be seen in a brief article by Avon Neal, "Molas: Jungle View of Civilization," *Smithsonian*, November 1975. H. Lester Cooks, *Molas: Art of the Cuna Indians* (Washington, D.C.: The Textile Museum, 1973) is an exhibition catalog that includes history and descriptions of the methods used. See also Clyde Edgar Keeler, *Cuna Indian Art: The Culture and Craft of Panama's San Blas Islanders* (New York: Exposition Press, 1969).

GLOSSARY

Bast: Fiber from plant stems.

Batik: Dyeing method using wax as a resist agent.

Beam: An end bar for a loom.

Binding Yarns: Complementary sets used in plain, twill, or satin weave to hold pattern sets in place. Used in compound weaves.

Block printing: See printing.

Brocade: Fabric patterned with supplementary weft. Term used generally to mean a richly patterned textile, often with gold or silver yarns.

Byssus: Fine cloth made of flax, cotton, or fiber secreted by a mollusk. Also a shade of purple known in the ancient world.

Calender: To smooth or press a fabric. A roller used for finishing fabrics.

Calico: Originally a plain white or printed plain weave cotton from India.

Carding: An operation used to prepare fibers for spinning.

Chintz: A plain weave cotton cloth originally painted and resist dyed in India.

Combing: An operation used to prepare fibers for spinning by laying them parallel to each other. *See* woolen and worsted.

Complementary sets of yarns: Additional yarns that are essential to a woven construction and cannot be removed without destruction of the base fabric.

Compound weave: A construction with more than one set of warp and (or) weft. One set usually appears on the face, the other on the reverse. A general term for a complex weave.

Copperplate printing: See printing.

Count, thread: Number of warp or weft per unit of measure.

Count, yarn: Measure of yarn size.

Damask: Cloth with a flat, reversible design made by combining warp-faced and weft-faced satin or twill weaves. A drawloom or jacquard textile.

Discontinuous weft: A pick not carried the full width of the cloth; it turns back upon itself to form a pattern. Seen in tapestry and brocade.

Diffusion: The spread of cultural elements from one geographical area to another.

Distaff: A stick for holding unspun fibers.

Double weave: Construction that produces two textiles, one above the other, with at least two sets of warp and two sets of weft. A combined weave structure.

Drawloom: A handloom with a system of cords for lifting warp in order to make the weaving of complicated repeat patterns possible.

Drop spindle: A simple spindle that is allowed to fall to the ground as yarn is spun. Its weight attenuates the yarn.

Dyeing: Cloth is dipped in the dyebath, or coloring solution. Both sides will have same intensity of color.

Fabric: Woven and nonwoven material. Cloth.

Fiber: The basic, hair-like material used to make fabrics.

Filament: Fiber that is very long. Silk is the only natural filament.

Float: A yarn carried over two or more yarns of the opposite set between interlacings. A warp float is a warp that goes over two or more weft. Conversely, a weft float goes over two or more warp.

Flyer: A U-shaped device that rotates around the spindle on some spinning wheels and winds the yarn on the spindle.

Fulling: A shrinking and felting process for wool fabrics.

Great wheel: See spinning wheel.

Hand or handle: The drape or feel of a textile.

Harness: A frame that holds the heddles, also called a shaft.

Heddle, headle, heald: A string, metal, or bone eyelet through which individual warp are threaded in an order determined by the pattern.

Ikat: A process by which pattern is resist dyed on warp and (or) weft before weaving.

Jacquard: A loom with a punch card mechanism used to make complicated patterns.

Knitting: Interlooping of yarns.

Kufic lettering: Arabic script often woven into or embroidered on textiles.

Linen: Cloth made from flax fiber.

Moiré: A ribbed fabric with a rippled or watered effect achieved by flattening the rib in patterned areas.

Mordant: A chemical agent that fixes a dyestuff to a fiber.

Napping: The teasing up of fibers from woolen cloth to make a soft surface.

Net: General term for an open mesh fabric. Yarns twisted, knotted, or interlaced.

Pick: Weft.

Pile weave: Construction with extra sets of warp or weft making a three-dimensional surface. Velvet, corduroy, etc.

Ply: Yarn made of two or more single yarns twisted together.

Printing: Application of color to the surface of cloth. Block printing employs carved wood blocks; copperplate printing, incised metal plates; roller printing, incised metal rollers.

Raw silk: Reeled silk, or greige, that has no twist. The gum, or sericin, has not been boiled off.

Reeling: Unwinding silk filaments from cocoons.

Resist dyeing: The process by which an agent such as wax or clay is applied to the surface of cloth to prevent the dyeing of patterned areas.

Roller printing: See printing.

"S" and "Z": Direction of yarn twist. The spindle is turned clockwise for "S" and counterclockwise for "Z." Formerly, "S" was a left twist; "Z," a right twist.

Saxony wheel: *See* spinning wheel.

Selvage: The lengthwise, finished edge of a woven fabric.

Sericulture: The cultivation and processing of silk.

Set: A group of yarns all used in the same manner.

Shaft: Loom harness.

Shuttle: The holder for weft as it is interlaced with warp.

Single yarn: The result of twisting fibers together.

Spindle: A shaft for spinning fibers.

Spinning: Formation of yarn or thread by drawing out and twisting fibers.

Spinning wheel: A simple hand- or foot-operated device with a spindle rotated by a belt and wheel system. Jersey, great, high, long, or wool wheels spin intermittently: they must be stopped to wind yarn. Saxony, Brunswick, or flax wheels use flyers to spin continuously.

Supplementary sets of yarns: Extra design yarns that can be removed leaving a fabric intact. Brocade is an example.

Tapestry: A weave with many more weft than warp. A woven pictorial hanging.

Textile: A woven fabric. The term is commonly used interchangeably with *fabric* and *cloth.*

Thread: A continuous strand of twisted fibers.

Throwing: Twisting silk filaments.

Tiraz: A Muslim textile workshop. Also the name of fabric made in a tiraz.

Twining: A method for making linen yarn in ancient Egypt. A fabric construction in which pairs of warp or weft are twisted around each other as they encircle yarns of the opposite set.

Warp: Lengthwise yarns in woven fabric. Ends.

Warp-faced: Said of a fabric with many more warp than weft. Weft are covered by warp.

Weaving: Interlacing warp and weft at right angles to each other.

Weft: Crosswise yarns in woven fabric. Also referred to as picks, filling, and woof.

Weft-faced: Said of a fabric with many more weft than warp. Warp are covered by weft.

Whorl: A disk of wood, clay, metal, etc., that serves to keep a spindle in rotation and that holds spun yarn on the spindle.

Woolen: Yarn or fabric made of carded wool.

Worsted: Yarn or fabric made of carded and combed wool.

Yarn: A thread used for weaving or knitting.

"Z" twist: *See* "S" twist.

INDEX

Page references followed by a "*b*" refer back to information in the chapter bibliographic essays.